EMINENT JEWS

EMINENT JEWS

BERNSTEIN, BROOKS, FRIEDAN, MAILER

DAVID DENBY

HENRY HOLT AND COMPANY

NEW YORK

Henry Holt and Company
Publishers since 1866
120 Broadway
New York, New York 10271
www.henryholt.com

Henry Holt® and Ⓗ® are registered trademarks of Macmillan Publishing
Group, LLC.

Parts of this book appeared, in a different form, in the *New Yorker*,
the *Atlantic*, and *Harper's Magazine*.

Distributed in Canada by Raincoast Book Distribution Limited

Library of Congress Cataloging-in-Publication Data

Names: Denby, David, 1943– author.
Title: Eminent Jews : Bernstein, Brooks, Friedan, Mailer / David Denby.
Description: First edition. | New York : Henry Holt and Company, 2025. |
    Includes bibliographical references and index.
Identifiers: LCCN 2024030918 | ISBN 9781250193407 (hardcover) |
    ISBN 9781250193414 (ebook)
Subjects: LCSH: Jews—United States—Intellectual life—20th century. |
    United States—Civilization—Jewish influences. | Bernstein, Leonard,
    1918–1990. | Friedan, Betty. | Brooks, Mel, 1926– | Mailer, Norman.
Classification: LCC E184.36.I58 D46 2025 |
    DDC 973/.0492400904—dc23/eng/20241126
LC record available at https://lccn.loc.gov/2024030918

Our books may be purchased in bulk for promotional, educational, or
business use. Please contact your local bookseller or the Macmillan
Corporate and Premium Sales Department at (800) 221-7945, extension
5442, or by e-mail at MacmillanSpecialMarkets@macmillan.com.

First Edition 2025

Designed by Meryl Sussman Levavi

Caricatures of Leonard Bernstein, Mel Brooks, Betty Friedan,
and Norman Mailer by David Levine © Matthew and Eve Levine

Printed in the United States of America

1 3 5 7 9 10 8 6 4 2

To Susan

A Jew survived the gas chambers, having lost every one of his relatives. The resettlement officer asked him where he would like to go.

"Australia," he replied.

"But that's so far," said the officer.

"From where?" asked the Jew.

—refugee quoted in Jeremy Dauber, *Jewish Comedy*, 2017

Once, in the late seventies, when I was on my high horse for radical feminism, I was invited to give the commencement address at a small women's college. I called my mother to let her know that this honor had been bestowed on me . . .

"You mean someone writes the speech and you give it?"

"No," I said, "I write the speech and I give it . . ."

"Do you have to show the speech to them before you give it?" she asked . . .

"No . . ." I sighed. "I don't have to show it to anyone . . ."

"Nu," she said at last, "if they don't like what you say all they'll do is tell you to go home."

Meaning: After all, it *is* America, they can't kill you.

—Vivian Gornick, *The Odd Woman and the City*, 2015

CONTENTS

PREFACE

This is a celebratory book, a happy book, but a note of mourning must be sounded nonetheless. American Jews know that anti-Semitism is a foul underground stream that bursts into sight now and then. No American Jew can be complacent when Hamas, backed by Iran, carries out a barbaric massacre of civilians in southern Israel, and then an enraged Israel, eager to destroy Hamas, kills thousands of civilians in Gaza. The events of October 7, 2023, and the war that followed it, made Jews everywhere feel miserable and unsafe. In response to Israel's campaign in Gaza, restaurants, businesses, synagogues, and cultural centers in the United States have seen bomb threats; some have been vandalized or covered with anti-Semitic graffiti; anti-Zionist college students, often ignorant of the Israelis and the Palestinians, have harassed and insulted their Jewish classmates. Leftist students have denounced Israel as a "settler-colonial" state and have demanded what amounts to the end of the Jewish homeland. In response, many American Jews have ended their support for the Netanyahu administration without relinquishing their love for Israel as a country. Israelis will change: they must recognize that the Palestinians have a humanity equal to their own for reasons of survival as well as justice.

No American Jew can be happy when anti-Semitism surfaces among white Christian nationalists attracted to Donald Trump and the MAGA-dominant Republican Party, or when Kanye West's anti-Semitic idiocies reach millions on social media, or when significant parts of a great national party disdain the Constitution and democratic norms. The death of democracy would almost certainly mean trouble for the Jews (as well as for everyone else), a minority protected in America by laws, customs, and sentiment.

Perhaps something useful can be learned from the assertiveness of this book's four subjects. They lived in the "Golden Era" of relative safety and abundant achievement for the American Jews after the Second World War, and they took advantage of liberty in every possible way. They did not suffer from the confusion and constraint of so many American Jews in the 1930s, a time when, as fascism arose in Europe and anti-Semitism gathered strength in this country, many Jews thought it best to keep quiet and not draw attention to themselves—most notoriously the Hollywood moguls, who kept Jewish characters and any criticism of Germany completely out of the movies all through the decade.

The same kind of shrinking back, the same kind of fear and silence, would be a disastrous Jewish response to the present moment of danger. Betty Friedan took all sorts of chances, Leonard Bernstein made music everywhere, Mel Brooks risked offending the Jews with his humor, and Norman Mailer told his sister Barbara, "Act stronger than you feel, and you will soon feel as strong as you act."

—JULY 2024

EMINENT JEWS

PROLOGUE:
AT HOME IN AMERICA I

The two million or so Russian and Eastern European Jews who came here between 1880 and 1924 usually brought very little with them—clothes, cooking tools, hammer and file, maybe some musical instruments (a violin!), a few religious items and books, not much more than that. They arrived with very little money in their pockets—some with fifty dollars, others as little as nine dollars. They also brought, many of them, an enormous drive, the desire to make a good life in this country. Living in the Lower East Side and other heaving urban ghettos, they worked in sweatshops and factories, rolled damp cigars, sewed piece goods at home while avoiding jobs in domestic service and such hard-muscle occupations as breaking rock or digging tunnels for the new subway lines. Among the boldest and luckiest, the situation of being outsiders only sharpened personal habits of risk-taking and entrepreneurship. To start a business! It was a common desire among the Eastern immigrants and their children.

This book is devoted to the flowering of that ambition in the next generation—the cultural achievement of postwar American Jews as embodied in four famous and intricately composed individuals: Leonard Bernstein, Betty Friedan, Norman Mailer, and Mel Brooks. As the general prosperity of American Jews increased, and anti-Semitism began to fade (in part because Jews organized against it), these four stormed through

the latter half of twentieth-century America, altering the way people listened to music, comprehended the relations of men and women, understood the nation's soul, and defined what was vulgar and what was not. I
hope to show how a Jewish *vantage* shaped their creativity without making the parochial error of assuming that what they accomplished was
entirely due to their being Jews. It wasn't. America poured into them, and
they, as Jews, poured into America, a happy intermingling made possible
by freedoms that Jews had never known before. My subjects expressed
themselves in the public arena as forcefully as they could, and they hoped
to shape the country they loved.

They were born just after the First World War and emerged as public
figures after the Second World War, in part by taking advantage of such
new media as television, the long-playing record, the comedy album,
and the paperback revolution, as well as easy air travel from one place to
another. Their talents, and their newly won freedom as Jews, meshed with
the exhilarations of a rapidly developing commercial culture.

Like almost everyone else, the American Jews were scarred by the
Depression, but they emerged from it with their sense of themselves as
a community largely intact. After the war, it became obvious (if a little
frightening) that America had become the greatest power instrument in
the world, perhaps in human history. (In 1950, for instance, real GDP
increased by 8.7 percent.) In memoirs of the postwar period—as sky-
scrapers were flung up; new communities laid down; new media developing; a new enemy, the Soviet Union, to be "contained" (the Truman
Doctrine)—one can feel giddiness mixed with unease. The unspeakable
slaughter of the European Jews in the Holocaust and threats of nuclear
war in the future produced, in some, a new kind of dismay, a kind of over-
hanging dread (Norman Mailer's favorite word). An abyss had opened
up; existence itself was in doubt. Still, as the economy took off, these four,
and many Jews like them, became convinced that this country was a place
in which they could flourish. (There were, of course, discontented, pessimistic, or impoverished Jews who didn't feel at home; I'm trying to get
at a large-scale mood, which nevertheless did not—could not—include
everyone.)

They little needed to observe the discretion of earlier years, when Jews
were generally unwilling to say out loud that their kind (at least the men)

were doing well in America. Though generally banned from management positions in large industrial corporations (railroads, oil, steel, chemicals, automobiles, aviation, engineering in general, etc.), the Jews in the United States were creating not just business and academic success but an abundance of good work in science, medicine, investment banking, literature, publishing, theater, movies, journalism, humor, intellectual and expressive life of all kinds—and also, of course, crime. But *shush*! Boasting was forbidden. No need to rev up the always waiting engine of Jew hatred. The fear of expressing Jewish chauvinism, joined to the fear of arousing anti-Semitism, produced what has been called the "booster-bigot trap," a double prohibition enforcing silence. After the war, as anti-Semitism receded, Jewish reticence faded as well. This book is about the moment of confidence, the breakout period when shame and silence were vanquished. My subjects were neither sequestered as Jews nor silent as Jews; they were "assimilated" without giving up a certain exuberant brazenness derived from their Russian and Eastern European lineage. No one could confuse them with German Jews.

THEY HAD THEIR first serious success in New York, a city whose openness to brash and talented people of all kinds was central to the immigrant story. "Without New York," as critic and memoirist Alfred Kazin put it, "there would have been no immigrant epic, no America." They worked in different fields, and apart from clinking glasses now and then at parties—intellectuals and people in the arts drank a great deal in New York sixty years ago—they hardly knew each other. But they share a common temperament—a bounding unapologetic egotism marked, at the same time, by a generous temperament and a stern sense of obligation. Both shameless and responsible (not a common pairing of qualities), they began as hungry outsiders and ended up as sages. They engaged the spirit of the times, gathering into their own readiness for action the cultural and economic currents swirling around them, and then, working as artists and intellectuals, they altered those currents. Of course, these four were preceded by many talented American Jews in the arts and intellectual life, including jurist Louis Brandeis, journalist Walter Lippmann, anthropologist Franz Boas, and a raft of Broadway composers. But my subjects, in

the special media-age shape of their temperaments and the public character of their acts, cannot be imagined in any other time or place.

Leonard Bernstein wrote classical music and Broadway shows and
became one of the great conductors of the twentieth century; he was also
a nonstop teacher of music to the nation, bringing music into the center
of our emotional lives. Betty Friedan, uncertain of her interests for years,
wound up kicking off second-wave feminism; she taught women to dis-
miss humiliation, confront anger, and say what had been hard or impossible to say. Norman Mailer freed up American prose, engaged the soul of
the country in condemnation and prophecy, and turned intellectual and
physical risk into a lifelong project of self-transformation. Mel Brooks
aimed low, grabbing audiences not by the throat but by the *kishkes*, making popular comedy a celebration of the body and an assault on death.
They all expanded expression, created new aspects of American temperament and being. They were unafraid and unaccommodating; they were
little affected by that famous lingering disease "Jewish self-hatred"—guilt,
in some cases, but not self-hatred. Except for Leonard Bernstein, they
were not obsessed with Israel. America was Zion enough, though the
mere existence of the vibrant young Jewish state may have allowed them
to feel stronger.

Tremendous talkers, irresistibly engaging for many, they could be
among the friendliest people in the world. They could also be a pain in
the neck or worse, and there was a dark side to their personal lives. Bernstein's homosexuality brought sorrow to his wife, and then, after she died,
his public behavior became crass, even lewd (while his musicianship was
better than ever). Betty Friedan, perhaps the most famous feminist in the
country, remained in a mutually abusive marriage for more than twenty
years; Friedan tried to dominate every feminist meeting she was part of.
Norman Mailer slept with more women than a harem master and stabbed
his second wife, Adele Morales, almost killing her, an unforgivable act; he
made speeches in faux-redneck accents that embarrassed almost everyone who loved him. Mel? He could be greedy about the credits on his TV
shows and films, edging out some of his collaborators. At twenty-five, he
was the noisiest man in New York (which is saying something), a begin-
ner who took over rooms and shouted down everyone else. In brief, all
four demonstrated the range of selfish behavior so often characteristic of
talented people determined to have their own way. I love them, I glory in

them, I converse with them (mostly in my head), but I am a biographer, not a hagiographer.

WHATEVER PREJUDICE AND hostility the Eastern Jews (and earlier German Jewish immigrants) encountered here, they had entered a land without centuries-old traditions of persecutions and pogroms. "The United States had no medieval past," in the words of sociologist Marshall Sklare in *Observing America's Jews* (1993). "There is no history here of the Jew existing as a pariah people." The defeated people in America were the Native Americans; the pariah people were enslaved Africans and their descendants; the Jews, accepted or not, escaped the extreme prejudice that African Americans faced every day. And they were, putting it mildly, better treated here than in Europe. The Jews would not be expelled from New York or Boston at sunset, or forced to convert, or press-ganged into the army, or forced to billet troops, or hit with special taxes, or rounded up and sent to camps.

They entered a bounding new capitalist society, brutal in many ways, but a society in which the skills (of white people) found a fair chance of employment and reward. Christian Europe had gone through centuries of distaste for the practice of lending money with interest (usury)—a practice essential to the growth of capitalism. America had no such distaste. The immigrant Jews, largely an urban group, were literate; adaptable; more than fluent with information, trade, and the basics of finance. They were, as historian Yuri Slezkine wrote in *The Jewish Century* (2004), shaped by their past in a way that made them adept players in the economic and civil life of the modern era.

In the first and second generations, the Eastern Jews cultivated habits— sexual propriety and a general inclination to go to bed sober—that bolstered steady work. The most adroit and adventurous of them drew on limited financing ("shoestring capitalism") with the help of Jewish-run credit unions. They built small and then midsize businesses—clothing (my mother's business), printing, costume jewelry (my father's business), small factories of all kinds, merchandising in general, retail of every kind, scrap-metal and waste-management firms, real estate; and they entered vaudeville, Broadway, and Hollywood entertainment, industries dominated by Eastern Jews from the beginning of the twentieth century. An informal ethos took hold in the second and third generation: to become a useful person, you needed to master something—if not the family business, then finance, law, medicine, entertainment, accounting; an academic discipline, or teaching and writing, the civil service; perhaps religious training as a rabbi or cantor. Some sort of trade, a profession! *Something.* This was true for many Jewish boys before the war; it became increasingly true for Jewish girls in the sixties and after.

After the war, in the wake of Hitler's infamies, Judaism suddenly became one of the major religions in America: the country was discovered to have a defining "Judeo-Christian heritage." The reigning popular stereotypes of Jews moved from pushy and clannish to . . . respectable members of the American community. Many Americans regarded with amused appreciation "the Jewish doctor" and "the Jewish husband." Almost everyone enjoyed the innumerable Jewish entertainers on TV—the exceedingly dry Jack Benny, the alarmingly damp Milton Berle, the brilliant, tormented Sid Caesar. A minority enjoyed the *shpritzing* venom of Lenny Bruce as he tore through politics, the Church, soft Jewish liberalism.

Psychoanalysis—"the Jewish science," as the Nazis called it—served as a frame of reference for millions, including many who would never dream of undergoing treatment. Not just American-born Jews, but Jewish émigré physicists, social scientists, and literature professors, burdened but often exhilarated refugees from Europe, triumphed in great American universities. At least part of the country looked fondly on such demanding writers as Saul Bellow, Cynthia Ozick, Allen Ginsberg, Norman Mailer, Bernard Malamud, Philip Roth, Grace Paley. What became known as "the New York Intellectuals," centered in the city in the mid-1930s and after, marked the first time, as Irving Howe put it in 1982, "that a self-confident group of intellectuals did not acknowledge the authority of Christian tradition." The New York group was an erudite, quarrelsome cohort of men and women, entirely secular but given to wrestling with one another as if God Himself were judging the outcome. As Edward Shapiro wrote in *A Time for Healing: American Jewry Since World War II* (1992), "A Jewish community without intellectuals was simply inconceivable."

With the exception of Mel Brooks, my subjects were middle-class kids. The emancipatory, up-from-the-ghetto narrative of so much Jewish American memory was not their story. Their parents had made that dif-

ficult journey before them. Business dominated the family background
of these four, not creative or intellectual work. Yet their parents offered
them one of the greatest benefits of middle-class American life: a good
education. Mailer entered Harvard at sixteen, Bernstein at seventeen,
and Friedan entered Smith also at seventeen. Mel went to the Mountains—
the mighty Catskills, northwest of New York—where he learned the not
inconsiderable skill of entertaining vacationing Jews in the slumbering
hours between lunch (Chilled Schav with Sliced Egg, Grilled Eggplant
Steak à la Meyer, Strawberry Cheesecake) and an equally modest dinner
(Colossal Ripe Olives, Boiled Yearling Fowl en Pot, Vienna Almond Cres-
cent). The entertainment business was his university.

The cultural disdain for Jews expressed by such American mandarins
as Henry Adams, Edith Wharton, and T. S. Eliot meant nothing to them
(if they even knew about it). They may have been children of Yiddish-
speaking immigrant families (Betty's and Norman's mothers were
American-born, the rest of the parents foreign-born), but they assumed
that the Western tradition of literature, philosophy, art, and music
belonged to them. Mailer loved Tolstoy and Dostoevsky as well as American writers like James T. Farrell and Ernest Hemingway; Bernstein became
a major interpreter not only of the Americans (Ives and Copland) but of
the German-Austrian classics (Haydn, Beethoven, Schumann), and in
particular he devoted himself to conducting and explaining the work of
Gustav Mahler. Betty Friedan loved and fought with Freud her entire life.
Mel Brooks told *Playboy* in 1975, "Where would I be today if it wasn't for
Nikolai Gogol?" He said virtually the same thing to me forty-three years
later. The great Russian writers brought out the pessimistic side of Mel's
burlesque. In Russia, however, he would have been a provincial buffoon, a
nuisance, or a man who should be suppressed altogether. In America, he
attained complete self-expression.

IRVING HOWE'S CLASSIC *World of Our Fathers* (1976) re-creates the abundant social, political, and religious life of the new immigrants and their
children on the Lower East Side. Stephen Whitfield's *In Search of American Jewish Culture* (1999) dramatizes, with great wit and erudition, the
interplay of Jewish tradition and American art forms—music, literature,
and theater—as they developed in the early and mid-twentieth century.

There needs to be more work, both celebratory and critical, devoted to the American Jews exercising liberty after the Second World War. What are the conditions that led to cultural achievement? What kind of personal qualities enabled it?

I had little desire to write about Jewish scholars, jurists, scientists, religious leaders—the usual subjects of (entirely deserved) veneration in Jewish culture. The notion of eminence among Jews, I thought, needed to be expanded, which meant ignoring the lure of Jewish respectability. *Eminent Jews* is a fractured group portrait of unruly Jews living in freedom. The four portraits, I hope, will throw light on one another, allowing something like a composite picture of time, place, and temperament to emerge, a composite picture of the ideology and practice of postwar Jewish cultural achievement.

These four were not very observant, but the Jewish religion, even in its absence in their personal lives, shaped each of their temperaments. Having said so, I need to insist that soulfulness and spirituality may take worldly as well as religious forms—as achievements of intellect and art and character. At times, I speak of "Jewish values" and "Jewish character"; such notions become more than empty generalities only when embedded within the idiosyncrasy of individual lives.

I will dramatize these four people in their messy intricacy, emphasizing their early years, when their ambitions burst out, praising their best work and best habits without ignoring their confusions, contradictions, and defeats. They were not saints; they were Jews. The most famous group biography ever written, Lytton Strachey's *Eminent Victorians* (1918), offers four disconnected portraits held together by ironic amusement; Strachey's subjects were often ignorant, hypocritical, or both. *Eminent Victorians* is a skeptical, sometimes wicked book. But my task is to celebrate.

A PERSONAL NOTE

My mother's parents came from Belorussia and Austria; my father's grandparents from Vilna (Lithuania). My mother, Ida Eve Harkavy, one of seven children, grew up in the Washington Heights section of Manhattan, dropped out of high school at fifteen, and worked as a retail clerk in New York. In her mid-twenties, she became a buyer for chain retail stores. She was good at calculating what American women would need ten months or a year down the road and then backing up her judgment with enormous orders. One of her specialties was traveling to Paris, "knocking off" (copying) an expensively designed blouse for mass production in America, and selling the garment in stores for (maybe) $7.95. In other words, an American Jewish woman with very little education made extravagant dreams available to millions of American women. In midcareer, she jumped the fence and worked for a Seventh Avenue manufacturer. Her husband, my father, Ezra Lawrence Denby, attended City College for one semester but dropped out to work. For decades he ran the Fifth Avenue showroom (his partners ran the factory) of a costume-jewelry outfit—bangles, baubles, necklaces, cultured pearls.

After the stock market crashed in October 1929, my father and his brother, a stockbroker, were afraid the disaster would be blamed on the Jews. They changed their name from Dembosky to Denby, an English pottery company that makes never-drip teapots. You can't get more respectable than that. My parents were businesspeople who (as far as I could see) thoroughly enjoyed their lives. They worked hard, came home at six, poured themselves a double scotch (J&B), put their feet up on a Louis Quinze–style bolster, read the papers, and had a good dinner; they went to the theater, traveled a few times to London, Paris, and Rome. They were aware of prejudice and "restricted" country clubs (but who cares?). They did not speak of ghettos. They were members of a Reform Jewish synagogue, upper-middle-class Americans, prosperous but not wealthy. We lived in two-bedroom Manhattan apartments, nothing special in size but located at deluxe-sounding addresses: Park Avenue, Gracie Terrace, Sutton Place.

It apparently never occurred to them—or to me—that I would follow them into the garment business. The subject never came up. In the 1950s and '60s, many middle- and upper-middle-class Jewish parents looked for serious intent in their children. Parents in that era were pleased with their children if they had a book in their hands, as if the book cast a kind of protective shield over the child's destiny. You had to *prepare*—or at least read, fasten your curiosity to a rising star or at least a stable trade. In my case, after some delay, it was movie journalism. Failure was always a possibility, and it threatened me and engulfed others, but it wasn't much talked about. After much scrambling, dented shins, bruised elbows, I made my way from Park Avenue to . . . West End Avenue. (A New York joke, but I think you get it.)

My story is unremarkable, which, of course, is the most remarkable thing about it. How many Jews throughout the two-millennia diaspora grew up in families that hoped, even assumed, that their children would get a good education and enter a profession? Yes, some entertained that hope in nineteenth-century emancipated Berlin and Vienna, in Warsaw and Budapest, in London and Paris. In those cities Jews might actually succeed—but only after facing threats, restrictions, demands that they abandon Judaism as the price of entering professional ranks. I faced none of that. By any measure, I was privileged and lucky, yet I knew almost nothing about what had come before me. In my own nightmares, I never tasted the rotten food of a long passage or breathed the damp, choking air of a sweatshop. I understood virtually nothing of the years of misery, struggle, and anxious commercial activity that had made possible my leisure to "find" myself. I'm a generation younger than my subjects, but we are all lucky products of the migration to the New World, ending in American abundance and general American goodwill toward the Jewish people.

I NEVER MET Leonard Bernstein, but I attended his concerts, saw his shows, read his books, and have listened to his recordings and lectures for decades. One of his concerts, as I shall explain later, changed my life. Outside the concert hall, I saw him only once: sometime in the sixties, after a Friday afternoon performance with the New York Philharmonic, he was riding down Fifth Avenue in the back of a silver Lincoln Continental convertible, his arms stretched out along the top of the seat; he took possession of the scene, nodding vivaciously this way and that, openly acknowledging the greetings of people on the street. He was dazzling in the sun, a modern prince. I never met Betty Friedan, either, but I remember agreeing with her anger when I encountered it (later than I should have) in her breakthrough book *The Feminine Mystique* (1963), which reset my own expectations of women and offered an escape from the unwelcome burdens of machismo.

Reading Norman Mailer as a teenager and college student filled me with a sense of hope. Who knew you could write that way about America? His prose made me feel stronger. I can attest that he had the same effect on many young men. There were many women in Mailer's generation and the next (including Diana Trilling, Lillian Hellman, Joyce Carol Oates, Doris Kearns Goodwin, and Joan Didion) who admired his work, but few in later generations, which is both Mailer's tragedy and a cultural loss. I ran into him once or twice when I was young, spent two companionable days interviewing him in Provincetown for a *New Yorker* profile in 1998, and saw him several times after that. And I saw Mel Brooks for a piece in the *Atlantic* for a couple of hours in his Culver City office when he was ninety-two, and I've spoken to him many times since then. I have always responded to the harshness and even pessimism beneath his humor, his sturdy, this-world realism ("Praying is good, but penicillin is better"), the freedom offered by his try-and-stop-me bad taste.

For the record, I am nothing like any of them. I do not make hilarious vulgar jokes; I am not contentious and aggrieved; I do not constantly test myself and have never, dear God, boxed with my sons; I love music but do not play or sing. Yet these four have a powerful shadow existence for me; they represent the full development of lives I have not lived, cannot live. In some mysterious way, much of what I have become as a writer, husband, and father has been fueled by the relationships I have maintained with them in my head. They are possibilities that have enlarged my life; they are an imagined bounty of existence. This book is my way of making an account and offering praise.

1

MEL BROOKS AND THE END OF SELF-PITY

JEW COMIC

I n 1983, Mel Brooks, a very famous man, went on *The Tonight Show Starring Johnny Carson* to promote his new movie—*To Be or Not to Be*, starring Anne Bancroft and himself. After the usual banter, Mel suddenly turned to Johnny and said, "You know, I'm not Jewish." Johnny Carson tucked in his chin. "I didn't really know that," he said. So Mel explained:

This is one of the great charades. It's one of greatest fabrications of all time. I was five eleven, blond, a Gentile, with a perfect little nose. I went into Mount Sinai for over thirty-six hours. They knocked the . . . *stuffings* out of me. They pulled out my nose, they turned it, they bolted, they shortened my hair, they took two inches out of my legs because I wanted to make it . . . as a Jew comic!

There you have it. He was prouder of being a five foot six, stocky, barrel-chested man with a spreading nose, a wide grin, a coarse voice—prouder of *that* than of being an American physical ideal. Notice that he says to Johnny Carson "Jew comic" and not "Jewish comic." In a quirk of the language, "Jewish" always seems anodyne, merely descriptive, but "Jew" still has the power of a brand hitting flesh. Fifty years earlier, a Jewish store owner in an American small town might have been known contemptuously as a "Jew butcher" or a "Jew tailor." Mel turned an insult into a boast. A Jew comic was all of his identity as a Jew and as a performer. In the end, there was no loftier calling. In 1975, he told *Newsweek*, "Unrelieved lamenting would be intolerable. So, for every ten Jews, beating their breasts, God designated one to be crazy and amuse the breast-beaters. By the time I was five, I knew I was that one."

Cheering up the Jews! What a job! It never really ends, though Mel Brooks has done his best to go beyond just cheering people up. Mel would actually like to terminate Jewish sorrows altogether, but only in his own complicated and seemingly perverse way. His ambitions, which he will not always admit, have made him a significant figure in Jewish history.

But first he is an entertainer, the master of many forms of show business, including *tummling* at Catskill resorts, TV-skit parody, comedy concept albums, talk-show appearances (nineteen times on Carson alone), and, late in his life, Broadway musicals. He embodies the traditions of vaudeville and burlesque, the memories of roughhouse and travesty going back to medieval street fairs (if not further), the influence of Russian literature here and there, all of that pouring into some of the messiest and funniest movies ever made: *The Producers, Blazing Saddles, Young Frankenstein, History of the World, Part 1,* and *Robin Hood: Men in Tights.* Mel Brooks the lovable Jewish clown! Vulgar in expression, good-hearted in spirit—that would be the common summing up, and in some ways it is true.

But then consider something strange. Consider an episode from *History of the World, Part 1,* which came out in 1981. Most of the movie is fine bawdy burlesque. With all appropriate pomp (trumpets blasting,

Orson Welles narrating), Brooks revisits the Great Historical Moments of the Past. He feasts on each age's ceremonies, turning splendor and power into spoof. Mel himself, white-bearded, clad in Charlton Heston's scarlet robes from *The Ten Commandments*, appears as Moses, descending from a shabby crevice in Mount Sinai. In his arms, he holds three stone tablets. "All pay heed!" he cries. "The Lord, the Lord Jehovah has given unto you these fifteen"—here Moses accidentally drops one tablet—"these TEN . . . ten commandments for all to obey." Brooks appears later as a lecherous Louis XVI living among aristos and deep-cleavaged courtesans in licentious Versailles. "It's good to be de king," he confides to us, which became Brooks's motto.

But in the midst of the pranks and happy lewd jokes, there's a scandalous episode. It's called "The Spanish Inquisition," and it takes place in a dark fifteenth-century castle. Jews in skullcaps are variously strung up and tormented with all the inventiveness of Spanish cruelty as well as Mel's own mock-sadistic variants—such as Jews spun around in a giant slot machine. Mel appears as Torquemada, the Grand Inquisitor, leading a chorus of gleeful monks in an up-tempo, Broadway-style production number, "The Inquisition." It has such lyrics as "The Inquisition / Let's begin / The Inquisition / Look out sin / We have a mission / To convert the *Jewwwsss!*" Torquemada is a friendly guy, a tease: *Why won't you convert?* Nuns emerge from the shadows and remove their habits, revealing white bathing suits; they dive into the castle pool and pull Jews by their feet down into the depths. A more crushing image of Jewish humiliation would be hard to imagine.

If you're watching the episode for the first time, you may be seriously alarmed. It's beyond bad taste; it's a bloody outrage. In 1981, citing this episode, many critical stiffs (including me, in *New York* magazine) panned the movie. I have since changed my mind but, still, the entire sequence makes you wonder what in the world Mel was up to. Back in 1967, he had created a similar mad jest in his hilarious "Springtime for Hitler" number in his first movie, *The Producers*—Mel triumphing over the Nazis by turning them into high-kicking Broadway guys and girls. "Springtime" has become so familiar that people sing it at dinner parties. But the musical-comedy "Inquisition" is a much more aggressive joke. Who's being mocked? If the Jews have suffered a great deal in their history, why should they have to watch their ancestors tortured, even as part of a joke? Mel's staging is blustery and hearty, the meanings of the scene elusive, even antagonistic.

One cannot accuse him of Jewish self-hatred. Throughout his career, the word "Jew" has popped out of him like nuggets from a gumball machine. He may tease the Jews, but he doesn't make self-deprecating jokes, as other Jewish comics of his generation did. He is the opposite of the cringing Jewish *shlemiel*. Yet in *History of the World, Part 1*, he mocks the suffering of the Jews in an episode of far-out black comedy. Mel Brooks certainly enjoys breaking the tablets. Where does this rage and daring come from? There were signals along the way that Mel Brooks was a more complicated Jewish clown than the world was ready to acknowledge.

OLD GUY I

I went to see him in Hollywood in 2018, and I've gone back and forth with him numerous times since then by telephone. In 2018, Mel Brooks was an old man. As I write this in 2024, he's a still older man—ninety-eight years old. One does not want him to die, which is a generous and unkind request to make of anyone. One wants him to stay old forever, the surviving Jew, two thousand years old in his most famous comedy routine, "The 2000 Year Old Man"—two thousand years, not coincidentally, is roughly the length of Jewish survival in the diaspora after the birth of Jesus, something Mel explicitly reminds us of in the skit again and again. In his haphazard and rambunctious way, Mel's old man shoves Christianity out of the center of Western civilization. *We were here first.*

He has blue-gray eyes and a rakish smile; his hair is white and full; his voice remains powerfully hoarse, with maybe a touch of Louis Armstrong filtering through the back-of-the-deli guttural tones. (When he sings, however, he evokes easeful Bing Crosby or hyper-stylized Sinatra.) He has a genius for brief narrative, for rhythm and emphasis in storytelling, with never an extra beat, nothing half-hearted, nothing extraneous. "We comics had only a few minutes out there, so we learned to say things very quickly," he told me. Whenever he's *talking*, his go-ahead rhythm is so insistent, the pungency of his stories so striking (fear and death are his favorite characters), that it's impossible to stop listening to him. Which is why hundreds of people he's shouted at or shouted *down* have forgiven him. Something has been clarified for them—a truth of temperament, of human nature, a strangled bit of Jewish wisdom, a wild fantasy. Mel Brooks is not just a comic performer and moviemaker, he's a walking instrument of American Jewish culture and life.

When I went to see him in 2018, he was enjoying the London success of a shortened version of the stage musical *Young Frankenstein* (initially, of course, it was a 1974 movie). Preparing the show, he spent months in Newcastle during tryouts and then additional months in London, living it up at the deluxe Savoy Hotel, where he got to know hotel staffers by name, even meeting some of their parents.

Another stage hit in his tenth decade? Entertaining a London hotel staff? He cannot rest, and something about his drive is almost demonic. He has to entertain everyone in the world, in every possible medium, and he has to take over their bodies while doing it. In interviews and in his autobiography, he describes his jokes and movies causing people to slide off their chairs and fall to the floor. Some spill their food or get coffee dismally trapped in their nasal passages. Watching *Blazing Saddles*, employees of the studio that made it, Warner Bros., left their seats and flew through the air upside down. "It was like a Chagall painting," he told Johnny Carson. How hard you laugh is almost a test of your humanity: if you're only mildly amused or, God forbid, *silent* . . . no, your body has to be inhabited like the bodies of religious celebrants at a tent revival. You have to be conquered. He wants to do more than just entertain you. Where does the drive come from?

THE STREETS OF BROOKLYN

"I'm lucky," Brooks said to me. "Gertrude, my mother's mother, left Russia, left Kiev, and Abraham on my father's side left Danzig, and they brought their children to Henry Street, where Max Kaminsky and Kitty Brookman met, and then they made *us*," by which he meant his three older brothers and himself. Henry Street was in the middle of the Jewish Lower East Side, a tenement district near the Manhattan Bridge in which families of five or more crowded into tiny, cabbage-smelling apartments shaped like dumbbells (two rooms with a corridor in between). Max Kaminsky and Kitty Brookman met in 1915 when Max was twenty-two and Kitty nineteen; they married the following year and quickly moved to Brooklyn. On the Kaminsky side of the family, there was a successful herring import business, with pushcarts distributing fish all over the neighborhood. But Max and Kitty weren't part of the business. They were poor.

Their son Mel was born on a kitchen table in the Brownsville section of Brooklyn on June 28, 1926. He doesn't remember his father, a process server. Max Kaminsky died of kidney disease when he was thirty-four and Mel was an infant. In a long *Playboy* interview from February 1975, Brooks said, "I can't tell you what sadness, what pain it is to me never to have known my own father, who died when I was two and a half. All I know is what they've told me. He was lively, peppy, sang well. Isn't it sad that that's all a son should know about his father? If only I could look at him, touch his face, see if he had eyebrows!"

But there was always his mother, Kate Brookman, or Kitty. She was three when she arrived from Russia, landing in the Lower East Side not among the Jews but among the Irish. In 1970, on a famous episode ("How to Be a Jewish Son") of David Susskind's late-night talk show, Brooks said of Kitty, "She speaks no known language, but she speaks it with an Irish accent." Kitty was small, determined, very hardworking, always scrubbing; the floors were washed and then allowed to dry under Yiddish newspapers; the living-room furniture was covered with sheets (Mel claimed he never saw his family's furniture). No tiny crawling creature was safe on Kitty's floor. Speaking of Jewish mothers in general, Brooks said on the Susskind show, "Until they die themselves, they *clean* and *kill* . . . they *clean* and *kill*."

But before any further jokes about Jewish mothers go down, let us say of Kitty that she was a marvel. Every morning, she went off to the Garment District for a ten-hour workday (she also brought piecework home in the evening). But before leaving she woke up her sons. All four slept on a single bed, not lengthwise, but straight across the width, and Mel, her favorite, was the last of the four to be awakened. On cold winter mornings, at 365 South Third Street in Williamsburg, Kitty would warm his clothes on the radiator, and then get him dressed under a blanket, kissing him and singing to him all the while.

In 1931, when Mel was five, one of his brothers took him to see the original *Frankenstein* movie, with Boris Karloff. He was frightened by it; he was sure the monster was coming to get him. On a hot summer night, he closed the window near his bed. But Kitty wanted some air in the fifth-floor apartment, and, according to Mel, held forth as follows: "In order for Frankenstein to bite you, he's got to leave Russia, Transylvania, wherever he's from. . . . First he has to catch a train to a seaport. Then he's got to have money to get on a boat, a ship, to go all the way from Romania to America. Then when he lands in America, in New York, he's got to know which subway to take to get to Williamsburg. Then he's got to know which apartment to go to. If he climbs up the fire escape, any of the windows . . . he'll eat someone on the first floor, why would he climb to the fifth floor?"

Most parents would have (mistakenly) tried to tease their children out of fear. Kitty told a *story*, both literal and absurd, and it worked. Mel went to sleep, and forty-three years later he made his own Frankenstein movie. His version of the monster was not frightening but more like an over-grown kid searching for love.

No single explanation could account for a phenomenon like Mel Brooks. Still, you would have to be blind not to notice that his life was at least partly driven by a constant presence and an eternal absence: Kitty was always there; Max, his father, was never there. Mel gained enormous confidence from being his mother's favorite son; at the same time, his desire to entertain, to touch everybody in the world, would always fall short, frustrated by his inability to reach the one person he wanted to reach the most. That inability can't tell us everything, but it's suggestive, and it may be linked to his conviction that laughter is the only real answer to death. "Vive! Vivre!" he said to me. "The joy of life. Comedy is central to it. . . . Comedy is the realization of being alive."

He cannot bring his father back, he can't see him or touch him, but he can avenge that loss with comedy that became an all-out assault on taste, a celebration of the living body in all its gross happiness—an assault on death. *Take that! I'm alive!* Yes, you could say that the work of any great comic is an assault on death, but Mel Brooks means it literally. He attacks such supreme proponents of death—especially Jewish death—as Torque-mada and Adolf Hitler. The Jew killers have to be brought into Jewish entertainment again and again; they have to be kept alive in order to be humiliated by mockery. Reviving and ridiculing these tormentors is one way of cheering up the Jews, even if it makes the Jews squirm at times.

THE FAMILY MOVED from Brownsville to Williamsburg when Mel was still two; later they moved to Brighton Beach (all in Brooklyn) and then back to Williamsburg, which was then a neighborhood of cobbled streets and horse-drawn milk carts offering pickles, lox, and memorial candles. The men wore black; their wives were often in rose-colored wrappers. *Luft-menschen*, adrift in the New World, their heads filled with Jewish text and argument, wandered around, looking for someone to talk to. Many of the family's neighbors, including the Orthodox, spoke Yiddish. It was essentially a nineteenth-century city with twentieth-century media (the radio, the record player) pouring into courtyards strung with laundry. Mel was a child at precisely the moment, in the early thirties, when "media" were encroaching on life in the streets; he devoured both, and later transformed the excitements of street life into his own kind of all-media assault.

At home, Kitty had a lot of help from her husband's clan and from the neighborhood women. "I was adored," Mel told *Playboy*. "I was always in the air, hurled up and kissed and thrown in the air again. Until I was six, my feet didn't touch the ground. 'Look at those eyes! That nose! Those lips! That tooth!'"

He didn't take school (Williamsburg's Eastern District High School) very seriously. The notion of homework shocked him, and, in class, noisy and disrespectful, he got smacked by his teachers. School was something to be endured, and so, apparently, was his bar mitzvah, performed at a tiny Williamsburg synagogue on Keap Street. His friends celebrated the event by throwing hard candies at him, which was a Jewish custom, though it's difficult to believe that the neighborhood *bonditts* wished him a sweet life. In all, Mel's time in Brooklyn suggests silent comedy. He was always running. He ran from the toughs who wanted his lunch money; he ran from a five-and-dime store after he had stolen a yo-yo or maybe a whistle or a pen-sized flashlight ("Let's go *taking*," he and his friends would say). When he couldn't run, he talked his way out of situations. "He was never a quiet boy," noted Kitty, who was not famous for irony (her son was inca-pable of attaining the state of being known as quiet). He was small, he needed protection, and he kept his mouth going. "I became accepted and was allowed to hang out with bigger kids because I made them laugh. . . . You don't hit the kid that makes you laugh."

The street life was an ongoing festival—mockery of teachers, of rabbis, of other kids, of highfalutin attitudes. Before Mel's time, on the Lower East Side, this cauldron of happy derision had produced some of the greatest performers in vaudeville—Eddie Cantor, Al Jolson, Fanny Brice—as well as a New York population of fast-talking taxi drivers, argumentative waiters, motor-mouthed grifters, and criminals of all kinds. New Yorkers *talk*. On the street, the competition could be brutal. The principal arena of combat was a corner near a candy store. From *Playboy* again:

> The corner was tough. You had to score on the corner—no bullshit routines, no slick laminated crap. It had to be, "Lemme tell ya what happened today. . . ." And you really had to be good on your feet. "Fat Hymie was hanging from the fire escape. His mother came by. 'Hymie!' she screamed. He fell two stories and broke his head." Real stories of tragedy we screamed at. The story had to be real and it had to be funny. Somebody getting hurt was wonderful.

Throughout his work, large projects and small, Brooks displays an endless fascination with such experiences as fear and cruelty, accident and death. Such are the sources of his humor—for him, the sources of humor, *period*. He makes that clear in "The Stone Age," one of the early episodes in *History of the World, Part 1*. The Homo sapiens gather in an uncomfortable-looking cave. Out in front, a fellow in ratty pelts tries to put on a show. He tumbles and kicks up a leg and gets little response. It's definitely a slow night in the cave. Suddenly, T-Rex appears; he grabs the entertainer in his jaws and carries him off screaming, and the audience falls into hysterics. It is the Birth of Comedy.

Mel Brooks's view of life is essentially gloomy, or at least morose. In the past, as Jeremy Dauber pointed out in his *Jewish Comedy: A Serious History* (2017), oppression has always been a principal source of Jewish joking. Mel Brooks in America has hardly been oppressed, but the weight of Jewish humor, in all its morbid persistence, hangs on him like a thick robe and feeds energy into his body. Death must be conquered; he resists and resists, he springs laughter out of calamity by facing it over and over. In the "2000 Year Old Man" comedy routine, Carl Reiner, a terrific straight man, earnestly asks the ancient survivor, "How do you differentiate between tragedy and comedy?" Brooks answers: "If I cut my finger, that's tragedy. . . . Comedy is if you walk into an open sewer and die."

A CAREER KNOWNST TO GOD

In the 1930s and '40s, some of the more ambitious boys and girls in Mel's neighborhood went to the great public institutions, City College or Hunter, both parts of the City University of New York. But there was a more likely destination for many. As I heard Mel say at a public performance in 2018, "Unbeknownst to them but *knownst* [he savors the word] . . . *knownst* to God, they were heading for the Garment District." Jews owned many of the firms on Seventh Avenue, employing men and women of all ages as shipping clerks, seamstresses, tailors, pattern cutters, secretaries, rack pushers. (A little later, my mother attained the serious position of *buyer*.) It may also have been knownst to God that Mel Brooks would *not* go there; nor would he enter the Kaminsky family herring trade. He went into show business, just as an earlier generation of talented immigrants and children of immigrants, including Irving Berlin and George Gershwin, as well as the vaudevillians, had done—in their case to avoid not only the Garment District but also the metal workshops and the cigar-rolling factories. Mel was one of the kids in the neighborhood who was seized by artistic ambition, or at least by artistic appreciation.

To a degree that seems amazing now, the working-class Jewish neighborhoods in New York in the thirties were suffused with longing for culture. Mel told me that in many poor families in Williamsburg, someone played an instrument or sang or wanted to be an actor or a playwright. The sound of people playing or declaiming bounced off the courtyard walls, mingling with the music from the radio. What created this longing? As Hannah Arendt has noted, the Jews throughout their history have demanded that everyone in the community had to read. (Without the ability to read sacred texts, identity would dissolve.) Among the immigrant Jews, that insistence was joined to the absolute need to speak and write a new language. Language classes were everywhere—how could one survive without English? And for some, the practical demand for literacy was joined to an overlay of respect—something remembered from Warsaw or Vilnius or even a shtetl in the countryside—for European high culture. Even a Lower East Side workman might want to read Tolstoy. No one would make fun of him if he had that desire.

In the immediate way, the neighborhood was obsessed with education, which, as we know, had little effect on Mel's school attendance. Yet the general atmosphere left him with unfulfilled desires. He absorbed popular entertainment, but he longed for great things as well. He read very little as a boy, but years later, when a fellow writer, Mel Tolkin, on the Sid Caesar TV program, *Your Show of Shows*, suggested that he read the Russians—Tolstoy, Dostoevsky, Gogol—Mel took the advice and was hit very hard by what he read. Some part of the Russian pessimism melded with his own cruel knowledge of what was funny.

Across the Williamsburg Bridge, there was "New York," a place both attractive and frightening. (Mel and his friends never called it "Manhattan." It was always "New York.") The Yiddish theater was still going strong in the thirties, and much prized for its emotional extremes. He told me he went "once or twice, on Second Avenue on the Lower East Side. It was a lesson in *peaks*. They would end the act with some sort of revelation. 'She's pregnant!'" As for burlesque, he remembers "a few shows in which the comics wore the same elongated jacket with stripes. They all wore the same jacket!—it must have been some sort of reward for becoming a comic in burlesque." His actual experience of burlesque was minimal; yet his spiritual devotion to low comedy was enormous. He responds to the condition of the body in every way—as a patient, as a gatherer of medical lore and remedies (even as a young man, his medicine cabinet was famous), as a proponent of blatant jokes about farting, defecating, organs, emissions. To paraphrase Pascal: the body has a mind of its own which the mind knows not of.

IN 1936, WHEN Mel was ten, over 40 percent of the adult American population went to the movies every week. For a dime, or maybe eleven cents, Mel would go to the Marcy or one of the other Brooklyn neighborhood houses, with their broken seats and sticky floors, their mentholated gents' rooms and patrolling matrons with thick white shoes. Kitty would give him a salmon-and-tomato sandwich, which would get him through a double bill and perhaps a chapter in a serial, and hours later one of his older brothers would pick him up. The movies were life, freedom, imagination. Mel told me he remembers best the Hoot Gibson and Ken Maynard Westerns, the Fred Astaire–Ginger Rogers and the Dick Powell–Ruby Keeler musicals, and Universal Pictures' horror films, especially *Frankenstein*, which, as we know, scared him badly until Kitty came to the rescue. He would eventually make his own versions of the genres he remembered best. He also saw comedies with the Marx Brothers, the Three Stooges, and the nearly forgotten Ritz Brothers, Al, Jimmy, and Harry.

The Ritz Brothers were good-sized guys from Mel's neighborhood who appeared in the backgrounds of many movies in the thirties. They would dominate the interlude sets at nightclubs, and Harry Ritz also appeared in nearly unwatchable (for me) pictures starring skater Sonja Henie and the Andrews Sisters. "Harry had a physical insanity and freedom that no other performer had," Mel wrote in his autobiography, *All About Me!* (2021). "He was the master of wild, bizarre walks, facial contortions, and wacky sounds." The Ritz Brothers may have been the unacknowledged fount of much later comedy, here and in England, including, perhaps, John Cleese's Silly Walks and other *Monty Python* skits. They were certainly the inspiration for Mel's later mentor Sid Caesar.

On the radio, Mel listened to Jack Benny and the vaudevillian Eddie Cantor. "The difference between a good and great comic is the degree of confidence," he told me. "Comics without confidence rush to the punch line. Jack Benny, Eddie Cantor, Myron Cohen—the confidence shows in how much they paused." In particular, he learned from Cantor how to emphasize a certain word and sometimes strike off the beat or even after the beat. Except for the dryly witty Fred Allen, another radio hero, these were Jewish teachers.

In all, it was a loud, blatant, sometimes brilliant era of popular culture. New York had multiple newspapers, including the mass-circulation *Brooklyn Eagle* and such Yiddish papers as the *Forward* (as well as other Yiddish-language dailies). Neighborhood barbershops were decorated with bawdy calendar art and yellowing pictures of Franklin Roosevelt. Comic books, by the late thirties, had sprung out of newspaper strips and had landed on newsstands as separate publications. There was much more—dance halls, carnivals, traveling magic shows and street theater, open-air debates about socialism and Zionism. Later in life, Mel, exploding, seemed to embody many of these entertainments at once.

Through a chance meeting in Brooklyn, in 1939, he got to know the great drummer Buddy Rich (then in Artie Shaw's band), and Rich gave him some informal lessons, teaching him the importance of rhythm, which, as Brooks always says, is central to comedy. (As for drumming, he never really gave up on it: well into middle age, his thick hands would pound out complicated grooves on the desk of one talk-show host or another.) Kitty bought him a drum set, and he changed his name from Kaminsky to Brookman (Kitty's name); he then tightened Brookman to Brooks, so the lettering would fit on the head of a bass drum. He could be accused of anglicizing his name like so many other Jews, including my father. But has any other performer ever been so publicly Jewish?

APPRENTICE IN THE MOUNTAINS

Mel Brooks's life as a performer and comedy creator revved up in the summer of 1940, when he was fourteen. An actor friend in the neighborhood worked as a social director at one of the Catskills resorts; he put in a word for Mel at a neighboring place, Butler Lodge, in Hurleyville, New York.

The Catskills? The Borscht Belt? *The Mountains*? The words have a remote sound to us now—soft, withered, like pot cheese gone bad. Photographer Marisa Scheinfeld, in *The Borscht Belt: Revisiting the Remains of America's Jewish Vacationland* (2016), has granted us pictures of abandoned lodges, ripped and jumbled dining chairs, a tattered queen-size bed—remnants of blessings once enjoyed. Apart from such memorials, the phenomenon has so completely vanished that it seems a Jewish hallucination—a low-cost Eden a hundred miles northwest of New York, a place of cooling breezes and woodland walks, swimming pools, open-air ballrooms, and enormous piles of kosher food served by Yiddish-speaking waiters. Blintzes were put on the table *every day* and were served with sour cream—definitely holiday food. For some, it was a social paradise with many unattached men and women, a place for the pale Jewish body to meet the sun and please itself and other Jewish bodies. Most poor urban Jews generally married within a twenty-block radius of their homes; the Catskills opened up the possibility of finding mates from other neighborhoods, other cities.

Grossinger's, the Concord, Kutsher's—those were the monster hotels, with their private airstrips and their dining rooms seating hundreds. But there was every kind of smaller place, including lodges, inns, cottage colonies, boardinghouses created from old farm buildings (*kucheleins*, where families on a budget cooked for themselves). It was a Jewish summer colony—five hundred establishments in all. In the 1920s, working-class and lower-middle-class Jews from New York and other East Coast enclaves began going there en masse, arriving by bus, by train, and increasingly by car. The collective caravan moved north on Route 17 to such towns as Liberty and Hancock and then spread out. "Everywhere you went, there were Jews in the mountains," Mel said years later. "I'm sure the deer would say, 'I've never seen so many Jews.'" In part, they came because they didn't have many other places to go. They were excluded from resorts all over the country, and the Catskills were a companionable retreat. In the forties and fifties, some of the refugees from Europe, having survived unimaginable horrors, went to the Mountains for comfort and solace and the sound of Yiddish. Even Jewish gangsters—Louis Lepke and Dutch Schultz—went there for peace and quiet, and perhaps to hide. The gangsters left big tips.

The social director of a given resort, commanding sizable troupes of actors and musicians, would put on plays, musical revues, and every kind of comedy, from slapstick to "dirty" monologues and satirical sketches. People went to the Catskills to eat, to meet the opposite sex, to play cards, and to laugh. Vaudeville, dying in big cities after the onslaught of radio and the movies, was reborn in a very different form in the Mountains. Many of the entertainers came from neighborhoods familiar to the guests. After youths spent razzing authority figures and entertaining friends with monologues and impressions, kids from the slums suddenly faced new audiences, sometimes tough, sometimes easy, at the resorts. Sid Caesar was there when he was seventeen; Danny Kaye (born David Daniel Kaminsky, but no relation to Brooks) worked there as a teenager, as did, at one time or another, Jerry Lewis, Milton Berle, Jackie Mason, and Buddy Hackett; and, later, Joan Rivers, Woody Allen, Jerry Seinfeld, Sarah Silverman, and just about every other Jewish comic you could name, most of whom later performed in Las Vegas or Atlantic City or on television. What began in the Mountains as entertainment for a knowing audience was later broadened to include the entire country. From 1948 to 1971, the weekly *Ed Sullivan Show* was the most important goal for new talent, a kind of national comedy-and-music revue on television every Sunday night. In his book *Seriously Funny* (2003), comedy historian Gerald Nachman insists that the *Ed Sullivan Show* "was almost a wing of the Catskills hotels."

* * *

IN 1940, MEL Brooks worked at the Butler Lodge for eight dollars a week. He washed dishes, rounded up rowboats, ladled out sour cream. He ate a great deal, and, in a blessing for which he would always be grateful, achieved the position of pool *tummler*. In general, a *tummler* is a noisy fellow whose job is to entertain in different corners of the resort—perhaps in dining rooms, or on the lawn, or in the resort's nightclub. The position of pool *tummler* is not of the highest rank. Mel's job was to keep the guests awake in the afternoons. He vamped the middle-aged ladies (the men were often playing pinochle), ingratiating himself as best as he could. "Here I am, I'm Mel Brooks. I've come to stop the show," he sang. "Melvin, you're terrible, but we love you!" the women said to him. One of his moves when he was fourteen—he told the story many times—was to walk out on the diving board in a heavy winter coat and a black derby. Holding two heavy suitcases, he would cry, "Business is terrible! I can't go on!" and then jump into the water, only to be rescued by a large Gentile person serving as lifeguard. (Brooklyn Jews in those days did not swim.) In all, it's a grim bit of fun. Even when he was fourteen, he made a joke out of death. You joked about it, and you beat it.

Talking to a Jewish audience, Mel could try things out, play around, even turn against the audience at times. He was performing in a reassuring environment; he didn't have to do the sordid things that Al Jolson, a great Jewish entertainer of an earlier era, had to do. Jolson, born in 1886, initially entertained in the streets with his brother Harry. As Richard Bernstein re-creates their lives in *Only in America* (2024), at the turn of the century they lived among prostitutes, pimps, thieves, and bums; they sang and told jokes in beer halls and restaurants; they appeared in rough-and-ready vaudeville shows all over the East Coast. One of Jolson's most famous routines (which he recapped in the first talkie, *The Jazz Singer*) was to perform in blackface. Another was to make brutal fun of the mangled English of recent immigrants, including the Jewish immigrants from Russia, Poland, and other Eastern European countries—great amusement for Gentile audiences (who themselves may have been recently arrived Irish or Italians). "Ethnic comedy" was a standard bit; the comics doing Jews showed up with hooked noses and false beards, and said things like,

"Oy, I gedt troubles." But forty years later, vaudeville was dead, the Jews had their own retreat, and Mel told jokes *about* Jews, *for* Jews, but without nasty mimicry. The difference in Jewish entertainment in the two eras is as good a marker as any of Jewish success.

There was one memorable bit when he was fifteen. He would stand on stage with a female member of the hotel staff and say, "I am a masochist." She would say, "I'm a sadist," and haul off and smack him across the face. "Wait a minute, wait a minute. Hold it," he would say. "I think I'm a sadist." Pain always worked for Mel. And so did Hitler jokes. In the 2016 documentary *The Last Laugh*, directed by Ferne Pearlstein, Mel, then ninety years old, held a black comb to his upper lip and spouted German gibberish. "When I was a kid in the Mountains, I would do Hitler. And I would get a lot of laughs with Hitler. But a few Jews after the show would say, 'You know, that wasn't in such good taste.' And I would say, 'I don't care. I really don't give a shit what's in good taste.'"

His remark suggests not only the strength of his Hitler obsession but a certain difficulty for a comic in the Mountains, great as the place was for a young Jewish performer. If you came back for too many years, you could give in to the audience. You could make them laugh with stale, tired jokes. "Good evening, ladies and germs, I just flew in from Chicago. Boy, are my arms tired." That line is not a joke, it's a genre of jokes, and the audience laughs because the *form* of the words is funny. But is that kind of laughter a sign of generosity? Or is it a kind of contempt that envelops both a lazy comic and a bored audience? It's a strange question, and I would never have raised it, yet here was Mel in 1985, more than thirty years after he last appeared in the Catskills, talking to Johnny Carson.

> One night, *one night*, I really wanted to turn the Jews around, to do something insane. So I did everything—but no punch line. "Good evening ladies and germs, I just walked in from Chicago. It was . . . a little nauseous. I met a girl in Chicago, she was so skinny . . . I was worried. I got a room in Chicago, the room was so small, I called up, I said . . . "Change the room." I did every single joke known to man, but just straight, no punch line.

It's rebellion of a sort, even an expression of anger at his audience, and perhaps also a dare, recapitulated on *The Tonight Show*—a dare not to be funny, which, of course, is a dreadful risk for any comic, possibly a disastrous risk. The nonjokes played oddly on national television. Johnny Carson was puzzled at first, but then, as Mel gave one example after another, he began to laugh; Ed McMahon (of course) also began laughing, and the studio audience joined in. The moment of nonexistence had been faced and overcome. Mel was a comic again.

The Catskills were his school and his proving ground, and he certainly admired such virtuosos of the one-line joke as Henny Youngman. When I talked to Mel, we agreed that Youngman, with the long, sad face of permanent middle age, the violin he scratched or just tucked under his arm, his way of telling joke after joke without a break, never wrong-footing himself—Henny Youngman was an extraordinary performer. (Mel has twice told me a Youngman joke in double tempo: "*My wife used to tell me, you don't take me anywhere, I want to go somewhere I've never been, so I took her to the kitchen.*") But stand-up comedy, as well as the Catskills, were things Mel Brooks had to get away from. In his twenties, he had no desire to "work the toilets," as the comics say—the ordinary little rooms in cities and towns all over the country—and no desire, either, to work the big plush rooms (the Copacabana or the Latin Quarter in New York). Those were among the roads not taken. Mel Brooks did not do tales of life among the Jewish poor like Sam Levenson; he didn't make comedy out of his own neuroses (he didn't have any neuroses); nor did he insert corny "Jewish" lyrics into familiar folk songs and show tunes—"Seventy-six Sol Cohens in the country club," and so on. He became a writer and a performer of his own kind of explosive *comedy events*, and his dreams were always of the big time.

A JEW AT WAR

In April 1944, all three of Mel's older brothers were in the service, and Mel, though still in high school, enlisted in the US Army. He was first sent to Virginia Military Institute, perhaps a strange place for a Jewish boy from Brooklyn but a place he came to admire. At VMI, he studied electrical engineering for a semester, learned to ride a horse, and ate the worst mashed potatoes he had ever tasted (they turned out to be parsnips). Then the army sent him to Fort Sill, Oklahoma, where he was placed in a field artillery unit. In his autobiography, he claims a friend told him to tear a cigarette (unfiltered) in half and stuff it in his ears to dull the sound of the howitzer 105s. Finally, he went through basic training in Fort Dix, New Jersey, which was a bit of a shock: "I'd never gone to the toilet before with sixteen other guys sitting next to me." On the chow line, he learned to eat chipped beef and creamed gravy on toast, sometimes with sliced peaches piled on top. He couldn't believe he would long so much for noodles, kreplach, and egg creams.

Some of the army stories in Brooks's memories have the happy-complaining sound of many works about army life in the Second World War era; not the great ones, like *The Naked and the Dead* and *From Here to Eternity*, which were anything but happy, but the popular accounts of army life that spilled into movies and TV shows—service comedies—in which recruits grouch about endless drills, terrible food, incomprehensible orders. But the toilets and the food are only part of what Mel chooses to remember. He told Mike Wallace, on *60 Minutes*, in April 2001, that soldiers said things like, "Jewboy! Out of my way, out of my face, Jewboy." He smashed one anti-Semitic jerk on the head with a mess kit and served a day in the stockade as punishment.

In 1945, just after the Battle of the Bulge, he was sent to Belgium as a "combat engineer." Part of his job was identifying the locations of land mines (other people defused them). There were many terrifying moments—such as pulling a toilet chain without knowing what might be lodged in the water closet above the toilet. Describing his time in Belgium, he told Kenneth Tynan in a *New Yorker* profile (October 22, 1978) that he saw the following:

Along the roadside, you'd see bodies wrapped up in mattress covers and stacked in a ditch, and those would be Americans, that could be me. And I sang all the time; I made up funny songs; I never wanted to think about it. Some guy would say "We're gonna be killed, we'll never get out of this war," and I'd say, "Nobody dies—it's all made up." Because otherwise we'd all get hysterical, and that kind of hysteria—it's not like sinking, it's like slowly taking on water, and that's the panic. Death is the enemy of everyone, and even though you hate Nazis, death is more of an enemy than a German soldier.

These are not a hero's memories. These are a performer's memories, and they sound authentic. He fought against death by singing and telling jokes, and he doesn't want to go beyond that. He says he hated death more than Nazis, and I believe him, but he still punched out Hitler into his nineties.

SID AND THE REST OF LIFE

"When I met Sid," Mel told me, "I found heaven."

Mel Brooks first met Sid Caesar in 1940, when he was fourteen and Sid was all of seventeen, a sax player in the house band at the Avon Lodge in the Catskills. Broad-shouldered, swarthy—a sizable, good-looking teenager—Sid Caesar was certainly impressive compared to the skinny and pale Mel Brooks. You might have thought of him as a mature-looking young man, a future businessman or lawyer who would dominate his community. He certainly didn't look like a comic. But within a few years it became clear he could do anything with his face. Calling him "rubber-faced" doesn't do justice to the violence of his grimaces, his sly grins widening into savagery, his eyes popping, almost fish-tailing in rage, his jaw distorted into off-angle tilts like a swinging boom. Sid Caesar was a silent comic working in sound: even as he did weird things with his face and body, alarming noises emerged from his stomach and throat; he could imitate internal organs at work and machines of all kinds. He didn't emote, he exploded, though he could be subtle, too, his flickering eyelids and twitching mouth indicating innumerable shades of disgust and bafflement. He may have been the greatest performer of pantomime since Chaplin.

Peppy little Mel latched onto him from the beginning, amusing him with nonstop jokes and nonsense (and obvious adoration), and Sid remembered him. Mel visited him at the Copacabana nightclub in New York in 1947, and Mel in his memoir recalls him doing "a satire of a war picture playing both the good-looking American pilot and the evil-looking German pilot. And the sounds he made were amazing: the plane's engines, the machine guns, and the hero's dialogue as well as the villain's guttural crazy German." His encounter with Sid Caesar set his ideas about comedy for the rest of his life. "Sid's comedy," he wrote, "was not a bunch of one-liners, but a satire of the human race." Sid Caesar played characters; he satirized lust and appetite; he enacted frustration and loss—a starving, carnivorous husband, say, whose wife drags him to an alfalfa-rich health-fetish restaurant. When his characters were in pain, Sid Caesar nearly strangled himself with grief. He was more than impressive; at times, he was terrifying. "Sid brought a tragic element to what he did," Mel said to me. But he also said that by writing for Sid Caesar, "I couldn't have had a better vehicle to spew my own thoughts." Some of Sid's intensity came from the young Mel Brooks.

Caesar was a protégé of Max Liebman, who was born in Vienna in 1902 but grew up in Brooklyn. Wit was a great value among Jewish men in the 1930s: it was as much a way of distinguishing yourself as success in some burgeoning profession. Groucho Marx was a hero; everyone wanted to be like him, as later young men wanted to be like Woody Allen or Jerry Seinfeld. Max Liebman, mastering English, became a writer of sketch-comedy material. After working the Catskills, he turned himself into an impresario of talent in the Pennsylvania resort area the Poconos; his specialty was the Broadway-style revue, a mix of comedy, music, and dancing with only a slender line of continuity or none at all. In the Poconos, and later on television, Liebman was capable of assembling in one week a production that would take anyone else a month to pull together. There were simple ideas for skits with one or two characters sweetly or barbarously playing off each other; and complicated scenes, with many characters creating (satirically) an entire way of life. In the early years of television, Liebman's crew would throw together material building on and surpassing earlier versions of the same forms they had developed in vaudeville or summer-revue shows.

In 1950, a little less than four million households owned television sets. The black-and-white images could be unstable and blurry, the reception uncertain, the programming feeble. As the technology improved, however, and the audience expanded, the field was open to the hungry. Marshall McLuhan famously wrote in *Understanding Media* (1964), "the medium is the message," but in the early days of TV a distinct part of the "message" was fresh talent. Hollywood and the big movie studios hadn't quite got their hands on the new medium yet; the best programming originated in New York. Max Liebman thought of television as a cultural revolution, a way of bringing young performers to a large audience—opera singers and ballet dancers as well as comics and pop vocalists right out of the clubs and resorts. The optimism and ambition of the early years of TV ("The Golden Age"), however naive, now seem stirring to us.

In 1950, Liebman created *Your Show of Shows*, starring Sid Caesar and one of his discoveries, Imogene Coca, and later Carl Reiner, who was tall and handsome but also a tremendous comic performer; and also Howie Morris, small and light like Imogene Coca, both of them foils for the mighty Sid. Meeting Howie Morris for the first time, Sid Caesar picked him up to eye level, asked him a few questions, and then put him down and hired him. *Your Show of Shows* debuted on NBC in February 1950, in the middle of the season. Critics and audiences loved it. In comedy, nothing like it had ever been seen before. But Mel, at first, couldn't get past the door.

STORMING INTO THE WRITERS' ROOM

Sid's manager, policing the rehearsal rooms, took Mel for a hanger-on and threw him out. He would show up anyway, grabbing Sid in the hallway, adding a joke to some existing sketch. He would shout "Fuck!" into Liebman's meetings with writers and then slam the door. On occasion, when Liebman's dancers were rehearsing, he would slide across the shiny floor, hit the far wall, and shout "Safe!"

"Who is this *meshuggener*?" Liebman inquired. He threw a lit cigar at him more than once. "He would blow on his cigar to make the end hotter," Mel told me. "That's when I knew he was going to throw it at me." Mel was twenty-four, and he didn't have an agent; he was not equipped to negotiate with Max Liebman. "You make a lot of noise, but you're *nothing*," Liebman informed him.

"Every once in a while," Mel writes in his memoir, "I would suffer an attack of no-holds-barred madness." In 1950, officials from NBC and RCA (NBC's parent company) were having a serious meeting about *Your Show of Shows*. Mel had no business being there, but he still demanded a place in the room. Liebman was determined to keep him out. In his autobiography, Mel writes as follows:

I ran around the rehearsal area, which had a lot of props. I saw a straw boater hat and then I grabbed a white duster coat (a long coat that people wore to drive cars in 1893) that Carl [Reiner] used to wear sometimes in sketches. I put on the hat, coat, and a pair of goggles, and I burst into the meeting! I jumped up on the long conference table and yelled, "Lindy landed! He's in Paris, he made it!" And I hurled my hat out the open window.

Mel called me in January 2023 and said, "I want to correct something. I waited until the meeting was *over*. I wouldn't have interrupted the meeting while it was going on." Okay, and *then* he jumped up on the table. It's still impressive. We all need to be noticed, but Mel's table-jumping masterpiece goes beyond need. At that moment he could have thrown his career as well as his hat out the window. Too many people in show business get stuck and have minor careers or disappear; Mel, unwilling to be one of them, was seized with inspiration—a sudden accession of power— the way warriors on a battlefield or religious people in a moment of crisis are seized and then transcend themselves. "I wanted to have something brazen to say," he told me.

Anyone meeting him later (including me) has the impression of an enormously strong-willed man, but Mel Brooks should not be called, as he often has, "a force of nature." After all, nature can be benign, and he was often ferocious, deafening, shouting until he had worn down everyone's resistance. Nature rests; Mel never rests. Making people laugh was a way of earning a living; it was a way of fighting off death; and it was a way of asserting Jewish survival. *You tried to kill us all, and you failed!* Liebman, Sid Caesar, Carl Reiner, Howie Morris, everyone in the writers' room—all the principals involved in *Your Show of Shows* (except for the great Imogene Coca) were Jewish. Jumping on the table, Mel may have instinctively wanted to protect the Jews doing the show as well as advance himself.

But the overwhelming question of his early years was this: How do you get from "Me! Jew! Me! Jew!" to writing a script, having your own TV show, directing a movie? He didn't know, and his uncertainty may have been yet another reason he burst into scenes like an illegal fireworks display.

HIS FIRST WRITING credit, in the truncated 1950–51 season of *Your Show of Shows*, was "additional material by Mel Brooks." He was finally in the room, but it wasn't until the full 1951–52 season that he attained the status of a regular writer. Liebman had put together a team that included Mel Tolkin as head writer; Tolkin's writing partner Lucille Kallen; Larry Gelbart, later the creator of the TV version of *M*A*S*H*; Joseph Stein, who later wrote the book for *Fiddler on the Roof*; future hit playwright Neil

Simon (*Barefoot in the Park*, *The Odd Couple*, etc.), who came on with his brother, Danny; and, near the end of Sid Caesar's run as a TV star, Woody Allen.

That room, filled as it was with enormous talents, could be a brutal place. Someone would suggest an idea, and the idea would be debated, acted out, thrown down on the floor and danced on, only to be revived in some later form. The writers were out to top one another, destroy one another—laughing at someone else's jokes was usually disdained, though truly great ideas would crack everyone up. *Fou rire*, in this crowd, was the only *rire* worth having. They were Jewish intellectuals and comic talents determined to avoid the clichés and easy laughs of the Catskills. They created satire on television; they created television itself as a medium for artists.

The full season of *Your Show of Shows* ran for thirty-nine weeks, each show beginning at nine o'clock on Saturday night and lasting ninety minutes, all of it staged in front of a live audience. The cast had neither cue cards nor pretaped episodes nor serious breaks (the commercials lasted one minute). The writers, including Mel, especially Mel, were overstrained, exhausted, both gleeful and despairing. During the day, when not in the room, Mel would wander around, sometimes running in the streets of New York in order to combat dizziness and nausea, only to vomit, as he told Kenneth Tynan, "between parked Plymouths." At night, unable to slow down, he would try to think of bits for the show while dropping in on Village clubs to hear music and comedy, finally drifting off in front of a TV set early in the morning, as if he could dream his way into the medium. Waking up with a start, he would jag himself into life with coffee, pick up a bagel and some rugelach, and hit the writers' room an hour or two after everyone else, shouting out ideas, jumping on tables (the leap was habit-forming). His taste was for wild exaggeration, the grotesque, the lampooned ideal, an idea snatched out of the air and then turned inside out.

Almost four decades after working with this gang, Neil Simon was still drawing on his memories of it. His 1993 play *Laughter on the 23rd Floor* is one of the funniest things he ever wrote. The Mel Brooks character, known as Ira Stone, is a self-dramatizing mock hypochondriac. He storms in late complaining of a brain tumor, a spinal injury, an attack of some sort. The others first ignore him and then insult him. "Do you realize you monopolize every minute you're in this room?" one of the writers asks him. "Who better than me?" Ira replies. He throws another writer's shoes, as well as his own, out of an open window (an echo of Mel's Lucky Lindy hat toss). He demands love from the Sid Caesar character, who is known as Max Prince, and threatens to quit if he doesn't get it. As Neil Simon imagined Mel Brooks at twenty-five, he was a viciously funny, self-approving hysteric, and the other writers couldn't stand him. "He got most of it," Mel told me. "Not all of it." They may have hated him because they needed him. Max Liebman, Mel says, put his arm around him one day and said, "'I was wrong. You were the funniest, you were necessary.' That made me cry."

Mel adored Sid Caesar, feared him, flattered him, longed for him (perhaps) to be the father that he never had. In his wrath, Sid could be an Old Testament God—more father than most of us want. On one occasion, in 1950, after putting on a live show in Chicago, Sid was relaxing and drinking in a hotel room. Mel kept yammering that he couldn't breathe, it was too hot, he needed air. When he couldn't get the window open, Sid yanked it open and, grabbing Mel by the feet, slung him outside, where Mel had a clear view of the taxis below. "Is that enough air?" Sid asked.

In the writers' room, Mel Tolkin, the oldest and most traditionally cultured of the writers, took a benevolent interest in the turbulent young man. He advised Brooks to slow down and enter psychotherapy (a very fifties kind of advice) and to read the Russians (also a fifties kind of advice)—Nikolai Gogol as well as Tolstoy and Dostoevsky. Mel has always described this moment as a turning point in his life. "Gogol . . . read *Dead Souls*," he instructed me.

I can see the most important things he took from Gogol—a cheerfully pessimistic temperament and the notion that conventional life (including officialdom and all of authority) was just a facade for fraud and corruption. He picked up the master's way of dropping the fantastic into realistic presentation. In Gogol's story "The Nose," a minor official wakes up one morning to discover that his nose has disappeared, only to see it later stepping out of a carriage and wearing a uniform. Mel imitated Gogol's way of teasing the act of storytelling, undermining narrative consistency with a sudden insolent aside to the reader. In *Blazing Saddles*, the last scene in the dusty plains of the Old West suddenly gives way to . . . a musical that is shot on a Warner Bros. soundstage, complete with fey male chorines in top hats and tails. I don't mean to suggest that Mel Brooks is an artist of the stature of Nikolai Gogol, only that his immersion in Gogol affirmed his most aggressive and disruptive comic instincts and licensed his bouts of formal daring.

GIBBERISH BECOMES MUSIC

The slapstick horsing and miming on *Your Show of Shows* was sometimes so bizarre that you can't imagine anyone writing it down (though much of it *was* written down); nor can you imagine how the actors pulled it off without the benefit of retakes and editing. Mel told me it was hard to remember who was responsible for what, but he definitely wrote monologues for Sid, including the classic "German General" skit, in which the imposing Caesar wears a dress uniform, including brass buttons and epaulets, and the twittering, tiny Howie Morris, his adjutant, scampers around him. "*Das Monocle is vershmutzige,*" roars the general, who demands perfection. It was the early fifties, and the war was only recently over, and enraged German accents were ripe comedy material; adding Yiddish to the German seasoned the joke.

Sid Caesar excelled at foreign-language gibberish, as did many Jewish comics after the war, including Danny Kaye, Lenny Bruce, Carl Reiner, Howie Morris, and Mel Brooks. They generated a rush of syllables, appropriately pitched and emphasized, abrupt and harsh in German (a dog whose food bowl has been removed); intimate and insinuating in French (a lover arguing someone into bed); angry in Russian (a step away from violence). I can remember rolling on the floor as my father and I watched Sid and his group do a Yiddish-Japanese skit called "U Betchu," a parody of Mizoguchi's masterly film *Ugetsu*, from 1953. Why this skill for foreign-language mimicry among Jews? The comics grew up in Yiddish-speaking households, but they needed to master English to succeed at school and at work; they were necessarily bilingual. Sid spent his childhood in his father's diner in Yonkers, where he heard immigrant workers and truck drivers speaking Polish, Italian, and many other tongues. He learned the music of foreign languages without speaking an intelligible word in anything but English. More centrally, Sid and the other comics needed to master rhythm and intonation to tell a joke or create a scene. Lilt and momentum as well as rhythm were central to their attack; great comedy is always *sung*.

In the end, the singing of these comics had an enormous influence outside of comedy. The Jewish comics, not just Caesar and his gang but the vaudevillians who came earlier—Eddie Cantor, Fanny Brice, and the Marx Brothers—in their practice of parody, exaggeration, and spoof, developed the obsession with exultant *voice* that would bear fruit in the literary work of Saul Bellow, Philip Roth, and Norman Mailer. In a 1966 essay (the introduction to *The Commentary Reader*), critic Alfred Kazin insisted on it: the demanding postwar Jewish literature was derived not from high culture or academic tradition but from the joking of popular comics. There is a complete historical cycle here, which goes like this: street insults and profanity early in the last century move into classic vaudeville comedy; then into cleaned-up versions on the radio in the thirties and forties; then into postwar mimicry and satire on television; all of it winding up, transformed, in Saul Bellow's *The Adventures of Augie March* and Philip Roth's *Portnoy's Complaint*. Vulgar exaggeration and parody eventually ceased being gibberish at all.

The Caesar gang loved European culture, admiring it and lousing it up at the same time. They did immortal parodies of "art films," including the heartbreaking neorealist Italian film *Bicycle Thieves* (1948), in which Caesar, Carl Reiner, and Imogene Coca passionately fight and love one another in eloquent Italian double-talk. Mel says, "Max Liebman kept yelling. 'You're satirizing films that no one has seen!'" But they persisted, in part, because they had faith in the audience—*their* audience, the early TV buyers, often culturally knowledgeable viewers in New York, Boston, Chicago, California, and the college towns, who would get the allusions, the combination of mockery and respect. Mel learned much about genre parody, and he stored what he learned deep in his pocket.

Satire and parody have become endemic in our digital world. The spoof, the mash-up, so easy to pull off, is our daily breakfast. But seventy years ago, it was startling, and, in the Caesar show version, it was produced by habits of quick-wittedness and a refusal to be taken in by anything—temperamental qualities that had (and still have) a high cultural value among American Jews. In the post-Holocaust period especially, a Jew could not act like a fool without feelings of intense shame.

Life was treacherous, and idiots endangered themselves and everyone else. Men and women became aggressively funny partly as a way of showing they had survived the lure of stupidity. In particular, the Yiddish that Caesar and his writers sprinkled into the imagined German and Japanese of their skits was both a proud signature and a way of creating a knowing audience.

In this new medium, a bunch of Jewish comedy talents, children of immigrant families, working with both broad comedy and delicate wit, put a significant part of Jewish sensibility in front of millions of Americans. Yet it couldn't last. In 1954, NBC canceled *Your Show of Shows* and then reshaped it as a sixty-minute show, *Caesar's Hour*, which ran until its ratings began falling in 1956 and 1957. Television was becoming a true mass medium in the late fifties, penetrating 83 percent of households by 1958, and many of those households preferred Lawrence Welk's bubble-music *kitsch* to Sid Caesar on Saturday night. The ending was bitter. As far as Neil Simon was concerned, the writers slaughtering each other in the room while creating art in the show were a fount of free expression in the Joseph McCarthy era, a time when so many were frightened into silence and blandness. In Simon's re-creation of the faltering moment, Max Prince (as Sid) has a kind of violent breakdown, punching holes in the wall; he tells the other writers that the top brass's message to all of them was, "Give the people shit." Later on, Mel never gave the people crap, but he also never tried satire that wasn't broad enough to be understood by everyone.

Mel Brooks has always been intensely proud of what they all accomplished. At the 1958 Emmy Awards dinner, after the second Caesar show had been canceled, the writers for *The Phil Silvers Show* (a rival) won the award for best comedy series for 1957. They won *for the third year in a row*. When the winners were announced, Mel Brooks leaped onto a chair and shouted, "Nietzsche was right! There is no God!" and proceeded to cut up his tuxedo with a pair of manicure scissors.

"I was drunk," he told me. "The Emmys were in a theater, and I went to a wardrobe room and found some kind of medieval costume, and my wife and I took a taxi home." And here he rolled off the names of Caesar's writers. "We were in the trenches, taking on modern life. We were the cream of the crop. We were extremely bright, very well-read . . . and all of us were in analysis!"

Shredding one's clothes is a traditional Jewish demonstration of mourning. In his tuxedo-cutting lamentation, Mel was at one with David mourning the death of Saul and Jonathan. Mel told me he wasn't aware of this, so let's call it a case of tribal memory. What he remembers thinking is, "I swore I would never wear a tuxedo again, get dressed up and go to those phony baloney events . . . in which I wouldn't win." But he did dress up again, quite a few times in later years, and he often won.

PERFORM HOW? PERFORM WHERE?

Back in 1950, when he was still trying to break into the writers' room, Mel had met Florence Baum, a dancer in Broadway musicals (and later on television). At first, they had a gentle espresso-and-cannoli courtship: long walks in the city, foreign movies, museums (Mel adored van Gogh). They discussed literature: she liked Stendhal; he liked the Russians. The relationship became romantic. She was half-Jewish, a very good-looking woman, tall and dark, and when he was away from her (during a fruitless trip to Hollywood in 1952 and then a vacation in Europe), he longed for her and wrote her obsessively.

They were married in 1953, and they immediately had children: Stephanie, Nicky, and Eddie. But Mel as a young man was too restless, too worried about his career to be a decent partner or father. How stable, after all, was the position of "TV writer"? At night, he roamed around the Village, and he probably saw other women. According to Mel's (unauthorized) biographer Patrick McGilligan (*Funny Man*, 2019), Mel would arrive home late, and if Florence was talking to friends, he would throw them out and fall into a morose silence. He told *Playboy*, "I think my first wife needed more. I needed more attention from the world, and less attention from a wife."

The attention from the world was no more than intermittent. He might storm into a room like Zeus with a brace of thunderbolts, but in the fifties he had developed a reputation around town as a "talking writer" who couldn't complete a skit by himself (Neil Simon demonstrates that inability in his play). In any case, writing would never be enough for him. He wanted to perform, but Sid Caesar's greatness inhibited him. Perform how? Perform where? As early as the mid-fifties, he was telling Sid Caesar that television was not the right medium for their comedy.

"I want you to quit," he remembers saying. "I want us to get on a plane and fly to Hollywood." He thought they should be making movies, so their work wouldn't evaporate overnight. Happily, DVDs and various electronic revival houses—Amazon, YouTube, and the like—have proven him wrong. You can now see many of Caesar's skits whenever you want.

In 1954, when not working for Sid, he tried to write for the mild-mannered TV comic Red Buttons, but Buttons, off-camera, was an ego-maniac, and some of his signature shtick as a performer left Mel cold. He walked away from him. Later on, in 1958 and 1960, he tried to write for Jerry Lewis. The great man was also a table jumper; he grabbed good ideas from his writers and merged them into his own screeching manias, treating writers as gag writers. Mel drifted away from him, too. (Two table jumpers in one room leaves a script hanging in the air.) He worked on "specials" for Sid Caesar in the late fifties, and on an attempted revival of the regular program in 1962, *The Sid Caesar Show*, which didn't last. In any chronological account of a hero, there is a tendency to see every setback as a momentary pause in the journey to inevitable success. But in fact success was not inevitable for Mel Brooks. In the fifties and sixties, he contributed to other people's doomed musical projects and worked on TV scripts. If he wound up succeeding in every form of show business in the end, it's also right to point out that, early in his career, he failed at almost every form of show business. He risked failure, knew it, loathed it.

It turns out, however, that in Mel's case something had been there all through the fifties, through all the misfires as well as his great work in Sid Caesar's writers' room. It was part of his very being, part of his soul. Was it not a very Jewish soulfulness that saved him? Expressed as comedy, of course, but comedy that poked into the corners of Jewish history, per-sistence, and survival, soulfulness that was funny as hell but also seething with resentment and pride.

OLD GUY II: MOVING THROUGH HISTORY

Origin stories vary, so you may have to choose your favorite creation myth. The Revised Standard Version, which the late Carl Reiner expounded in his elder years, goes as follows: Reiner encountered the very young Mel Brooks in Sid Caesar's writers' room. Mel said he was depressed. He was a Jewish pirate, and the price of sailcloth had gone up. "I can't afford to set sail anymore. It's been weeks since I pillaged." Reiner had come in that day exercised over a pompous TV program, *We the People*, in which celebrities were interviewed, including a fictional Joseph Stalin encountered in his kitchen. Reiner complained about the show, and then, pausing no more than a beat, he turned to Brooks and said, "Here is a man who was actually at the scene of the crucifixion two thousand years ago."

Mel (in a thin, tired voice): "Oh *boy* . . ."

Carl: "You were there? Did you know Jesus?"

Mel: "Lovely. Thin lad, right? He wore sandals, walked around with twelve other guys. They always came into the store, never *bought* anything . . ." At which point everyone cracked up. *Fou rire* is the only *rire* worth having.

This encounter, I believe, took place early in the fifties. At parties for show-business folks, just to have fun, the two men would do interview skits with different kinds of material (for instance, Mel as a film director at Cannes). But once the "2000 Year Old Man" was born, it became a sensation, the best party entertainment in town. Question after question, period after period, the prehistoric past, the ancient past, the Inquisition, the conversation running backward and forward in time. In advance of any given occasion, they would set out certain areas to cover, but then the rest would be ad-libbed. Reiner, the straight man, was informed, rapid, literal. His questions were often high-minded, but Mel's answers brought everything back to the body—back to fear, sex, hunger, and death, and also back to commerce, Jews making a living through the ages. Reiner later remarked that "I always tried for something that would force him to go into a panic, because a brilliant comedy mind in panic will heroically defend itself."

Mel channeled his grandparents and family friends—not, as some people assumed, his mother, who spoke "no known language, but spoke it with an Irish accent." He channeled the anxious family sages who held forth on every topic—most of all, his uncle Joe, who walked into a room and uttered such sentences as "Don't buy a cardboard belt" and, of course, "Never eat chocolate after chick'n." Mel took over the sound of an elderly, lower-middle-class Jewish immigrant with a thick Yiddish accent. His 2000 Year Old Man speaks a charmed English, with syllables dropped, parts of speech scrambled, but always clear enough in meaning. Through the ages, this gentleman often owned a shop of some sort (during the

Inquisition, he had a *yarmulke* store). Fearful about many things, he had miraculously survived life in the caves, a relationship with Joan of Arc, a mistaken investment in Shakespeare's lost play *Queen Alexandra and Murray* (Carl: "This was probably the only one that didn't come to light." Mel: "Come to *light*?—it closed in *Egypt*"). Over the years, he fathered more than forty-two thousand children, "and not *one* comes to visit me." As Kenneth Tynan pointed out, the old man, more than twice as old as Methuselah, has conquered death, a fate Brooks feared more than any other.

In the fifties, Reiner believed that the material, drawing on jokes among Jews about crabby relatives, was too specialized for a wider public. He was even afraid that a Jewish accent, after the war, could fuel anti-Semitism. Brooks himself thought the material worked only for show people. But the late-night TV host Steve Allen thought otherwise. In 1960, after hearing the routine at a Los Angeles party, Allen, a good comic in his own right, offered to pay for two hours of recording time at a local studio. Brooks and Reiner worked together before an audience of friends (who were mostly convulsed), and the album, issued in November 1960 and widely played on FM radio, sold a million copies.

Many of us have savored the irony that only twelve minutes in the initial album were devoted to the old man, the rest to other Brooks-Reiner interviews. Yet it was the twelve minutes that made the record famous. Mel was then thirty-four, Carl Reiner four years older. They made four additional albums, the last in 1997, recorded when both men were in their seventies. (The entire set, along with other Brooks-Reiner material, can be heard on a CD compilation, *The 2000 Year Old Man—The Complete History*.)

"THE 2000 YEAR Old Man" is very explicitly a Jewish creation, and perhaps a creation more central to Jewish survival than has been widely recognized. If you listen to the entire run, a composite history of man appears. In the beginning, the old man and his friends stared at the sun and the stars. "We didn't know *anything*. We were so *dumb*." You hear about the discovery of sex. "Bernie discovered it in the night. Such a *story*. Hundreds of years later I still blush." Also the origins of transportation: "Mostly *fear*—an animal would growl and you'd go two miles in a minute." And you hear about the origins of humor, which—no surprise—occurred when "a tiger ate up Murray in a minute, and we got hysterical." Death, always death.

The two men do not ignore religion. "I knew the head writer of the Bible. He lived two caves away." The actual apostles were named Ben, Murray, Al, Richie, Sol, Abe, and the like, which is only one of many blasphemies intended to put Jews, not Christians, at the center of Western history. "I could hear my antecedents," Brooks said later. "I could hear five thousand years of Jews pouring through me." According to Jeremy Dauber, in his scholarly *Jewish Comedy*, there were medieval Jews who ridiculed Christianity as absurd. A virgin who gives birth without insemination? *What?* A God who exists in three versions? *Please!* Mel did not engage in medieval studies, but he was working in that tradition.

Carl Reiner, it turns out, had little reason to worry about the material seeming strange. By the 1950s, as we know, immigrant accents were all over TV variety shows. Sarah Silverman still does it—the mock-complaining tone, complaining and making fun of complaining at the same time. That sound was once so familiar to Americans that it's easy to pass over its historical and emotional significance. The Yiddish-speaking Eastern European and Russian Jews who arrived en masse between 1880 and 1924 struggled to understand a country that was entirely new to them. A few things may have quickly become familiar: the corner candy shop where you got egg creams and Eskimo Pies, the grocery store for soup greens and challah. But everything else had to be mastered. Manners, culture, street life, the ways of making a living. All of it was new, and anxiety and complaining were a defense against ignorance, a protest against the bewildering variety and abundance of an unfamiliar country. Wonderful America! But crazy, too! The Yiddish-influenced English of the immigrants and their children was a mode of baffled complaint. The next generation, however, was sure that the aging parents, aunts, and uncles worried too much. Don't go *here*. Don't go *there*. By the 1960s, the worried-about-everything tone sounded funny to young people. America was no longer a mystery, and life in general was simply not that dangerous. The endless prohibitions and cautions were mostly beside the point. "*Whose* law? *What* law?" Portnoy shouts. The Yiddish-inflected complaint had become cranky.

*   *   *

IN 1963, BROOKS, drawing on that accent again, joined up with a friend, filmmaker Ernest Pintoff, and produced a three-minute classic. The tiny movie, called *The Critic*, captures the exasperation of the old generation in a way so funny that it produces tears of heartbreak. We never see Mel. We see only some modest abstract images—blocks, circles, triangles, and squiggly lines, gently moving and sometimes joining—but we listen to Mel, speaking as an old Russian-immigrant Jew sitting in a movie theater. He came to see a French picture, and instead he gets an abstract cartoon. He's trying to find a plot, a story, *anything* that makes sense in the images before him. "Dis is cute, dis is cute, dis is nice. Vat da hell *is* it? Oh, I know vhat it is. It's *garbage*, that what it is." The old man is wretched. After everything he has had to face in America, now he has to deal with *this* nonsense? Mel Brooks concentrated all the immigrant woes into an absurd dilemma—a Jew baffled by art that his literal demand for meaning can't take in.

The old critic is a philistine, lost in America, but his commentary set off uncontrollable laughter in anyone who had ever stood before an abstract painting that arrogantly refused to yield up its meaning; or anyone, for that matter, who had endured a pretentious short film—they were not hard to find, playing between features in sixties art houses. In order to make *The Critic*, Brooks asked Pintoff to assemble his own series of images. He then sat in a studio, commenting on the film without rehearsal. He watched it twice—that was enough. He and Pintoff then chose the funniest comments, added some tinkling mock-baroque music, and *The Critic* was complete. A simple masterpiece (it won the Academy Award for best short subject in 1964), the movie offers rebellion against the tyranny of appreciation. Some part of us longs not to respond to art. The elderly critic is our surrogate, even if he's a peevish guy who doesn't know what world he's living in.

The 2000 Year Old Man is much better equipped than the elderly moviegoer. He faces something new and threatening in each era, but he always survives. He *is* Jewish persistence, the ultimate diasporic Jew. He travels through time rather than through Russia and Europe to America. He carries tribal memory along with him, the memory of learning things that make it possible to live. "He's got to know all the answers," Mel has written, "because it's about survival." Mel, so to speak, has always been old, has always embodied Jewish history and resistance.

Most of the Jews of Eastern Europe were murdered in the Holo-caust, their Yiddish-language culture—theaters, newspapers, Talmudic academies—disappearing with them. In this country, the survivors, the grief-struck, and the historical minded have established research insti-tutes and Jewish studies departments; and a few blessed American groups have revived the old language. Mel Brooks's straggling old Jew wandering through history is very different from the work of religious and secular scholars—and very different from the work of great Yiddish writers like Isaac Bashevis Singer—but it's nevertheless a significant act of remem-brance, a tree planted in America, the best place for memories of old dead Jews to hang on and even to blossom.

THE NEW COMEDY AND MEL

The success of the Brooks-Reiner records was part of the general efflores-cence of funny albums, a new way of producing and marketing comedy. Introduced in 1948, the long-playing record was a boon to classical music, jazz, Frank Sinatra, and every kind of ambitious pop artist. The forty-minute length also allowed a comic to gather together his best material—either bits from different gigs or an entire act as it was recorded at a comedy club. The hungry i, in North Beach, San Francisco, was a modest place for a rev-olution—no more than a smallish room in a hotel on Jackson Street. But history was made there. In the mid-fifties, the jazz combos, folk singers, and beat poets at the hungry i began to give way to the hip new Jewish comics—Mort Sahl, Lenny Bruce, the satirical songwriter Tom Lehrer.

The new comics represented a startling shift in taste, really a shift in sensibility. Young audiences—especially the educated young audiences in the clubs and in colleges—were growing tired of Bob Hope, Jack Benny, and George Jessel, the "boring immortals" as Pauline Kael called them, who were still appearing on late-night TV and not doing much of anything. The comedy showing up in the clubs was aggressively satirical. It included suave or snarling ridicule of the Eisenhower administration and McCa-rthyism; mockery of public relations and advertising and such commer-cialized, soul-shaping places as Disneyland; impatience with everything that was bureaucratized and massified into blandness. The comics hated the bullying dullness that Norman Mailer hated, but he called it *total-*

itarianism, while the comics, less apocalyptically, saw it as an insult to spontaneity and intelligence.

Mort Sahl, nervously intense, a newspaper in his hand, didn't do routines but just talked, flashing his tiger-shark teeth as he chewed up whatever was fresh in the news; Lenny Bruce needled sensitivities about race and religious hypocrisy in a spasmodic rush that was sometimes brilliant, sometimes obscene, convoluted, and nearly incomprehensible; Tom Lehrer, at the piano, sang his own music or adapted well-known songs with charmingly naughty lyrics devoted to such liberal-intellectual obsessions as nuclear war ("So long, Mom, / I'm off to drop the bomb, / So don't wait up for me"). Many of these albums were played in dorms, enjoyed as a kind of conspiracy. College students were beginning to see their own tastes as separate political and cultural turf. As Gerald Nachman has said, the fifties and early sixties comics anticipated both the explosive rock and roll and the anti-war protests of the middle and late sixties. They set the tone of rebellion and disbelief.

When he was very young, Mel went to the hungry i and heard Lenny Bruce say the following: "If Jesus had been killed twenty years ago, Catholic school children would be wearing little electric chairs around their necks instead of crosses." It is perhaps Bruce's most famous blasphemy. "I had never heard anything like that," Mel says. "It made me want to be a comic. He was in a puritan culture. He fought against it." Mel has taken his shots against the Church, but he didn't go in the direction of political satire; and though he fought against puritanism, he was certainly never hip. Yet Lenny Bruce allowed him to know his own temperament and his own capacity for committing outrages—which he did so thoroughly and vigorously that he absolved vulgarity of its defensive shame. Like the club comics, he reached the smart college students, but in his own way. He turned sophomoric profanities, pranks, and lewd dorm fantasies into something genuinely funny. The hip club comics spoke to a compact audience of liberal intellectuals and student rebels; Mel, working with the broadest possible humor, spoke to everyone. Utterly different from Lenny Bruce, he was still one of Bruce's heirs. "I broke through," he told me, "and it showed the way for a lot of comics."

ANNA MARIA LOUISA ITALIANO

After the lovely New York courtship, Mel's marriage to Florence Baum was never in good shape. At night, he was in clubs, he was with pals, he was with other women, he was *somewhere*, but he was not much at home. In 1959, Florence threw him out. Mel made periodic attempts to patch things up, but the marriage was effectively over. In February 1961, when he was still married to Florence, he met the woman he would live with for more than forty years.

Anne Bancroft was born Anna Maria Louisa Italiano in the Belmont section of the Bronx. She was thirty years old, tall, with a mass of magnificent dark hair and a dazzling smile. She was slender—certainly not "voluptuous" in the Jayne Mansfield–Jane Russell–Marilyn Monroe style of Hollywood in the late fifties and early sixties. She had gone out to Hollywood in 1952 at the age of twenty-one, and, after a number of small roles in which, she claimed, she learned absolutely nothing as an actress, she returned to New York in 1958 and took acting classes with famous teachers, first Herbert Berghof and then Lee Strasberg at the Actors Studio. In New York, she could be serious about acting in the way many New York–based actors in the fifties were serious. Acting was a search for truth—personal truth as well as authenticity in a given role. In 1959, working with director Arthur Penn, she created, in William Gibson's *The Miracle Worker*, the role that would make her famous: Anne Sullivan, the visually impaired therapist who took in hand the blind, deaf, and speechless little girl Helen Keller—the Helen Keller who eventually would become a world-famous celebrity. Penn also directed the movie version of *The Miracle Worker* (1962), and Anne Bancroft, re-creating her stage performance, won the Oscar for Best Actress.

Anne Bancroft could sing and dance, and she could do comedy, but people thought of her as a tough, demanding woman, quick to get angry (in life and in her roles). She was formidable, but, amazingly, in no way ladylike. She and Patty Duke, who played the seven-year-old Helen Keller, wrestled on the floor, whacking at each other, flinging each other around. The violence of it was shocking, and it left both actors and audiences exhausted. In other roles, Bancroft had an intimidating skepticism, almost insolence. In *The Graduate*, her Los Angeles *bourgeoise*, Mrs. Robinson, lusts after a young man and manages to insult him at the same time. The performance has a heartbreaking moment when Bancroft and Dustin Hoffman are in bed together and he asks her about her college interest in art, and her mask of contempt fades to sadness, betraying her regret for a life wasted. As an actress, Bancroft had temperament, power, and range.

The match with Mel Brooks seemed improbable at the time. "She was around handsome guys," Mel says. "I was a little street pug." What held them together? Her parents were immigrants from Muro Lucano in south central Italy; the section of the Bronx she grew up in, Belmont, was known as Little Italy (not to be confused with Little Italy in Manhattan). Mel grew up in Williamsburg, so they were both children of immigrants living in poor ethnic neighborhoods. Neither of them had gone to college; they learned about life by entertaining on the street. "Ever since I was old enough to open my mouth," Anne said in a 1961 interview with Lewis Funke and John Booth, "I was singing and dancing. And I'd rather do that than eat or sleep, and I often did. My mother would be looking for me, and I'd be on a street singing for somebody." Years later, they shared the ready good cheer of people who had survived tough city neighborhoods.

When they were together, they were both eager New Yorkers, moving around on the streets, in the parks, at restaurants, and they shared the unembarrassed, unironic culture hunger of New York in the fifties and sixties, when revivals of Brecht and O'Neill and the New York poets and the abstract expressionist painters and Leonard Bernstein's enthusiasms were in the lives of people who cared about such things. Finally, they both had been through failed marriages—hers in the past, Mel's ongoing (he and Florence weren't formally divorced until 1962). Anne was angry and proud but also earnest and inquiring, an unusual combination. Mel Brooks expressed the extremity of what she felt at times—and also the release from it. She saw his noisy tumult not as an imposition but as an act of generosity. After spending a lot of time together, they got married in a rush, in August 1964, at the Manhattan Marriage Bureau, with one of Anne's wire earrings, untwisted and then retwisted, serving as a wedding band.

SPRINGTIME AT LAST

In 1961, as Mel was working on other people's unsuccessful musicals as well as many other things, he would talk with friends about a novel he was writing, a novel about two producers who create an intentionally awful play and make off with the funds they had raised for the production. The idea was not as original as he imagined. Moss Hart and Irving Berlin had collaborated on a Depression-era show, *Face the Music* (1932), with a similar theme. After a while, the novel became a play called "Springtime for Hitler," a farcical idea which, Patrick McGilligan suggests, Mel may have lifted from Lenny Bruce. In his 1959 comedy album, *The Sick Humor of Lenny Bruce*, the comic did a monologue, called "Adolph Hitler and M.C.A.," in which two German Jewish casting agents, in the 1920s, are looking for an actor to play a dictator. They settle on a wall painter named Shickelgrubber, whom they dress up, rename, and launch into the world. In Bruce's take, Nazism is entirely a form of show business, a sardonic and sorrowful idea. But is Bruce's monologue an influence on *The Producers*? Let us say that it was natural to both these extreme personalities to make comedy out of Nazism, the force most upsetting to Jews. Yet the tonalities are utterly different: Lenny Bruce was brilliantly amoral, a ruthless and self-tormenting martyr, death-bound from an early age, whereas Mel is a pleasure maker, an entertainer—pessimistic, maybe, but eager to defy death in every way.

At the same time as he played with the idea for a novel, Mel was contemplating a farce about the young Hitler in love. It was no better than an unstable joke, teetering on the edge of disaster. Next, when neither the novel nor the farce worked out, he thought of a stage musical ("a Gay romp with Adolph and Eva at Berchtesgaden"). But that didn't work either; the producer Kermit Bloomgarden told him it had too many scenes for a play. At last, in 1965, working with Alfa-Betty Olsen, his secretary and amanuensis, he dropped the farce about Adolf and Eva, brought back the terrible-show idea, and transformed the ideas into a movie script in which "Springtime for Hitler" became the name of a ridiculous Broadway show and also a production number *within* the show.

He never left off making Nazi jokes. He had made fun of Hitler when he was a kid in the Mountains, whipping out his handy black comb and placing it under his nose. Decades later, in the epilogue to *History of the World, Part 1* (1981), he put der Führer on ice, skating gracefully under a spotlight (such a graceful young man). A couple of years after that, he made a video to promote his Nazi-era comedy *To Be or Not to Be*, in which Mel, wearing a mustache and uniform, holds forth as a rapper on stage center while a crowd of partially clothed dancers, male and female,

carry on behind him—sort of MTV on the Reeperbahn. All this was funny
enough, but it was only when the idea was lyricized and theatricalized—
joined to music and Broadway—that Hitler spoofing attained real power.

The plot is now so familiar it feels like a story we were told as children.
The moth-eaten producer Max Bialystock, who raises money by seduc-
ing rich old ladies, is joined by a repressed young accountant, Leopold
Bloom, who has never done much of anything. You know the rest. The
character names were chosen for their historical resonance. Białystok is
a city in northeastern Poland, a transfer point between East and West,
once a Jewish-dominated place that became the site of pogroms and Nazi
slaughter; the very word also conveys Jewish baked goods and the notion
of bulk. Leopold Bloom is the name of James Joyce's wandering-through-
Dublin Jewish everyman in *Ulysses*. In 1966, Mel took this very Jewish
script to an independent producer in New York, Sidney Glazier, a man
who, like Mel, had not known much of a father. Abandoned at five, Glazier had grown up in an Orthodox orphanage in Philadelphia. When Mel
met him, he was an ambitious and unfocused *macher* of forty, the producer of a documentary, *The Eleanor Roosevelt Story*, which had won an
Academy Award in 1965.

As Mel read the script to Glazier in a New York restaurant, the producer spit out his tuna fish and coffee. Poor Glazier had to be helped back
to his seat. Against the advice of his intimates, he raised about half the
budget, with Louis Wolfson, a financier, philanthropist, and sometime
scoundrel, chipping in. The financing was most irregular. Glazier and
Brooks went to the movie studios looking for the rest.

They got turned down everywhere. Among other things, Hitler's name
in the title was a problem. The head of Universal, Lew Wasserman, trying
to be useful, suggested they change the title to "Springtime for Mussolini."
In the end, the project was saved by another up-from-the-bottom guy,
Joseph E. Levine, who was born desperately poor in Boston, the child of
Russian Jewish immigrants. Levine had begun as a theater owner in New
England. By the mid-sixties, he had made a fortune importing beefcake
movies with Steve Reeves in his near-naked glory, *Hercules* and *Hercules Unchained*; at the same time, Levine had attained class by distribut-
ing De Sica's *Two Women* (1960), Fellini's *8½* (1963), and Schlesinger's
Darling (1965), the swinging-London film with Julie Christie. Levine was
short, he smoked cigars, he spoke profanely; he was in every way the heir

of such coarse-grained but shrewd immigrant movie moguls as Adolph Zukor, Samuel Goldwyn, and Louis B. Mayer. Levine put up the rest of the money, creating a total budget of $941,000, which is not much for a full-length feature, even in 1967.

Levine also insisted that Mel change the movie's name to *The Producers*. No Jewish theater owner, he reasoned, would put the original title on a marquee. He then agreed that Brooks should direct the movie himself. The noisy, expansively unrefined Boston Jew may have known exactly what he was doing—at the time, Levine was bankrolling *The Graduate*, which went on to make a fortune. Let us say that both Sidney Glazier and Joe Levine understood what it was to be hungry, physically and emotionally, and they saw that appetite in Brooks and in his mangy script. According to legend, Joe Levine said to Mel in his office, "My job is to get the money for you to make the movie. Your job is to make the movie. My job is to steal the money from you. And your job is to find out how I do it. Here, have an apple."

AS *THE PRODUCERS* was being shot in New York, the movie business, as Mark Harris has established in his excellent 2008 book *Pictures at a Revolution: Five Movies and the Birth of the New Hollywood*—the movie business was in turmoil in a variety of ways. The studios were falling under conglomerate control. The old Production Code (known as the Hays Code), which limited what could be represented of sex and violence, was losing its grip (in a few years it would be gone). A new sensibility, influenced by the French New Wave, was emerging among American writers and directors eager to work for a vibrant young audience that demanded different kinds of entertainment. The spirit of the sixties, in its culturally sensational and exploratory mode, was in full swing.

In that same year, 1967, Mike Nichols's *The Graduate* satirized New Money boorishness and adults in general. Arthur Penn's *Bonnie and Clyde* made violence glamorous (and very bloody), shredding our conventional responses to crime. Like the hip club comics, those movies were looking forward. But Mel's hearty vulgarity looked backward—to burlesque and the emotionally overwrought Yiddish theater, backward to the traditional Broadway musical, whose tropes he was fully prepared to violate. *The Pro-*

ducers looked back so violently that it created a new kind of American movie comedy, in which exuberant bad taste and exaggeration broke the bounds of form and structure. What was flagrantly old or obvious was presented so forcefully that it became radically new.

Chomping down hard on Joe Levine's apple, Mel summoned all his disparate energies—his love of singing and dancing, of making crass, noisy jokes; his love of slamming through everyone's patience. On the set, he was nervous: he began the first shot by shouting "Cut!" instead of "Action!" Bullying the actors and crew, he stuck, however fitfully, to his vision of the material. Central to that vision, Mel's first claim on immortality, was the musical number "Springtime for Hitler." Brooks composed the song himself, humming the notes and lyrics, turning them this way and that, until he and composer John Morris were happy; Morris then wrote everything down.

If we are honest about our initial reactions, we may remember being startled. We are in a Broadway theater with a tuxedoed and coiffed first-night audience. The curtain goes up. A rather swishy young Nazi in a black uniform—not just a Nazi but a member of the SS—swaggers down a white plastic staircase and sings, with lilting upbeat happiness, "Springtime for Hitler and Germany / Deutschland is happy and gay / We're marching to a faster pace / Look out, here comes the master race! / Springtime for Hitler and Germany / Winter for Poland and France."

Nearly naked chorines, wearing pasties on their breasts and floral arrangements on their heads (also German pretzels and beer), glide down the staircase, passing before the camera with ghastly fixed smiles. The taunting and fey exuberance of "Springtime for Hitler" recalls the shape and sound of Florenz Ziegfeld's *kitsch*-erotic stage extravaganzas from earlier decades and klutzy Broadway production numbers from the fifties and sixties, complete with an advanced Broadway cliché—rapid spoken interludes in the middle of the big song ("Don't be stupid, be a smarty. Come and join the Nazi party"). The banality of Brooks's tune and the clunky staging and choreography (Alan Johnson worked with Brooks on the movements) are very much part of the joke. Brooks humiliated Nazism by embedding it in the moldiest conventions of the commercial theater.

The Producers came out twenty-two years after the end of the Second

World War, when consciousness of the Holocaust (a relatively unfamiliar term in the late sixties) was approaching a new intensity. At the time, the shock created by the movie was considerable. Some found it insensitive, even offensive, and their way of dealing with their emotions was to say that Brooks, the first-time director, was crude, that he didn't know how to stage anything or where to put the camera. There's some literal truth to these descriptions, but it's a joke on criticism that Brooks's crudities made *The Producers* the classic that it is. Suavity would have killed this movie. It's a story about appetite.

As Bialystock, the great theatrical star Zero Mostel—huge head, sloping gut, bellowing or caressing voice—was not, putting it mildly, an appealing camera subject. Yet the greatness of Mostel's performance lay precisely in its gross volatility. As he looms into the foreground and overwhelms the frame, all the usual complaints about theater-based movie performances—"overacting," "mugging," "hogging"—fall by the wayside. If Brooks had held the camera back from the engorged Mostel, he would have blunted the actor's almost terrifying force. Gene Wilder, curly-haired and blue-eyed, trembles before him, shies away from him, and then bursts out into full-fledged hysteria. Violating the canons of good movie acting, Mel Brooks brought the Yiddish theater into movies but added a satirical edge—the "overacting" revealed the appetitive truth beneath conventional good manners: we are out for ourselves. What's original and even classic about the movie grows out of its exhilarating bad taste, taste so bad that it reorders the ground on which taste operates. Aesthetically, something this funny can't be ruled out. People who laugh aren't in the best situation to insist on aesthetic rules.

One can sense the confusion and panic beneath Renata Adler's jumbled review in the *New York Times*. She thought the movie was funny but "shoddy and gross and cruel" (but weren't the gross and cruel elements the source of the fun?), and she touched only glancingly (and irrelevantly) on the Nazis at the center of it. Pauline Kael, normally so attentive to every aspect of a movie, didn't describe the production number at all in her *New Yorker* review. She thought the picture was "satire of the theater," which, of course it *is*, but how does Brooks unleash the satire? With what? There's some kind of avoidance going on here. Both Adler and Kael were Jewish. *The Producers* was a Jewish movie aimed at the Nazis—but also aimed partly at the Jews, which is why it was initially so upsetting.

You have to remember that the Broadway musical, at least until the

1970s, was almost entirely a Jewish American creation. Irving Berlin, Jerome Kern, George and Ira Gershwin, Richard Rodgers, Harold Arlen, "Yip" Harburg, Kurt Weill, Frank Loesser, Fritz Loewe, Alan Jay Lerner, Leonard Bernstein, Jerry Bock, Stephen Sondheim, Jule Styne, Jerry Ross, Jerry Herman, Burton Lane, and many, many more. The composers were all Jewish except for the great Cole Porter, the wealthy Episcopalian from Indiana who had a few flops at the beginning of his career before he rue-fully concluded that he had to "write Jewish songs." Which he did in the classic "My Heart Belongs to Daddy," from the show *Leave It to Me!* (1938), a song whose lyric "da-da-da-da" has struck many people as quintessen-tially Yiddish-sounding. Not only the creators but the audience for those musical comedies was heavily Jewish, at least early in a given run (every-one else came next and made some of the shows long-running hits). So Brooks's joke was partially aimed at them and at Jews in general—an audi-ence inclined to feel itself a victim of history.

"Did you think," I asked him, "Oh, my God, people are going to have a fit over 'Springtime for Hitler'?"

"I got letters," he said. "I must have gotten a hundred letters from rab-bis, students, scholars, and I would write back to every single one, and try to explain to them, the way you bring down Hitler . . . you don't get on a soapbox with him . . . but if you can reduce him to something laughable, you win. That's my job."

He came too late of course to do any actual damage to the Nazis. Not even Charlie Chaplin could do that with *The Great Dictator*, which was made in 1940, as the war was underway. Comedy can't stop murder, but it can change the way we think of murder. In the late sixties, as the Holo-caust became a constant topic of public discussion, memory and emotion remained vibrantly at issue, and Mel was teasing and provoking those memories in a movie spoofing the prime Jewish art form. "Deal with it," he seems to be saying to the Jews. Anger, yes. Self-pity, no. Comedy can help us deal with murder, stop us, perhaps, from murdering ourselves. We can face terrible things in comedy to the point where they hurt us less.

SOMETHING WAS RADICALLY changing in the way a few key Jewish artists portrayed their culture and themselves. Around the same time as *The Producers*, Philip Roth was struggling to find a publishable form for a

scandalous idea—a hysterical Jewish son spilling his erotic life to an analyst. Earlier in the decade, at dinner parties with friends, Roth had done
extended monologues devoted to his unstoppable hero. Subsequent versions of the material included a two-hundred-page manuscript called
"Jewboy"; a play called "The Nice Jewish Boy"; another prose narrative,
called "Portrait of an Artist"; and so on, until pieces of *Portnoy's Complaint* in its final form began emerging in magazines in 1967 (when Mel
was shooting his movie). Roth's novel existed in so many different shapes
that it's rather like a creature that takes on aspects of other organisms (tail,
gills, etc.) as it struggles toward birth, only to burst forth triumphantly
in the end as itself. *The Producers* went through the same kind of shape-
shifting slow birth. In both cases, the transgressive idea (the production
of a Hitler musical; an obscene, guilty rant) struggled to find a way to exist
against every caution, bursting every form that tried to contain it until it
found the only form that in the end seems possible.

Portnoy's Complaint was published as a book in 1969, two years after
The Producers came out, and, like *The Producers*, it caused an infer-
nal uproar among rabbis and Jewish community leaders. It provoked
serious attacks as well from such Jewish literary critics as Diana Trilling and Irving Howe. Suddenly, fictional Jews (like Portnoy and Max
Bialystock) could be shown as lustful and greedy. The myth of Jewish
moral superiority—always the suffering people and therefore ethically
privileged—had taken a serious hit. "Do me a favor, my people, and
stick your suffering heritage up your suffering ass—*I happen also to be
a human being!*" Portnoy cries, in what are perhaps the most shocking
sentences in the book.

In *The Armies of the Night*, which was set in 1967 and appeared in
1968, Norman Mailer described how he made a drunken speech on a solemn occasion—the eve of an anti-war protest in Washington, DC. It was
a necessary part of his identity; he needed to acknowledge his bad behavior in order to qualify as a truth teller. In the late sixties, some American children of Jewish immigrants, braving disapproval from their own,
relinquished the old guilts, the old anguish, the old fears. The disorder of
the late sixties—assassinations, riots, anti-war protests—no doubt loosened the harness keeping Jewish circumspection in place. Looking back
to the period in 1974, Philip Roth wrote, "Not even a Jew could put up

a successful fight any longer against non-negotiable demands of crude antisocial appetite and vulgar aggressive fantasy."

SIGMUND FREUD WILL get knocked around in this book. But Freud immortally placed sexuality at the center of our lives, irritating Gentiles and Jews alike; he dramatized the unconscious, the needs and buried memories roiling beneath the surface; he analyzed the body in all its wants, irrevocably connecting urges, emanations, renunciations to psyche and soul. If Freud, so to speak, came down to the body in his writings and practice, down from philosophy and academic medicine, Mel came up to the body from the street, from Harry Ritz and Sid Caesar; he came to the body from his own explosive idea of what was funny. Somewhere in the middle, the two met in a liberationist embrace.

"I like that," said Mel when I proposed the Freud–Mel Brooks alliance. "There was more room in bad taste for me than in good taste. I found out the walls were made of cardboard, not of steel. It was easy to break through them."

"Weren't you also sending a message to the Jews: 'The Nazis can now be made ridiculous. Haven't you suffered enough? Can't you get over it and laugh?'" But he demurred. "Yeah. Maybe . . . I'm just an entertainer. A very good one, mind you. You may be right . . . maybe."

Yes, maybe. Never trust the teller, trust the tale, as D. H. Lawrence said. I thought of "Springtime for Hitler" again when *History of the World, Part I*, with its torturing-the-Jews musicale, "The Inquisition," came out in 1981, some thirteen years later. That bit of entertainment makes "Springtime" feel like a soft warm-up. And I wondered what Mel would say when I pressed him again about his intentions.

TREADING WATER AS THE PERFECT GUEST

Mel Brooks spent a great deal of time promoting *The Producers*, but the film didn't initially make much money, except in New York and a few other big cities, where it played at small art houses (in Manhattan, at a single house for eight months). At a preview, Joe Levine watched a few scenes and walked out. He may have been obsessed at that moment with

The Graduate, which was set to open a month after *The Producers*. If the movie was about a Broadway show that was meant to fail, the actual movie failed initially and then became immortal. Still, Mel claims he never made much money from the picture. He told Charlie Rose that years later he asked Joe Levine at one point if he could see the books, and Levine said he could see them at any time he wanted—they were in Fairbanks, Alaska.

To Mel's amazement, *The Producers* won the Oscar for best original screenplay. At the time, however, he was forlorn. "I guess they don't want me in movies," he remembers telling Anne. In the few years after 1968, he engaged in additional projects that didn't go anywhere. He was obviously some sort of comic genius, but not quite a writer, not quite a star performer, maybe a director—or all three of these things. In 1970, he directed a movie farce set in the Soviet Union right after the Revolution, *The Twelve Chairs*, in which the single joke of avarice is repeated again and again—avarice as calculation, as stealth, as violence, most of all as slapstick desperation. Like Woody Allen's *Stardust Memories* (1980), *The Twelve Chairs* is a mediocre movie, the black sheep that its creator always mentions as a favorite.

It's not that Mel Brooks was obscure. Anything but. The first "2000 Year Old Man" album had come out in 1960, followed by its sequels. And he appeared on television a great deal and sometimes said things that people repeated for years. He was the most reliably funny of guests, appearing on *The Jack Paar Program*, *The Mike Douglas Show*, *The Arlene Francis Show*; much later, he joined the new generation of talk-show hosts—Conan O'Brien, Jimmy Kimmel, David Letterman, and others. He worked well with Dick Cavett, a comic himself and always a great fan of comics, but most memorably with Johnny Carson. His appearances on Carson's show became a minor art form. On one occasion, on February 13, 1975, Brooks came out from behind the curtain, acknowledged the applause of the audience, waved to Johnny as he crossed in front of the set, but then kept going, exiting on the other side of the set and waving goodbye. An NBC producer corralled him and shoved him back into the arena. He grabbed Ed McMahon's coffee, took a sip, and spritzed it out in front of him, as if it were rotgut purchased on the street. "Are you *kidding*? On the *air*?" he said to McMahon.

He spat out McMahon's coffee on other occasions, complaining indignantly of Gentile taste in booze, an opening to what often followed—

updates on his movie projects and then, needing to return home, tales of the Jews. "How do Jews die?" he asks. "It seems that in the Mountains they eat tons of sour cream and indigestible chopped vegetables. Then they sing 'Dancing in the Dark'"—and here Mel sings it in Bing Crosby's easy baritone—"but they sing it in the wrong key, starting too high, then going higher and higher until they run out of breath on the highest notes and drop dead." Death in the Mountains.

As Johnny urged him on, offering a quick running commentary in his rapid undertone (no one talks *over* Mel Brooks), Mel acted out everything with his hands, legs, ears, torso, tongue, eyebrows—his shoes, even. You got a feeling of the entire man, his body an expression of a mind that never stopped working. Only Robin Williams was more dynamic on *The Tonight Show*, and Williams went so fast—slamming from one voice to another, jumping, crouching, preaching, cork-screwing his neck and torso—that he was unintelligible about a third of the time. His appearances were nerve-racking flights. Listening to him, you thought, "What a crazy genius!" Listening to Mel, you thought, "What a smart, funny man!" Mel was easier to watch.

Johnny Carson had special qualities that made Mel go back those nineteen times. "They're all good," he told me (meaning the late-night talk-show hosts), "but the others were too busy worrying about the next guest or reading questions to respond to what the guest was actually saying. And they tried to get their own jokes in while you were doing something, and Carson never did that. Johnny Carson *listened*."

His greatest TV appearance—definitely a case of TV performance art—was in that legendary 1970 episode of *The David Susskind Show* entitled "How to Be a Jewish Son—or—My Son the Success!" Among the other Jewish sons, comic David Steinberg tried to hang in there, but actor George Segal looked stunned by Mel, as if he had been walloped by a salami; the other participants were mostly silent as Mel took over the show. He told unsentimental tales of home life in Williamsburg, praising the incredible energy and caringness of Jewish mothers, their obsession with safety and cleanliness, and he shouted the line that became famous, "Until they die themselves, they *clean* and *kill* . . . they *clean* and *kill*." He interrupted, clamored, jumped out of his chair. This was not some screwed-up Jewish son, self-hating like Alexander Portnoy. No, the message bursting through the TV cameras was that having a Jewish mother meant you could be very aggressive in your life and always get away with it. Mel Brooks may have been excitable, but this Jewish son was free. He was untroubled by the crippling, folkloric Jewish neuroses of guilt and shame.

He was not troubled by narcissism, either. In his 1914 paper, "On Narcissism: An Introduction," Freud proposed that criminals and humorists shared a similar temperament. They both "manage to keep away from their ego anything that would diminish it." We know what he means. Working their mouths, humorists can be as mean as the vilest hoods. But the category of narcissism doesn't fit Mel Brooks, for all his earsplitting ego. He cares about many things beside himself. Susan Stroman, the choreographer and director who worked with him on the stage-musical versions of *The Producers* and *Young Frankenstein*, told me, "No one loves Mel Brooks more than Mel Brooks. But when he comes into a room, he has to know who everyone is, what they do. He finds out."

JEWING AND JIVING THE OLD WEST

Two years after finishing *The Twelve Chairs*, Mel, depressed, was walking on the street in New York when he encountered his agent, David Begelman, then of Creative Management Associates (later the embezzling head of Columbia Pictures). Begelman took him to lunch and told him about the draft of a screenplay called "Tex-X" written by a young man named Andrew Bergman, then a publicist for United Artists and later a writer and director of his own movies—*The Freshman*, *Honeymoon in Vegas*, and others. Bergman had written "Tex-X" as a novella, and then rewritten it as a screenplay.

"It was a story," he told me, "a story powered by an image that had gripped me for years. A dusty, low-rent town awaits its new sheriff, expecting Tim Holt. In rides H. Rap Brown." The idea combined time travel and culture shock: Tim Holt was the genial boyish beauty who starred in innumerable B-movie Westerns in the forties; H. Rap Brown was a sulfurous Black civil rights leader in the sixties and seventies. Intrigued, Brooks assembled a writing team that included Bergman; a neophyte named Norman Steinberg who had been bugging Mel about writing for a living; and another neophyte (and Steinberg's friend) Alan Uger, a dentist—at which point Brooks said, according to Patrick McGilligan, "I see four white guys here. Four Jews. We need a person of color."

The person of color turned out to be the most brilliant comedian of the day, Richard Pryor, then thirty-two years old, a profound and profane creative mind spilling in every direction. Bearing Rémy Martin and small amounts of white powder, Pryor joined the band of Jewish irregulars at the New York headquarters of Warner Bros. At the time, he was still developing his stand-up routine, a thrilling, somewhat nerve-racking affair that became more and more candid as he got older. He made fun of everyone, including whites, Blacks, Africans, and most of all himself. Richard Pryor was a dirty-mouthed humanist who propounded a vision of the end of racism. To the "Tex-X" script, he added disreputable jokes and a liberal use of the N-word, a word he renounced a few years later, in 1979, after a trip to Africa. But in 1974, when he was working on the script, the word was alive for him—and for Bergman, too. "The 'N-word' was very much a part of my original 'Tex-X' novella and first draft," Bergman says, "because that was both the vernacular of the era and the emotional engine that drove the piece. What Richie did was liberate us to use it freely. A guarantor, if you will."

Uger, the dentist, dropped out quickly; Pryor, after about six weeks of work, also dropped out, but a good deal of his shiv-like humor remains. In the writers' room, Brooks told his crew to throw in whatever crazy ideas they could come up with. "We will all be in jail for making this movie," he said. He wanted scandal, tumult, uproar. By this time, he had drawn certain strategic lessons from his TV experience and the fading audience for Sid Caesar's comedy. In order to survive, he knew he had to work for the broadest variety of tastes—which meant, in his case, going low, going to the body, to desire, to greed, to the physical and psychological truth beneath ordinary social intercourse, the truth hidden, for instance, in the conventions of one genre film after another.

In its slovenly and profane way, *Blazing Saddles* (as it was eventually called) is an alarming piece of pop culture. It's also a moving example of Black-Jewish collaboration in an exciting time of liberalism. Blacks had appeared in a few Westerns before *Blazing Saddles*—most notably Woody Strode, the athlete-turned-actor, in John Ford's *Sergeant Rutledge* (1960); and Sidney Poitier in *Buck and the Preacher* (which Poitier directed), from 1972. But those were both solemn affairs. Ford and Poitier came to redeem the Old West; Brooks, Bergman, Pryor, and the others came to violate it. If comedy is often the way minorities make a claim on the majority culture, here you have *two* minorities making a claim, saying, in effect, "We've had it with this stuff, stop making fools of us."

THE WESTERN IS a great American art form, but it's an art form that embodies a self-congratulatory myth—the vision of a virgin land where good people and righteousness triumph. The myth was repeated in books, in radio dramas, in comic books, in epics, and in mild Saturday matinees. There were disturbing masterpieces like *The Searchers* (1956) and *The Wild Bunch* (1969) that certainly complicate our feelings about righteous violence, but most Western movies and TV shows, even the ambitious ones, were formally and emotionally conservative. Audiences loved the genre in part because it was so reliable and reassuring—the empty space conquered, savagery tamed, civilization advancing.

Nothing is more stirring in Westerns than the horses. Beautiful and noble beasts, always our friends, they carry Indians, villains, and heroes across open plains; they stand on rocky buttes expectantly, always ready for action. In *Blazing Saddles*, a big, dopey cowboy, played by ex–football great Alex Karras, comes into the town of Rock Ridge and punches out a horse—roundhouses the animal right across the muzzle, causing it to fall on its side. It's one of Mel's scandalous city-boy jokes, mock heartless, a shocker. A little later, an old lady repeatedly gets punched in the stomach. She turns toward the camera and asks, "Have you ever seen such cruelty?" Well, no, actually, we *haven't*. As always, the joking borders on savagery. Madeline Kahn, as Lili Von Shtupp, does a parody of Marlene Dietrich's bored S&M vamping in *The Blue Angel*, *Destry Rides Again*, and other movies. Her song, which Brooks wrote, is called "I'm Tired" ("I've been with thousands of men / Again and again / They promise the moon / They always coming and going / And going and coming / And always too soon"). Stretching out Dietrich's German drawl, Kahn buggers her consonants and captures the goddess's uncertain relation to pitch, her voice running out of steam in the held notes. Unfurling her legs, Madeline Kahn is lewd and mock-lewd at the same time.

In 1974, when the movie was finished, Ted Ashley, the head of Warner Bros., wanted all the tasteless things thrown out. Mel took careful notes, agreed, then deposited the notes in a garbage can. The picture was then shown to Warner's regular employees, and, as Mel later said, men and women started floating toward the ceiling like figures in a Chagall painting. At that point, Ashley's objections were dropped.

Blazing Saddles is an indelible triumph of coarsely satirical pop culture. But one has to ask: Would Ashley's objections now prevent the picture from being made? The issue is not "taste" so much as it is our sensitivity to all kinds of hurt. Wouldn't the inspired Madeline Kahn number be shelved as a rude assault on women? When I asked Mel if *Blazing Saddles* could be done today, he wouldn't answer. But the answer is probably no, it couldn't be done. The language, the attitudes, the outrages large and small, the nervous-making jostling of whites and Blacks, the jokes about Black male genitals, and, finally, the grand-scale surreal messiness of the settings, the West giving way at the end to a Warner Bros. soundstage where a musical is being shot—most of this is out of the question. Mel Brooks of course always meant to shock. The playful-dirty tone, the seemingly spontaneous, tossed-off barbarities began in that writers' room. But some kinds of shock have become inadmissible. From our cautious and respect-laden vantage, the movie is funnier and more dangerous than it was fifty years ago. It's like some jewel-encrusted dagger (okay, a jewel-encrusted *plastic* dagger) recovered from a long-ago civilization, too threatening for our more fretful time.

If cruelty is the source of Mel's comedy, racism itself, one of humanity's nastiest jokes, was a great big target. "When you parody something," Mel wrote in his autobiography, "you move the truth sideways." In the beginning, white cowboys ask for a song from Black workers on a railway gang. Rather than "Camptown Races," the minstrel-show favorite that the whites want from them, the workers sing Cole Porter—"I get no kicks from Champagne . . ." A little revenge is playing out here: the Blacks are suave, modern, musically sophisticated, the whites crude and dumb. Like all the whites in town, they happily sling the N-word around. Sometimes the whites start to say the N-word and stop themselves after the first syllable—a pre-correctness kind of joke on correctness.

No one, as I remember, missed the point in 1974, but recently the picture has been buzz-bombed on social media as racist. The sound of the N-word hurts too much even when the people using it are shown as jerks. But *Blazing Saddles* is anything but a racist movie. Whoopi Goldberg got it right (on *The View* December 7, 2022) when she said, "It deals with racism by coming at it right, straight, out front, making you think and laugh about it." It does so by clothing social satire in crass, funny jokes. You laugh at the outrageousness before realizing that it's your own attitudes that are being mocked. Brooks's excesses have a cleaning force; he's a great exposer of hypocrisy.

Richard Pryor, who certainly thought racism could be funny, wanted to play the sheriff, Black Bart, but he was freebasing cocaine and Warner Bros. couldn't get insurance for him. His substitute, the handsome and charming theater actor Cleavon Little, has an easy way about him—he looks great on horseback in his Gucci Western range wear. In this Western, the new sheriff in town, the man with the star, makes friends with an alcoholic gunslinger, the Waco Kid (Gene Wilder). And the Waco Kid describes the racist townspeople as "people of the *land*. The common clay of the New West. . . . You know, *morons*." That's a more relaxed version of the acid sentiments one can imagine H. Rap Brown expressing, and we think, well, yes, Jew and Black can show up in the Old West only as interlopers and satirical myth busters. They can't be insiders; nor do they want to be. In the end, the two men ride off together in a Cadillac.

Mel Brooks is not given to political statements or political comedy. Like most comics, he's an opportunist; he goes where the laughs are. (The big campfire farting sequence is not as bold as he claims; he knew well enough that young audiences would howl with delight when they were pushed.) Yet the Black-Jewish alliance against the racist white settlers not only works very well as comedy; it becomes, by means of its energetic warmth and contempt, a political statement. "What would all the ornaments be without the tree for support?" Mel said to a reporter after the movie opened. "They'd just be a lot of shiny baubles on the ground." The tree he was talking about is race prejudice and the friendship between a white and a Black man; the ornaments are the mock-vicious gags. Mel and his gang suggested that hypocrisy lies beneath so much supposedly moral violence in Westerns, that contempt lies beneath genteel manners. If the movie seems funnier now than in 1974, it also feels more heartfelt, too. For all its crude jokes, *Blazing Saddles* is a sweet liberal dream of companionship and soul-brotherhood triumphing over the bigots and the squares.

THE MOST TOUCHING SICK JOKE IN THE HISTORY OF THE MOVIES

In early 1974, after editing *Blazing Saddles* at Warner Bros. all day, Mel Brooks would have dinner and then go to the Hotel Bel-Air for an assignation with Gene Wilder. They would have tea and English biscuits and then work until late.

As much as two years earlier, Wilder had been thinking about a project called "Young Frankenstein." He had even, at Mel's urging, worked up a draft of the script. Both he and Brooks had read Mary Shelley's classic from 1818 (written when she was nineteen), *Frankenstein; or, The Modern Prometheus*, but they relied for inspiration principally on the old James Whale movies, *Frankenstein* (1931) and *The Bride of Frankenstein* (1935). Both pictures feature the elongated, beautiful Boris Karloff as the monster and Whale's gnarled trees and German-expressionist towns. As they worked, Wilder would write down bits of dialogue and action on a yellow legal pad, and Brooks's secretary would type it up the next day. Their time together could be tumultuous. Some scenes were written over and over. According to Wilder, on one occasion Mel screamed at him and stormed out, only to call from home and say, "WHO WAS THAT MADMAN IN YOUR HOUSE? I COULD HEAR THE YELLING ALL THE WAY OVER HERE!"

Brooks and his producer Michael Gruskoff took the finished script to Columbia Pictures. The studio executives liked it and offered a budget of $2 million. According to Brooks in *Young Frankenstein: The Story of the Making of the Film* (2016), the following happened: "On the way out, I shouted, 'Oh, by the way, we're going to make it in black and white.' Then we shut the door. A thundering herd of Jews followed us down the hall from the meeting room." The Columbia executives insisted that no one in world cinema shot in black and white anymore ("No black and white! Peru just got color!"). The deal quickly fell apart, and Gruskoff gave the script to Alan Ladd Jr., at that time vice president of creative affairs at Twentieth Century–Fox. He and Gordon Stulberg, then head of the studio, green-lit the project with a $2.8 million budget. At Wilder's insistence, Brooks kept himself out of the movie, so he could concentrate solely on direction. By contract, he was guaranteed complete freedom on the set and final cut, all of which meant that *Young Frankenstein* was a big-studio movie made in a rare state of liberty. At the end of 1974, as Brooks and his crew were working on the new movie, *Blazing Saddles* opened big. Brooks and Wilder knew they were on a roll.

They extended the basic *Frankenstein* structure further into craziness, combining horror-film fantasy with sex spoof, lyricism with palpitating erotic nonsense. They stuck to the central idea: a mad scientist (Franken-stein's grandson Frederick), playing God, creates a monster out of limbs foraged from grave sites, adding, by mistake, a criminal brain. Mel Brooks was now getting comically serious about defeating death, his old enemy, fighting it literally with the fantasy of rebirth; and fighting it with the most touching of horror tropes, the easily hurt monster—especially touching as Brooks and Wilder fashioned the material. This monster, played by Peter Boyle, longs to have such human qualities as intelligence and sensi-tivity. He's not death come to life; he *is* life, Mel's hatred of death become flesh. He wants to be loved, and his creator, Frederick Frankenstein, wants to love him. *Young Frankenstein* is a Jewish monster movie.

As everyone has said, *Young Frankenstein* is the smoothest, most skill-ful of Brooks's pictures. In something like *Blazing Saddles*, you might say that Brooks as a director achieved great expressiveness in sloppiness. But *Young Frankenstein* is highly controlled—a sustained narrative with its serious themes introduced, developed, and resolved, even as the shlocky generic elements are caressed and amplified to the point of mania: the filthy dark castle with its sweating walls and treacherous stone staircases; the dials and switches and bottles in the laboratory flashing and popping like cheap sparklers; the tormented woods, the cobbled town, the police inspector with his mechanical arm jerking up like a semaphore. It's a very *patient*, very expository comedy, and even as Brooks lets loose and starts pushing the ideas over the edge (Gene Wilder, soaring with experimental ecstasy, his mustache quivering, shouts "Tonight, we shall hurl the gaunt-let of science into the frightful face of death itself. . . . Give my creature . . . LIFE!")—even at its craziest, *Young Frankenstein* is better made than the famous James Whale movies it takes off from. The old movies were poetic but also clunky. Brooks fills the spaces more comfortably, moves the cam-era more fluidly; the backlighting is even more creepily effective, and the actors perform as a happy unit.

Exhilarated by the high-octane nonsense, the supporting cast, includ-ing Teri Garr and Marty Feldman, play off each other's shtick—there's a lot of rhyming and echoing, reaction and counterreaction, some of it improvised on the set. This is a family, frightened by their creation at first, but then fussy and concerned, for they've got a big, ungainly kid on their hands, and they have to protect him from an uncaring world. Peter Boyle is bulkier than Karloff but even more gentle, a giant alarmed by his own strength. Brooks uses him for a great dirty joke: Madeline Kahn, as the doctor's trembling-with-lust fiancé, finds ecstasy with the monster and his remarkable *Schwanzstucker*, and she bursts into "Ah sweet mystery of life, at last I've found you . . . ," a fruity love anthem that Jeannette Macdonald sang in the movie version of Victor Herbert's operetta *Naughty Marietta* (1935). The idea to sing operetta was Kahn's. The dirty joke was Mel's.

The approach is absurdist and heartfelt at the same time. Together, before a crowd of stuffed-shirt scientists and their wives, Dr. Frankenstein and the monster, dressed in white tie and tails, rapping their canes on the floor (like Fred Astaire in *Top Hat*), perform "Puttin' on the Ritz," one of Irving Berlin's masterpieces of complex rhythm and delayed stress. As Peter Boyle howls the refrain, "*Puhhtin on the Riitttss . . . ,*" the number becomes at once the funniest and most touching sick joke in the history of the movies. It's a moment beyond satire—it's close to anguish, a scene about aspiration, the desire to create art against every discouragement. Mel Brooks conquered death by creating life anew. He exercised his penchant for mean fantasy and then transcended it. "Puttin' on the Ritz" is a Jewish triumph: family love and Irving Berlin make the monster sing.

FAREWELL TO NEW YORK (FOR A WHILE)

After many visits to Los Angeles, Mel and Anne and their baby son, Max, moved to Los Angeles in 1972. The subsequent box-office triumph of *Blazing Saddles* in 1974 and then *Young Frankenstein* in 1974 and 1975 gave Mel Brooks the enormous success that had eluded him up to that point (he was almost fifty), and it set both of them rolling through the rest of their professional lives.

Anne Bancroft never had another role as great as Anne Sullivan, but initially, when she and Mel were still in New York, she worked a great deal, appearing in revivals of plays by Bertolt Brecht, Lillian Hellman, and Thornton Wilder, and in such movies as *The Pumpkin Eater* (1964), *The*

Slender Thread (1965), *7 Women* (1965), and *The Turning Point* (1977). She appeared in TV movies and in a special created for her by Mel, Martin Charnin, and a whole bunch of friends, *Annie: The Women in the Life of a Man*, in which she sang, danced, recited poetry, and performed a great comedy skit about a woman who has a nightmare of throwing a party for the Peruvian soprano Yma Sumac. Her delivery was so exactly right—elocutionary yet slightly goofy—that it makes one mourn the comedies that weren't written for her.

From all accounts, she and Mel fought a lot and laughed a great deal. She was forty when Max Brooks was born in 1972. It was a difficult pregnancy; she spent the last three months of it in bed. According to Max, who is dyslexic, his mother took a lot of time off from acting to work with him on his reading and his general intellectual skills. He went on to become a bestselling author (*The Zombie Survival Guide* and *World War Z: An Oral History of the Zombie War*). In all, the union of Mel Brooks and Anne Bancroft was among the most moving and beautiful show-business marriages one can think of.

AT MIDCENTURY, MANY of the New Yorkers who had success in the arts were devoted to the city. New York had art, music, and theater, publishing houses and magazine offices, galleries and studios, agents and production companies, Carnegie Hall and the Brill Building ("Tin Pan Alley"), where the pop hits were written. As well as good bagels and great Chinese food, both hard to find elsewhere, the city offered poetry readings and jazz clubs, friendly bars, wealthy patrons, chamber music on Sunday afternoons. New York Jews in particular were a good part of the audience for the arts. The city itself served as both the molten core of American capitalism and a thriving connection to Europe—a culture older than ours, with perhaps a more complex and dangerous sense of pleasure than we had, a sense of tragedy that was not ours. The last part of that changed after the war. After the news of the European catastrophe was understood, Jews would say, in effect, "The tragedy was ours, even if we didn't experience it directly." The Holocaust left permanent heartbreak and unappeasable anger. Mel Brooks left New York, but he took his anger with him—and his admiration for traditional high culture, too, even as he made his eruptive comedies.

Hollywood offered long sunshiny days, the ocean and the mountains, the palm-studded open sky; it meant sleek cars and some of the most beautiful women in the world—the eternal LA siren song. Most of all, it was the home of the movie business, with its (sometimes) high-paying jobs, its historic acceptance of Jews, both as founders (Carl Laemmle, Louis B. Mayer, Adolph Zukor, the Warner brothers, et al.) and as immigrant European directors and composers looking for a home (Josef von Sternberg, Ernst Lubitsch, William Wyler, Billy Wilder, Otto Preminger, Erich Wolfgang Korngold, Max Steiner, et al.). Directors and composers often did well in Hollywood, the writers not so much. The prolific and proudly cynical Ben Hecht played the system to his advantage, but the other New York Jewish writers who moved there—Daniel Fuchs, Nathanael West, Clifford Odets, Dorothy Parker, and Herman Mankiewicz—were often stymied or betrayed. They would return to New York, complain about stupid movies, interfering producers, and studio bosses, and then, caught by money and the possibility of perhaps doing something good, they would go back to Los Angeles. They were caught in a cycle of hope and self-contempt. But Mel Brooks, whatever his anxieties and early troubles, was given neither to self-pity nor to self-contempt. In all his dealings with Hollywood, he fought openly, with almost insulting candor, for freedom and money.

And he insisted on a network of support. In New York, Mel and a group of friends, including novelists Joseph Heller and Mario Puzo, had met for years at restaurants in Chinatown ("The Group of the Oblong Table"), a consortium with famously strict rules for how much of the main dish—lobster, chicken chow mein, Mongolian beef—each could take before suffering the contempt of the others. The rule-bound behavior was part of a regimen that licensed a ferocious competition of wits. In person, Mel Brooks could talk earnestly and quietly, but not in company. He dominated the table as he dominated a writers' room.

In Los Angeles, Mel's groups consisted entirely of show-business folks. As Patrick McGilligan puts it, "He frequented favorite delis and restaurants and places where he counted on seeing familiar faces (many displaced New Yorkers with ties to his own past)." By the seventies, a good part of television production had moved to the coast. He and Anne hung out with members of the old writers' room—Carl Reiner, who became a major writer and director (*All of Me*, *The Man with Two Brains*), and

Larry Gelbart, who created the TV version of *M*A*S*H* and wrote most of *Tootsie*. Apart from an occasional gig with Carl Reiner, Mel wasn't performing in public, but he couldn't live without an audience.

Mel now says he occasionally misses New York, especially the "irregular streets and beautiful nineteenth-century houses in the Village." He misses the old jazz and comedy clubs and also "a degree of rudeness." That rudeness could be a New York Jewish style of wit. For instance: at delicatessens Mel knew well, the Carnegie Deli and the Stage on Seventh Avenue, near Carnegie Hall (both now gone), the irritable old waiters had a certain surly panache. Shuffling over to the table with aprons tied around their midriffs, stubby pencils gripped like weapons, they could hardly take down an order for pastrami and Swiss without morose complaints, threats, terrible jokes. If you missed the rhythm of it or failed to come back at them—which is what they wanted—they could seem merely hostile. They would certainly have seemed so in California, where hostility, mock or genuine, was hardly the style.

"There are many nice people in Los Angeles," Mel says, "a great swath of politeness that's missing in New York. New York is very real. No lying. People say what they mean." Like the decrepit waiters, they often say it in jokes. Mel has twice insisted to me that what he does "is not Jewish humor." He was very clear about this. "It's not soft, it's not *Yiddishkeit*, singsongy, tweedledee. It's New York humor. New York has its own drumbeat, its own march. It's the big city. But Jewish humor is shtetl humor. Isaac Bashevis Singer got that in his stories [Singer is tough as nails, but never mind]. We were not whimpering little Jews afraid of the Cossacks. We were out there fighting. The Italians were on the north side of Williamsburg. We were on the south side. We held the line."

SILENCE: UN-JEWING HIMSELF

A man who could do pretty much what he wanted in Hollywood decided to make a silent movie. The idea was pitched to him in 1975 by Ron Clark, a Canadian-born TV writer and playwright, and Brooks was intrigued: it engaged his considerable fund of perversity, and he could also star in it. When he took the idea to Alan Ladd Jr., Ladd said, according to Mel, "So with *Young Frankenstein* you take away color and now you're coming to me and you say you want to make a movie that takes away sound? If I let you go unrestrained, you're liable to turn Twentieth Century–Fox into a vaudeville house."

Ladd knew Mel Brooks well. He may have sensed that Mel's heart was yearning for live performance of some sort; and he may also have detected, buried in the idea of the picture, more than a little hostility to movie studios. The story that Brooks worked out with Ron Clark and two writers from *The Carol Burnett Show*, Rudy De Luca and Barry Levinson (who went on to have a long career as a writer and director)—the story was devoted to the adventures of a contemporary director, Mel Funn (Mel himself), who decides . . . to make a silent film. Mel Funn tools around Los Angeles with two maladroit chums (Dom DeLuise and Marty Feldman) in a yellow sports car (a hand-built Morgan), looking for big stars to appear in his picture. So: a silent movie about the making of a silent movie. The studio chief of "Big Pictures Studios" is played by Sid Caesar, who smokes two cigars at once and cares about nothing but money. At the same time, Big Pictures is threatened with takeover by "Engulf and Devour," a sarcastic reference to the conglomerate Gulf and Western Industries, which had indeed taken over Paramount in 1966.

Silent Movie is perfectly pleasant, but it lacks Mel's usual bruising brash insolence. Apart from the teasing of big studios, its tone is winsome and ingratiating. Driving all over town, Mel and his companions stumble and fall; they get slapped, whomped, dumped. Silent comedy is about mishap, and Mel takes advantage of silence's two natural friends, momentum and gravity. There's a funny scene in which the three men, trying to woo stars for their picture, come across Liza Minnelli in a studio commissary. They approach her wearing heavy suits of armor, breaking every chair they try to sit on, falling onto her table, falling onto her and each other. It's the kind of silly-clumsy thing that cracks up kids. Each of the men also does a wild flamenco dance with Anne Bancroft, who enters the shenanigans with initial sullenness (the Bancroft stare) and exits it with great brio. The rest of the movie is only mildly amusing. Mel Brooks is not a physical poet, and by going silent, he un-Jews himself. Without his voice—without jokes, stories, rage, Yiddish, Melvillian clamor—he's a moderately inventive comic with a wide smile and active arms and elbows.

The plot of *Silent Movie* suggests that something was roiling around inside him. Alan Ladd Jr. was a good friend and certainly no philistine, but at this point in his life Mel didn't want to answer to any master at all. In 1967, when he became producer of *Bonnie and Clyde*, Warren Beatty said, "Some things that you care about you have to control."

BECOMING A MINI-MOGUL

It was not enough for Mel to direct; he needed to join the ownership class, movie-colony division. He needed to become a producer. In 1979, three years after *Silent Movie*, he set up Brooksfilms Limited, and he kept it going for years, producing not only his own movies (*History of the World, Part 1, Robin Hood: Men in Tights*, etc.), but a number of what can only be called class projects. He took on such serious and interesting films as *Frances* (1982), which features a great performance by Jessica Lange as Frances Farmer, the talented, neurotic Hollywood actress of the thirties; and David Cronenberg's Tristan-und-Isolde horror romance *The Fly* (1986) with Jeff Goldblum and Geena Davis. He was drawn to dark versions of his own irrepressible death-insulting exuberance; drawn to grotesque subjects—humanity pushed to the edges. In 1979, he and producer Jonathan Sanger purchased an original script written by Christopher DeVore and Eric Bergren, *The Elephant Man*, which told the story of Joseph Merrick, a man terribly deformed by neurofibromatosis and exhibited as a freak on Whitechapel Road, in London, in the late nineteenth century. (The film is not to be confused with the play of the same name by Bernard Pomerance, which was staged in London and then in New York.) Brooks took a chance on the young director David Lynch, whose best-known film at the time was the malignant, creepily impressive midnight-movie sensation *Eraserhead* (1977).

"At first, they wouldn't accept movies from me," Mel says. "They had a Pavlovian response. It's Mel Brooks, it has to be funny. Some crazy guy with an elephant trunk?" But *The Elephant Man*, starring John Hurt and Anthony Hopkins, was a dignified and tender film, a box-office success that went on to be nominated for eight Academy Awards. The love that Mel extended to the made-up monster in *Young Frankenstein* got transferred, in this soulful movie, to a man whom many considered an actual monster, a man who suffered every day of his life.

If directing occasionally brought out Mel's bullying side (the actor Lewis J. Stadlen described him as "a street tough trying to escape the body of an elderly Jewish woman. It's like he's holding a knife to your throat and demanding that you eat chicken soup"), the job of producing, in a surprise, brought out a gentle and respectful side. He developed the scripts with different writers and chose the directors, but then largely stayed out of the way.

A mini-mogul now, he enjoyed life in Los Angeles as a wealthy man. He and Anne lived (initially) in the Beverly Hills flats, and then, exercising the geographical prerogatives of the rich, bought or rented a spacious Malibu "beach cottage," an apartment on the Upper East Side of Manhattan, a shack on Fire Island for August vacations, and a condo on Fisher Island, so Mel could visit his mother, Kitty, who lived in nearby Hallandale Beach, Florida. Later, in 1986, they built a large stucco house in Santa Monica; Mel still lives there. In the strenuous style of Hollywood royalty, they jogged and played tennis. They liked good food, and Mel lugged his private stock of French red wines to Beverly Hills restaurants. Showing off in this way may have had some serious emotion behind it. In Italy and Poland (the Old Country for these two), and in working-class Brooklyn and the Bronx, dining out was virtually unheard of. Who could afford it? Surging up from the bottom, Mel and Anne joined the celebrity class, triumphing over the poverty of previous generations. "Little by little, we raised ourselves," Mel told me.

RE-JEWING THE GENRES

In his own movies, Mel recovered from the innocuous *Silent Movie* by offering, in 1981, the lewd, morally hazardous *History of the World, Part 1*, with its merry-vicious "Inquisition" scene. Yet I'm going to hold that movie to the end. In some ways, it *is* the end—the end of humor, for some people; for me, the end of American Jewish self-pity, which will take some explaining.

For Mel, offering his Jewish take on the world—and for him, "the world" meant Hollywood genre films—was the way to be funniest in his own voice while baiting the myths and tropes that America loved. He Judaized his genre parodies, mocking the *goyishe* straightness of their heroism. In *Spaceballs* (1987), Mel's parody of the *Star Wars* movies, he teased the pomposity of the franchise by casting, in place of David Prowse as Darth Vader (with James Earl Jones's imposing yet snuffling tones), tiny Rick Moranis (glasses, nose, whine) as the ominous warlord "Dark

Helmet," who miserably spits hot coffee inside his shell and can hardly draw a breath in there. Some of the jokes are juvenile, too easy, crappy even. You feel Brooks's disgust with the flimsy/monumental mythmaking in Lucas's epic. It's as if he were saying, "Jews don't go in for this stuff. We deal with too much complication in this world to worry about grand-scale baloney in other worlds."

Brooks himself showed up in the 1993 *Robin Hood: Men in Tights*, this time as Rabbi Tuckman (in place of Friar Tuck), wearing a black suit, a black beard, a black hat, and side locks (the side locks rise when he lifts his hat). Driving a cart through Sherwood Forest, the rabbi sells sacramental wine and does circumcisions on the spot. Hollywood had made Robin Hood movies since 1908, most stirringly with Errol Flynn in *The Adventures of Robin Hood* (1938), and, just before Mel's venture, *Robin Hood: Prince of Thieves* (1991), starring solemn Kevin Costner, who made a point of insisting in public that the Merry Men had not worn tights. (Kevin, calm down.) Brooks had adored the legends ever since he was a child; he had made a farcical TV series in 1975, *When Things Were Rotten*, but it was canceled after one season. His take on Robin Hood was a little different from other people's. "Did Robin Hood really steal from the rich and give to the poor?" Carl Reiner had asked the 2000 Year Old Man. "No, no, he didn't," Mel said. "He stole from everybody and kept everything." It is the voice of the New York streets, where there are no saints.

In every way, Brooks gives us the unheroic Jewish view of the legends: Robin is played by beautiful Cary Elwes, good-hearted but dumb, and when Robin battles Little John, the staves keep breaking until the two could be fighting with toothpicks. Errol Flynn played swashbucklers, but in this version of Flynn's material, buckles are unswashed, archers have trouble springing arrows from their quivers, and the arrows, finally launched, fly all over the place. A blind man fights heroically against a post. Yes, Mel makes blind-man jokes; he makes fat-lady and mute-man jokes. Jeremy Dauber in his book *Jewish Comedy* insists that mocking physical handicaps was in fact a feature of Jewish humor for centuries, starting with the Bible, but Mel's jokes are—how shall I put it?—somewhat more aggressive than anything in the book of Judges. In all, Mel's view of the Middle Ages appears to be that nearly everyone was maimed or handicapped in one way or the other. If you had two arms and a tongue in your head, you should be happy. Jewish burlesque romps through the forest, savage, hilarious, brushing against nearly everything with enliven-ing disdain.

What comes through as a positive force in *Robin Hood* is the urge to sing and dance. An ensemble of Black rappers in green clothes and feath-ered caps perform at the beginning and end, busting a move right there in Sherwood Forest; Robin's cohort, the Merry Men, at one point break into song and dance. Mel had always put music in his movies, and now he was becoming insistently lyrical. The art critic and historian Walter Pater said, "All art constantly aspires towards the condition of music." This might be slightly amended as follows: all of Mel Brooks's later movies aspire toward Broadway. The best thing in his 1983 remake of the Ernst Lubitsch clas-sic *To Be or Not to Be* is the opening scene, in which Mel and Anne sing "Sweet Georgia Brown" in Polish. After *Robin Hood*, he made one more genre parody (*Dracula: Dead and Loving It*, 1995), and it felt tired, the jokes stale. He was ready to return to New York and to pursue the goal that had eluded him years earlier as he worked on other people's musicals that flopped: a Broadway hit of his own.

RETURNING TO NEW YORK: THE ULTIMATE HIT MUSICAL

None other than David Geffen, it seems, came up with the idea of doing *The Producers* as a musical. Geffen thought the show "would be the fun-niest ever done on Broadway," and, according to Mel, he called about it again and again. Geffen, the great record producer (Joni Mitchell, Elton John, et al.) and studio boss partner with Steven Spielberg and Jeffrey Katzenberg (SKG), had a Broadway hit in 1981 with *Dreamgirls*, and, in the late nineties, he was eager to invest in the theater again. He suggested that Mel ask Jerry Herman, the composer of *Hello, Dolly!*, *Mame*, and *La Cage aux Folles*, to write the music. Mel went to see Herman, but Herman refused to work for him; instead, he sat down at the piano and played a certain composition of Mel's called "Springtime for Hitler." Bring back the spangled Nazi chorines, advised Herman. "That's your second act cli-max," he said, and suggested that Mel write the rest of the songs, which he finally did, both music and lyrics: seventeen songs in all.

As we know, the movie version of *The Producers*, thirty-five or so years earlier, had begun (in Mel's mind) as a novel, then as a show—not a musi-cal, but a comic play on the stage. Mel was returning the conception to its roots. He summoned Thomas Meehan, who had written the book for the hit musical *Annie* (1977), and the two men worked on the book, on and off, for two years, often in Mel's office in the Culver Studios, and then later in New York, repairing after sessions to Madame Romaine's Omelettes on East Sixty-First Street (their favorite omelet: cheese and tomato). Meehan has been quoted as follows: "He doesn't really write; he talks. I would take notes, then go away and write." In 2000, their eyes turned toward Broadway, Mel and Anne moved back to New York. They settled into their Upper East Side apartment and bought a new house in the Water Mill section of Southampton.

AS MEL TELLS it, he had a lot to learn. "Max and Leo have to sing and dance about their wants, needs, and dreams rather than do it just through dialogue," he writes in his autobiography. "The music drives the emotion. That was a huge revelation. And in the musical more than the movie, you root for their friendship and their success as failed producers because the emotions are being heightened by the music." Heightening was always the goal—everything from the old movie was enlarged, including the size of the cast, the number of jokes, the number and Amazonian stature of the dancing girls.

For director, Mel wanted British-born Michael Ockrent, who had put together, in 1992, *Crazy for You*, a reborn and refashioned Gershwin musical. He went to see Ockrent and his wife, the choreographer Susan Stroman, in their West Fifty-Seventh Street apartment. As Stroman told me, "He brushed past me without saying hello, ran down a corridor in our apartment singing 'That Face,' a song which he had written for the show." He concluded his trek by jumping on a sofa and saying, "Hello, I'm Mel Brooks." There's that jump again: he jumps when he needs or wants something desperately; he jumps when his future is at stake.

Mike Ockrent died tragically of leukemia in 1999; he was fifty-three years old. After a pause, Mel, in his own account, bullied the grieving Stroman to get back to work rather than sit alone in dark rooms. She had never directed a show before, but he persuaded her to take over as both director and choreographer, promising her (as she later told John Lahr in the *New Yorker*) that she would "cry in the morning, and you'll cry at night. But when you are with me during the day, you will laugh. And that will save you." Apparently, it did, since Stroman has not stopped working as a theater director in the last twenty-five years.

Brooks, Tom Meehan, Stroman, and music arranger Glen Kelly gathered together, sometimes in Brooks's apartment, sometimes in Stroman's. The working nourishment had switched from omelets to fresh bagels, lovingly toasted and sliced in thirds (in thirds?) by Mel. That was brunch. According to Meehan, late-afternoon lunch invariably consisted of "tuna fish on toasted rye, dry with no butter or mayonnaise, with a slice of tomato, no lettuce." The proper maintenance was very important to Mel. He insisted on it. At the same time, as Stroman told me, "Mel was unbelievably respectful of musical theater, of what theater people do. At first, we did a reading in my living room. Mel would play all the parts—Max Bialystock, Leo Bloom, Roger De Bris [the gay theater director]. We invited some producers we wanted to invest, and Nathan Lane sang a song as Max with lyrics like 'I'm a shyster,' putting down producers. But these Broadway producers couldn't wait to produce it!," which rather sounds like Mafia dons eager to invest in *The Godfather*. For the small roles—showgirls, Bavarian peasants, storm troopers—everyone came in for an audition. "They had to sing, they had to dance, and they had to tell a joke—in front of Mel Brooks!" It was trial by fire.

It's no cliché to say that the rest is show-business history. *The Producers* was brought to the stage at a cost of $10.5 million, about eleven times the cost of the original movie. David Geffen, it turned out, was too busy with his film company, SKG, and dropped out, at which point Mel divided the costs among *fourteen* investors. Everyone in town wanted in. There were five weeks of rehearsals in New York, an anxious three-week tryout in Chicago (the sustenance had shifted to gut-saving bran muffins), followed by the New York opening on April 19, 2001, at the very large St. James Theater on Forty-Fourth Street. In the early weeks of the run, an extraordinary thing happened: *people were cheering and laughing before the curtain went up*. Mel had created a national cult of people determined to laugh. Nothing could stop them.

In June, two months after the opening, *The Producers* won twelve Tony Awards. The production wound up running six years at the St. James; it received productions in London (also directed and choreographed by Susan Stroman) and touring companies in both the United States and Great Britain. "You know the phrase," Stroman told me, "'he had them rolling in the aisles'? Well, I actually saw people fall out of their seats and tumble down the aisles. I couldn't believe it." Geffen's prediction that *The Producers* would be the funniest musical ever on Broadway had turned out to be right.

WHEN MEL BROOKS was nine, his uncle Joe, who drove a taxi and would come into a room and utter such sentences as "Never wear a cardboard belt"—*that* uncle Joe took him across the bridge and into "New York." Joe kept his taxi light off, and Mel lay down in the back seat. They went to see the Cole Porter musical *Anything Goes* with stentorian Ethel Merman belting out songs easily heard by the two theatergoers in the top balcony. That was a thrilling experience for a nine-year-old, and his ambition to create a hit show had never left him. "I've always loved the Broadway musical," Mel said to me. "It uses all of me. To write songs, to write lyrics. The stage is so *personal*. It's live, it connects heartily, heavily. When you're watching a movie, there's always a disconnect. It's up there on the screen. Stage connects." Yes, stage frees the body even more than film does; the last remnant of "realism" is gone, the story can be stretched, danced, enlarged, undermined—the only constraint is laughter.

In his review of the show in the *New Yorker* (May 7, 2001), John Lahr noted, "After *Oklahoma!* (1943) raised the hegemony of the musical's score and book over the idiosyncratic high jinks of its comedians, the genre became increasingly sophisticated and artistically ambitious; 'musical comedy' became 'the musical.' Humor, if there was any, was relegated to the subplot or to an eleven-o'clock number." In brief, Brooks was returning the Broadway musical to the kind of show, popular in the thirties, that featured lots of singing and dancing, guys cracking jokes, and beautiful girls wearing as little as possible. Mel doesn't name names, but he was clearly gunning for Stephen Sondheim's sour-mash, hyper-knowing *Follies*, *Company*, and *Sweeney Todd*; gunning also for such serioso-banal Brit epics as *Jesus Christ Superstar* and *Cats*. His show would be dedicated to the frivolously entertaining essence of the form itself, the musical as *play*.

A MIXTURE OF Broadway blue humor, Borscht Belt gags, and abundant large-scale production numbers, the show exudes an unending delight in its own freedom, like a porpoise wriggling in water. Perhaps it's principally Nathan Lane's wriggling body I mean. Zero Mostel, the original Max, was a great actor; his roar and simper had the conviction of despair. Nathan Lane is a farceur, with a circular open mouth, a flexible collapsing spine, eyebrows reaching skyward like the two sides of a bridge. Matthew Broderick, as Leo Bloom, is a more upright, able-bodied man, though he dances and falls adroitly enough. The musical version amounts to Mel's last liberation of the body, the joining of burlesque's flagrant lewdness with Broadway tradition.

"When you got it, flaunt it!" says Max Bialystock, shouting out the window. That could be Mel Brooks's working assumption: if there's something you are good at, we can use it. The performative gay swishiness of the movie version of *The Producers* now fully flowers into a number called "Keep It Gay." This time the no-talent director of "Springtime for Hitler," Roger De Bris (Gary Beach in the show), introduces his set designer, his costume designer, and so on, and they are all dressed in different street-gay outfits, like the members of the disco group Village People. When the show opened, there was a small outburst of protest about "gay stereotypes." But most people (rightly, I think) took the flamboyance as an expression of Mel's appreciation of gay theatricality. Calling the displays hostile "fag jokes" isn't right: Mel goes so far into hip-twisting pout and smirk that each movement becomes a proud emblem of spirit (as well as funny). These men are glorious in their gayness—a straight man's testament to the healing powers of exaggeration.

In a similar enlarging spirit, the grasping old ladies who are eager for a last bit of joy with Max Bialystock (in return for investment in his shows) are now a dancing and singing *cohort* of old ladies, banging their walkers on the stage in unison. "I took a walker to a dance studio," Susan Stroman told me. "I realized you could dance with a walker, sit on it, flip over it." The old ladies (played by young women) are no longer stooges in a sour joke; now they have what academics call agency, boasting that they are sexually alive. In its bad-taste audacity, the joke rivals "Springtime for Hitler."

At times *The Producers* feels like a musical revue, but the songs, dances, and jokes lead to the scorching early climax that Jerry Herman wanted: storm troopers, in a chorus line, goose-step their way toward the audience, arms raised in Nazi salutes, singing "Springtime for Hitler." By 2001, when the show opened, the number may have become a widely shared joke, but some of us still feel a twisting discomfort in our bellies. At the age of seventy-five, Mel had his longed-for triumph in the theater, but he had not become a completely lovable Jew. When *The Producers* musical finally opened in Berlin, in 2009, the ushers placed into the hands of the first-nighters little Nazi flags printed with pretzels in the form of swastikas.

OLD GUY III

In the early eighties, Anne Bancroft had breast cancer, something she mostly kept secret as she fought it. Late in 2003, a doctor's visit revealed that she had a new malignant tumor but, after surgery, she appeared to be all right. In the previous decade, she had appeared often on television and in small roles in movies, but not in the kind of great theater roles she had enjoyed much earlier. In this period of their life together—the early years of the new millennium—Mel worked on the movie version of the musical *The Producers*; collected awards of all kinds; appeared on the Paul Reiser–Helen Hunt sitcom *Mad About You*; and appeared as himself (with Anne) in season four of Larry David's crankfest *Curb Your Enthusiasm*. He voiced commercials and animated characters in cartoons. He did all sorts of things just to keep busy and make a little money.

By 2005, it was clear that Anne also had uterine cancer and was seriously ill. She underwent chemotherapy treatment, but in public appearances she looked tired. Anne Bancroft died, at the age of seventy-three, on June 6, 2005. She and Mel had been together for forty-four years. They shared everything: no thought that either of them ever had was complete until it had been conveyed to the other—it was that kind of marriage.

There were memorial events in Los Angeles and New York. Distinguished friends from theater and the movies made testimonial speeches. Mel will not talk about their final years together, and, according to one of Mel's biographers, James Robert Parish, at both events Mel said, "If any of you are grieving, keep it to yourself. I don't want to hear it." He needed to possess his own feelings. "I have never got over Anne's death," he told me. "But somehow I survived."

His son Max had a new baby, Henry, whom he visited a lot, and Max took him out to eat in a small New York restaurant where they wouldn't be recognized. Mel drew closer with his three (grown) children from his first marriage; he reverted to his old habit of visiting someone and falling asleep in front of a television set. For a while he seemed lost.

IN 2007, TWO years after Anne Bancroft's death, Brooks, Thomas Meehan, and Susan Stroman made a Broadway musical out of *Young Frankenstein*. The show received mixed reviews and was only a moderate hit. Brooks insisted, as he told me, that the show was "lugubrious." Yet Susan Stroman says that the New York theater it played in (the Hilton, now the Lyric) was simply "too large for the jokes to land." She and Meehan aided Brooks in cutting forty minutes from *Young Frankenstein*, and it was mounted at the (much smaller) Garrick Theater in London in September 2017. In this shortened form it was a smash. So Mel had his second West End hit, at the age of ninety-one.

He had also become one of the rare EGOT winners, those who had received at least one of each of the big awards: an Emmy (television), a Grammy (albums), an Oscar (movies), and a Tony (the theater). He won lifetime awards from the American Film Institute and the Kennedy Center. In 2016, President Obama placed around his neck the National Medal of Arts, a clunky piece of embossed metal that Mel later said he used as "something to put a hot cup on, so it doesn't burn the table." It was a sentence worthy of Kitty Kaminsky, who had died on August 19, 1989, in Hollywood, Florida.

During these later years, when he was in his late eighties and then nineties, Mel also did something quite surprising—though not at all surprising after you've seen him doing it. Way back in 1978, he had told Kenneth Tynan that the last thing he wanted was to wind up as "a white-belted, white-shoed, maroon-mohair-jacketed type" headlining in Las Vegas. This vision, I suspect, was always a warning to himself more than an actual possibility. But he did have a desire to go live again, something he hadn't done except for appearances on late-night talk shows or in special interview-and-jokes sessions with his friends Dick Cavett and BBC producer Alan Yentob. He needed to hear the sound of laughter. He began to hear it in 2015 at the age of eighty-nine. Nattily dressed (no maroon in sight), he appeared in such places as the Kennedy Center, the Microsoft Theater in Los Angeles, and Radio City Music Hall. In these outings, he was accompanied onstage by his producer and manager Kevin Salter, a forty-ish WASP from the Northwest with an encyclopedic knowledge of Brooks and his work.

"De facto manager," Salter told me. "No one really ever *manages* Mel Brooks." Salter fed him questions and cued certain memories. "There are some greatest hits," Salter said, "but he would quickly become bored if I asked him the same questions each show. He's best when nothing is planned."

At a number of appearances, Brooks asked for questions from the audience. One urgent inquiry went as follows: "What do you wear: briefs or boxer shorts?"

"Depends."

In May 2018, when Mel was ninety-two, I caught his act at, of all places, New York's Temple Emanu-El on Fifth Avenue, the home of America's most status-conscious and proper Jews. "These are German Jews," I warned him just before the show, meaning they wouldn't laugh as easily as the Russian Jews. I needn't have worried. Brooks turned the vast, fretted hall into an intimate space. On the dais, he sat for short periods in a club chair, holding back as if exhausted, listening to Kevin Salter's questions. Then he would jump up ("He must have steel springs in his legs," my wife marveled), pacing back and forth on the synagogue's narrow stage, ranging over his life and experience, acting out his stories with arms, hips, shoulders. He killed.

There was no dying fall in Mel's life, no tepid, easy nostalgia, nothing equivalent to the soft appearance of George Burns and Jack Benny on talk shows at the end. It was full-out Mel, pungent, aggressive, slightly dangerous, all the way. In April 2023, I asked him about his regrets—anything he did that he considered *bad*. He told me two stories. In the first, he was in his twenties, entertaining at Grossinger's, the enormous Catskills hotel, and he began a routine by announcing, "'This is for Jews, only Jews. If you're not a Jew, you can't understand this material, so stand up and get out.' I think three people started to get up . . . 'No! Kidding! Kidding!'" And here his voice trailed off into uncharacteristic pleading. "Of *course* you're as good as Jews! Of course!"

The other story took place on West Fifty-Seventh Street, near Carnegie Hall. It was some time in the early fifties, and Mel was walking with two colleagues from Sid Caesar's writers' room, Larry Gelbart and Neil

Simon. They were all young sketch writers, not yet famous, working for Sid. As they walked, three nuns were approaching.

"No, Mel, no!" said Gelbart.

"*What?* Nothing."

"Get hold of yourself!" said Simon.

"No worry," said Mel. "*Nothing*." But as the nuns drew close, he thrust himself forward. "Take off those costumes!" he shouted. "The nuns sketch is OUT!"

"How did they react?" I asked.

"They fell to the ground," he said. Notice that both anecdotes reveal an attitude less than respectful to the composure of Gentile Americans.

IN HIS EARLY and middle nineties, Mel Brooks came to his office in Culver City from Monday to Friday. He would write every day (on unlined paper, with pencil), both at home and in the office, and bounce ideas off Kevin Salter. "He is endlessly gauging the level of my reaction," Salter told me in an email. "Titter or guffaw? He loves to throw ideas back and forth. That process allows the joke to build. Then he arrives at the cherry on top of the sundae. Sometimes he makes you cry. But mostly he makes you laugh." On Fridays, Brooks had lunch in Beverly Hills with his former buddies from 20th Century Fox (Alan Ladd Jr., Michael Gruskoff, Richard Donner, Jay Kanter), where he spent many productive years. At night, he went out to dinner with friends or to Carl Reiner's house in Beverly Hills, where the two of them, as has been widely reported, watched television shows and old movies together as they ate dinner on trays. At these sessions, the wit was known to fly about the room.

Reiner died at the age of ninety-eight in June 2020. "Carl was like a blood brother," Mel told me. "He would always try to trap me. 'Prove it. Prove that you're the 2000 Year Old Man.' He was like my brother, my father. He was unusually gentle. He directed Lily Tomlin in *All of Me*, and Tomlin was not easy to work with."

Back in the sixties, Carl Reiner had asked the 2000 Year Old Man the secrets of living so long a life. Brooks cited the excellence of nectarines ("half a peach, half a plum, a hell of a fruit . . . even a rotten one is good") and the importance of staying out of Italian sports cars. In his office, in 2018, Brooks enlarged on this advice a bit: "Walk a mile a day and sing

Broadway songs, you'll live forever. And the last thing," he added mysteriously, "is chicken chow mein."

"Do you ever think about dying?"

"All the time."

"Is there an afterlife?"

"Carl Reiner is a flat-out atheist. He says, 'It's a joke! There is no one. It's
made up to make people feel good.' But I like the tribal aspect of religion.
It's like a school song. [Singing] 'We welcome you to Sussex Camp, we're
mighty glad you're here. We'll send the air re-ver-ber-ating with a mighty
cheer. Rah rah!' . . . It's like that. It's fun to be part of something. That's the
best part about it. But to really believe in an afterlife, that's a stretch. That
don't work, not for me."

I didn't waste time telling him that artists needn't worry about an afterlife.

"THE INQUISITION" ONCE AGAIN AND THE END OF JEWISH SELF-PITY

In her 2016 documentary *The Last Laugh*, Ferne Pearlstein interviews a
great many professional comics. What jokes can be made about painful
subjects? What about the Holocaust? Is it off-limits? We hear a variety of
taboo jokes (from Sarah Silverman, the late Gilbert Gottfried, and others), some of them actually funny. But Mel holds forth seriously.

> Comics are the conscience of the people, and they are allowed a wide berth
> of activity in every direction. Comics have to tell us who we are, where we
> are, even if it's in bad taste. I like dirty comedy, and I like filthy comedy,
> and I like BAD comedy. I do like a fat lady slipping on a banana peel and
> falling on her ass. I do like that. It's good, but you can't get me on the
> Holocaust.

No, he couldn't make any such film, and he makes it clear that he
detested Roberto Benigni's 1997 comedy about a concentration camp,
Life Is Beautiful. But in the same documentary, asked again about the
Holocaust, he answers a little differently. "I, personally, who have done
a musical called 'The Inquisition,' with Jews floating around and being
dunked in water and tortured, I cannot go THERE." That answer, however, suggests that "The Inquisition" came pretty close to *there*. "It wasn't

fun," he said on another occasion, describing the number. "And it certainly wasn't fun for all those Jews who were tortured, you know, but it was a delicious way of REMINDING the world that not only were Hitler and the concentration camps indescribable and despicable, but there was a time in the history of the Jews when this happened before." He was reminding the world, and reminding the Jews, too, in his own astonishing way.

The episode, no matter how many times I've seen it, remains discomforting as well as excruciatingly funny. Mel wrote the music, singing it into a tape recorder. His old colleagues then helped him out. Rudy De Luca worked with him on the lyrics; composer John Morris wrote down the notes and turned them into a performable number; and Alan Johnson, who had choreographed "Springtime for Hitler" back in 1967 and later directed *To Be or Not to Be*, worked out the dance patterns for Mel and an ensemble of singing and dancing monks.

It certainly is a jolly scene. The Jews are strung up, turned on spits, spun in a gigantic slot machine, xylophone-tapped on their heads. Mel, as Torquemada, sings and dances right through it, ending the number with his arms thrown up in the air in a Broadway boffo finish. All of which suggests a filmmaker pushing Jewish suffering and a Jewish audience—not to mention everyone else—as far as they can go. Whatever my gripes in 1981, I now think "The Inquisition" is the craziest thing Mel Brooks has ever done and also the greatest—certainly the closest he has come to a dangerous kind of modern art, a work dependent on extreme irony, the dislocation of representation and emotion. The French avant-garde thinker Antonin Artaud advocated for a "theater of cruelty." Somehow, I don't believe that this jubilant bit of shenanigans is exactly what Artaud meant, but it *is* cruel—and gleeful, too.

When I was thinking (again) about "The Inquisition," and trying to work through my misery over it, the resemblance of Mel's spectacle to another piece of fiction was shadowing my thoughts. What *was* it? . . . Something outrageous in its demands on its audience. And of course, with a little more pushing, I knew it had to be Kafka—Kafka's terrifying story "In the Penal Colony."

Kafka published it 1919. It was one of the few things of his that pleased him. In the colony, men who have committed trivial rebellions against authority—men guilty without trial—are punished by being strapped into a machine that inscribes with glass needles the lesson of their crimes onto their bodies, torturing them with this lesson before they acknowledge it and die. I know, I know: Kafka's grim humor (composed, dry, distanced) couldn't possibly be further from Mel's Broadway burlesque (noisy, musical, ebullient). How can a furiously neurotic Czech Jew, convinced of his inadequacies, eager to destroy his own work—how could this strange hidden man ("I have constructed my burrow") be linked to the deafening American entertainer who campaigned all over the world for his movies? When I asked Mel, he said he hadn't read that particular Kafka story. But no matter. Jewish minds sometimes think alike. In both cases, torture is presented with agonizing irony as the way to knowledge. The prisoners in the penal colony are "taught"; the Jews in the Inquisition number are made to renounce their faith or be killed. Both works of art could be called attacks on official domination—punishment justified solely by authority's claims of right.

But this kind of literal-minded moralism is hopeless. The meanings can't be easily pinned down. In both cases, the audience is challenged— and almost stranded. The Kafka story is a morose satire of "justice" and some sort of allegory—but of what? To paraphrase critic Walter Benjamin, some of Kafka's stories feel like commentary on a doctrine that doesn't exist. As for Brooks, the usual interpretation of the scene trails off into commonplace remarks about "sick" humor, remarks that get us nowhere. Both pieces are elusive, and taunting. At the least, Brooks is saying, *You stiffs, don't you have the strength to find this funny?* Well, maybe some of us do have that strength in the end. But the question remains: What is the intention of the joke? What's being released by it?

Think of Kafka again. He wrestled with Judaism and Jewish identity his entire life. For years, interpreters of his work have seen in his dire and comical mysteries the expression of extreme states of Jewish homelessness and alienation. "As Gregor Samsa awoke one morning from uneasy dreams he found himself transformed in his bed into a gigantic insect." So goes the opening line of Kafka's most famous story, *The Metamorphosis*, which Mel actually quoted in *The Producers*. The stories and novels Kafka wrote in the early twentieth century reverberate backward and forward. "Kafka *knew*," Mel said to me. A few decades after *The Metamorphosis* was finished, the Nazis, very literal-minded indeed, treated the Jews exactly as "insects"—vermin to be exterminated. Kafka himself died in 1924 (of tuberculosis) at the age of forty-one; his three sisters were killed in extermination camps. He is the sovereign prince and exemplar of Jewish consciousness and suffering transformed into art.

Mel Brooks's entire showbiz career, intentionally or not, is a triumphant answer to such miseries. His temperament and his work—proclaiming the Jews, teasing them—is a way of announcing that the Jews will now suffer and be happy as other people suffer and are happy. He is free to make jokes *on* the Jews and *for* the Jews (as well as for everyone else). He makes them in a way that is unique. Many Jewish comics get us to laugh at Jewish traits while avoiding the Jewish past; he violently reverses the process, restaging the calamities of the past as musical comedy or, in the "2000 Year Old Man" skit, restaging the past as comedies of survival. Of course, the laughter at "The Inquisition" does not come easily; it has to be squeezed out of every Jewish impulse to cry out in rage. The innumerable murdered children, the books burned from a hundreds of libraries, the culture destroyed—none of that can be undone. Yet our responses to life as it's lived now can be changed. Is not Mel Brooks saying, "Deal with it. Be tough enough to face it"? And is not his noisy work just as valuable as the writings of moralists and historians? Mel Brooks's robust life and art are propelled by anger but not by self-pity. "The Inquisition" is a very harsh joke. What's released and chased away by it is precisely the Jewish habit of self-dramatizing misery. Remember what he told *Newsweek* in 1975: "Unrelieved lamenting would be intolerable. So, for every ten Jews, beating their breasts, God designated one to be crazy and amuse the breast-beaters. By the time I was five, I knew I was that one."

Brooks wouldn't put it as I have. He conforms to the frequent bland refusal of American popular entertainers to make higher claims for themselves. (Introducing himself on a public occasion, a great movie director said, "My name is John Ford. I make Westerns.") When I asked Mel again, in 2022, about sending a memo to the Jews, he said, "Yeah . . . *Get over it.*" That's about as far as he will go, and after the massacres of October 7, 2023, in Israel, he might not be willing to say that anymore. I don't want to put words in his mouth. But I'm sure of this: the two scandalous musical numbers are both audacious and life-enhancing examples of comic art. Whether he meant it or not, they function as exorcism, or at least as powerful shots in the arm to a people subject to the tyranny of history and memory.

* * *

IN ONE OF our conversations, in August 2022, Mel Brooks said to me, "I've done everything I set out to do. I've done everything I've wanted to do. I can't think of anything I haven't been able to do." It's a remarkable statement, one that few of us could make. But eight months later, in April 2023, when Mel was pushing ninety-seven, he suddenly said: "I'm always looking for that impossible joke that no one ever thought of. I'm still looking for it."

2
BETTY FRIEDAN AND THE END OF SUBSERVIENCE

THE JEWISH FEMINIST I

In 1958, George Brockway, the publisher of W. W. Norton and Company, gave Betty Friedan an advance of $3,000 for a study of contemporary women. Friedan worked on the book for five years. *The Feminine Mystique*, as she decided to call it, came out in February 1963, in the middle of a New York newspaper strike. The book still sold about sixty thousand copies—a very good number, though Friedan and her husband, Carl Friedan, believed that Norton had been stingy and half-hearted in promoting it. Betty composed a fourteen-page complaint to Brockway ("You should not have published this work if you were not aware of its significance"). In the next year, the Dell paperback edition sold one million three hundred thousand copies; altogether, the paperback sold about three million copies during Friedan's lifetime. Coffee-stained and dog-eared, *The Feminine Mystique* was passed from one woman to another, on movie sets, in teachers' lounges, in doctors' offices. It is widely considered one of the most influential American books of the twentieth century. Friedan was hardly the only feminist in the early sixties, but she was the one who kicked second-wave feminism into life.

After *The Feminine Mystique* became a paperback bestseller, George Brockway, eager to retain his star author, took Friedan out to lunch. Brockway asked her about her next book.

"What next book?" she said. "You're not going to have my next book. George, you made me feel so Jewish for trying to sell my book. Go fuck yourself."

BETTY FRIEDAN WAS not religiously observant or much interested in Jewish doctrine or ritual—at least not until late in life. Yet she certainly never hid her identity as a Jewish woman, and if she detected an undertone of anti-Semitism in the room, she would torch up like acetylene. In 1979, when she was fifty-eight, she made explicit what she had always felt. Friedan was addressing a national gathering of Reform rabbis in Arizona.

> I had this burning feeling. I had this feeling as a Jew first. First as a Jew before I had it as a woman. All that I am I will not deny [the words are from Joan of Arc]. And if I've had strength and passion, and if that has somehow helped a little bit to change the world or the possibilities of the world, it comes from that core of me as a Jew. My passion, my strength, my creativity, if you will, comes from this kind of affirmation.

Friedan may not have been observant, but she lived, as novelist and essayist Cynthia Ozick would put it, within the shadow of Sinai; she was determined to create a community of justice. What do we live for? What makes for happiness? What would *personhood* look like in a woman? She took literally Reform Judaism's injunction *tikkun olam*—the necessity of repairing the world, the notion that Jews need to do more than just look out for themselves but need to look out for other people as well. In individual Jews, this demand produces both ethical ardency and presumption, both philanthropy and gall, both social activism and harsh, excessive moralism. It's a strenuous calling, and Friedan's life was marked by both the thrillingly triumphant and sourly negative sides of it. Her Jewish inheritance made her great and, in the end, may have grievously limited her greatness. But greatness, no matter how compromised or saddened, cannot be taken away from her.

BOURGEOIS REVOLUTIONARY

Betty Friedan liked men, she liked sex with men, and when she got older she enjoyed hard-drinking parties, but, essentially, she was an American Jewish Victorian, with an unrelenting focus on the matter at hand. Her ethical passions were derived not just from Jewish traditions but from her father, a Jewish freethinker in a conservative town (Peoria, Illinois); from the traditions of left-wing protest in the thirties (anti-fascist and pro-labor), much of it created by Jews; and, finally, from her own aggrieved sense of herself—her past, her uncertainties, her need to prevail in every situation.

In the late 1950s, she was living in the middle of an extraordinary situation, all the more remarkable given that many people accepted it as normal. The number of American women working in the late fifties was actually rising, but about two-thirds remained home, either because they wanted to or because they had to. They took care of children and served as companions, mates, cooks, and house cleaners for wage-earning husbands. During the Second World War, hundreds of thousands of women had worked in the defense industries, but most of them were pushed out when the war ended. The postwar economy was booming, and a single income was enough for many families. Still, the millions of women choosing to live at home—or trapped at home—constituted an enormous pool of unused labor, a situation with economic costs to the nation and, for some of the women, spiritual costs that wore them out.

In the affluent suburbs, women had "everything"—husband, children, house, cars, appliances, clubs, churches, synagogues, volunteer work—and yet many were miserable. They suffered from "the problem that has no name," as Friedan called it; an "eerie restlessness," according to *Life* magazine. For years, psychiatrists and social analysts as well as innumerable magazine writers addressed the issue of women's unhappiness, sometimes with teasing whimsy: Why couldn't women accede to the glory of being a wife and mother? In 1960, in an excruciating attempt at wit, *Newsweek* observed that "American women's unhappiness is merely the most recently won of women's rights."

As many have pointed out, Betty Friedan's reporting in *The Feminine Mystique* was devoted solely to middle-class and upper-middle-class white suburban women. It's as if Friedan noticed no one else—for instance, the working-class women who needed to take a job in order to survive. Or the Black women who led civil rights protests. Ever since 1963, a variety of scholars and activists, irritably charging Friedan with racial and class bias, have filled in the picture, chronicling the situation of urban women, working-class women, women of color. All this work has greatly expanded the portrait of American women after the war. In relation to Friedan's text, however, the critique misses the point.

Along with her reporting about suburban women, Friedan analyzed and criticized studies and opinions about women *in general*—condescending attitudes that turned up in the work of psychiatrists, rabbis, ministers, sociologists, educators, novelists, screenwriters, movie and TV directors, magazine editors, advertising men, motivational researchers, and many others. These men thought they were writing about women's essence, the nature of *all* women, not just suburban white women. They were experts, weren't they? Betty Friedan took them on, and many kinds of women, immersed in decades of professional male contempt, hitched their own experience to Friedan's strong-shouldered prose. You didn't have to live in Greenwich or Shaker Heights to know what she was talking about. Women who merely heard about the book were affected by it.

No act of consciousness can ever be complete. Betty Friedan was partially defined by her class, her color, her situation on the East Coast. But her critics might consider that she knew what she was doing. Could not a report on suburban women offer some truths about the estate of women in general? And she was bolstered by historical truth: most revolutions are begun by the middle class, by people with the education and means to make public their demands. In the event, she and her feminist cohort (women like herself) were enormously successful in getting things going.

In the last sixty years, feminism has produced a tectonic change in the economic, moral, and spiritual life of the nation.

BETTY FRIEDAN'S STORY is glorious and sad. In the years after publication of *The Feminine Mystique*, she fought for women to have good jobs, political power, the right to abortion; she advocated radical revision of the law and the workplace; she pushed for new roles for both men and women in marriage. For a while, her head-down, immigrant-family drive was enormously effective in building organizations, leading protests, and pushing for new laws. Standing before a crowd, she'd issue a boiling stream of social accusation, personal assertion, demands for action. She wrote and spoke without a lyrical strain or a transcendent impulse—or more than an occasional flash of humor. She was not blessed with the gift of irony: there was only one way of being understood, and that was her way.

In the late sixties and seventies, younger feminists began moving away from her. In writing that could be witty and wrathful as well as boundary breaking, radical feminists attacked capitalism and the nuclear family as the twin vessels of women's oppression; they attacked the institutional denigration of women, the widespread acceptance of rape and abuse. They wanted new lives, new ways of living in their bodies and minds, not just jobs and equal pay. Betty seized up. Stiff with anger, she insisted that the young feminists, especially gay young women, had joined a sinister conspiracy to destroy both the movement and herself. She was too immersed in struggle, and perhaps too egotistical, to see that women turned away from her as a leader in part because of her own character and ideas. Betty Friedan—the thought is impossible to ignore—may have had the wrong temperament for the particular revolution she unleashed. Yet could it have been unleashed in the first place without her pile-driving manner?

However much she was rejected in her later years, Friedan's *Feminine Mystique* is still exciting and necessary; indeed, her later preoccupations remain central to us now. She was an intelligent and courageous Jewish woman, irritable, vain, harsh, blind to herself and to her effect on others—in other words, a heroine. At her best, she radiated purpose and hope. I will not turn away from her failures, but it's the heroic element I'm looking for.

A JEWISH GIRL IN PEORIA

> I must have known I would have to leave Peoria. My favorite sound, as a
> child, was the sound of the train whistle and the clanking of rails as the
> Santa Fe to California came within earshot of our house on its way from
> Chicago. I would stand at the window of the bedroom, waiting for the
> sound of the train. Another favorite game, in winter, was to open the win-
> dow very wide and stand there in my nightgown until I couldn't bear the
> cold any longer (*Life So Far*, 2000).

We are in the mid-1930s; Betty is perhaps ten or twelve. At those moments,
listening to the trains going to and from Chicago, or standing in the cold,
she seems a nightgowned Winged Victory of Samothrace, ready to fly off
into the future.

She was born Elizabeth (Bettye) Naomi Goldstein, on February 4,
1921. (The *e* at the end of her name was a genteel touch that her parents
favored; she dropped it at the end of college.) Peoria, located 130 miles
south of Chicago, was then a city of some one hundred thousand people—
the second-largest city in Illinois, and a place dominated by Protestant
churches and a conservative social ethos. The catchphrase "But will it
play in Peoria?" had been around since the early part of the century.
Meaning: will this product, or this vaudeville act, or that radio program
become a hit in the squarest part of the country? The joke was wounding
and perhaps a little unfair, since Peoria, a river town with distilleries and
a red-light district, certainly had its wild side. Men working barges on the
Illinois River stopped there to drink, gamble, and visit brothels. Still, if
you grew up in Peoria in the 1920s and '30s with critical attitudes toward
your society, you could find yourself in trouble.

The drive to move out of restricted social circumstances is central to the
Jewish immigrant story—central to Betty's family, too. Her grandfather
(on her mother's side) Sandor Horwitz was born in Hungary and took his
medical degree in America; he served as a doctor in the army, and eventually led public-health efforts in the Peoria area. Betty's father, Harry Goldstein, has a similar tale. Born in 1888 in a village near Kiev, he arrived in
the States when he was six, moving with his family to St. Louis. Still in his
teens, he took off for Peoria, and he became, like many immigrant Jews,
a peddler, selling collar buttons from a street-corner stand. In America,

where Jews were kept out of many business enterprises, the way to success, from the middle of the nineteenth century on, was to create one's own retail establishment. After a few years, Harry had enough money to open Goldstein's Jewelry Store, just off the main street in the center of Peoria. The store was a personal and family triumph. Betty herself called it "the Tiffany's of Peoria."

On the male side, then, the family story was one of entrepreneurial and professional energy leading to substantial success. But women were not encouraged to perform in the same way. The Jewish immigrant experience may have been inspiring, but Betty Friedan grew up in a man's world.

The chief victim of that world, in Betty's life, was her mother, Miriam Leah Horwitz Goldstein. Born in Peoria in 1898, Miriam, an intelligent and good-looking woman, wanted to go to Smith, but her parents insisted that she stay close to home and attend a two-year program at Bradley College (now Bradley University). After school, she worked on the local paper as a writer-editor on the women's page, a job she apparently liked very much. But at Harry Goldstein's request, Miriam quit work when they got married. In Peoria, amid proper families, women did not work—a "rule" that may have been particularly commanding for socially ambitious Jews in a Protestant town.

Harry Goldstein had been married before. By the time he met Miriam, he was a widower, twenty years older than his new wife, a bulky man with a large nose and a Russian Jewish accent. To our ears, after Mel Brooks's immortalization of those tones, Harry's voice was a blessing. But not to Miriam's ears. According to Betty, her parents were unhappy much of the time, and the central problem was that Miriam was ashamed of Harry's Jewishness, ashamed of his foreignness.

Miriam may have absorbed the attitudes around her. In the Midwest, bigotry was common enough. Henry Ford's anti-Semitic weekly, *The Dearborn Independent*, from which Hitler and the Nazis took many ideas, was published in nearby Michigan. The weekly paper, which had an enormous circulation, published excerpts from *The Protocols of the Elders of Zion*, a forgery concocted by the czarist police at the beginning of the twentieth century. As well as excerpts, Ford published the entire text in an edition of five hundred thousand copies. Jews, it seems, wanted to replace capitalism with communism; they were leftists who somehow controlled world banking and the money supply; they were determined to rule

Christian America. Personally, they were greedy, unclean, and aggressive. There's no way that the Goldsteins, living in Peoria, could not have been aware of these commonplace attitudes.

AFTER QUITTING WORK, Miriam joined the local Hadassah group and took up golf and riding; she became a champion mah-jongg and bridge player, and she shopped—endlessly, according to Betty, but with never enough money to buy what she wanted. She and Harry argued about money all the time. Frustrated, Miriam became a household tyrant, superb in all the business of place settings and linens, a cold, censorious woman, "charming" but distant. Betty longed for her mother's touch—a simple physical embrace—but Miriam, often suffering from colitis, gave little to other people. Betty saw her with an acuteness that perhaps only a semi-unloved child would have: Miriam, she noted, was sugary on the phone with a friend, but would then say, after hanging up, "that bitch!" Years later, in the women's movement, no one ever accused Betty Friedan of being sugary. She was direct, blunt, and often inconsiderate. From her point of view, however, she was just being honest.

In the 1920s, when they had money, the Goldsteins employed a nursemaid, a cook, and a man who doubled as a butler and a chauffeur. In the dining room, Harry, like Leonard Bernstein's immigrant father, Sam, held forth on the issues of the day, soliciting opinions from his children. The family joined Peoria's Reform synagogue, Anshai Emeth, but Harry was a freethinker—a fan of attorney Clarence Darrow and the great nineteenth-century orator and agnostic Robert G. Ingersoll. Betty was his chief intellectual companion; they argued over politics and social justice. But Miriam hoped to induce the social graces in her children. She enrolled Betty in golf, tennis, riding, and dancing lessons—a failure, since Betty was not coordinated enough for such things. Most grievously for Miriam, Betty was not pretty. Her sister Amy was the pretty one; Betty had Harry's nose. And her room was a mess. Miriam thought that order was the essence of happiness, a belief common, perhaps, to people who control no more than a small corner of their lives. Years later, guests arriving at Betty's house in Sag Harbor, Long Island, would discover the bedclothes tossed about. Domestic order was never a big priority for her; disorder at home may in fact have pleased her more.

School provided something of a relief. A terrific student, she studied English, Latin, physics, and chemistry. She raided the local libraries, read poetry, and acted in plays. As a teenager, she talked like a revolutionary intellectual in old Russia—quickly, and in spurts, with an enormous fluency about facts, conditions, and opinions. She made friends among the girls, and when she was accepted, a gregarious nature came out, but she didn't get the kind of attention she wanted from boys. Years later, she wrote, "When I still used to say prayers, even as a child, after the 'now I lay me down to sleep' and the Shema Yisrael, I would pray for 'a boy to like me best' and 'work of my own to do' when I grew up. I did not want to be discontented like my mother was." She had the same aspirations that many women would have five or six decades later, but without feminist sentiment, which was unknown to her.

At fourteen, she was rejected by Central High School's sorority. Some might say, "So what?"—but for Betty it was a serious blow. To be excluded was to be demeaned. In a 1988 interview, recorded half a century later and published in the liberal Jewish magazine *Tikkun*, Betty came to terms with the entire business.

> I remember very distinctly that [being Jewish] was first oppressive to me when I was in high school. Sororities and fraternities dominated social life in this Midwestern town. All my friends got into sororities and fraternities, and I didn't because I was Jewish. . . . So being Jewish made me an observer, a marginal person and I made one of those unconscious vows to myself: "they may not like me but they're going to look up to me."

In the Depression era, Harry's business fell off, and the servants disappeared. Desperate for cash, Miriam went out at night and gambled in some disreputable corner of Peoria—and lost her money. In all, there's an element of sad comedy in the family's social ambitions. Betty boasted that they ate fresh vegetables and good steak; they had standards, they had taste. But socially, they were successful only within their circle of middle-class Jews. Before Betty failed to get into the school sorority, Harry and Miriam were denied membership at the Peoria Country Club. Assimilation, as the sociologists say, is not binary; it moves along a spectrum. The Goldsteins were entirely American in their outlook. Like many families descended from immigrants, they took advantage of America as an open society, a field of opportunity. But Gentiles thought of them as Jews who needed to be restricted. Harry's business friends would not speak to him after closing time.

Yet how bad was all this? The Goldsteins weren't prevented from running a business; they weren't publicly mocked or chased from their homes. To use Hannah Arendt's terms: they were treated as parvenus but not as pariahs. Surely many children in the Depression had a worse time than Betty Friedan. Her father loved her, and her mother may have loved her, too, though Miriam was so badly crippled by personal chagrins that she found it hard to express her feelings. Miriam's most serious problem was not a shortage of cash but a shortage of opportunity and encouragement. That late-developing gambling habit makes one wonder: Did Miriam need adventure, some sort of semi-scandalous activity outside the house? Did she need liberty more than cash? When she started leaving the house again, she did it successfully: as Harry's health began to decline in the late 1930s, Miriam took over management of the jewelry store. Betty said that her mother's colitis, which had been bothering her for years, gradually went away.

As Betty Friedan admitted, she only began to understand Miriam many years later—how little freedom she had, how much of her tyrannically proper behavior was caused by rage at having been made to give up a good college and a career. But what she didn't quite say, and couldn't say, even after decades, was that desperate Miriam was the necessary agent of her own fate. For it was Miriam, not Harry, who insisted that Betty apply to Smith College, which Miriam's own parents had prevented her from attending years earlier. And landlocked Miriam was the perfect model of the bored, unhappy women whom Betty re-created years later in *The Feminine Mystique*. Inspired by her mother's negative example, Betty acted on her own determination to be free and eventually worked for the freedom of millions of other women.

A JEWISH WOMAN AT SMITH

For liberal college students, and especially for liberal Jewish college students, the late thirties were a tumultuous time. In September 1938, during Betty's first weeks at college, France and Britain appeased Hitler at Munich, and within days the Nazis took over the Sudetenland—the

German-speaking periphery of Czechoslovakia. In September 1939, Germany attacked Poland; the war had begun, and the Jewish population of Europe and the Soviet Union (as well as millions of other people) were under threat of death. At Smith, one of the best of the women's colleges at the time, the students were expected to take themselves seriously and to form opinions of fascism and communism as well as attitudes toward labor unrest and even capitalism.

Not all the students, of course, were serious-minded. Many of the young women, as social historian Daniel Horowitz notes in *Betty Friedan and the Making of "The Feminine Mystique"* (1998), were at Smith because their East Coast Protestant parents wanted them there for social reasons. The fathers were often in banking or corporate business; only a few of the mothers worked for pay. By accepting many such students, the college put itself in an odd position. It may have urged the women to arm themselves with knowledge and opinions, but it did not prepare them for professional careers. In this matter, social conservatism was reinforced by a truth that everyone could see: university teaching was partway open for women, but law, medicine, and corporate business were closed (and even more tightly closed to Jewish women); the idea of entering such professions, rather than marrying well and raising children and perhaps doing some charity work, attracted no more than a minority of the students. "We were expected to be responsible, competent community leaders," Betty wrote later, "good wives and mothers, and cultured patrons of the arts, hostesses for our husbands. I don't think I ever heard the word 'career' until 'career women' became a term of opprobrium."

Betty exulted in the intellectual resources of the college, and, at the school paper, the *Smith College Associated News* (*SCAN*), she and her friends pushed the "society girls" out of the way. Betty became news editor of the paper in her junior year and editor in chief the following year, setting policy and writing (unsigned) progressive editorials. She was accepted, even admired, by many women, some of whom sought her out and asked for advice or chatted her up in extended bull sessions on art and politics. As an undergraduate, she was a great success.

Anti-Semitism was common among wealthy Protestants, and it existed at Smith, too, though Betty's driving intellect protected her. What incensed her was the seeming anti-Semitism among some of the Jewish students. In November 1938, Betty's freshman year, the president of the college, William Allan Neilson, a Shakespeare scholar and lexicographer, urged the students to sign a petition that would press President Roosevelt and Congress to alter the immigration quotas that were drastically restricting the number of Jewish refugees entering the United States. In Betty's residence, Chapin House, some of the students signed, including Protestant students, but four wealthy Jewish girls from Cincinnati did not. Did their refusal echo, for Betty, the kind of discomfort with Jewishness that Miriam felt about her immigrant husband? In any case, Betty regarded the docility of the wealthy Jewish girls as an outright betrayal, and it taught her, I believe, bitter lessons about the occasional safe playing of well-off women.

BINARY CHOICES

Betty had surpassed Peoria, killed it, escaping, at least for a time, her unhappy childhood. Yet she had an odd mishap in the last weeks of school. She was taking the final exam in a psychology course—material that she knew and loved—and for a solid hour she froze, unable to write a word. The event was not a disaster; she completed the second half of the exam and subsequently graduated summa cum laude. Still, she was shaken up. In *Life So Far*, she professes not to understand what happened but, for the reader, the reason for the freeze-up seems obvious enough: she was at the end of a brilliant undergraduate career, and she didn't know what to do next. She had successfully applied for a fellowship at Berkeley in psychology, but she wasn't sure she wanted to go. Should she go to medical school instead? Should she become a psychiatrist, even an analyst?

Her indecision was exacerbated by her father's attitude, an odd mixture of love, condescension, and resentment. Something Harry said at that time threw her for a loop. "If you're just going to be another doctor with a shingle, you might as well be a woman." It's a strange remark. Did Harry mean that she should become a specialist rather than an ordinary MD? Betty assumed he meant that she had to choose between being a professional of *any* sort and being a woman, since the two, in his view, were mutually exclusive. In *Life So Far*, she writes that "I knew enough psychology by now to be devastated with horror and dread and unspeakable shame by that remark, which I could never forget. Then, I wasn't a woman? He didn't see me as a woman? He wouldn't let me be a woman?"

In the late thirties, as Harry's health failed, Miriam began running the jewelry store, and he lost his sway in the family; he abandoned his free-thinking ways, and a surly intolerance took over. Among other things, he became obsessed with Betty's sex life. In 1942, he thought she had casually slept with a man on the way home from Smith to Peoria (she hadn't), and he shouted at her and called her "a whore." The charge was absurd (she was a virgin), and she left the house in a rage, without saying good-bye. That leave-taking later distressed her a great deal, because she never saw him again. In January 1943, Harry Goldstein died, at the age of sixty. Betty went home for the funeral, but what she mainly remembered of the visit was her anger at her mother. "Why couldn't she give him the love that he needed?" And, she added, "if I didn't say so then, why couldn't I give him that kind of love?"

IN 1942, AFTER months of miserable indecision, she entered the graduate program in psychology at Berkeley on her fellowship. She studied with well-known professors and was offered additional support for the next few years. Yet graduate school was wrong for her. She missed the stir of undergraduate days, the excitement of being at the center of things. A lot of the young men, both students and faculty, were away at war. The intellectual action on campus was not in psychology but in physics, especially in a mysterious building in the hills at the top of the campus, the Lawrence Radiation Laboratory. Several graduate students she was interested in, including David Bohm and Robert Loevinger, were working there, under the supervision of J. Robert Oppenheimer, performing, as it turned out, part of the secret experimental work on enriching uranium that led to the Manhattan Project and the development of the atomic bomb. But none of that was out in the open. Bohm was both ardent in his admiration of Betty and sexually shy. After her father died, she was determined to sleep with someone—anyone—in order to lose her virginity; a law student unfit for military service was her choice. Meanwhile, she and Bohm fumbled at the edge of a romance.

In *Life So Far*, she says she quit Berkeley because the other man she was interested in, Robert Loevinger, was jealous of the financial support she was offered. In her telling, Loevinger made her choose between him and the second fellowship. What is notable in this period is that two men she was very fond of asked her, within the space of a year, to choose between intellectual ambition and "being a woman." In the early forties, this kind of binary choice was forced on women who wanted to get anywhere. You might achieve something of value, but you had to give up something of equal value. At that moment, Betty decided to abandon both things— she gave up Loevinger and the fellowship as well, leaving Berkeley for New York. Her struggles for self-definition, it has to be said again, did not include a specifically feminist consciousness, though she had noticed that the women professors at Smith didn't have much clout on campus. They were single and mostly lesbian, and therefore in her eyes unhappy.

Something was holding her back—a lack of clarity or focus, though certainly not a lack of ambition. She didn't know where she was going, yet she couldn't shake what she later referred to as "my existential guilt, which I have used to this day when I'm just coasting and not using my powers to meet serious new challenges," a bedeviling pressure she associated with being Jewish. It's a curious formulation: notice that she employs "use" twice in one sentence, which I'm guessing was an unconscious declaration and not mere sloppiness. *We are here for use. Jews do not waste time, lolling about; if we do, we will be ashamed.* She flirted with joining the Communist Party, and for a while she lived with some party women in Berkeley. They taught her how to make delicious avocado sandwiches but, as she later complained, they "didn't seem to wash or comb their hair all that much." No longer indifferent to clothes, she wore stockings and a garter belt. Applying to join the party twice, in New York and San Francisco, she was laughed out of the office both times. Despite her Left politics, she was bourgeois through and through. She would have to find ways to become useful without giving up the comforts of life.

AT BERKELEY, SHE was having what later became known as "an identity crisis," a term invented, as it happened, by one of her teachers at the university—Erik Erikson, who had escaped with his wife in 1933 from anti-Semitic Vienna, where he had been studying child psychology with disciples of Freud. Erikson later wrote *Childhood and Society* (1950) and studies of Martin Luther and Mahatma Gandhi; he became famous in the United States for his development of "ego psychology" and the notion that human beings go through distinct stages in which identity issues take over their emotional lives, issues that are sometimes successfully resolved, sometimes not. The identity crisis, in Erikson's thinking, principally happened to men.

Erikson's reputation is in eclipse. He believed that girls were born with a determining "inner space" and that boys had to conquer an "outer space." Lamentable opinions aside, Erikson was a very strong writer, and something he wrote had a serious bearing on Betty Friedan's career. In 1958, Erikson brought out *Young Man Luther*, an erudite psychological portrait of Martin Luther's youth and early manhood. In considerable detail, he captured Luther's long period of hesitation—roughly from 1507 to 1517—when he refused his father's desire that he become a lawyer and instead lived as a monk, developing his critique of the all-too-worldly practices of the Catholic Church. In 1517, according to legend, Luther posted his ninety-five theses on the door of the All Saints' Church in Wittenberg and began his long history as a heretic and religious leader. The decade of hesitation before 1517 Erikson called a "moratorium," a time for Luther of withdrawal, introspection, gradual awakening, and refashioning of personal ambition and ideology. At last, armed and ready, the hero bursts into the world in the most aggressive and disruptive way possible.

At first glance, any comparison between Martin Luther and Betty Friedan seems absurd, and I don't want to push it past the point of suggestion. He was a spiritually electrifying malevolent genius convinced that something was seriously wrong with man's relation to God and Church, and she became a talented middle-class journalist equally convinced that something was wrong in our common marital and employment structure, our consciousness of women's abilities. And yet, Betty Friedan, before writing her significant work, had to create a new psychology of female success; she had to overcome the frustrations and uncertainties of her ambitions as a writer, her inability to exist in the world in a way that mattered. Why shouldn't a "moratorium" and an "identity crisis" apply to women as well as men?

UNION PAPERS

She left Berkeley in the summer of 1943, and moved to New York's Greenwich Village, where she joined Smith friends in a small house on Grove Street. She was free of home and school; she was free of sexual inhibition, too, her virginity issue having been settled at last. Her father was dead, her mother cold and remote, she was no longer an academic star; now she had to create herself on her own.

She needed a job badly, and soon after arriving in the city she went to work for the *Federated Press*, a daily news service that was sent out (by mail) to labor unions and radicals all over the country In 1946, she moved to the *UE News*, the official organ of the United Electrical, Radio and Machine Workers of America—the UE, which once had been the most radical big union in the country, with many Communists among the leaders and membership. Betty was hardly a Communist. Her central concern was the situation of labor, including one labor issue new to her. She made a trip to a New Jersey plant that had an all-female workforce. The women, she realized, were being paid less than men would have been paid for the same work. As she wrote later,

> There was nothing I had studied, at economics class at Smith or in the classes in radical economics I now took, along with other Smith sisters, at the Jefferson School of Social Science in New York—the educational enterprise run, I suppose, by the Communist Party—that explained or even described the special exploitation of women.

In 1952, in an article for the *News*, she pointed out an enraging contradiction: corporations glorified the role of women as consumers while paying them poorly in their factories and offices. Women were being groomed, courted, and flattered, not just as a way of selling them dishwashers but as a way of sanctifying them in their household function. This perception of the psychological victimization of women was central to the aggressive critique that Betty produced later. The moment marks a near awakening: in that 1952 article, she argued for women's skills, and she established, as an ideal, a workplace in which gender no longer mattered. She was on her way, though it took another decade of working and living before she realized all the ways in which women were being "underpaid"—undervalued in general, their intelligence slighted, their possible contributions erased in advance.

In her autobiography, she says she was no more than half-interested during her early days in what she was writing. She sounds a little bored, calling herself "quite miserable often with that hair shirt I'd put on, choosing to write for the union papers instead of *Time* or *Life*." In New York, she was enjoying "a kind of cashmere Marxist life," as biographer Judith Hennessee put it (*Betty Friedan: Her Life*, 1999). She wanted to live well, eat well, dress well. The UE office was on Fifty-First Street in Manhattan, just opposite St. Patrick's Cathedral, and, in her lunch hour, Betty would shop at Bergdorf Goodman or Henri Bendel, two luxury women's stores a few blocks up Fifth Avenue. But there is no contradiction here. She was a bourgeois Jewish liberal, a progressive who enjoyed good things without giving up her sense of social injustice. In the end, she poured her outraged sense of wrong into her belief that women were getting a rotten deal.

SCENES FROM A MARRIAGE I

The fit young men were mostly away at war, so she had short affairs with married men, a way, perhaps, of overcoming her sense that she was unattractive, and perhaps also a way of competing with other women. Still, she was lonely, and she was afraid she would never get married, which, in the immediate postwar years, was considered a terrible fate for an American woman, particularly for a Jewish American woman. To be without a family! For Jewish women, it was a disgrace.

Betty met Carl Friedan on a blind date in 1947. He was slender, of medium height (though taller than Betty), with reddish hair and a nervous rapid walk. One wants to be kind to the young Carl Friedan (his name was Friedman, but he dropped the *m* in order to sound less Jewish), since parts of his marriage with Betty come off terribly. As a boy, growing up in Boston in a poor family, he taught himself magic tricks, and, while still a teenager, he traveled around New England to vaudeville shows and summer hotels and did sleight-of-hand material wherever he could. In all, he was extremely energetic and, according to friends, spontaneous in temperament, even rebellious—a promising young man.

After a couple of years at the University of Massachusetts, he knew that theater was his passion, and he transferred to the theater program at Emerson College. He joined the Army Signal Corps in 1942, fought in the European theater, and, after V-E Day, helped stage entertainment for the soldiers overseas, working, at times, on shows featuring Mickey Rooney and Danny Kaye. No longer a performer but a producer, he returned home and ran summer stock productions in New England; he produced a few experimental productions in New York. But at that point, in the late forties, his career in the theater fell apart. An independent producer is always trying to shake money out of reluctant backers, and Carl Friedan was neither bold nor charming enough to succeed at this difficult job. In fairness, it should be said that many people failed in the little-theater movement in the forties and ever after. It's a tough business. Carl Friedan needed to earn a living, and he started a small advertising company.

"He brought me an apple on our first date, and made me laugh," Betty wrote later. In this encounter, the Adam-and-Eve polarities get reversed: a man brings the apple to a woman. But the intellectual polarities are not reversed. Carl may have made Betty laugh, but he did not bring her knowledge, which Eve brought to her mate. Betty was better educated and brighter than he was. What he brought her was sex. They were both lonely and, as it turned out, needy—two awkward solitaries in the big city—and they became lovers almost immediately. In *Life So Far*, published when Betty was seventy-nine and had been divorced from Carl for almost thirty years, she writes as follows.

> I loved going to bed with him. I loved our sex. We were silly and cozy, had pet names for his cock and my diaphragm. I loved giving myself over to sex, letting him take over. Later the feminist critique of heterosexual sex seemed crazy to me. It denied my own experience. I loved kissing, and when he put his tongue hard down my throat, I loved the whole melting feeling, not just the clitoral orgasm.

The last sentence is a swipe at the feminists who insisted that sexual pleasure in women was confined to one place alone. Her assertion of wider pleasure was her own kind of liberation. She wanted the world to know how sexual a woman she was, how many things made her happy. The passage is also an act of gratitude, a gift to her long-ago husband.

The marriage was certainly happy in the beginning. They went hiking and camping; they partied in Betty's basement apartment on West Eighty-Sixth Street in Manhattan. In 1950, they moved to Parkway Village, a UN-built encampment in Queens with a congenial international population. As Susan Oliver points out in her expert short biography, *Betty Friedan: The Personal Is Political* (2007), Betty may have been living in New York City, but at Parkway she became a de facto suburbanite, enjoying grassy lawns and easy sociability with other parents as they watched their kids play together. Yet Carl and Betty were at war. She was an anxious, ambitious woman who didn't quite know what to do with herself, he a failed theater producer—not a combination tending toward harmony. They argued frequently about money, which must have been mortifying for Betty, since her parents had argued about money all through her childhood. And, after a while, they began hitting each other.

EGO AND VANITY

In 1952, when Betty was pregnant with her second child, she was fired by the *UE News*. It was a serious blow. She lost steady income ($100 a week; the equivalent now would be $1,160) and any remaining illusions about the American Left, which was clearly not going to do anything for women.

According to legend, God spoke to Martin Luther by sending a lightning bolt crashing down next to him on the street. Thereafter he could not be a lawyer, as his father wanted; he had to devote himself to religion and the truth of man's relation to God. The lightning bolt, mythical or not, suggests a surge of fresh consciousness—a decision point. In Betty's case, no message came from heaven. For her, as for most of us, major change was a matter of one step forward, one step back, and then, finally, a lurch into a new life. She was a liberal journalist; she needed to write something that engaged both her moral energies and her vanity as a writer.

She loved being a mother (Daniel was born in 1948; Jonathan came in 1952). The children, she wrote later in *Life So Far*, seemed like "a *bonus* in my life, an unexpected, maybe an undeserved, bonus." When she was fired by the UE, she felt, as she admitted later, a sense of relief as well as chagrin, for she could now spend more time with the children. She was also affected by the omnipresent "pejorative that women who worked, had professional careers, were losing their femininity." To some degree, Betty Friedan, as she insisted, was herself oppressed by "the feminine mystique." But she pulled herself together, took a course in magazine writing at Queens College, and found herself an agent, who began selling her writing to the women's magazines (*Ladies' Home Journal*, *McCall's*, *Redbook*, et al.), which then had enormous circulations (almost five million in the case of *Ladies' Home Journal*) and considerable cultural power. She loved motherhood, but she needed to write.

In 1956, when Betty was pregnant with her third child, Emily, the Friedans moved out of the city—first to a rented stone barn in Snedens Landing, north of New York City, on the west side of the Hudson River, and then, taking advantage of Carl's GI status for a low-interest mortgage, to a large Victorian house farther upriver, in Grand View-on-Hudson, just south of Nyack. Betty was a suburbanite—and a magazine pro. She hired domestic help so she could be free to go in and out of the city. For magazines, she wrote profiles of actresses and artists; she did some serious science reporting as well as articles about marriage and families ("Millionaire's Wife," for *Cosmopolitan* in 1956). But she also suffered humiliating setbacks: if she wrote a piece on an independent woman managing family and work together, it was altered by her editors into an article about a "happy homemaker."

To anyone who writes more than routine copy, vanity is just as important as ego. What I mean by ego—confidence and skill—encourages you to put words on a page. Satisfied vanity, a tingle of pleasure along the neck or in the hands, as well as praise and money, provides the hoped-for rewards. By 1956, Betty's vanity was under assault, and she resolved not to write any more articles for the women's magazines (not a resolution that she kept). In her collected papers, which are available at the Schlesinger Library at Harvard, there is an undated bit of writing marked "Notes to Myself," which includes the following: "I must have my own identity—to be able to go out to others, to live outwardly, to be able to surrender the self. Otherwise, fear of emptiness, death . . ."

BIRTH PANGS

One of the many forces impelling Betty Friedan to emerge from her funk was a noxious old slander—a slander earnestly believed by a variety of serious people in the 1950s. Back in 1947, the psychologist Marynia Farnham and the journalist Ferdinand Lundberg (who later became famous for his attacks on the American super rich) published a study of purportedly scientific nature, *Modern Woman: The Lost Sex*. Farnham and Lundberg were among the writers busily analyzing women's unhappiness. They laid special blame on education. Since women's natural state required them to be wives, mothers, and homemakers, women who went to college suffered from an excess of intellectual ambition that led to neurotic unhappiness and bad sex. Women were destroying their femininity by *competing with men*, a domestic crime that hurt the husbands as well as themselves. These notions, encountered now, seem merely stupid or disingenuous—the authors' actual intent, as some have said, was to persuade women, many of whom worked in factories and offices during the war, to get back to the kitchen and bedroom, leaving men free to resume their former positions. The poisonous Farnham-Lundberg thesis was echoed for years in magazine articles, in psychiatrists' advice, in jocular male conversation. The idea was enraging to Friedan. At Smith, she had embraced "the life of the mind," as she unapologetically called it. Was her education to be considered a burden?

In 1956, when she was thirty-five, she finally stepped forward. In cooperation with the Smith College Alumnae Association and two classmates, Anne Mather Montero and Marian Ingersoll, she composed a survey of her graduating class. The results were aimed at the class's fifteenth reunion in 1957. The women had been out in the world. How happy were they with their lives? How had they used—or not used—their education? The seemingly routine questions—which almost any alumni association might have come up with—of course concealed a critical intent. If graduates of a superb women's college weren't happy, was it because of their education? *Why* weren't they happy?

About 40 percent, or two hundred women, answered the survey. Most of them said that education had given them the equipment to do many things in their lives and their communities. Their regret was that they hadn't used it better. The ones who were busy were reasonably happy. But the ones who conformed entirely to the conventional notion of feminine fulfillment—wives and mothers who lived through husbands and children—were "either depressed or outright frustrated." In any case, it certainly wasn't education that was making them unhappy.

In June 1957, after presenting her findings at the Smith reunion, she ran into some women on campus who were just graduating. To her amazement, they talked not about intellectual passions or career but about marriage and property ("What I'm interested in is where we're going to live and [my fiancé's] career.") Jolted, she wrote an article for *McCall's* called "Are Women Wasting Their Time in College?" She asked the old Farnham-Lundberg question but reversed its conclusion. Women, she said, were not serious *enough* in college. The twenty-one-year-olds she had met were swallowing the women's-magazine pablum of "togetherness"—a dominating *McCall's* rubric in the fifties. "Togetherness" was the notion that men should pitch in and do some childcare and housework without giving up their actual precedence in the family. Friedan was against "togetherness."

Her piece was rejected by *McCall's* and then by *Ladies' Home Journal* and *Redbook*. All the editors were male; the editor of *Redbook*, Jim Stern, wrote Betty's agent that Betty had "gone off her rocker." These men, one imagines, were neither slow-witted nor malicious but were protecting their franchises and their readership from any possible threat. They had to squash even the most minimal protests. Fully aroused now, Friedan began interviewing older women in her part of Rockland County. "I never set out to write a book to change women's lives," she wrote later. Ambitious and anxious—she had three kids, a big house, a husband of uncertain income—she vigorously backed into the subject that made her famous.

HER AGENT SENT her to meet George Brockway at Norton. After Brockway gave her a contract, she grabbed a carrel in the newly opened Frederick Lewis Allen Room of the New York Public Library and worked there when she needed books. At home, in Grand View-on-Hudson, she spread out on the dining room table and other places, claiming the house for work. She wrote on anything that was handy—on the backs of envelopes, on checkbook stubs, on yellow legal pads, on IBM Fortran coding forms. And she did something curious. She would take sheets of unlined paper, white or yellow, turn them sideways, fold them at the center, and then write on the freshly created pages—sometimes only on the right side of the fold, sometimes on both sides. On each page she scribbled just a few lines, writing in a slanted script pulled way down to the right. The words, like someone heading into the wind, rushed toward the goal, which was to fill the pages and move on.

For an outsider, the writing, so angular and bent, is very hard to decipher, but words like "MASLOW," boxed and in caps, stick out—that's Abraham Maslow, the existential psychologist and prophet of "self-actualization," a man who, some years later, would play an important role in Friedan's thinking about women. Something else, set down nearby, also sticks out, a magisterial sentence written almost straight up: "The awe that keeps us from questioning a great mystique keeps us from seeing the strange mirror-like resemblance at any time between our great ideas and our personal choices." In other words, when we are inside a powerful ideology, we can't see it *as* an ideology—we can't break free of it. That is a stunning insight—the kind of insight that makes a revolution.

Friedan would lay these folded pages on top of one another in a thick wad of paper. She was willing a book into existence, literally making a book with her hands. A myriad of questions became obvious to her: Was it healthy that 60 percent of women in the late 1950s were dropping out of college? Was it right that women were getting married at younger and younger ages? As she did her research, one reason after another for women's alleged natural weakness fell to the ground. The process was intensely demystifying, clarifying, energizing, and it produced a shift in consciousness, a surging realization of her own situation and her own powers.

"Something possessed me there that I cannot really explain," she said to her son Jonathan thirty years later. What possessed her, of course, was the truth, or at least an explosive series of revelations. Anyone submitting to a new reality feels impatient with everyone around her. Unpossessed, the others appear dull, unfocused, irrelevant. In such a state, you believe in your own sanity even if you're acting like someone mad. She wrote all the time, and everywhere, including on the marital sheets, in the middle of the night, in black ink.

HEROINE: THE BOOK I

In the late fifties, Betty read women's history and was thrilled to discover that many of the nineteenth-century feminists were not the dry spinsters of hostile legend but passionate women like herself. In her own time, as social historian Stephanie Coontz has established in *A Strange Stirring: "The Feminine Mystique" and American Women at the Dawn of the 1960s* (2011), there were other women at work on feminist critique—Betty's was not the only game in town. But the overall coolness and indifference of the atmosphere may be gauged by noting that such literary intellectuals as Mary McCarthy, Hannah Arendt, and Elizabeth Hardwick had little interest in feminism. Their attitude was that any woman who worked hard and had the stuff would be recognized—*they* had made it, after all. They were embarrassed by the subject. Diana Trilling, however, was an exception; she considered herself an old-fashioned suffragist-type feminist who believed in the equality of the sexes.

Betty was bolstered not by what other American women were doing but by an old masterpiece—Simone de Beauvoir's *The Second Sex*, published in France in 1949 and translated into English in 1953. Beauvoir summoned forth anthropology, biology, psychology, and literature to characterize the ideology of male predominance. Women are formed not just by their bodies but by their social situation, by economics and history, and they conform to what is expected of them. Their temperament as feminine (passive, emotional, and so on) is *constructed*, not defined by nature. Canonically: "One is not born, but rather becomes, a woman." In that process, women subside into "immanence"—a notion of their essence that they absorb in childhood and that remains beyond question, limiting their freedom.

Biology alone, Beauvoir insisted, is insufficient for setting up a hierarchy of the sexes. Women can be free. To do so, they have to seize for themselves the powers of self-definition and will, committing many assertive acts, ending in what Beauvoir called "transcendence." In all, the moral demands that she placed on women are quite daunting. "I am interested in the fortunes of the individual as defined not in terms of happiness but in terms of liberty"—a statement that placed human destiny well beyond the comforts or discomforts of American middle-class women. That sentiment remains troublesome. The essence of it—liberty, not happiness, matters most—was something Betty Friedan had to confront a decade later at the end of her own book.

Beauvoir's enormous volume hovered in the background of so much American feminist writing in the sixties and seventies—always acknowledged but often in a surprisingly perfunctory way that masked the writer's true indebtedness. Friedan knew the book and learned a lot from it. She took extensive notes on it, including on the last chapter, in which Beauvoir wrote (of women) that "Society in general—beginning with her respected parents—lies to her by praising the lofty values of love, devotion, the gift of herself." Louis Menand, in his chapter on feminism in *The Free World: Art and Thought in the Cold War* (2021), reports that he discovered a reference to this passage in Friedan's papers. The reference was accompanied by Betty's note: "Mystique of femininity." That appears to be the moment when Betty found her title.

Beauvoir was a philosopher, a novelist, a historian of culture, and *The Second Sex* remains an event in modern consciousness. Yet her book did not kick off a vast movement, and Betty Friedan's did. Why is that so?

Friedan began her work not with philosophical definitions of being, but with the actual experience of white middle- and upper-middle-class women similar to herself. It was time for their voices to go public. "A bitter laugh was beginning to be heard from American women. They were admired, envied, pitied, theorized over until they were sick of it, offered drastic solutions or silly choices that no one could take seriously." A few years later, she wrote that "My methods were simply those of a reporter on the trail of a story, except I soon discovered that this was no ordinary story." In other words, she extended the working methods of someone who wrote professionally for magazines. She spent two years interviewing women in the eastern and midwestern parts of the country, and she saw signs of discontent everywhere—"in suburban ranch houses and split-levels on Long Island and in New Jersey and Westchester County; on patios in Memphis; in suburban and city apartments; in living rooms in the Midwest . . . at suburban cocktail parties, in station wagons waiting for trains, and in snatches of conversation overheard at Schrafft's."

What she heard was a repeated cry of boredom and frustration. "I feel as if I don't exist," said one woman. Many of her subjects had been to college and didn't know what to do with that part of themselves not devoted to taking care of husband, children, and households. "Their voices were dull and flat, or nervous and jittery," Friedan says. Again and again, she encountered her own feelings in the women's complaints, recovering, for instance, her teenage griefs in the high school girls she listened to. In this way, she not only created her book through reporting; she created herself, turning her working methods into an existential journey. She began with personal hurt and frustration and ended with a new consciousness of how social reality was constructed.

Corey Robin, the eminent political scientist at the City University of New York, has recently called attention to the originality of Friedan's way of listening. In a long article for the *New York Review of Books* ("What People Power Looks Like in a Pandemic Democracy," April 13, 2020), Robin insisted that her listening tour recorded a new form of social discourse, a kind of rebellion in solitude. Friedan's text, Robin writes, brought together "a commonality of unacknowledged interests, a shared situation that lacks only a story (and a storyteller)."

In her methods, there was nothing particularly Jewish, but her temperament, as she asserted, was Jewish in its insistent, even tormenting, moral energies. There was that "existential guilt," she spoke of—a pretentious phrase, no doubt, but a very real force for her, drawing as it does on a peculiar American Jewish contempt for time wasted, a life wasted. In all, *The Feminine Mystique* was produced by multiple forces: Betty Friedan loved to work, and she was wounded by a lack of recognition. Aroused by her own plight, she needed to listen to the plight of others, and she had to repair both. Vanity was the motive for her actions; Jewish ethical seriousness and impatience provided the tone of her inquiry; magazine professionalism provided the means. In this country, in an expanding postwar economy, that trio of energies made a bourgeois revolution.

She linked together the many tales of woe and doubt; she categorized and assailed the forces that caused the condition. The collection of suburban voices is only one part of the book. *The Feminine Mystique* is also an encompassing review of anti-female ideology—the insulting views of women buried in the corners and folds of midcentury culture. Friedan investigated the social sciences, advertising, psychiatry, religious instruction, the media, and centuries of unconscious male supremacy. Big data, infinitely analyzable, was not available to her, so she used what sociological and demographic studies she could find, depending for the rest on her interviews and intuitions. She consulted experts, but she was essentially working on her own, and she held forth as a bold amateur on diverse subjects—medical, psychological, cultural, and practical.

Like many obsessional texts, *The Feminine Mystique* is garrulous and unrelenting. But despite its length and repetitions, it remains satisfying to read as a portrait of a culture we thought had vanished. Friedan evoked and deplored the ghastly side of the American fifties—the bland mediocrity; the fearfulness; the pomposity; the coarse, sometimes virulent hatred of women. What remains of these attitudes now, in the actions of right-wing politicians, judges, and media pundits, attacks our lives as a returning nightmare.

THE JEWISH FEMINIST II: WHY SO MANY JEWS?

At a 1979 conference of Reform rabbis, Betty Friedan spoke in an affectionate yet rousing way.

You can see why so many Jewish women particularly gave their souls to feminism, when you think of all those girls brought up by the book, brought up to the book, to the worship of the word, as our brothers were. When you think of all the passion and energy of our immigrant grandmothers, in the sweatshops without knowing the language! When you think of mothers rearing sons to be doctors, and coping with all the realities of life! When you think of all that passion, all that strength, all that energy suddenly to be concentrated in one small apartment, one small house, as happened with Portnoy's mother! . . . A lot of women realized they were not alone and we broke through the feminine mystique.

It's hardly a secret that a remarkable number of American feminists in the sixties, seventies, and eighties—the founders and intellectual stars and activists of the second wave—were Jewish. Along with Betty Friedan, their ranks include Justice Ruth Bader Ginsburg; Congresswoman Bella Abzug; Gloria Steinem (half-Jewish); poet and essayist Adrienne Rich (half); Robin Morgan (poet and editor of the anthology *Sisterhood Is Powerful*, 1970); Susan Brownmiller (author of *Against Our Will: Men, Women and Rape*, 1975); Shulamith Firestone (*The Dialectic of Sex*, 1970); psychologist Carol Gilligan; artist Judy Chicago; novelist Erica Jong; poet and novelist Marge Piercy; historian Gerda Lerner; psychotherapist Phyllis Chesler (*Women and Madness*, 1972); essayists Ellen Willis, Vivian Gornick, Letty Cottin Pogrebin, Andrea Dworkin, Susan Faludi, Katha Pollitt; English professor, novelist, and biographer Carolyn Heilbrun; literary theorists Eve Kosofsky Sedgwick and Judith Butler. Those are just the famous ones; there are many others.

What a list! Poets, artists, cultural essayists, politicians, academics, journalists, many as driven and contradictory as Betty Friedan—wrathful, some of them, or perhaps angry and playful at the same time (not much play in Betty, alas). They constitute a literary generation, a generation of leaders and writers emerging from different class backgrounds, possessed of different skills and temperaments. I can describe Betty Friedan's circumstances and hope that certain elements of her nature will shine a little light on the others. But the question remains: Why were so many second-wave feminists Jewish? Readers interested in the details should

consult the books by Joyce Antler and Daniel Horowitz and the antholo-
gies edited by Hasia Diner and Susannah Heschel listed as sources at the
end of this volume. But here's at least a rough sketch.

A fair number of American Jewish women of Russian and Eastern
European descent freed themselves from what their parents experienced—
clogged, ill-shaped ghetto apartments and suffocating workshops and factory rooms. Those who were able to leave home in the twenties and thirties
worked in entertainment, teaching, the Garment District; in civil service
and welfare work. Some became union organizers; some worked in corporations (mainly as secretaries). The next generation (including the women
above) often became openly feminist.

One cause of Jewish feminism is that many American Jewish families of the thirties and forties were small. According to sociologist Erich
Rosenthal, writing on "Jewish Fertility in the United States" in the *American Jewish Yearbook* (1961), the longtime evidence was that the fertility
of American Jewish wives was 78.8 percent of that of Protestant wives
and 76.6 percent of that of Roman Catholic wives. Putting it another
way, American Jewish families, mostly living in cities in the thirties and
forties, averaged 2.1 children per family, compared to 2.5 for Protestant
families and 3.2 for Catholic families. Eager to move up the social ladder,
first- and second-generation immigrants regarded education with a passion approaching mania. Boys got the most attention, but certainly not
all of it. According to the Jewish Women's Archive, "by 1957, when many
second-wave feminists were girls, among Jews aged twenty-five and over,
twenty-three percent of women had at least some college studies and ten
percent had four years or more of college, versus thirteen and six percent,
respectively, of all American women."

As Joyce Antler has written, Betty Friedan—and by implication other
educated Jewish women—couldn't help noticing the difference in status
between men and women, and were likely to act with hurt or anger. A
painful realization: many did not want to be like their mothers—certainly
not like Betty's Miriam, stymied, distant, and unhappy; nor like the legendary Jewish mother of a thousand jokes, a woman producing endless
love, flinging kreplach at her sons, crippling them with guilt, dominating the household with her fears and opinions because she had so little
power outside of it. (The "Jewish mother," one hastens to add, is a New
World invention. In the Old World, Jewish women did business outside

the house and were not necessarily obsessed with their sons.) In the sixties, the daughters of such mothers, aroused to the dangers of injustice
and victimization, miserably conscious of the Holocaust, joined the civil
rights or anti-war movements, where they quickly realized they were
highly valued as cooks and bed partners but not as thinkers or warriors.
Many got out and joined the women's movement. Schooled in Marxist
analysis, they developed a radical vision of women and power. Some
became fierce critics of Betty Friedan's "liberal" feminism, which, they
believed, didn't go far enough in ending misogyny and reshaping social
structure. Betty was known as "the mother" of the women's movement (a
phrase she disliked). Some younger feminists, it would seem, in rejecting
Betty, rejected a second mother.

The women from Orthodox families couldn't so easily change their
lives. They first had to deal with the patriarchal thunder of Jewish tradition. Judith Plaskow, the notable Jewish theologian and feminist, defin-
itively stated the matter in 1973: "The Bible was written by men. The
myths from which the Bible borrowed and which it used and transformed
were written by men. The liturgy was written by men. Jewish philosophy is the work of men. Modern Jewish theology is the work of men."
Orthodox women could not be called to the Torah; they could not form a
minyan. Women, as novelist and essayist Cynthia Ozick has pointed out,
are not protected by the commandments. "There is no mighty 'Thou shalt
not lessen the humanity of women' to echo downward from age to age."
And Ozick went the next step: "Torah—one's heart stops in one's mouth
as one dares to say these words—Torah is in this respect frayed." Some
Orthodox women in the last fifty years have responded to this "fraying"
by repairing Judaism along feminist lines—moving ahead despite severe
criticism from the male Jewish authorities who found them "egotistical"
and "narcissistic" and guilty of "attacking the family." The issue, of course,
is power: Who will control women's lives?

Those Orthodox women who became feminists, or whose daughters became feminists—were they flouting Jewish traditions or fulfilling
them? Their brothers and fathers may have been steeped in close analysis
of the Torah and rabbinical texts (the Talmud and others), immersing
themselves in unending commentary, parables, and interpretation (mid-
rash); or, at a significant worldly remove, mastering some complex body
of knowledge in science, medicine, law, music, or finance. How could

some of the young women not have picked up the habit of close reading? Feminist polemic in the sixties and seventies became defiant, critical, often witty, an argument with oppressive social systems rather than with an unfathomable God.

IN PEORIA, BETTY Friedan attended the Reform synagogue Anshai Emeth, but as a young woman, she was not observant—her formal interest in Judaism came later in life. Betty Friedan wanted to join the congregation of educated professionals. Yet the diminution of women within traditional Judaism was something she was angrily aware of. In the early eighties, for instance, she noted that the Hebrew Bible's phrase for sex—a man "knows" a woman—left out a woman's experience of sex. She told the rabbis in 1979 that if they wanted the next generation of women to have children, they had better support women's desire to get a good education, a startling piece of advice. In all, the "otherness" that she felt as a Jew when she was young was reinforced by the subordinate position of women. That double negative was a motivating force for her and for many Jewish women who became feminists. A positive force was what many feminists called "Jewish values." But what is meant by that familiar phrase?

There are Jews who go to shul and Jews who are secular; Jews by heritage or by adoption or marriage; Jews who join Jewish associations or contribute to Jewish charities; Jews who love the history and culture of the Jewish past; Jews who ignore all of this but know they are Jewish. They are many different kinds of men and women. There are not enough Jews to insist on exclusive definitions. Identity should require, at a minimum, an assertion, either public or silent, that one is Jewish, that one acknowledges, in doubt or belief, the power of monotheism in the Jewish version—a single, indivisible, overpowering God whom one cannot see but one has to imagine; and that one further acknowledges that the Messiah has not come and that the gifted young man who taught in Judaea and Galilee two thousand years ago was not the son of God. It should also mean, one hopes, that one accepts the burden and glory of Jewish history and perhaps some of the humor and complication of a Jewish temperament; and that, given the persistence of oppression in that history, you understand the situation of the outsider and the scorned. (*Thou shalt not oppress a stranger . . . seeing you were a stranger in the land of Egypt.*) "Ever since I was a little girl," Friedan said in an interview with *Lilith* magazine in 1976, "I remember my father telling me that I had a passion for justice. But I think it was really a passion against injustice which originated from my feelings of the injustice of antisemitism."

In the past, Jewish women had experienced contempt and estrangement in a double way—as anti-Semitism from outside the community and, for some, as diminished status within the community. Jewish women drew on their knowledge of the past even as they fought for selfhood in the present. That so many second-wave feminists were Jewish seems, in the end, no great mystery at all. And now, thanks to them, as anthropologist Melvin Konner put it in *Unsettled: An Anthropology of the Jews*, "the history of Jewish women in some ways is just beginning."

THE BOOK II: A WEALTHY COUNTRY

The situation of Friedan's suburban women could have emerged only in a wealthy country, a country in which happiness, not survival, was the central issue for a fair number of Americans. After the Second World War, as the United States manufactured goods for a shattered Europe and Japan, mass affluence—not wealth but middle-class comfort—became a central fact of national life. For many, a house of one's own became not just a possibility but a need. Middle-class couples, their numbers rapidly expanding in the baby boom, moved into such instant communities as Levittown, Long Island, or growing suburban communities like Mesa, Arizona. It is estimated that the number of Americans living in the suburbs increased from 19.5 percent in 1940 to 30.7 percent in 1960. American Jews, in particular, fled the cities. According to religious leader and social historian Arthur Hertzberg, in his estimable book *The Jews in America* (1989), one of every three Jews moved to the suburbs between 1945 and 1965.

A house needs a vacuum cleaner and a lawn mower; it needs a washer-dryer and a blender. Betty Friedan was enraged, however, by all the *extra* goods women were constantly persuaded to buy—"red stoves with rounded corners, and synthetic furs, and waxes, and hair coloring, and patterns for home sewing and home carpentry . . . and bleaches to keep the towels pure white." In these suburban catalogs of the unnecessary, one hears the disgust of a woman who had triumphed over physical plainness and anti-Semitism by studying hard and learning what really mattered in

life. The Jewish workhorse was offended. She certainly liked to buy things—
she liked comfort, food, good company—but shopping, she knew, wasn't
much of an achievement.

In the suburbs, Betty was sure that women were being traduced. She
arrives at the heart of darkness: the work of a sinister expert in "motivational research," unnamed but certainly the notorious Ernest Dichter, a
Viennese psychologist who had emigrated in 1938. Dichter made a fortune applying Freudian theory and focus groups (a new invention) to
the task of selling convertible cars and cigarette lighters. Dichter allowed
Betty to read many of the reports his group had generated for corporate
clients. The entire operation was stunningly cynical. "We sell them what
they ought to want, speed up the unconscious, move it along," Dichter
told her. One of the reports to advertisers read as follows: "Identify your
product with the physical and spiritual rewards she derives from the
almost religious feeling of basic security provided by her home." The anxiety men had about not having the right job, or any job, was transferred to
women: they might not have the right goods in their home. The fix was in.

Women were told by advertisers that their consumer choices were
"creative"—that the freedom to buy was freedom itself. And though wealth
gave women power, it was no more than a limited power. In the suburbs,
as Friedan exhaustively chronicled, isolation often reduced women to
their consumer choices alone, a largely negative exercise of freedom that
left many frustrated and anxious. There had to be something more. Soul
was at stake—spirit, health, something like a valuable life.

THE JEWISH FEMINIST III: A HARDHEADED WOMAN

Betty Friedan was quick-tempered, driving, ungracious. Some of her abra-
sive spirit was produced by her personal needs, her chagrins and disap-
pointments. But that wasn't all of it. She was an American middle-class
Jewish woman; the tribe had left its marks on her.

In past centuries, religious Jews, refusing to acknowledge Jesus as the
Redeemer, son of God, expected the Messiah to appear in the here and
now. They waited and waited, and He never came. What then? The rabbinical writers of the Talmud had their mystical passages, their speculations about the beyond, but the Hebrew Bible, which is what most people
know, does not speak of an afterlife. Except in a personal way, and an idio-

syncratic way—each individual case standing for itself alone—redemption is no more than a fond thought for Jews. Even considered as a joke, the afterlife turns Jews back to this life. In a Hasidic tale, the following lines appear: "Before his death, Rabbi Zusya said, 'In the coming world, they will not ask me: "Why were you not Moses?" They will ask me: "Why were you not Zusya?"'" The rabbi should have been a better Zusya.

In American terms, for the Jews to be useful (Betty's word) meant, to begin with, knowing exactly what their situation was. In the past, they had known. For centuries, the Jews were the victims of a bizarre joke, the ultimate double bind: they were God's chosen people, yet they were defenseless. In America, no longer defenseless, Jews could nevertheless be wary and demanding: a life had to have a shape and some meaning; an anecdote a clear significance; a joke a solid punch. For the immigrant and second generations, haunted, many of them, by historical memories of being outsiders, certain qualities of temperament—ambition, quickness, disdain for magical thinking—became central to success in the most dynamic capitalist country in the world. "Pushy" became a standard epithet, vaguely insulting and vaguely admiring at the same time. A pushy Jew got things done.

That admiration of drive and quickness included contempt for people who were ineffective. In Yiddish, a *luftmensch* is a man with his head in the clouds, an intellectual dreamer, or even worse a sap, a mark. There is, however, a serious complication here: an unwillingness to be fooled requires perception and cunning, but it offers little guidance for ever trusting *anyone*. Trust requires intelligence, too. All in all, the need to attain the balance between wariness and openness—the balance known as *sechel* or judgment—is virtually one of the Jewish commandments. It's the sense of reality that Jews constantly appeal to—in life, in jokes, in everything. "We who are Jews practice a living religion that is never finished," Betty Friedan said when visiting Israel in 1984. "There is no 'pie-in-the-sky' for us. We are charged with our own being to make life better, not only for ourselves, but for future generations as well."

Call it the temperament of *impatience*. In her dealings with other women, Betty was baffled by indecisiveness and stupidity. In meetings, she demanded that people get to the point (*her* point, often enough), and her great book is filled with outrage and sometimes contempt, for here were women all over America literally being sold a bill of goods. "A baked potato is not as big as the world, and vacuuming the living-room floor—with or without makeup—is not work that takes enough thought or energy to challenge any woman's full capacity. Women are human beings, not stuffed dolls, not animals." Her anger was split between the exploiters and the women who allowed themselves to be sold. The distaste for a life of illusion, joined to an equal distaste for ineffectuality, produced the steady pulse of Betty Friedan's temper.

THE BOOK III: SIGMUND FREUD FOR GOOD AND FOR ILL

As she gathered together her examples of anti-female ideology, Friedan was most exasperated by the sins of the educated—priests, ministers, sociologists, and psychiatrists—many of whom, swathed in authority, earnestly persuaded women to give up their dreams. She took on Talcott Parsons, a famous sociologist at Harvard who offered elaborate reasons why women should stay in their place; and Margaret Mead, the great anthropologist who turned her back on her own dynamic, willful, and rebellious behavior as a young woman and wrote, after the war, that she found it "very difficult" to imagine women making "their full and special contributions in . . . medicine and law, education and religion, the arts and sciences."

And Friedan was obsessed with Freud, the most powerful voice denigrating women's ability and courage, a situation that presented a painful trial for her. She had undergone Freudian analysis not once but twice; she had even considered asking a Freudian analyst—her own doctor, William Menaker—to collaborate with her on *The Feminine Mystique*. She was more than indebted to Freud for her understanding of why people acted as they did. Whatever his mistakes and failures, he was a great modern intellectual hero. That it now seems necessary to make such an assertion suggests how much Freud's reputation has slipped in the last sixty years. But when Friedan was a young woman, Freud was the man who mattered.

One part of Freud's thought—his views of Judaism and Christianity—played, I believe, a significant role in Betty Friedan's outlook. A lifelong atheist—a "Godless Jew"—Freud nevertheless expressed a considerable respect in his last book, *Moses and Monotheism* (1939), for Judaism as a religion. The Jews in the time of Moses had chased out idolatry and magic, rejected earth goddesses and other semi-deities. By insisting on a single blindingly powerful God, a God who could not be represented (the second commandment's ban on graven images), a God *one could not see,*

Judaism caused men and women to rely on imagination, a purely mental activity. Jews, Freud implied, established the basis of the most rigorous aspects of modern intellectual life—conceptual and abstract thinking, the foundations of science and philosophy.

Friedan did not explicitly say so, but it's hard to believe that her critique of representation in popular and middlebrow culture was not influenced, in part, by Judaism's rejection of sacred depiction and explicitly by Freud's dislike for iconography—the Christian religious painting and statuary Freud regarded as a kind of seduction. For Friedan, seduction by representation was very much the issue: the media and advertising operatives flattered women's weakness; they presented the American woman as a blonde beauty in her suburban salvation, passive apart from one significant strength, her endless willingness to buy keg fridges and waffle makers. Friedan, the critic of seductive salesmanship, was a child of Freud, the Jewish theorist and unmasker.

But there was a miserable problem: Freud's general views on women were condescending, patronizing, and they had the effect in America of hardening the existing prejudices against women into seeming science. He believed that women were subordinate to men in character, often fragile and passive, and he made, in particular, an odd mistake. In turn-of-the-century Vienna, Freud discovered in his upper-middle-class female patients an envious disposition toward men. Noting men's greater sway in the world, the women, beginning in childhood, had assumed it was the penis that gave men power. "Penis envy" now seems like a bad joke—one of Freud's outlandish ideas that turned out to be little more than outlandish. It may not have occurred to him that it was the men's freedom, not their organs, that his patients envied. In any case, the idea had a disastrous afterlife in the United States. From the forties through the sixties, penis envy ran riot over the land. It was the time of such fabulous monsters as the man-eater, who lives to compete with men; and the castrating woman, who destroys male potency. "I don't know why American women are so dissatisfied," a Westchester analyst said to Friedan. "Penis envy seems so difficult to eradicate in American women, somehow."

One of Freud's distinguished colleagues in Vienna, Helene Deutsch, moved to Cambridge, Massachusetts, in 1935, set up a practice, and issued, in 1944, her two-volume magnum opus, *The Psychology of Women: A Psychoanalytical Interpretation*. After Deutsch's book came out, common sentiment and jokes gave way to something like official doctrine. "Ambitious women," Dr. Deutsch noted grimly, suffered from "a masculinity complex," in which "warm, intuitive knowledge has yielded to cold, unproductive thinking." This kind of bullying rubbish was offered as a helpful guide to women seeking an active life. It was reproduced, Friedan says, "by those who suffered and those who cured and those who turned suffering to profit." She meant the local suburban shrink, a kind of secular rabbi in the fifties and sixties, a professional who may well have needed to believe that women were weak in order to maintain his hold over them as paying customers.

Betty Friedan broke with Freud and his followers in the most important way; she, along with many other feminists, diminished his authority over half the human race, an act of rebellion not as great as Luther's rejection of the Church but certainly, for her, an enormous intellectual and moral step forward. Freud was the most radical and demanding of modern Jewish patriarchs—for Betty, the patriarch who mattered far more than her father. Feminism could not exist until he had been killed, or at least refashioned, adapted for use in a great modern social movement. Freud had defined happiness as *"Lieben und Arbeiten"*—to be able to love and to work. Friedan and the others insisted that women, no less than men, could not be happy without achievement.

THE BOOK IV: ABRAHAM MASLOW AND THE WAY OUT

The Feminine Mystique, as Louis Menand has pointed out, is really addressed not to Friedan's generation of women but to the next generation, the daughters. In search of daughters, Friedan went back to ground zero—to Smith as well as to other elite colleges whose students had made her angry a few years earlier. And she found more listless and defeated women, women afraid that if they got too involved in biology or literature they would somehow never find a husband. ("The idea is to be very casual, very sophisticated," one student told her. "Don't be too enthusiastic about your work or anything. People who take things seriously are more or less laughed at or pitied.") At Sarah Lawrence, a leading college for women, students in the past, Friedan writes, "had taken a large responsibility for their own education and for their own affairs." But the new generation of students "was helpless, apathetic, incapable of handling such freedom."

She found some guilty parties: the women's high school guidance coun-
selors, in many cases, had advised girls against taking tough courses, and
now, in college, some of the students were studying "Family Life" and
"Life Adjustment" rather than history or chemistry.

As Friedan admits, college women had some good reasons to be
wary of professional life. In the early sixties, getting a good job was hard
enough, and those who did find good work were often passed over for
promotion in favor of less-talented men. Successful or not, they would be
punished in undermining ways. Having chosen to pursue a career, they
were informed by journalists and psychiatrists, in the spirit of Helene
Deutsch, that they faced endless loneliness. Betty at her most forlorn:

> When a culture has erected barrier after barrier against women as separate
> selves; when a culture has erected legal, political, social, economic and
> educational barriers to women's own acceptance of maturity—even after
> most of these barriers are down it is still easier for a woman to seek the
> sanctuary of a home. It is easier to live through her husband and children
> than to make a road of her own in the world.

Who wants to face loneliness? It was a possibility that had once dismayed Friedan herself.

In such moments, she is patient, even-tempered, and exploratory. She
admits, for instance, that "the feminine mystique" arose after the war
partly out of genuine needs. "In the foxholes, the GI's had pinned up
pictures of Betty Grable, but the songs they asked to hear were lullabies.
And when they got out of the army, they were too old to go home to their
mothers." Their nerves jangled, they wanted comfort and peace and family
life. In the suburbs, the men were often engaged in corporate work, the
notorious site of fifties unhappiness—a "rat race" in the slang of the day.
Friedan never underestimates how difficult it is for men to find satisfaction at work. For that reason, men were eager for the solace of quiescent,
attentive women at home.

Friedan writes with bitter satisfaction—she's a strong writer—but there
isn't a trace of gaiety anywhere in *The Feminine Mystique*, not a hint of
satirical enjoyment or profane merriment. She makes a catalog of follies,
but each of those follies hurt women so much that she could not bring
herself to sharpen her rage into wit. (Germaine Greer's blunt and funny

The Female Eunuch, from 1970, provides an obvious contrast. Greer has the gift of spontaneity.) The stick-to-the-point earnestness may be one reason that some women now find *The Feminine Mystique* boring. Nothing regarding the unhappiness of married housewives was irrelevant to Friedan—women suffering from open-plan living spaces, which gave them little privacy to work and think; women suffering from depression, excessive fatigue, obsessive and destructive love affairs; from menstrual irregularities, homosexual sons (a serious affliction, according to Friedan), mysterious blisters on their hands—the blisters, she tells us, were not caused by washing dishes.

Friedan had, perhaps, the Jewish vice of worrying too much about everything. Her lack of humor—and her faulty sense of proportion—suggests one reason why she got into trouble with women in her later years. The humorlessness was a kind of incapacity—blindness, even. At one point in *The Feminine Mystique*, her overzealous moralism leads her into a serious blunder. Chapter 12, devoted to the ways that housewives give up initiative and will, is called "Progressive Dehumanization: The Comfortable Concentration Camp," by which Friedan meant that suburban women amid their furniture and appliances suffered a loss of self and the desire to resist akin to what Jews and other prisoners experienced during Nazi incarceration. Even as a metaphor, the comparison is stunningly insensitive—an insult to the actual victims of the camps. How could she make so serious an error? Jewish women were not an explicit subject of *The Feminine Mystique*, but the concentration camp comparison suggests that a specifically Jewish fear and anger lay behind her general portrait of women's estate. She later apologized for the comparison. Her grim misstatement nevertheless poses the question: How do you escape?

BOXED AND IN caps, Abraham Maslow's name pops out of Betty's scrawled and often indecipherable notes. Maslow was one of the "humanist" postwar psychotherapists (along with, among others, Carl Rogers, Karen Horney, and Rollo May) who analyzed a patient's neuroses not in the Freudian way of casting back into childhood memories and interrogating psychosexual development but by dealing with patients in their current reality. What made for unhappiness in adults? How do you change your habits? Maslow's parents were from Kiev, but he was born in Brooklyn in

1908, and he was educated, like so many Jewish intellectuals of the twenties and thirties, at City College in New York. Maslow had survived hard times in the Depression but had passed into an affluent society. Looking around him, Maslow and the other humanists had begun to think that happiness was attainable for those who had the courage to reach for it.

The humanists substituted a philosophy of growth for Freud's grim biological and psychosexual determinism and arduous self-exhumation. Adults had an unlimited ability to change and expand, they insisted, if their fears and inhibitions were cast aside. (Such thinking planted the seeds for the self-help and human-potential movements of the sixties and forever after.) Maslow and his cohort, to Friedan's relief, didn't put much stock in "adjustment"—the goal of so much Freudian analysis in the fifties. For women, "adjusting" to their role in society meant relinquishing any feelings of revolt. Adjustment was for saps.

During the war, Maslow developed what he called "a hierarchy of needs." At the lowest level, human beings needed food, shelter, and sex; next, passing upward, came the desire for safety; then the need for friendship and love; then esteem (a sense of accomplishment); and finally, arriving at the peak, what Maslow called "self-actualization"—the full creative expression of one's potential. A blessed state indeed, and in Maslow's estimate few people get there. His historical examples included Abraham Lincoln, Thomas Jefferson, Sigmund Freud, the socialist Eugene Victor Debs, Franklin Delano Roosevelt, Walt Whitman, and, to Friedan's chagrin, only two women, Eleanor Roosevelt and Jane Addams, the founder of the settlement-house movement.

But Friedan's chagrin led her, by degrees, to find a way out of "the feminine mystique." Maslow and other psychotherapists, relying on clinical data, were sure that men who did not move beyond basic needs, men who had never achieved competence and self-esteem, suffered from guilt and depression and even physical illness. "The unused capacity or organ," Maslow wrote, "can become a disease center or else atrophy, thus diminishing the person." (Our current version: "Use it or lose it.") Friedan demanded to know: What about women? They had not received the same clinical attention. Those women who had "everything" but were mysteriously falling apart—were they not subjected to an enforced passivity, and was that not ruinous, in many cases, to their health? Women had to grow, or they would fall ill. She could not have forgotten that her mother,

Miriam, after suffering from colitis for years, gradually got better when she took over Harry's jewelry store. Betty drew as well on her own history: if she had not broken out of her unsatisfactory life as a suburbanite and a freelance writer for women's magazines, she might have failed in her own eyes in a way that led to death.

Maslow did not think the hierarchy of needs much applied to women. But he changed his mind after reading *The Feminine Mystique*. In *Life So Far*, Friedan offers a moment of justified pride: "When I sent him an advance copy of my book, he called me in the middle of the night, in great excitement over my use of his concepts." A signal moment for Friedan: Abraham Maslow realized that self-actualization, a state of ego-rich sufficiency without crippling aggression, was a possibility for women as well as for men, and he added a bonus—better sex—which Friedan encapsulated as, "The transcendence of self, in sexual orgasm, as in creative experience, can only be attained by one who is himself or herself complete, by one who has realized his or her identity." Not the most elegant formulation, nor the most convincing, but still, it offers the equality between men and women that Friedan had always been looking for. The old canard that intellectual and hard-driving women would miss out on pleasure had been overthrown at last.

IF *THE FEMININE MYSTIQUE* was intended as a warning and a prompt to the next generation, what about her own generation—the unhappy women she repeatedly describes and quotes? The last chapter, "A New Life Plan for Women," is a bit of an anticlimax. Betty Friedan did not call for women to walk out on their husbands and children. She knew that professional fulfillment for women was most likely to be attained by a full-time career, begun in college or soon after; that few married suburban women had the training or the connections to get serious jobs; that getting back to academic work at the age of forty would be hard. And she admitted that any new ambition—especially creative ambition—was bound to be painful, risk-laden, possibly defeating. She had arrived at her own version of Beauvoir's daunting statement, "I am interested in the fortunes of the individual as defined not in terms of happiness but in terms of liberty." Betty Friedan was a realist: a liberated woman was inevitably heading for trouble. Yes the risks had to be taken: married women had to do some kind of socially or personally meaningful work. The last paragraph begins, "Who knows what women can be when they are finally free to become themselves?" And the book ends, "The time is at hand when the voices of the feminine mystique can no longer drown out the inner voice that is driving women on to become complete."

CELEBRITY

In her useful study *A Strange Stirring*, social historian Stephanie Coontz describes the extraordinary reception of Friedan's book. Apart from the many readers, there were women galvanized by merely hearing about it. A mystique of femininity that condemned women to a diminished experience? They recognized elements of their own lives in the critique, and it changed them. Letters poured in, both to the magazines that published excerpts of the book (*The Ladies' Home Journal* and *McCall's*, finally relenting) and to Friedan and her book publisher—vivid, sometimes angry, sometimes aroused letters. She had wanted to "wake the sleeping beauties," and she had.

The sixties were an exhausting time to live through. Rapid economic change, convulsive anti-war protests, civil rights upheaval, the "sexual revolution," the drug culture! Ernest demands and political debates jostled for public space with mind-blowing insanities and fervent beatitudes. The sixties were also a time of serious media expansion, which increased the palpitating notoriety of everything in the public sphere. The sixties marked the beginning of the complete mediaization of everything that is our reality now.

The relatively modest means of book publicity before the war—newspaper and magazine ads, radio, posters, billboards—gave way to the capital-driven data and calculation of marketing after it. The publishing industry hardly had the resources of, say, General Electric selling refrigerators, but it was shaking off its gentlemanly ways. Norton, prodded repeatedly by Betty and Carl, hired a press agent for her, and she went on a book tour, a recent invention.

After the hardcover sales died down, in 1964 Dell brought out *The Feminine Mystique* in a cheap paperback version. The mass-market paperback was a rather recent invention. Simon and Schuster had established Pocket Books in 1939; it began by reprinting Shakespeare's tragedies and classy bestsellers by James Hilton and Pearl S. Buck. But Dell, Betty's publisher, had always worked down-market. Starting in the thirties, the house had published pulp fiction (romance and war stories) in magazine form, and then, in 1942, it began issuing paperback novels—whodunits and bodice rippers—to millions of readers. By the early sixties, Dell had hundreds of titles in print, some of them serious, all of them available on newsstands and on metal racks at the front of grocery stores and drugstores. One reason the book sold three million copies in the Dell edition was that it was available almost everywhere. An angry book had gone mass market.

Television had become ubiquitous, reaching 90 percent of American households by the mid-sixties, and Betty appeared on national talk shows. Despite a distaste for flying, she traveled all over the country, giving bellicose interviews in her raspy voice to local stations and newspapers, which were then potent shapers of attention and opinion. The big-time players, of course, apart from the TV networks, were the national weeklies, *Time*, *Newsweek*, *Life*, and *Look* (a biweekly), which ran excitedly after new trends, promoting fresh currents (sometimes nascent or stillborn currents) in social, political, and sexual behavior. The news magazines wanted to get out ahead of everyone else. Defining "the culture" became a prime journalistic form in the sixties, and feminism was hot copy.

Militant feminism—later "women's liberation"—was framed by many men as a sensational joke. *The feminists were silly, shrill, deluded, ungrateful.* For women hearing such things, the media attention, particularly by the end of the sixties, could be exhausting and humiliating. As historian Ruth Rosen put it in *The World Split Open: How the Modern Women's Movement Changed America* (2000), "It was a shock to go home, turn on your television set or read your morning newspaper and discover that everything you cared about was summed up in the image of a zany hysteric who sought, through flamboyance, what she was unable to achieve through physical attraction." *They were butch, they wore boots.* Still, feminism was something men had to deal with, and, for millions of women, the moment of attention and reexamination, as well as the new bonds with other women, was electrifying—and remained so for years. In brief, riding a crest of emotion and media expansion, Betty Friedan became a celebrity.

"Don't be an appliance, a vegetable or a service station," she advised women in *Life*, about six months after her book came out. "As for me, I'm very unbored. I'm nasty, I'm bitchy, I get mad, but by God, I'm absorbed in what I'm doing." She lectured in synagogues, in women's clubs, at policy conferences. On campus, she rattled the young men by telling them they were being bullied by macho images; she rattled the young women even more by telling them they were facing entrapment if they didn't wake up. As she held forth, her hands working up and down in parallel, she advanced some notions, furiously denied others. Strenuous, onrushing, overwhelming, she did not analyze the way things were so much as *announce* them.

Wherever she went, literally for decades, women recognized her on the street and said things like "It changed my life!" Later, in 1976, she used that phrase as the title of a book she devoted to the writing and reception of *The Feminine Mystique* and the 1966 founding of the National Organization for Women (NOW).

"The book," she wrote in her notes, "has catapulted me into a moment of history."

SCENES FROM A MARRIAGE II

In 1963, when *The Feminine Mystique* was published, Carl Friedan ran around to bookstores, pulling copies from the back shelves and moving them to the front of the store. He seemed, for a while, to have recovered the energy he had as an itinerant teen magician. He screamed at Norton publisher George Brockway on the phone, urging him to do more promotion, calling so often that Brockway refused to speak to him. His activity on Betty's behalf was a happy interlude in a marriage that had been going sour for years. Back in 1952, when Betty was pregnant with their second child, Carl had stayed out some nights, seeing a woman who had been his girlfriend before he met Betty. As before, they quarreled about money. In 1963, they had three kids and two cars; the Grand View house, an American Victorian mansion, was large and expensive to heat.

On one occasion, back in 1956, as biographer Judith Hennessee reports, Betty gave a dinner party for friends, and Carl, upset with the menu, picked up the fish platter and threw it at his wife. A few years later, as the children listened in wonder upstairs, the couple hurled crockery at each other. This sort of thing may be exciting as an expensive form of sexual arousal, but eventually the broken dishes became all too symbolic of the marriage. At social events they drank heavily, and Carl would say things like "I'm the bitch's husband." They fought on the street, embarrassing people who were passing by. For both of them, rudeness became a dare, a challenge, a necessity. They were locked in an obsessive, emotionally demanding, but, in some ways, emotionally satisfying American marriage. As Judith Hennessee puts it, "The freedom they gave each other to behave badly had surely bound them together." Whenever the violence began at home, it appears, at least on some occasions, to have been mutual. Carl showed up for an important job once with a scratched face. On another occasion his hand was scarred from a mirror Betty threw at him. On still a third occasion, Betty was seen chasing him on a Fire Island beach with a butcher knife.

Some people close to Betty knew about the violence. In February 1969, six years after the publication of *The Feminine Mystique*, a group of women in fur coats from the recently formed National Organization for Women set out to invade the all-male sanctum of the Oak Room restaurant in the Plaza Hotel. It was part of an action that also brought NOW invasions of the Polo Lounge at the Beverly Hills Hotel and McSorley's Old Ale House in New York. Among the NOW women was Muriel Fox, Betty's longtime friend and cofounder of the organization. "Betty showed up with a black eye," Muriel said to me. "Cameras were there, so Dolores Alexander"—another power in NOW—"took her off to the bathroom and applied makeup." (In the standard version of the events, Alexander prepared Friedan's face earlier at Betty's apartment; then the two of them invaded the Plaza.)

CARL FRIEDAN TURNED down two major advertising firms that tried to hire him. Yet he did not have the drive—or perhaps the necessary shamelessness—to turn his small company into a major ad firm. It's hard not to sympathize with him—at least part of the way. In the business world, he was teased about his wife, which must have been humiliating. As Betty became famous, however, his response was to make dumb remarks, repeatedly calling her a lesbian, which was absurd on the face of it and particularly wounding, since Friedan hated lesbians and was convinced they were a danger to the women's movement.

She was frequently on the road, though her book tours were scheduled with two-week breaks, so she could get back to see the kids. At home, she tried to be a full-bore mother and wife. Looking back on the period in *The*

Second Stage (1981), she relates that during the writing of *The Feminine Mystique*, she would stop working "when my little daughter came home from school, or my boys were in Little League or basketball game, or to make a martini when my husband got home, fix dinner, go to the movies, make love, join an expedition to the supermarket or a country auction on Saturday . . ." Physically active, the family was devoted to hiking, camping, sailing, and clamming. There were quiet moments, too. Of their days in Grand View-on-Hudson, Jonathan Friedan, Betty and Carl's second son, recalls the following: "I could sit on the covered porch on a rainy day and watch the barges going under the recently built Tappan Zee bridge where during an intense freeze we went ice-skating at night along the banks of the river, carrying torches and singing with neighbors."

She and Carl gave the children a secular education with a particular emphasis on science. They also raised them as Jews. Daniel Friedan, their firstborn, told Rachel Shteir, author of *Betty Friedan: Magnificent Disrupter* (2023), that "Carl would put the children to bed and tell them that of the five greatest men in the world, four were Jewish—Einstein, Jesus, Freud, and Marx. Daniel remembered that while there was no 'connection to religious Judaism,' his mother taught him to 'think for himself and not swallow someone else's line,' qualities he considered intrinsically Jewish." But Jonathan Friedan, Daniel's younger brother, tells me it was himself, not Daniel, who got put to bed this way and told about the greatest men. The fifth man, Jonathan says, was Charles Darwin.

NEWLY ENRICHED AFTER the success of *The Feminine Mystique*, the couple left Grand View-on-Hudson in 1964 and bought, at virtually the same time, a house on Fire Island and a seven-room apartment in the Dakota, the famous old building on Central Park West, eventual home of Leonard Bernstein, John Lennon, Jason Robards Jr., Lauren Bacall, and other intellectual and artistic celebrities. In the city, Betty engaged in expensive redecoration and threw big parties, spending money she didn't have. "She was her mother's daughter," Hennessee says.

Maybe, but she was a much better mother than Miriam. Betty gloried in her children as much as any mother anywhere—loudly praising their promise and achievements in her interviews and books. She fought for them when she had to. After the Friedans moved back to New York,

Jonathan was a student leader of anti–Vietnam War protests at the prestigious Dalton School. The headmaster, Donald Barr—father of Trump's attorney general William Barr—was outraged by Jonathan's anti-war activities. In general, Barr thought such protests at Dalton were a profanation. He also made nasty and sexist remarks to female students. In 1970, as Marie Brenner reported in *Vanity Fair* (December 2019), Betty Friedan and other parents tried to get Barr ousted. He retaliated by writing a negative recommendation for Jonathan's college applications. A top student, Jonathan was turned down by eight schools, though he eventually entered Columbia and graduated with an engineering degree. Jonathan works for the city of Philadelphia; Daniel is an award-winning theoretical physicist; Emily is a pediatrician in Buffalo.

Wherever they lived, Betty was a negligent housekeeper, which, given her mother's obsession with neatness and her own distaste for housekeeping in *The Feminine Mystique*, is hardly a surprise. Like many obsessed people, she was maladroit. On one occasion, when the family was in the Dakota, Emily's boyfriend put a box of Kodak film in the Friedan refrigerator. Betty, mistaking the yellow box for food, opened it and exposed the film. Her son Jonathan told me that "She was not good at general management. She didn't bake cookies. Boiling hot dogs was a challenge. We had Haitian housekeepers, and I grew up on shrimp and rice" (which doesn't sound so bad). Betty actually indulged a rare bit of humor on this issue, telling a friend, "I affirm the right to make chicken soup, even though I might take it out of a can."

HER HUSBAND WAS an ordinary man who had stepped into an extraordinary situation. Carl Friedan's designated role—not the one he chose but the one that fate assigned to him—was to play the sympathetic mate of a famous and distinguished woman. It is a role that would in time have brought him a kind of glory (the jokes would have subsided) and in the end historical renown. But Carl was overwhelmed—not just by his volcanic wife but by the onrush of cultural change, the sense of old supremacies fading away. Not all men, however, performed as badly as he did. A few years later, Paul Child, husband of Julia Child, gloried in his wife's success, as did Martin Ginsburg, husband of the Supreme Court justice; and also Paul Pelosi, husband of Nancy; and Martin Abzug, Bella's proud mate; and many unknown men, including my father, Ezra Denby, who revered my aggressive mother through a forty-three-year marriage.

As a girl, and many times as an adult, Betty had expressed her longing for a union of equals. But these two were not equals, and at this point understanding must confess its limits: Carl Friedan behaved badly for years, yet Betty Friedan wanted to stay married and at times acceded to his authority. "I used to think, what a phony I was in my personal life," she told an interviewer in the mid-eighties, long after they had split. "I was such a *worm*, such a masochist, unable to face my rage." It's hard to imagine Betty Friedan unable to face her rage. But her marriage fell into a different emotional range than the rest of her life. At one point, in the late sixties, according to Judith Hennessee, when Betty still wanted to keep the marriage together, Carl issued an ultimatum: unless she gave him control of all their finances, he would leave her. She acquiesced for a while and was thereby reduced to the humiliating situation of a prefeminist woman, dependent on her husband for an allowance. "Economic abuse," as we now call it, was added to the standard kinds of abuse. It was a strange situation and embarrassing, though Betty didn't talk about it in public. The most famous feminist in the country, fierce on public platforms, was locked into a violent marriage with a second-rate man.

In 1969, she spent a few days alone in Paris, enjoying both solitude and freedom. She and Carl had been litigating a separation, spending lots of money on lawyers, and she was out of patience. A few months later, after giving a lecture in Jackson, Mississippi, she slipped over the border to Chihuahua and got an uncontested divorce. They had been married almost twenty-two years. Two years later, Betty told journalist Lyn Tornabene for a *McCall's* article, "I went to a bar and sat and cried, not because I was alone but for all the wasted years." An extraordinary admission, but the unpleasant secret of violence within the marriage was not something she was able to address directly until years later.

HEROINE AGAIN: RELUCTANT, THEN FERVENT ORGANIZATION WOMAN

The Civil Rights Act of 1964, one of Lyndon B. Johnson's greatest achievements, included section Title VII, which prohibited discrimination in employment based on race, color, religion, or national origin. As the bill was debated in Congress, a southern segregationist, Representative Howard Smith of Virginia, inserted a phrase forbidding discrimination on the basis of sex, too. Smith intended the words as a joke, a kind of poison pill that would kill the entire bill. Indeed, there was much laughter in the House. Yet the bill passed with Smith's addition intact. Among other absurdities, three white southern congressmen, gallant racists, did not wish white women to be denied a right—protection against discrimination—that Black men would have. So they voted yes.

In parts of the press, the notion of women's equality was greeted with mandarin whimsy. An article in the *Wall Street Journal* asked its readers to imagine "a shapely, knobby-kneed male 'bunny' serving drinks to a group of astonished businessmen." Astonishment shaped the mood. A *New York Times* editorial ended with the words, "This is revolution, chaos. You can't even safely advertise for a wife anymore." The men were at wit's end.

The bill was passed in June 1964, about ten months after Martin Luther King Jr.'s March on Washington for Jobs and Freedom, when he gave his "I Have a Dream" speech. Black activism was roiling the capital, and Betty hoped to rouse women to comparable dreams about their future. But how to do it? What instrumentality, what organization could change the culture? In order to enforce compliance with Title VII, President Johnson set up the Equal Employment Opportunity Commission (EEOC), a federal agency that would process complaints from men and women who felt they had been on the receiving end of discrimination. But Johnson was preoccupied with the Great Society, the War on Poverty, and Vietnam. He had no real interest in the status of women; and the EEOC itself was more interested in helping Black men than women of any color. In 1964 and 1965, women from all over the country got in touch with Friedan, complaining that they had been passed over for promotion in favor of less-qualified men.

In this period, Friedan spent a good deal of time in Washington, operating as a spy reconnoitering the terrain. She discovered women of feminist conviction, many of them lawyers, working in such places as the Department of Labor and the Department of Justice. Some of them had been in place since the Eisenhower administration. They were a potent group, and she began to think of them as proto-revolutionaries at their desks, often unknown to one another.

In the spring of 1966, she made contact with a brilliant Black lawyer,

Pauli Murray, who had published, with Mary Eastwood, a Department of Justice lawyer, an article with the startling title "Jane Crow and the Law." Murray, a militant who believed, like Dr. King, in public action, spoke of marching on Washington. From all accounts the Friedan-Murray connection, however short-lived, was a key moment in the history of second-wave feminism. Friedan and Murray's first idea was to compel the EEOC to act in compliance with Title VII. But that notion, as other Washington insiders joined in, gave way to a more ambitious scheme: what was needed was a civil rights organization for women.

Over time, Betty became the hub, bringing professional women together and listening to their ideas and personal tales, just as she had listened to housewives' stories a few years earlier. In June 1966, some of Betty's cohort met in her room at the Washington Hilton. The meeting broke up late at night without agreement on what form a new organization should take—or whether there should be a new organization at all. Many things were working against such an effort. Not only did the women not know one another well, they didn't have the money to get going. They were at an impasse. As she wrote later,

> How many times had that process repeated itself—in me and all the others, each time we face a new necessity to act? And the very fury of our resistance may mask our underlying sense of the urgency of that action, and our reluctant awareness of our need and responsibility to take it. It is existential dread. And then acting, we evoke that dread in others until they too begin to act.

An extraordinary formulation: you get people to act by making them frightened (Norman Mailer might agree). Apart from practical issues and the fear of going forward, the women faced the possibility of genuine trouble: women starting a civil rights organization during an administration that many of them worked for (at a high time of liberal federal activism, too) could be demoted or fired. Someone had to make the first move. The next day at lunch with some of the same women, Friedan wrote down the words *the National Organization for Women* on a paper napkin. As Ruth Rosen says, the founding of NOW signified that the federal government—not even the most liberal federal administration since the New Deal—would never do enough for women.

The first formal meeting of NOW took place on October 29, 1966. Thirty women, representing three hundred charter members, met in the John Philip Sousa Community Room of the *Washington Post*. Military marching bands were not present. The NOW founders were a mix of midwestern labor organizers and white upper-middle-class professionals—the latter a group like Betty herself. Friedan ignored working-class women and, apart from her working relationship with Pauli Murray, she disregarded Black women altogether. Black women, she thought, would benefit from a general rise in women's economic position. This may have been naive (racism was not something she thought about very much), but she did not apologize, and ten years later, in *It Changed My Life* (1976), she let the bourgeois cat out of the bag.

> Other revolutions, despite the clichés of radical rhetoric, were also started by middle-class intellectuals (the only ones with education to put it into words), but they were always doing it for someone else: the poor, the working class, "them." . . . Doing it for *ourselves* is the essence of the women's movement: it keeps us honest, keeps us real, keeps us concrete.

That's as candid a statement about her way of acting as Friedan ever made. She did not have an office, so her apartment at the Dakota became the organization's de facto headquarters, much to Carl's chagrin. She was making a revolution both *with* and *for* a barely existing female professional class. She drew on friendships and associations, contacted college presidents, church leaders, female union officials, and nurses. It's as if she wanted to reach every woman in the country with a good job.

Once again, she made notes on odd pieces of paper, setting down a few lines across legal-pad pages or filling an entire pad, from beginning to end, with her heading-into-the-wind scrawl, crossing out whole paragraphs as she went. Much of the time she wrote on hotel stationery—forlorn, lonely-bedroom memos inscribed on tiny pages from the Washington Hilton, the Mayflower, the Drake in Chicago. You might say, "How else could one start an organization in 1966?" Friedan's labors in this period are primitive by our standards, yet she was extraordinarily successful, especially considering that collaboration was not her natural mode. "I'd never been an organization woman," she wrote later. "I was a writer who had written about women."

In group meetings, as it turned out, she could be testy and overbearing. When someone else was talking in a Manhattan meeting, her stage whisper could be heard in New Jersey. She was sure that she was the right woman to lead a new organization. Why wouldn't other women *listen*? As she solicited powerful people, including some men, she elbowed potential rivals out of the way, except for Pauli Murray, who wrote to her, after a contentious telephone call, "It was good to talk to you tonight, dear pepperpot."

Betty's victory at NOW was made possible, in part, by a Statement of Purpose she had written the previous summer. She composed it mostly alone (Murray made some contributions, and Mary Eastwood and Alice Rossi amended it). It's her most powerful piece of writing. There were at least three versions of the statement. One version began "We, men and women, gathered here in a new partnership of the sexes to constitute ourselves as a National Organization for Women." The phrase "new partnership" was moved to a spot later in the sentence and was altered to "a fully equal partnership of the sexes," though all versions began with "We, men and women." The final version of the opening went as follows:

> We, men and women who hereby constitute ourselves as the National Organization for Women, believe that the time has come for a new movement toward true equality for all women in America, and toward a fully equal partnership of the sexes, as part of the world-wide revolution of human rights now taking place within and beyond our national border.

The "fully equal partnership" reflected her desire that feminism liberate men as well as women. Yes, men had to step up and raise children, recognize talented women at the office, discard the macho instincts that made them foolish. Making men part of the revolution, she was sure, made it easier for women to demand the full rights of American citizenship. Later in the statement, attempting to guarantee those rights, Friedan refers to "the power of American law, and the protection guaranteed by the U.S. constitution." Protection, in other words, for everyone.

Black activists, pointing to the broken promise of the founding documents, made the same demands during the civil rights movement and for decades afterward. Inequality and discrimination violated the promises embedded in the Declaration and the Constitution—universal equality, promised but never acted on. Friedan wanted to make it clear that feminism was not some eccentric or marginal movement of shrill malcontents but a central claim on constitutional turf. The statement is straightforward, dignified, often factual, but it moves forward with a hurtling moral force.

NOW MOVED QUICKLY in the next few years, challenging the EEOC, and finally acting directly in a way that the EEOC did not. It picketed the *New York Times* (the rest of the press loved it), attacking the separate listings for men and for women in the paper's want ads, with its lower-paying jobs for women; it supported airline stewardesses in a civil suit calling on the airlines to drop age requirements (stewardesses all had to be young and unmarried). Friedan was learning on the job: sex discrimination in the workplace was the area, she thought, in which public pressure would work most effectively.

She was at the center of everything, planning, telephoning, writing strategic memos, working the press, working so obsessively that she ate on the fly or not at all. At times, she says, she forgot to go to the bathroom. Lawrence Lader, the longtime abortion-rights journalist and Betty's friend and ally, described her in this period in rapturous terms.

> Everything is in motion, not just her words which come so fast she seems to ignore the necessity of breathing. Her hands gesticulate, wave, flail. Her eyes are deep, dark, charged, and violent as her language. Her nose is long, her hair . . . often askew. Nothing fits the accepted model of beauty. Yet she exerts a powerful, haunting attractiveness—that special combustion which lights up a few, rare individuals interacting with their audience.

It is the language of a man in love with a Jewish woman. But women in the movement did not always feel the same way.

As Betty flung charged half sentences into the room and talked through everyone else, some women resented it like hell. She didn't understand that many feminists, especially the radical ones, insisted that sisterhood required a more relaxed, communal organization—perhaps a revolving authority rather than single leader. Within NOW, the opposition to Friedan became both personal and ideological, and by the late sixties some members were laying plans against her.

FRIEDAN, AS SHE admitted, found the idea of abortion distasteful. In the original edition of *The Feminine Mystique*, she did not mention it. A few years later, she worried that advocating abortion rights would hurt NOW's reputation and standing. Abortion wasn't respectable. But for the younger members of NOW, it was the central feminist demand, and they kept bringing it up. In the end, Friedan's wrath was stirred by the notion of men telling women what to do with their bodies. In this case, a moral issue became an organizing issue. After 1967, reproductive rights became part of NOW's program, as did the Equal Rights Amendment (ERA), a proposed constitutional amendment, first introduced in Congress in 1923 guaranteeing equal legal protections for women in matters of law, divorce, and property. Again, Friedan was learning on the job. A bristling NOW document called the Bill of Rights for Women, which she wrote in 1968, called for maternity leave, childcare centers, the right of women to control their reproductive lives, and the passage of the ERA. In 1969, she was one of the founders of NARAL, the National Association for the Repeal of Abortion Laws. Friedan built strong institutions that functioned for years—even though, sooner or later, she was removed from leadership of those institutions. Given her temperament, failure was lodged in the very foundation of her success.

The Bill of Rights for Women was a powerful document, but it omits mention of rights for gay women, and it says nothing about protections for women against harassment and rape. The first omission was intentional and, Friedan thought, politically necessary—the movement, she was sure, would be tarred and even destroyed by outsiders ridiculing lesbian members. The second omission may have been created by a guilty consciousness of her own violent marriage. How many of her actions in the late sixties—some would say prejudices—were produced by her personal history and difficulties, how many by the middle-class Jewish cultural imperatives that she embodied and that caused her to be flummoxed by what was happening? Both things were working in her, and she was stunned. She wanted changes in the law, but what she and other women had unleashed was a change in consciousness, a change in being. In the mid- and late sixties, and then into the seventies, the revolt of women became much more exuberant, intimate, contentious, witty, and encompassing than anything Betty Friedan was ready for.

RADICALS, LESBIANS, AND BETTY

In the middle and late sixties, in New York, Chicago, Boston, and San Francisco, young women began getting together and sharing their sorrows and ambitions. And not just in the big cities. "Consciousness raising" became a mass movement functioning through many small gatherings. As Carolyn Heilbrun put it in her biography of Gloria Steinem, *Education of a Woman: The Life of Gloria Steinem* (1995), "it was the brushfire through which the conflagration of feminism spread with enormous speed." As men looked on in wonder, some retreating into ridicule, others into silence, women took up taboo subjects, including bad and unwilling sex, faked orgasms, dark-alley abortions, shabby treatment at home and in the office. Shame, reticence, and anger gave way to relief and gratitude. The Old Left, both Communist and Socialist, was often silent about sexual matters. The new feminist Left was going to let it rip. The women's movement had morphed into women's liberation.

Betty Friedan's NOW was a dues-paying organization, operating top-down; it worked successfully to challenge workplace discrimination and to change laws (in fairness, some of the NOW chapters were quite radical). Women's liberation, if one speaks of it organizationally, was composed of innumerable small groups, spontaneous, leaderless, often theoretical, groups devoted to reimagining social bonds and developing new liberties. The younger women wanted decolonization—the end of a society dominated by men. They wanted to change child-rearing, dating patterns, workplace relations, the nature of narrative art, language—everything. They achieved a biting clarity in speeches, in mimeographed pamphlets, and tirade-scorched underground press articles. A lot of the writing was exhilarating even if you thought it overwrought or unfair. None less than Norman Mailer praised the terse, "mean" new style. For the younger women, the war against "the patriarchy" was on. But that was not Betty Friedan's war.

The famous sixties "sexual revolution" fed the mood. In 1962, Helen Gurley Brown had written the cheerfully vulgar bestselling *Sex and the*

Single Girl, which advised young women to party for the weekend, sleep with married men, and get back to work on Monday. It was life without shame, made possible by the widespread availability of birth-control pills. Yet how much power did women have in this "revolution"? Many women were uneasy. When a seismic shift in power finally occurred, in the middle and late sixties, its cause was not so much political as anatomical; or rather, first anatomical, then political.

That the clitoris was the principal location of sensation in women's sexual response was hardly news to women. Nor was it news to sex researchers. Alfred Kinsey, in *Sexual Behavior in the Human Female* (1953), established that the vagina had minimal sensory receptors; William Masters and Virginia Johnson's *Human Sexual Response* (1966) emphasized, with experimental data, the ability of the clitoris stimulated by a vibrator to yield one climax after another. Suddenly freed from its demure status, the clitoris moved to the center of feminist polemic. Mary Jane Sherfey's *The Nature and Evolution of Female Sexuality* (1972) and Anne Koedt's essay, "The Myth of the Vaginal Orgasm" (1970), and other such texts, were eagerly passed around among women. The news for men was not happy. Their situation was comic-tragic: the penis, strictly speaking, was not necessary for female sexual enjoyment, an idea that rattled the struts of male ego, Norman Mailer's struts most of all. Betty Friedan herself was made profoundly unhappy. Many of the young feminist writers were Jewish; some were fighting against their mothers, some were fighting against the sexual role that Jewish women were expected to play in marriage. Betty Friedan was devoted to that role.

Masturbation attained a new prestige, lesbianism an even greater prestige; gender separatism was a reasonable course of action, as was celibacy (at least as argument). The strongest assertion of power was the refusal to accept the nuclear family and biology itself. Shulamith Firestone, in *The Dialectic of Sex: The Case for Feminist Revolution* (1970), an enraged theoretical text still read today, merged Marxism with supercharged feminism. "Unless revolution uproots the basic social organization, the biological family—the vinculum through which the psychology of power can always be smuggled—the tapeworm of exploitation will never be annihilated." Rather than the revolutionary proletariat seizing the means of production, revolutionary women must seize the means of *reproduc-tion.* Pregnancy was barbaric, marriage a form of prostitution or even slavery, the nuclear family a prison house for women. Children should be raised collectively without strong ties, and so on.

Betty Friedan thought all of this was crazy—or worse. Attacking the family, she believed, was a disaster for feminism. As long as women were not imprisoned at home—as long as they had choices—they should certainly have children, a sentiment that, by degrees, turned into a fervent belief in the *necessity* that feminists have children. At the same time, the brazen sex talk bothered her. She was hardly a prig, and, in the seventies and eighties, she refused to join the feminist anti-pornography drive (in the later jargon, she was "sex-positive"). But she was sure the constant talk of sex would alienate middle-class women, who, after all, were the revolutionary class in the revolution she wanted to lead. And what in the world was meant by "sexual politics"? Politics required women and men working together and bringing pressure on corporations, cities, and states, changing laws, manners, and then, just maybe, the nation. "Such pressure," she later wrote, "required grindingly difficult organizational work, not 'navel-gazing,'" which was her term for consciousness raising. She could not understand that sexual freedom for women was in fact a political as well as a private issue. She was huffy over what she called "orgasm talk." But how could women not care about pleasure? After all, in her book, she had celebrated orgasm as the reward for liberated women.

Joyce Carol Oates, hardly a squeamish writer, was shocked by some of the new rhetoric. "We understand," she wrote in the *Atlantic* (July 1971), "slowly that what is being liberated is really hatred. *Hatred of men.* . . . Such crude, vicious jokes at the expense of men!" For Friedan, hating men was not an option. "Let's face it, men are here to stay. We have to live with them, work with them, have kids with them, love them if we can." In any case, some men were persuadable. "It is possible for men to put themselves finally in woman's place by an act of empathy or by guilt or conscience or simply by a human rights consciousness as it has been possible for whites to do it for Blacks."

There speaks the soul of sixties white liberal thought, drawing as it does on a universalist humanism in which we are all comprehensible to one another. What was needed, Friedan said, was a revolutionary theory that dealt with everyone—and with the world as it existed. In all of this, she was at her most insistently down-to-earth, pragmatic, and middle-class-Jewish. At Cornell University, in 1969, railing against the radicals, she spoke as follows:

> Endless self-pity or abstract discussions of a miserable situation that do not lead to a transcendence in action are no good if we are going to try to arrive at a revolutionary theory. But if we are going to address ourselves to the need for changing the social institutions that will permit women to be free and equal individualities participating actively in their own society—with men—then we must talk in terms of what is possible, and not accept what is as what must be. In other words, don't talk to me about test tubes.

She was wrong about test tubes—in vitro fertilization, surrogate motherhood, and many other kinds of assisted reproductive technology became major options for women, straight and gay, within a few years. And she missed the spirit of the moment: the late sixties and early seventies was a time in the women's movement of savage criticism and also of great generosity and warmth. Women opened bookstores, started journals, wrote plays and poetry with a feminist edge, created rape and abuse clinics, performed safe abortions (illegally, before *Roe v. Wade*). They *talked* to each other, not always an activity Betty favored when she was not doing the talking. If the goals of NOW were largely legislative and material, the goals of women's liberation were moral and grandly political—change both revolutionary and intimate at the same time.

Friedan couldn't see that her notion of "a revolutionary theory applicable to all" might be unnecessary or irrelevant. America is a country divided by class, race, ethnicity, religion, a country with a noisy debating hall of subcultures—in such a country, how can women speak in one voice? It turns out they didn't need to. Over the next few decades, through many individual battles, defeats, dead ends, improvisations, and victories, feminism flowed into the way men and women related to one another; it flowed into consumerism, hiring practices, literature, academic life, corporate life, medicine, law, entertainment, and a myriad of other things.

Part of the problem for Betty was generational, part geographical. Many of the radical young feminists were Jewish women who had grown up in New York, Boston, or Chicago, where they were protected, even cocooned. She was middle-aged and from Peoria (her anti-lesbian prejudice was the one way she had not beaten her hometown). They were in flight from student-Left politics and the anti-war movement; in flight, some of them, from marriage and domesticity. She was sticking to a violent marriage. Consciousness raising, for her, might have produced the most shameful of confessions.

Lesbianism in particular baffled her. Was it a perversion? A form of seduction aimed at Betty Friedan? A plot by the FBI or CIA to disrupt the movement altogether? "Lesbianism," she wrote, "does not empower women or enable them to change their lives," which is perhaps the dimmest remark this intelligent woman ever made. Friedan's statement remains true only if you expect gay women to stay hidden in the closet forever. Lesbianism alone could not be all of liberation for women, but if women couldn't be free to say they were gay, what could liberation mean? And where was her political sense? Gay women were a major part of the constituency.

Irony is inescapable. Betty Friedan's temperament was ill-suited to the revolution she had unleashed. But she couldn't alter herself. The second-generation immigrant drive that gets you to the top can't be shut down once you get there. Self-involved and impatient, she turned young women eager to work for her into servants—until they rebelled and walked away. She bullied even the older women on the NOW board, successful professionals who had triumphed over male indifference only to suffer one of their own shouting at them. They humored her, but only up to a point. In February 1970, the board set up a slate of officers for election, but Friedan, who had been president for four years (since the beginning), was kept off it. The board chose Aileen Hernandez, an African American union organizer and civil rights activist, as the new president. Afterward, Betty insisted she could have stayed if she had wanted to. "The only reason I did step down was a Black woman wanted to run," which was a disagreeable way of putting it, and untrue as well.

THE BEST MOMENT I: WOMEN'S STRIKE FOR EQUALITY, AUGUST 26, 1970

Yet there were several fine moments, several moments of personal and political glory—not redemption, exactly, but happy recoveries. In March 1970, presiding over her last NOW board meeting, Friedan, without any prior notice, issued a call for a strike—a national women's strike, in which women, for a day, would withdraw from men and cease to work, cook, make love. Betty was certainly not against sex with men, but Aristophanes's idea of a sex strike was irresistible. This event was to take place on August 26, 1970, on the fiftieth anniversary of women gaining suffrage, and it would feature three central demands: abortion rights; community-controlled, twenty-four-hour childcare centers; and equal opportunity in jobs and education. Making the announcement without warning was clearly a risk: time was short, NOW's resources were meager, and Betty had made enemies; the entire thing could be a flop. But she saw the strike as a dramatic event that would take the focus away from what she called "man hating" and attacks on the nuclear family and get it back to the issues that mattered.

During recent summer vacations, she had stayed with friends in the Hamptons, and now she engaged in a Hamptons specialty: the Big Liberal Party that raises money for a cause. At the same time, with a great deal of help from local NOW chapters, she galvanized parallel events all over the country. She electrified herself and everyone else, even wooing the young radical women in New York. Many of them, perhaps sensing that this was her last hurrah, or close to it, willingly joined in. And this time she triumphed, because the idea of a strike was outrageous and funny ("Don't iron when the strike is hot"). Women would make trouble, and they would get away with it. The Jewish moralist had turned radical, at least for a while.

The strike, it turned out, was impractical, too hard to pull off, so it became a march instead. At 5:30 p.m., Betty joined a mass of women in front of the Plaza Hotel, at Fifty-Ninth Street, and then led them down Fifth Avenue, right in the middle of rush hour, their numbers swelling as they went. The moment was brazenly happy. The young radical women distributed leaflets along the way and walked arm in arm with the NOW organizers. In Bryant Park, she found herself in the commanding position of the old Jewish labor leaders Samuel Gompers and David Dubinsky, exhorting a crowd to action—in this case, some fifty thousand marchers, including elderly suffragists, Kate Millett, Gloria Steinem, and women from such groups as the Lesbian Food Conspiracy and Black Women's Liberation. Her tone on that day was euphoric and universalist—all women, despite differences, were there to celebrate a political triumph. She began:

After tonight, the politics of this nation will never be the same. By our numbers here tonight, by women who marched curb-to-curb, down Fifth Avenue—women who have never marched before in their own cause with veterans of the first battle of the vote with young high-school students, Black women with white women, housewives with women who work in factories and offices, women whose husbands are rich and who discovered that all women are poor—we learned. We learned what none of us had dared to hope—the power of our solidarity, the power of our sisterhood. We learned we have the power to change the conditions that oppress us.

It was likely her greatest moment. As usual, some of the national press coverage was patronizing. Howard K. Smith, ABC's national news anchor, said the following: "Three things have been difficult to tame. The ocean, fools, and women. We may soon be able to tame the ocean, but fools and women will take a little longer." Yes, taming fools will take a little longer. Smith's bitterness may have been caused by men knowing—really understanding—that the women's movement could no longer be stopped.

THE JEWISH FEMINIST IV: GLORIA, BELLA, AND BETTY

By the early seventies, colleges, law schools, medical schools, corporations, and media outfits, often complaining, often grudging, taking one step forward, a half step back, were beginning to open their doors to women—mainly upper-middle-class educated women, which was always Friedan's cohort. Many young women, some consciously feminist, others simply seizing the opportunities that had opened up, put themselves forward and changed their lives.

Two attractive personalities emerged at the same time, not initially as feminist leaders but as accomplished professionals: Gloria Steinem, a very good magazine journalist, and Bella Abzug, a crusading liberal lawyer. Like Betty Friedan, Gloria Steinem and Bella Abzug were children of Jewish immigrant families. Yet they came out of that background with temperamental gifts much more generous than hers. The differences are illuminating—and nearly heartbreaking.

Before he opened his jewelry store in Peoria, Betty's father, Harry Goldstein, had made his living selling buttons from a street-corner cart. Gloria Steinem's dad, Leo Steinem, who was descended from German Jewish immigrants, pulled off a mobile, slightly upscale version of the same thing. Gloria was born in 1934 in Ohio. When she was a girl, the family lived in Michigan, and scraped along buying and selling antiques at auctions. Every fall, at the first breath of cool air, Leo would load his wife and both Gloria and her older sister into a house trailer and head south. More than sixty years later, in her autobiography, *My Life on the Road* (2015), Gloria Steinem wrote that "we never started out with enough money to reach our destination, not even close. Instead, we took a few boxes of china, silver, and other small antiques from those country auctions, and used them to prime the process of buying, selling, and bartering our way along the southern route to California, or still farther south to Florida and the Gulf of Mexico."

The contrast is stunning: Betty and her family tried to penetrate Peoria's inner social circle of Christians. They never made it, and Betty's way of being an immigrant's daughter was to furiously demand recognition for her entire life. Gloria Steinem partly grew up on the road, and part of her way of being the daughter of a Jewish immigrant family was to reach out to people again and again. She transformed the childhood habits of roving commerce into an easy way with strangers in need. Later in her life, for all her celebrity in New York as the beautiful feminist journalist dating attractive and famous men, she often headed for the airport and visited a struggling group of women, sometimes in a large city, sometimes in a small town—women hoping to organize a feminist group, a local feminist action. She visited poor communities, African American communities, the Lakota Nation. She also welcomed lesbians into the movement. It should be added that she became remarkably shrewd in managing the media, controlling her own story and, as much as she could, the feminist story. She was temperate, loyal, beautiful, and calculating. Reactionary buffoons and younger radical women made fun of her, but many men and women found her both thoughtful and likable, even admirable.

The all-cylinders-firing Bella Abzug was born Bella Savitzky, in 1929, of Russian-immigrant parents. She grew up working the cash register in her father's store on Ninth Avenue, in Manhattan, which was called—wait for it—the Live and Let Live Meat Market. At home, where her grandfather Wolf Tanklefsky dominated the proceedings, Friday night Sabbath was celebrated with prayers and songs, readings from the Torah, and iron-like moral lessons derived from Isaiah. "Cease to do evil. Learn to be

good. Devote yourself to justice." Bella Abzug took these injunctions literally; she also insisted on her own strength. After her father died, she went
to the synagogue every morning and recited the kaddish. She learned
Hebrew, and, at summer camp, spoke the abrupt old language with other
kids as they hiked, swam, and rowed together. From the beginning, she
associated Judaism with strenuousness: it was not enough to be good;
you had to have an effect on the world through the sheer expression of
energy. And she was lucky: there were patriarchs in Bella's life from whom
she took strength; at the same time, her mother vigorously supported her
ambitions.

After law school (Columbia), Bella Abzug became a resolute fighter
against racism; she fought for better housing for the poor and much else,
leading up to a passionate feminism. She was large and stocky, with a big,
handsome head topped by circular hats. (She wore hats so no one would
think she was a secretary.) Combative and funny, she got in your face.
Literally: sometime in the seventies, as I was having lunch at a West Side
restaurant, Bella, in full campaign mode, stuck her face over my newspaper, followed by her hand, which I took.

When Norman Mailer ran for mayor of the city of New York in 1969
(in part because of a suggestion from Gloria Steinem), he asked for the
support of Abzug and her cohort. "We're here to look you over," Bella told
him. "Your record against the war in Vietnam is okay . . . yet your views
on women do not impress us. We think your views on women are full of
shit." As Mailer recorded the meeting in *The Prisoner of Sex*, "she had a
voice which could have boiled the fat off a taxi-cab driver's neck. It was as
full of the vibrations of power as those machines which rout out grooves
in wood." Contrary to his reputation, Mailer was not always hostile to
female strength. In his writing about Abzug, the metaphors speak of love
and fear, united by amused appreciation. He approvingly described her
"wall-slamming style," which turned out to be less a metaphor than something close to truth. At a dinner party with friends, Bella, in mid-tirade,
smashed her fist down on the table, and the table collapsed.

It was a misfortune for Betty Friedan that she never accepted any
woman as her mentor (Margaret Mead's postwar reactionary turn hurt
Betty badly); it was an additional misfortune that she never made friends
with a woman whom she could admit was an equal. Her relations with
these two fellow children of Jewish immigrants were troubled, conten-

tious, close to tragic. In 1971 and 1972, she felt, literally, that she was being pushed out, as if there were only so much turf to stand on, not a widening ground that could accommodate many interests, many rebellions, large and small. *She* was the Jewish feminist, the leader; who were *they*?

When Betty Friedan and Gloria Steinem first met, at an anti-war protest in the sixties, Gloria found Betty "bossy and rude." On Betty's side, she thought she could use Gloria as an attractive advertisement for feminism. She was not prepared for how serious Gloria Steinem was, or how happily, with a collective sigh of relief, thousands of people would welcome her as a role model—not a role that Steinem campaigned for but one she accepted. In 1968, Steinem was part of the founding of *New York* magazine, and, in 1972, she created, with Letty Cottin Pogrebin, Mary Thom, and other women, *Ms.* magazine, which Betty disliked—or claimed to dislike (her own idea for a women's magazine had been rejected by publishers). *Ms.* was a companionable women's lib monthly packed with funny or painful stories about home life and child-rearing, as well as reporting on professional struggles, harassment, and rape. Betty thought it at once too militant and too attentive to lifestyle issues rather than jobs and wages and other bread-and-butter matters. But the movement had gone beyond bread and butter without quite leaving the kitchen. *Ms.*, with its commercial alertness and multifarious interests, demonstrated how feminism would burst through somber or enraged categories of protest and spread through the entire culture.

By the time of the Democratic National Convention—the Miami convention of July 1972—Betty's resentment of her younger rival was obvious to everyone. Nora Ephron, writing with exasperated humor in *Esquire*, demanded to know why Friedan was walking around the convention muttering, "I'm so disgusted with Gloria" and publicly accusing Gloria of "man hating," which was preposterous. "It is probably too easy," Ephron wrote, "to go on about the two of them this way: Betty as Wicked Witch of the West. Gloria as Ozma, Glinda, Dorothy—take your pick."

It was too easy because Betty had made it so. Judith Hennessee, summing up the contrast between the two women, writes, "Betty created scenes, blew up small things into huge, nerve-wracking dramas, forcing people to deal with her; Gloria salvaged situations, papering over the cracks, even denying that differences existed…Betty never made excuses for herself. She led armies; she was Joan of Arc." But this Joan would not be consumed by fire; her armies, irritated and restless, merely slipped away from her.

In 1972, Betty Friedan attacked both Gloria and Bella in a *McCall's* column as "female chauvinist boors," which was absurd. Bella defended herself; Gloria refused to respond but took revenge by never publishing anything in *Ms.* about Betty Friedan or even about the National Organization for Women. Betty compounded the *McCall's* debacle with more acid taunts. Gloria Steinem, she claimed, was "ripping off the movement for private profit. . . . No one should mistake [Steinem] for a leader." And, in 1973, she delivered a malevolent and egotistical piece to the *Times*, a newspaper where she had potent allies. It was called "Up from the Kitchen Floor," and in the course of its surly length she claimed credit for every victory of the women's movement and attacked, yet again, man hating and "disrupters." She could not rid herself of the notion that women who disagreed with her were plotting to destroy the movement. In 1975, she informed Simone de Beauvoir (no less) that the "over-focus on sexual issues, on sexual politics, as opposed to the condition of women in society in general, may have been accentuated by those who wished to immobilize the movement politically." The champion of common sense— *sechel*—in *The Feminine Mystique* had fallen into malice and paranoia.

For the children descended from Eastern European and Russian immigrants, making their way in America meant, among many other choices, settling on the right degree of aggression and accommodation. Getting that balance was hard. What Steinem and Abzug gained from their earlier lives was a bodily and spiritual ease with themselves, nonthreatening and reasonable in one case, hyperaggressive but good-humored in the other. In different ways, the two women dared you not to like them—they suggested there was something wrong with you if you didn't. Yet they made other women feel comfortable, grateful, amused, proud; Betty, dominating and needy, made other women feel resentful.

THE BEST MOMENT II—THE HOUSTON SPEECH, NOVEMBER 21, 1977

In late November 1977, something like twenty thousand women, Republicans as well as Democrats, journeyed to Houston for the National Women's Conference, a major event held under the aegis of the Carter administration. All fifty states elected delegates, and minorities were well represented. Gay women as well as hetero feminist women showed up. Lady Bird Johnson, Betty Ford, and First Lady Rosalynn Carter were there. In all, the conference was a celebration, almost a consecration: second-wave feminism had arrived as a national movement. At the same time, however, as the women gathered at the Sam Houston Coliseum, the indefatigable anti-feminist Phyllis Schlafly staged a kind of counter-event across town. Back in 1972, in her first statement on abortion, Schlafly had said the following: "Women's lib is a total assault on the role of the American woman as wife and mother and on the family as the basic unit of society," and so on. In Houston, Schlafly denounced the Women's Conference as "sick."

Bella Abzug was a prime mover in setting up the event; Friedan was excluded from the organizing meetings but attended as a delegate at large. During its four days of debates, the conference issued resolutions on reproductive rights and the rights of poor women, minority women, rural women. The event marked a kind of awakening for Betty. She came to Houston because she was obsessed with getting the ERA ratified (it was then three states short). But when gay rights were debated, the disagreements among the delegates were so acrimonious that Betty feared a resolution supporting the ERA would be derailed. Pulling herself together, she addressed the floor.

I am considered to be violently opposed to the lesbian issue in the women's movement, and I have been. . . . As a woman of middle age who grew up in Middle America—in Peoria, Illinois—and who has loved men maybe too well, I have my personal hang-ups on this issue. But now we must transcend our previous differences to devote our full energies to get the Equal Rights Amendment ratified, or we will lose all we have gained. Since . . . we know the Equal Rights Amendment will do nothing whatsoever for homosexuals, we must support the separate civil rights of our lesbian sisters.

When she finished, many people were in tears. In Houston, the ERA plank was approved; so was the resolution in favor of gay rights. According to historian Ruth Rosen, "Lesbian women shouted, 'Thank you, sisters,' and released hundreds of pink and yellow balloons in the air. On the balloons were printed the words, 'We Are Everywhere.'" That sentiment couldn't have made Friedan happy—she would rather that lesbians be nowhere. And there was trouble ahead. In the Reagan era, which began in 1981, Phyllis Schlafly, helmeted in stiff bouffant, vivid with rage and the excitements of power, organized against the ERA and feminism itself by constantly wielding the lesbian issue as a club. But for Friedan, the long struggle against gay women in the movement ended in the only way it could have, with public acceptance. Acceptance in her heart was a different matter.

THE LATER YEARS OF A WARRIOR

After the Houston speech, Betty Friedan lived for another twenty-eight years.

She continued to fight for the movement and its goals of equality, political power for women, abortion rights, childcare, and maternity leave. The institutions that she had founded, or collaborated in founding, carried on their work even though she had been thrown out of leadership positions. She insisted, again and again, that marriage and child-rearing should be at the center of feminism, a sentiment that effactually ended her influence among younger women, some of whom wanted children, some of whom didn't, but none of whom wanted to be lectured about it. She couldn't stop attacking radical (and some not-so-radical) women who were allegedly undermining the movement. She berated recalcitrant congressmen and senators, gingered the Democratic presidential candidates George McGovern, Jimmy Carter, and Bill Clinton. She was available by telephone for her opinions of such world-shaking phenomena as miniskirts. She was against them.

She turned the historical Reform Jewish injunction of repairing the world, *tikkun olam*, into something closer to setting people straight. Or rather, to put it more positively, she became a sojourner acting out a familiar saying from the rabbinical literature: "It is not up to you to finish the task, but you are not free to abandon it." One problem for her was that some of the young women who had broken through, attaining good jobs through the efforts of second-wave activists, no longer wanted to hear the old rhetoric; they were tired of being mobilized; they wanted to live and work. But from Betty's point of view, they were ungrateful. As a girl, she had wanted to be respected more than she wanted to be liked, and these late rejections hurt. As many people stopped taking her seriously, her old miseries over an unloving mother and a father who couldn't accept her, as well as the family's social defeats in Peoria, came back to her.

She taught a great deal, giving courses on modern sex roles and the mass media, and from 1986 to 1993 she conducted seminars on public issues and business management at the University of Southern California— seminars attended by some of Los Angeles's most powerful women. She began enterprises, study groups, symposia on experimental modes of group living in which work and career would run together more easily than they currently did. Most of these initiatives didn't go very far. She was a historical figure, tireless, always working, but an element of malicious comedy had overtaken her life: her very efforts to sustain power further removed her from power. Many American women had had enough.

BUT THERE WAS the rest of the globe. She tried to bring the feminist word and the tools for basic organizing wherever she was asked. Voyaging as "the mother of the modern women's movement," she wore her historical significance as a crown. Overseas, audiences knew little of her diminished influence at home.

No one could doubt her courage. In Rome, in 1973, she had a private audience with Pope Paul VI; the two politely exchanged views on the roles of women in the church and elsewhere. But then she gave a pro-abortion speech in the Piazza Navona and was menaced by motorcycle gangs and right-wing priests. In Brazil her ideas were seen as a threat to *machismo*, a national ideal. *Bom Deus!* A woman attacking *machismo*! The newspapers couldn't get over it. In Mexico City in 1975, at the UN-sponsored World Conference on Women, she grew so incensed at anti-Semitic comments directed at Israel that, according to her son Jonathan, "They had to get her out of the hall." In Israel itself, Golda Meir rebuffed her (a big disappointment), but Betty spoke to women in small groups and returned numerous times, helping to launch Israeli feminism. "She loved her trips to Israel," her daughter Emily told me. "She liked being connected there."

In 1966, she had conversations with Indira Gandhi, the first woman to be elected prime minister of India; she was impressed by how Mrs. Gandhi wielded power. The prime minister admired a Rudy Gernreich reversible cape that Betty wore (black on one side, camel on the other);

Gandhi had it copied and wore it to the White House a few years later, winking at Betty as she passed the press line. "The last time I saw her," Betty wrote in her autobiography, "was much later at some international conference and she said, 'How would you like to come back to India?' I told her I'd love to, but then she was assassinated." End of story.

In her travels, the diva at times overwhelmed the evangelist. If she didn't receive the treatment she wanted—the best room, a car of her own, the best seat in a restaurant—she threw tantrums and shouted things like, "Don't you know who I am?" Germaine Greer accompanied her to Iran in 1974, and later wrote (in the *Guardian*) that Betty carried on so angrily in Tehran that the state functionaries feared she was drunk. On that trip, she was impressed by the modernizing shah, Mohammad Reza Pahlavi, who listened gravely to her ideas about women. But Greer claims that Betty, noticing little but her own reception, insisted that the chador had been banned even as women were wearing it in the street outside her car. A few years later, the shah was overthrown and replaced, to Betty's fury, by ayatollahs pushing women back into the Middle Ages.

As Simone de Beauvoir had suggested, a change in women's standing would produce liberty but not necessarily happiness. In practical terms, liberty in America could mean uncertainty. Should women refuse to marry? Should they have children without husbands? Women, Phyllis Schlafly said, were in danger of losing their protections; the entire structure of deference, the belief in women's specialness and delicacy, would be shattered. On the male side, George Gilder, Ronald Reagan's favorite author, issued *Sexual Suicide* (1973), which insisted that feminism was destroying everything. "The whole sexual constitution is based on the maternal tie. Women's Liberation tries to reject this role." (Betty Friedan, of course, did no such thing.) But it was not just reactionaries who were attacking the women's movement. In the eighties, the liberal press and a variety of television shows renewed the derisive tones of years earlier, but with a new twist of recrimination. In the classic *Backlash* (1991), Susan Faludi bitterly chronicled the malice, opportunism, and misinformation of both media and politicians in the Bush-Reagan era. *Feminism is destroying the American family . . . Freedom has made women unhappy . . . Women can't get a man…The price is too high.*

With many expressions of weariness and boredom (not entirely convincing), Betty Friedan buckled on her armor and again mounted her horse. In her 1981 book *The Second Stage*, a collection of speeches and magazine articles, she makes the case for the family again and again and attacks the feminist radicals for the failure of the Equal Rights Amendment. (She thought the radicals scared people off.) She admits what everyone had noticed: women trying to balance work and family often have a tough time. Many more women were working than had been twenty years earlier, but some were having children alone. Real wages for male workers, whose muscle power was no longer needed in many jobs, were dropping in a changed economy, and women often saw little benefit from marrying. (In 1970, single-parent families amounted to 10 percent of all American families; now it's around 40 percent.) Whether married or not, women attempting to work while raising children were tying themselves in knots.

> What worries me today is "choices" that women have supposedly won, which are not real. How can a woman freely "choose" to have a child when her paycheck is needed for the rent or mortgage, when her job isn't geared to taking care of a child, when there is no national policy for parental leave, and no assurance that her job will be waiting for her if she takes off to have a child?

Back in 1967, four years after the publication of *The Feminine Mystique*, Betty was traveling in Sweden, and feminists there told her, "Without childcare, it's all just talk." Well, it's not all just talk, but the Swedish women had a point: universal, public-funded, community-controlled day care was the obvious solution to the motherhood-and-career dilemma of ambitious women, but in this country we were not close to it then, and we are not much closer to it now. Back in 1971, Walter Mondale and other senators created legislation that would provide early-education programs and after-school care across the country on a voluntary basis. It passed both houses of Congress as the Comprehensive Child Development Act, but President Nixon vetoed it. In the 2020s, those who can afford babysitters, nannies, and private day care centers get by well enough, while everyone else scrambles from one day to the next.

Friedan's logic in *The Second Stage* is clear enough: women have the babies, yet the work situation is based on male models. She wanted a new model—"a new paradigm"—in which men and women would share jobs or stagger their careers; she wanted women to receive paid maternity leave and the government to sponsor day care. "The solution is not the break with family—as the radical feminists would have it—but the reorganization of it." In the forty years since Friedan wrote these words, many more women have entered the workplace, but the new paradigm, except for limited situations, has not arrived. American capitalism rarely yields to moral persuasion.

The political impossibility of solving the childcare problem in this country left Friedan with an analysis but no course of action. She was not wrong, but she was tiresome, antagonistic, a woman who replaced workable solutions with moral overinsistence. In Susan Faludi's *Backlash* (1991), she shows up as an incoherent advocate, confused, even reactionary. Friedan grated on many. When she spoke, the evangelical cadences could be mesmerizing, but in print those speeches (as well as reprinted articles) come off as monotonous and shapeless. The sentences stretch on, gummy, colorless, bending back on themselves; the moments of strong argument are swamped by pages of sullen iteration. As a bourgeois feminist, she was rhetorically neutered. To praise bourgeois marriage successfully, one would need the lyrical gifts of a poet, or the dramatic gifts of a novelist, or perhaps the eccentric gifts of a witty wife and mother. These skills were not part of Betty Friedan's formidable equipment.

SCENES FROM A MARRIAGE III

In her own account of her marriage to Carl Friedan, Betty achieved, if not understanding, then a certain triumph of truth telling. Writing in her late seventies in *Life So Far*, thirty years after the breakup, she reviewed her old situation with discomforting candor. I will quote the passage at length, because any attempted editing could alter its meaning.

> Almost every time I got ready to go to Washington, and especially when I returned, Carl and I would get into an argument and he would start beating up on me.
>
> But for reasons that are still unclear to me, I still wasn't considering divorce. I didn't confront Carl. That's the reason I've always been uneasy, politically, about the battered wife issue, because I knew from personal experience that it wasn't that simple. When it was happening to me, if I am

honest about it, I think I colluded in it. I think if I had made it clear to Carl that I would leave him if he didn't stop hitting me, he probably would have stopped. But I didn't. I know I am blaming the victim, even if the victim was me, but I think I accepted the abuse because I didn't have the nerve, somehow, to get out, or make it clear that I would get out.

Was Carl really a vicious wife-beater? Or, taunting himself as he must have when my fame became just too much, did the slightest hint of taunt from me, when we were both drinking as much as we were drinking, then every night—a martini or two before dinner and brandy after—bring out pent-up rage? Looking back on it now, I was so into what we surely call denial that I didn't want to admit how much I really enjoyed my new fame or how angry I was at Carl for not letting me enjoy it. Guilty of all that, I suppose, I taunted him into finally beating up on me and giving me those black eyes, giving us both something to feel guilty about to make up for that incredible unearned fame (unearned? I *earned* it) that he couldn't really share.

In some ways, the passage is puzzling. After all, Carl Friedan was not a magician—he was a man more sour than charming—yet he cast a spell over his wife. However one reads it, the passage has the mixture of shame, anger, tenderness, and confusion that dramatists like Tennessee Williams and Ingmar Bergman have aimed for in their work. I don't mean that it's masterly as prose, only that it's extraordinary as an act of disburdening. Betty Friedan, at times the most famous feminist in the world, admitted that she was partly complicit in her own abusive marriage. However strong she was, she may still have felt some tinge of prefeminist belief that a woman with great success deserved punishment in some way. And she seems to take responsibility for her husband's behavior as well as her own, which is absurd. When the book came out, Carl Friedan was eighty and on his third marriage (with a woman more than forty years younger than himself). In press interviews, he conceded that he was violent with Betty Friedan, but claimed he was forced into it by her bad temper. He never came close to acknowledging who he was and what had happened to him.

Men and women stay in abusive relationships to protect children, to hold on to money; they stick together because they fear failure and social disapproval, because they fear losing friends. Some stay because they have lost themselves in a labyrinth of dependency—which certainly doesn't describe

Betty Friedan. Violence in marriage is a terrible kind of attention; for some it may be better than indifference. The passage can be interpreted in many ways, but the act of writing it figures for us, her readers, as Betty Friedan's last liberation of herself. Discomforting as it is, the passage is heroic. The moralist of marriage exposes the strange, almost sickening reality of her own marriage. But she doesn't say why she failed to pull away from Carl Friedan well before she did.

THE JEWISH FEMINIST V

Back in August 1970, at the end of her speech on Strike Day, Friedan, standing before an enormous crowd in Bryant Park, said something surprising.

> In the religion of my ancestors, there was a prayer that Jewish men said every morning. They prayed, "Thank thee, Lord, that I was not born a woman." Today I feel, feel for the first time, feel absolutely sure, that all women are going to be able to say, as I say tonight: "Thank thee, Lord, that I *was* born a woman."

Notice that Friedan set the prayer in the past—there *was* a prayer. But was the prayer from *her* past? As Daniel Horowitz has pointed out, Friedan's family was not Orthodox but Reform, so it's unlikely that Betty's father or the men in the Goldstein circle made such prayers. But let's not be literal-minded. Friedan's concluding remark has tremendous force. She may have disliked public attacks on "the patriarchy," but thanking God for being born a woman was her own way of dealing a death blow to male supremacy. Friedan offered a revisionist prayer that, coming at the end of a triumphal speech, had the weight of prophecy. Whatever the patriarchal tradition of the Jews, from now on women would insist that the Lord meant women to be as worthy as men.

The remark grows in curiosity and interest because it marks for Friedan not some new separation from her Jewish roots; on the contrary, it marks a return to them. Quarreling with God—Abraham bargaining with God over his destruction of Sodom, Jacob wrestling with the angel, Job and his questions—is a Jewish tradition, both stern and playful. Friedan was quarreling not with God but with God's authorities on earth, the men who entirely dominated traditional Judaism. Theologian Judith Plaskow, in *Standing Again at Sinai* (1990), writes of Judaism's traditional silence regarding women. "Hearing silence is not easy. A silence so vast tends to fade into the natural order. . . . Over time, we learn to insert ourselves into the silences."

No Jewish woman was ever less silent than Betty Friedan. Was she consciously rebelling against the behavior expected of her—not just in her maturity but as a girl as well? Early on, she lost the most important member of her audience, her father, but she never had any trouble talking boldly to men. When she addressed the Reform rabbis in 1979, she reaffirmed her identity as a Jew ("I had this burning feeling. I had this feeling as a Jew first. First as a Jew before I had it as a woman"), but she also told the rabbis that she had never felt "alien in the male culture of Judaism at that time." It was a proud boast, and it was fully justified. She was at home among men. Feeling at home among women was sometimes a problem.

When her son Jonathan told me about her rage at anti-Semitic comments at a UN-sponsored conference in 1975, he added, "she became more conscious of her Jewish identity as she got older." The speech to the rabbis came in 1979, when Friedan was fifty-eight. In the years following, she would spend time in Torah study groups with young women in a Los Angeles synagogue and at Brandeis University. "She had a spiritual sense," Jonathan says. "She suspected that there's more going on than appears to be going on." He hints at a mystical perception of the unknown, though I can't find much evidence of that in Friedan's words. Instead, there are hints of a more sensual appreciation of life.

In middle age, she became a habitué of the Esalen Institute in California, but what she explored there—group therapy, family therapy, communal bathing (she liked public discussion of intimate problems, role-playing, mixing it up)—all of that feels more like a return of her old interest in depth psychology mixed with New Age healing and sexual curiosity. It doesn't sound like religious belief. What one does find in her later years, however, is a grander sense of her role as a Jewish woman. "I would not be the first in the history of the Jews to play the role of a visionary or prophet, a female Moses leading women out of the wilderness," she said in 1987, when she was in her early sixties. "I wouldn't be the first in our history to take a sense of injustice and apply it to the larger, human category." Betty Friedan had not only refused to be intimidated by the male tradition of authority in Judaism; in her own mind, she had joined—even replaced—one of the greatest of all Jewish leaders.

All this points to an obvious question: How did her self-assured pride as a Jew affect her endless obsession with marriage and the family—her insistence on the family's necessary place at the center of feminist thinking?

IN THE EARLY part of the twentieth century, the unpleasant fact that some immigrant Jewish husbands deserted their families was discussed as a social, rather than a personal, issue. In the Yiddish-language paper *The Forward*, published in New York, men's faces were on display from 1908 to 1914—a rogues' gallery of deserters, the *Galerie fun farshvundene mener*. The disapproval of such *mener* was joined to contempt for men who drank heavily. Alcoholism was regarded not just as a personal failing but as an attack on the family. Men who drank were not reliable providers. I can remember my gentle parents expressing their contempt for *shikers*. They weren't family men.

In this country, as many have noted, the family, not the synagogue, became the center of Jewish life. As it might have existed in Eastern Europe, or in immigrant American neighborhoods around 1900, the family was often multigenerational and patriarchal. Grandparents lived with their children; the family itself was usually dominated by the father, and some of the families were pious—the sons, or at least some of them, studied Torah and Talmud. Within these families, women, as was often said, "lived for the children," a generalization hard to swallow since it ignores the women who did not live for the children. In any case, one can say that those older families were consciously built and sustained as a place to raise the next generation. The cultural pressures were severe. In Genesis, both Sarah and Rachel are bereft without sons—they have not fulfilled their social and tribal roles as women—until God hears their anguish, and they are able to conceive. In popular prefeminist Jewish sentiment, not to be married was a refusal of a woman's role. Betty's mother, Miriam, may have had contempt for her foreign-born husband, but she still had three children with him.

Lonely in New York after the war, Betty Friedan wanted to be married, and she was delighted, at first, with her husband. In popular Jewish sentiment, not only was marriage a duty, but raising children well was an imperative. Indifference as a parent was inexcusable—hardly an exclusive Jewish sentiment, of course, but still, very much a powerful Jewish belief binding together unhappy couples, including Betty and Carl. Their misery and violence ceased when raising their kids. Betty Friedan longed to be a great mother to her brood. Among her children, Daniel would not speak to me about personal things, Jonathan was amused and ambivalent, and Emily was the most intimate.

   She recalled an exhausting tour of Italy together—"something like five cities in eight days." Betty gave many talks, and Emily, who was thirteen, usually lugged the bags. "She was so demanding and impatient that to a teenager she was embarrassing." At times, their relationship was fraught. In 1974, sitting with Betty on Barbara Walters's TV show *Not for Women Only*, Emily had said, "I don't consider myself a feminist," a tough thing for Betty to hear. She responded four years later, as Emily was entering Harvard Medical School, with a written lecture to her daughter, saying, in effect, "Don't take success for granted." They reconciled and traveled together again. In a one hundredth birthday celebration for Betty, in 2021, the Veteran Feminists of America (mainly NOW alumni) put together a video with a variety of speakers, including Emily, who spoke of Betty as her mother and a movement leader combined: "She was a formidable mother, protective and hopeful and enmeshed and exacting and impassioned and possessive, giving it strength and guidance, always sure that she knew what was best."

A WOMAN OF action, Betty Friedan was not given to introspection, so by necessity one has to speculate about her feelings. She had written a book that more than any other book sprang women, especially future young women, from the home. She had contributed to an exciting and alarming new situation in which women were struggling to decide whether to marry, whether to have children, how much of themselves to give to career, and how to balance work and motherhood. By the 1970s, as so many women struggled to find the right path, how could her own role as an activist not have affected her sense of herself? *The Second Stage*, her 1981 compilation of speeches and articles, is obsessively an argument for marriage. The repetitiveness of the book suggests a profound and unceasing emotion. I would not say she felt guilty; I would say she felt accountable. Responsibility was the true north of her moral compass, and the new troubled situation for women was partly her doing.

In her later life and writings, she tried to reconcile the commanding traditions of the Jewish family with feminism's vaunting desire that women leave the home and conquer the world. As far as she could see, lesbianism was a threat to the family; childless devotion to career was another threat. She was pulled in two directions. Jewish ethical ardency carried her forward through her writing, her organizing, her speeches; at the same time, Judaism, as she understood it, affected her view of women's responsibilities. Her egocentric version of *tikkun olam*, her need to predominate in a movement that disdained predominance, cut her off from younger women in the movement. Since she did not cite Jewish tradition in these matters, her insistence, for those women, seemed merely irritable, obsessional, and cranky. Judaism as she understood it made her a leader but, in the end, Judaism, again as she interpreted it and acted on it, narrowed her sympathies and loosened her grip on leadership. The ironies are wounding.

But consider Betty Friedan at her ideal best: she would be both the new Moses, leading women out of the wilderness, and the new Jewish mother—not the overbearing panic-stricken hysteric of a hundred jokes ("Until they die themselves, they *clean* and *kill* . . . they *clean* and *kill*"), but a modern warrior-mother free to come and go, giving of herself equally to the world and to her home. Women, she was sure, could find freedom as world beaters; they could find freedom as mothers who worked; they could find freedom when in love with a man. They could nurture children without regret. She was sure that there were many ways for women to feel good about themselves.

HAPPY ENDING I

Betty Friedan never stopped working, and, after her divorce from Carl in 1969, she sought as much companionship and pleasure as she could find. "The pseudo-radicals in the liberation movement say that women should go to bed alone until after the revolution succeeds," she told the *Times* on March 23, 1970. "That's for the birds!" For a few summers, starting in 1970, there was a roving "commune" in the Hamptons (Sagaponack one year, Wainscott the next) in which Betty and a group of friends—including divorced men and women from the Manhattan media world, assorted intellectuals, and business executives—rented houses, debated policy and ideas, and drank together. "It was a time," Emily told me, "when families inheriting large homes could not afford their upkeep, so they rented them out." Betty and her friends didn't want to buy, so they took advantage of the situation. She wanted community but—big surprise—did little of the necessary housekeeping. Other people could make chicken salad.

After 1978, she had her own house in Sag Harbor, the lovely Long Island village just north of Bridgehampton. She spent a lot of time there with friends and children (and later grandchildren). All through the seventies she had a serious love affair with a married professor who taught at Boston University, David Manning White. She took White with her when she gave talks in Alaska and in Vienna, and on several occasions his longtime wife, Catherine, whom he had no intention of divorcing, came along with them. After the affair with White broke up, Betty, in her seventies, vamped men of appropriate age at parties. Her energy, her appetite for experience, her need for men never flagged.

And she partway reconciled with her mother, Miriam, who, it turned out, had married and buried two more husbands after Harry Goldstein. Settled in Leisure World, an assisted living community in Orange County, California, Miriam in old age had taken up horseback riding and was running bridge tournaments and selling health products out of her home. In her own way, she had achieved if not liberation then at least usefulness and pleasure. With multiple things to manage, she was happy. Betty had become a feminist partly in opposition to this cold and censorious woman, and for years they had little contact. But by the end, Betty understood how much of her mother's manner was caused by the disappointment of her hopes. In *Life So Far*, she writes with stiff admiration of Miriam nearing the end: "I had come to some sort of peace with my mother in our later years. I greatly admired her courage and her determined energy to live well right up to the moment that the structure [which sustained her] was taken away from her." Miriam died, at the age of ninety, on April 4, 1988.

IN 1993, AFTER ten years of work, Friedan published *The Fountain of Age*, her defense and celebration of aging, a process that had been slandered, she said, by specialists and the culture at large. The elderly were in fact being subjected to a new "mystique," an assumption of weakness, and they had to fight it as assertively as they could. A Jewish woman's work is never done. Betty wrote a short book, *Beyond Gender*, in 1997, in which she recapitulated and renewed her demands for a "new paradigm" for work and family life. And in 2000 she published her autobiography, *Life So Far*, which she wrote, she said, out of dissatisfaction with the unauthorized biographies of herself that had already appeared, including excellent books by Daniel Horowitz and Judith Hennessee, both of which, she claimed, were "in large or small part false, mistaken, sensational, and trivializing." Her own book is sometimes detailed and revealing (I've quoted from it here and there), sometimes maddeningly evasive and vague.

She worked and traveled into her eighties and was seen, in Sag Harbor, driving around town, very slowly. "She had a beat-up car," Emily Friedan told me, "because she knew she would beat it up." In 2001, she turned eighty, and her old friends Dr. Shepard Aronson and his wife Muriel Fox, Betty's colleague when NOW was formed, decided to give her a birthday party. The couple had rented a house in Puerto Vallarta on the Pacific coast of Mexico, and Betty flew there for the event. "She came alone, and she had to change flights, and I was a little worried about her," Muriel told me. "But she got there all right. In town, we were crossing a street—we were going to watch the whales from a boat—and I took Betty's arm. 'Fuck off, Muriel,' she said."

On February 4, 2006, in Washington, DC, on her eighty-fifth birthday, Betty Friedan died of congestive heart failure. Hillary Clinton told a reporter, "She defined the problem, and then she had the courage to do something about it."

HAPPY ENDING II

If she were alive, Betty would approve of the advances women have made in education, wages, and politics. As has been established by Nobel laureate Claudia Goldin in her 2006 study "The Quiet Revolution That Transformed Women's Employment, Education, and Family," American women, after the seventies, were beginning to see their careers as men did, marrying later and recognizing work as a key part of their identity (all ideas proposed earlier by Betty). Betty, in her rasping voice, would have demanded that women be paid as men are paid, not (in the current situation) eighty-three cents for every dollar a man makes.

Educated women, in some cases the first in their families to go to college, are now often doing well. Working-class women, however, are struggling to get by. The Left-ideological feminist critique of marriage as the prison house of women's hopes has run into a hard economic fact: given that many of the men they know have been dropped from industrial jobs or have low-paying service jobs, many working-class women cannot afford to get married, a situation that Betty regarded with greater and greater sympathy. Emily Friedan told me that in her later years, "Betty did think that families came in all sorts of configurations. I don't think she was specifically thinking of gay parents at that time but more of single-parent families, multigeneration families, divorced families, and one of her favorites, 'family by choice.' Families with same-sex parents would have been another of the variations." In other words, as long as people are having children and raising them with other parents, Betty would have accepted the many variations on the traditional nuclear family. Her long obsession with traditional marriage had faded.

Feminism goes through alternating waves of forward and backward movement, both sometimes occurring at once—a surge in the 2010s was accompanied, silently, by Republican efforts in state legislatures to limit abortion, and not at all silently by Donald Trump's appointment of conservative justices to the Supreme Court, leading to the 2022 *Dobbs* decision that overturned *Roe v. Wade*. Anti-feminism will always be a passion of men afraid of losing control. They may succeed for a while, but I don't think it's naive to assert that the anger of women and young voters in general will overcome them.

Stephanie Coontz, in *A Strange Stirring*, her 2011 book on *The Feminine Mystique*, writes that the revolution would have happened without Betty Friedan. A decade later, Louis Menand, in his chapter on Friedan and feminism in *The Free World*, implies the same thing. But these counterfactuals are mostly demeaning and beside the point. The point surely is that it happened *with* her. And that accomplishment can never be taken away from her.

3

NORMAN MAILER AND THE END
OF SHAME

MIDDLE-CLASS JEWISH BOY AT WAR

When Norman Mailer was inducted into the US Army in March 1944, he was twenty-one years old, a freshly married Harvard graduate, a slight young man of five feet seven inches and one hundred thirty-five pounds. In the previous few years, he had published some stories and composed a play and two novels (one of them published as *A Transit to Narcissus* in 1978). Even as a student, he thought of himself as a professional writer, and from the day Japan attacked Pearl Harbor in December 1941, he had wanted to write a big book about the war.

He was sent for basic training to Fort Bragg, North Carolina, where many of the men were from Pennsylvania, the South, and the Upper Midwest. Mailer was from middle-class Brooklyn; he had landed in the great working-class Gentile world and was eager to observe. He interrogated the recruits about their sex lives, taking notes on a yellow legal pad (he discovered that many of them did not believe in foreplay). Mailer knew that tough Jews served in the war, including criminals, louts, and bitterly determined, hardworking men, but Mailer was a Jew without physical skills. He had never worked a thresher, or manhandled heavy goods into a truck, or toyed with his father's jalopy—or any of the other things a poor country or city boy might have done.

FOR SEVERAL WEEKS in January 1945, Mailer sat around in a sweaty, foul-smelling troopship off the coast of Luzon, the largest of the Philippine islands. General Douglas MacArthur had landed with an enormous invasion force, and Mailer finally went ashore on January 27. A rifleman, he was thrown into the 112th Cavalry regiment out of North Texas, a former National Guard unit that had been federalized in 1940. The 112th had been through almost three years of combat in the Pacific, and many men in the unit had died. Mailer described those who remained as hardened, a little crazy, and physically messed up—some with jungle rot and open ulcers. The Texans were joined by men from other parts of the country, some of them bar fighters and casual anti-Semites (not by theory but by habit). "I didn't open my mouth for six months in that outfit," he later wrote.

"A nice Jewish boy from Brooklyn"—that was the one image of himself that Mailer famously said was "absolutely insupportable." It was insupportable because, for a while, it was true. A picture of him in uniform from early in his service reveals a young man with sweet lips, large ears, a gentle gaze. He did indeed write his big book, *The Naked and the Dead*, finishing it in 1948, and the novel presents a fascinating paradox: a tough, even pessimistic work, filled with an almost sordid sensuality—muck and detestable odors, bodily discomforts and mutilations, the tedium, exhilarations, and cruelties of an army fighting in the jungle—it was also a book that perhaps only a nice Jewish boy could have written; a nice Jewish boy, that is, in flight from his background.

After the war, his flight continued. In the 1950s, step by step, as doggedly as another puny American, Theodore Roosevelt, Mailer began transforming himself into a barrel-chested macho—a man six times married, the father of eight children (he also helped raise a stepson), the author of more than forty books, some of them American classics (*The Armies of the Night*, from 1968, and the supremely abundant and sympathetic "true-life novel" *The Executioner's Song*, from 1979), some of them clogged and all but unreadable. Attentive and sweet-natured much of the time (his letters to friends and even strangers are generously supportive), a social thinker allied (for a while) with New York political and literary intellectuals, he held forth for five decades on the state of the nation's soul. But this American-style prophet brawled and head-butted at parties; at one time or another, he was decked, hammered, billy clubbed, his eye gouged, his ear bitten. He believed that physical courage was necessary equipment for a great writer (Hemingway was the model) and that Jewish men in particular had to overcome all sorts of weakness. "In the first week / of their life / male jews / are crucified," he wrote in one of his poems.

An egotist of a peculiarly self-afflicting sort, he sailed into absurdities as if only reckless abandon could save him from his obsession—cancer, which he imagined as punishment for the timid. His recklessness also betrayed him into an abominable act: at the end of a drunken party in 1960, he twice stabbed Adele Morales, his second wife and the mother of two of his children. Morales lived to the age of ninety, but the assault will always be unforgivable. "I let God down," Mailer later said to Betsy Mailer, one of his daughters with Adele.

For good and for ill, that was the Mailer the world knew for over fifty years. Before he was done, he had exhausted nearly everyone. His genius, his follies, his love for America, his disgust with America, his wives, his mistresses, his Jewishness and anti-Jewishness, his gentleness and belligerence—there was too much of him to allow normal comprehension, and many gave up trying. When he died in 2007, at the age of eighty-four, his work and temperament seemed far from the preoccupations of many Americans; his reputation was at a low ebb. In particular, Mailer's reactionary sexual politics, expressed at length in the rapturously composed but morally fatuous polemic *The Prisoner of Sex* (1971)—perhaps the only defense of male chauvinism worth reading—has been at the center of searing critiques of the writer for a half century.

Yet he was a great American, extraordinary in the fecundity of his reinventions. Apart from *The Naked and the Dead* and *The Executioner's Song*, he was not a major novelist (such is the consensus view), but he wrote indelible essays and books on politics, literature, space exploration, movies, boxing, the Kennedy assassination, and much else. And for all his apostasies and rebellions, he was very much an American Jew, indifferent to the biblical Yahweh who thundered at Moses "I AM THAT I AM" but proudly attendant upon his own invention, a weakened God, unable to save the Jews in the Holocaust, a God who needed man's help. Mailer was there to help. Along with Vladimir Nabokov, Isaac Bashevis Singer, Flannery O'Connor, and Ralph Ellison; Toni Morrison, Saul Bellow, Philip Roth, Joan Didion, and Don DeLillo, he was the most talented American prose writer of the postwar years.

HE WAS BORN in Long Branch, New Jersey, on January 31, 1923, as Nachem Malech Mailer, which became Norman Kingsley Mailer (*melech* means "king" in Hebrew). His ancestry was Lithuanian Jewish on both sides. His maternal grandfather, Hyman Schneider, grew up near Vilnius, and trained as a rabbi in Volozhin. Arriving in the States in 1891 (his wife came later), Hyman Schneider worked as a newsstand operator in Manhattan and as a peddler in rural New Jersey, eventually opening a grocery store in Long Branch, a resort town on the coast. A humorous and tough-minded man, he read Torah at night, sometimes right through the night, and held forth as an informal religious authority while insisting that "rabbis are all *schnorrers*." The combination of obsession and skepticism was something Mailer inherited. In Long Branch, on the beach, Hyman's children went into the hotel business.

On the paternal side, Mailer's father, Isaac Barnett Mailer, also born near Vilnius, moved with his family to South Africa in 1900, where he served in the British Army during the First World War. In America, he spoke with a punctilious English accent. Barney Mailer was a strange bird—a mock-Brit Jew, formally dressed, a bit of a dandy even, an elaborately masked personality, ceremonious, polite, and duplicitous. An accountant by trade, he was also a passionate gambler, frequently in debt and away from home.

Barney was probably the source of Norman's insistent self-creation, his fatal way of dropping into redneck and other mangled accents in his public speeches. For all his faults, Barney Mailer had a mutinous streak that his son admired; an intermittent but powerful bond existed between them.

Barney married Hyman Schneider's youngest child, Fanny, in 1922. The couple lived on the Jersey coast but eventually moved to Crown Heights, in Brooklyn—the neighborhood east of Prospect Park that was then a central landing place for immigrant Jewish families on the way up. At home in Crown Heights, Fanny, a loving, physically capable woman, raised Mailer and his sister Barbara while managing a home-oil delivery company by telephone. The Jewish-folkloric combination of weak father and strong mother evidently benefited Fanny's son, who drew power from the love of his family through a seventy-year writing career.

All through his early boyhood, Mailer was surrounded by adoring women—not just his mother and sister, but also his New Jersey aunts and the neighborhood ladies, who lauded the studious child. Slight, with neatly parted hair and protruding ears (he looked like *Mad* magazine's Alfred E. Neuman), he was a quiet and obedient boy, too preoccupied with study to spend much time among the neighborhood *bonditts*, with their pranks and their passion for stickball. He built model airplanes, some of them extremely impressive, and spent his summers with his sister Barbara in one or another of the Long Branch hotels owned by his aunts. In a spare room, he wrote fiction.

IN SEPTEMBER 1939, Mailer, sixteen years old, showed up at Harvard sporting an outfit of orange-striped blue trousers, gold jacket, and saddle shoes. He was as ignorant of ruling-class undergraduates and the social rituals of the college as he would be of the habits of working-class Americans five years later. The clothes were soon discarded, though some of his regular laundry was sent home, washed by the family's Black maid, and mailed back. At school, in his first year, he ate dinner with other Jewish boys at the Freshman Union and began to feel his way around. Until the end of his sophomore year, he lived almost entirely within the protected boundaries of the American Jewish middle class.

Latin was a prerequisite for Harvard English majors at the time. He had never studied it, so he became an engineering major, learning much that would serve him well when he reconstructed the liftoff of the Saturn V rocket in *Of a Fire on the Moon* (1970), his impassioned report on the Apollo 11 moon landing. His major occupation at school was reading, particularly the American realists he discovered as a freshman—James T. Farrell (the Studs Lonigan trilogy), John Dos Passos (the USA trilogy), John Steinbeck (*The Grapes of Wrath*). Faulkner, Fitzgerald, and Thomas Wolfe came later, and, of course, Hemingway, who apart from his greatness as a writer served for years as Mailer's (distant) spiritual mentor. Hemingway's hunting, fishing, and boxing, his war exploits, his courageous and soulful physicality—boastful yet wounded—bore little resemblance to the habits of Crown Heights Jews. Mailer fell in love.

His problem as a writer, as he well knew, was a simple lack of experience. Escaping from Harvard's rich preppies and ambitious Jews, he journeyed around in the MTA, taking notes on working-class behavior, clothes, and accents. In the summer after his sophomore year, he left his hotel room on the Jersey shore with only a few dollars in his pocket, hitchhiking his way down to North Carolina, sleeping out at night. Voluntarily, and for only a brief period, he became that familiar Depression-era figure, a hobo. When he returned home, Fanny was not amused and made him take off his filthy clothes before entering the apartment.

His lack of sexual experience was particularly mortifying. "You bore a standard of shame," he later said of himself and his friends. But he at least lost his physical inhibitions. He played house football in front of Clavery Hall and later Dunster House and loved the bone-jarring contact. In his junior year, at a Boston Symphony concert, he met Beatrice ("Bea") Silverman, a very lively music major attending Boston University. She was argumentative, a passionate lefty, and a proto-feminist; she was also profane, and, in the appreciative slang of the day, "earthy." They carried on in the mattressed trunk of a Chevy convertible given to Mailer by his uncle and, at Dunster, they became famous for their love making in Mailer's dorm room. Bea would talk dirty in front of his friends; they were both showing off. They got secretly married in January 1944. His draft notice arrived a few weeks later.

MAILER WAS AN ordinary soldier, in no way heroic. At first, working at headquarters in Luzon, he typed reports, laid wire, built a shower for officers. Humiliated and bored, he pulled himself together and volunteered for a reconnaissance squad. He went on twenty-five patrols, many of them for fifteen miles, and he finally saw some combat—nothing much, as he admitted, but he knew what it was like to climb up a damp, rocky hill in the heat while bearing a rifle, ammunition, grenades, two canteens, a steel helmet, perhaps forty pounds in all. His real job was to see the worst and make an account of it. He wrote long letters to Bea (who had joined the WAVES), some of them detailed and harrowing. He was not just creating his book—working on it as it happened to him—but creating himself as a man. In February 1945, he entered a Japanese-held town that the Americans had overwhelmed with artillery and tanks.

> Right before us was a destroyed Japanese armored half-track and a tank. The vehicles were still smoldering, and the driver of the half track had half fallen out, his head which was crushed from one ear to the jaw lay reclining on the running board, and pitiful remaining leg thrust tensely through the windshield. The other leg lay near his head on the ground, and a little smoke was still arising from his chest. Another Japanese lay on his back a short distance away with a great hole in his intestines which bunched out in a thick white cluster like a coiled white garden hose.

> After a half hour or so we descended to the road, and mounted the Jeep again. As we drove along the road the destruction was complete. Fragments of the corrugated steel from the warehouses had landed everywhere, and the wreckage formed almost a pattern on the road. Everything stunk, and everything, the road, the wreckage, the mutilated vehicles had become the two colors of conflagration—the rust red and the black. The whole vista was of destroyed earth and materiel—that battlefield looked like a hybrid between a junk-yard and a charnel house.

Amazement contends with disgust: war meant the destruction of the body's unity, the collapse of physical structure, color, intactness.

After the Japanese surrendered in August 1945, Mailer became part of the American force occupying the home islands. He worked mainly as an army cook, which he enjoyed. Promoted to sergeant, he sent his family a picture of himself in uniform looking much older than in his earlier photos—now darkly handsome, with squared shoulders and a full head of hair in the style of actor John Garfield, a Jewish movie idol. But soon after that picture was taken, he got into a humiliating quarrel with a superior and decided to give back his stripes. He left the army in 1946 as a private, after a little more than two years of service. He and Bea settled down in Brooklyn and in Provincetown, on the upper end of Cape Cod. He wrote *The Naked and the Dead* at the rate of five thousand words a week, finishing in about fifteen months, though he subsequently added and rewrote sections. The book, published in May 1948, received rave reviews and was an overnight bestseller, remaining on the *Times* list for over a year. The Brooklyn Jewish boy was no longer abashed, no longer inadequate, and certainly no longer quiet.

THE NAKED AND THE DEAD is set on the fictional island of Anopopei, a kidney-shaped blob in the Pacific with trackless vegetation and withering wet heat—and thousands of Japanese defenders (who hardly figure in the novel). Mailer never tells us how the Anopopei campaign fits into American strategy. The absence is intentional: strategy is left to officers, who, in Mailer's estimate, are mostly ambitious, self-important stiffs. What matters most is the day-by-day life of fourteen soldiers in a reconnaissance platoon, men who find themselves trapped in the obsessions of two pathological egotists—the island commander, General Edward Cummings, a MacArthur-like military intellectual who thinks that men can be controlled only through fear; and, at the platoon level, Sergeant Sam Croft, a nerveless warrior who "could not have said . . . where his hands ended and the machine gun began." Killing, for Croft, seems no more than a natural expression of his being. In a limited way, he's intensely admirable. Writing to Bea, Mailer described the actual platoon leader whom Croft was based on—"the archetype of all the dark, bitter, inarticulate & capable men that America spawns." At that point in Mailer's life, capability meant a great deal.

He wrote a terrifying combat scene (units directly firing at each other across a river at night), but much of the novel chronicles the routine work of an army at war—unloading supplies, building a road, "harsh eventless days" followed by such exertions as pulling 37 mm anti-tank guns across a rooted jungle path in darkness. In the central action of the novel, General Cummings sends the platoon on a recon mission that turns out to be foolish, even superfluous, and Croft, ready to test himself, willingly carries it out, sacrificing men along the way. He tries to take the platoon over the island's big mountain—Anaka, which he thinks of as *his* mountain, as Ahab thinks of the whale. But somewhere near the peak, he stumbles into a hornets' nest, and the enraged insects cause the men to throw away their packs and rifles and scatter down the slope like children. Cummings's regular infantry, under the command of a mediocre officer (Cummings is away), wipes out the remaining Japanese garrison. The overall emotion of the novel is one of futility. Accident, not strategy, rules the events.

In 1960, looking back on the book, Mailer described his state of mind in a letter to his friend the literary critic Diana Trilling. "There is no meaning but the present," he wrote. "So of course I could do *The Naked and the Dead*. I had no past to protect, no habits to hold on to, no style to defend. My infirmity is that I had no emotional memory." This is an attempt at mythmaking. What he actually meant by "no emotional memory" was no memory he was proud of. Henry Roth in *Call It Sleep* (1934) and Alfred Kazin in *A Walker in the City* (1951) had done a great deal with the furtive behavior of a Jewish boy on the New York streets. Mailer may have believed that he was no more than a blank slate with senses, but he drew heavily on the American realists, especially Dos Passos, influences he reconstructed as his own version of wartime naturalism, piling up endless physical detail and moments of emotional suffering.

MAILER PUT A lot of the 112th Cavalry and his other mates into the fourteen platoon guys. As we discover in lengthy, bristling flashbacks, many of them have been knocking around in Depression America, working on farms, in stores, in ordinary jobs, or not working much at all. Vaguely rebellious yet defeated, they are callous and cynical about women while desperately needing women; they are routinely contemptuous of "Yids" and "Izzies." Mailer, perhaps unconsciously, saw the men from the point of view of his family and his family's friends—the vantage of successful middle-class urban Jews. Most of these guys aren't going anywhere. *The Naked and the Dead* has some courageous fighters, some generous acts, much endurance, but it has neither heroes nor innocent men. No one has any illusions to lose, which might be described as the ultimate condition of naturalist fiction.

For all Mailer's hard knowledge of failure, his prose is little like that of his hero Hemingway—not spare and stoical, with a strong lyrical pulse, but abrupt, obsessional, and grimly material. Two of the men attempt to carry a wounded buddy out of the jungle and back to safety, and Mailer unleashes the enduring achievement of the book, his portrayal of the male body at the outer edge of fatigue.

> Through the afternoon the litter-bearers continued on their march. About two o'clock it began to rain, and the ground quickly became muddy. The rain at first was a relief; they welcomed it on their blazing flesh, wriggled their toes in the slosh that permeated their boots. The wetness of their clothing was pleasurable. They enjoyed being cold for a few minutes. But as the rain continued the ground became too soft, and their uniforms cleaved uncomfortably to their bodies, their feet began to slip in the mud, and their shoes became weighted with muck and stuck in the ground with each step. They were too fagged to notice the difference immediately, their bodies had quickly resumed the stupor of the march, but by half an hour they had slowed down almost to a halt. Their legs had lost almost all puissance; for minutes they would stand virtually in place, unable to co-ordinate their thighs and feet to move forward. . . . The sun came out again, inflamed the wet kunai grass and dried the earth whose moisture rose in sluggish clouds of mist. The men gasped, took useless gasps of the leaden wet air, and shambled forward grunting and sobbing, their arms slowly and inevitably bending toward the ground.

On a bad day, a soldier may know every wretchedness of skin, lungs, arms, legs, bowels, kidneys. *The Naked and the Dead* is repetitive but at times very moving. As Mailer's letters to Bea reveal, he was shocked by the spilling corpses, the breakdown of physical distinction. But his writing about the male body amounts to a full-throated humanist response: the body under stress is heroic; consciousness remains intact, and the body lives in its wholeness even when vibrating with pain.

The two Jews in the platoon, Roth and Goldstein, struggle especially hard for dignity—an obvious point of concern for Mailer, who had his own anxieties to resolve. Roth has been to City College in New York; he's married, but he's not getting anywhere, an irritable guy, snobby, morose, too weak to survive—clearly Mailer's disapproving version of himself.

The other Jewish character, Goldstein, has greater physical and moral strength. Goldstein, along with Ridges, a very serious Christian, bears the body out of the jungle, and the words of medieval sage Judah Halevi jump into his head—"Israel is the heart of all nations." Goldstein's consciousness as a Jew keeps him from letting go, for if he fails, the men will think badly of him, badly of the Jews. In the character of Goldstein, Mailer's fear that he was not tough enough for the army gets resolved in a portrait of formidable staying power.

In his own life, everything was a test for him; everything he could put his body and spirit through was a test. He was sure he needed to escape not only the traps of his soft middle-class Jewish background but also the traps of postwar America—the desire for "security," the endless consumerism, and what he took to be the country's humiliating spiritual mediocrity. He had made himself into a novelist in the Pacific, and now he brought the war home. For the author of *The Naked and the Dead*, the truce never arrived.

THE JEWISH BODY

Did the immigrant Jews and their children—the generation of Mailer's parents—think of the body in such dramatic fashion? They certainly worried about health. In cities like New York and Chicago, diseases such as influenza, diphtheria, and scarlet fever were a terror for their children. If those children flourished into middle age, they regarded health as a moral victory. The immigrants and their children took pleasure in dancing and swimming, the men had sports and the *shvitz* bath—but the body itself, the *body*? Few thought of it in dramatic terms as a theater of pleasure and pain, an arena of heroism and failure. The entire subject made many Jews feel squeamish. In this and in so many ways, Mailer ran against the values of middle-class families descended from Russian and Eastern European immigrants. It's not as if there weren't any lawless, pleasure-seeking Jews. But even if one acknowledges the embezzling husband with an office mistress, the Jewish swindlers and gangsters (the bravos of Murder, Inc. and the *Undzer Shtik*)—even as one acknowledges the Jewish *shtunks* and worse—one has to say that most such families, eager for success in America, were cautious in their physical behavior.

Traditional Jewish morality was devoted to thou shalt not; Mailer was devoted to thou shalt. The children of immigrants abhorred drunkenness (a weakness of the *goyim*, they believed), and Mailer drank heavily; they admired reasonableness and feared violence, and he battled with his fists and forehead and was fascinated by boxers, murderers, and spies; they were often sexually reticent, and he was promiscuous; they retired to Miami, and he loathed Miami; they were realists and philosophical materialists (they believed, most of them, in the here and now and the sensuous world—the excited rush of New York or Chicago at night, the warming sands of tropical beaches), and he was obsessed with magic, the Devil, and karma. A psychoanalyst would say that by fighting middle-class Jewish habits so hard, he was, in his way, reaffirming them.

His emotions were complicated. He wanted to be known as "a writer," not "a Jewish writer," and because he mostly avoided Jewish themes and characters, at least on the surface, he was rarely mentioned at the time with the inescapable fifties and sixties trio of Saul Bellow, Bernard Malamud, and Philip Roth. "If you want a menorah-and-gefilte-fish Judaism," his friend Mashey Bernstein said to me, "you won't get it from Mailer." He hated the softness of *Yiddishkeit*; he escaped the "nice Jewish boy" by inventing the bad Jewish boy.

But if he was at home, spiritually, with outsiders and criminals, he admired at the same time the Jewish literary intellectuals who were among his friends in New York when he was a young man. In the last year of his life, 2007, he was asked, "What role has your being Jewish played in your being a writer?" and he answered, with great heat, "It played an enormous role. When you're born a Jew . . . it's almost impossible to take anything for granted. . . . We're here to do all sorts of outrageous thinking, incisive, fine thinking. If the Jews have brought anything to human nature, they developed the mind more than other people did." Almost twenty years earlier, he told his friend Bob Lucid, "I grew up with this idea that Jews were beleaguered and were people living on the edge of great peril."

Peril needed to be confronted with intellectual and physical effort. He interpreted that responsibility in his own way, by turning the habits and the ethos of his tribe inside out, creating a counter-morality of risk and appetite. The ways in which he was and wasn't Jewish run through his eighty-four years like a musical motif binding together an enormous symphony.

TOUGH ACT TO FOLLOW

In 1959, Mailer brought out *Advertisements for Myself*, a strange and won-derful mélange of essays, stories, poems, and commentary, in which he tried to create himself as both a public figure and a tormented private man. The different pieces in the anthology were written throughout the fifties, in the wake of *The Naked and the Dead*, and Mailer arranged them in groups and surrounded them with self-analysis, deploring and praising his state of mind when each group in the collection was written. He pleads for understanding of his most destructive and exalted moods, including greed, lust, envy, and, especially, infinite ambition. The book teased and then violated every notion of proper literary behavior; it had the self-delighting energy of outrage.

He candidly admitted that the tremendous success of his war novel put him in a difficult situation. He wasn't frightened as much as baffled. He not only insisted, as he told Diana Trilling, that he had no past he could draw on, he discovered that he could no longer observe the world unnoticed, as he had in the army. Now people looked at *him*. He had little choice, he said, "but to force myself to step into the war of the enormous present, to accept the private heat and fatigue of setting out by myself to cut a track through the new wild." The new wild was not a jungle patrol with a group of pals and jerk-offs but the literary thickets of New York and perhaps his own inchoate ambitions.

> If I had once been a cool observer because some part of me knew that I had more emotion than most and must protect myself with a cold eye, now I had to guard against arousing the emotions of others, particularly since I had a strong conscience, and a strong desire to do just that. . . . What could ambush me and did was the violence aroused in others by rip-ping into their secret places; they resented it precisely as they would have resented outrageous bad manners.

This is what Mailer *thought* he was doing—getting into people's faces in order to protect his gift. Yet nothing he set down in *Advertisements* could explain what he actually did in 1960 soon after writing these words—attack his second wife, Adele Morales, with a penknife, almost killing her. Despite the good essays and stories collected in *Advertisements*, the fifties had been terrible in many ways for Mailer, and the stabbing was a most terrible act. How could he be blind to the possible consequences of "ripping into [people's] secret places"? Norman the ripper. One must go back to the beginnings of the decade and look for intimations of disaster as well as for many acts of intellectual bravery.

IN MAY 1948, after Mailer finished writing and revising *The Naked and the Dead*, he and Bea moved to Paris. He took courses at the Sorbonne, worked on his French, visited Chartres and Mont-Saint-Michel. He read a great deal and made a friendship that would last for decades.

Jean Malaquais was a Polish Jew who had arrived in France in the 1920s (his parents almost definitely died in the Holocaust). He worked as a laborer in the French mines and fought (like George Orwell) in the anti-Stalinist POUM brigade in the Spanish Civil War. Malaquais had written highly praised political fiction; he had worked as a secretary for André Gide and was known to Stalin's chief foe Leon Trotsky. An intellectually weathered Marxist, he made Mailer read Marx and, at the same time, disabused him of any remaining affection for Soviet Communism. Malaquais's certitude about left politics irritated almost everyone. He would not stop talking. Fanny Mailer, for one, was astonished by the man's arrogant presence in the family; she thought he was a sponger. Yet Mailer revered him and kept him close for decades as his teacher and critic—his own private Jewish intellectual.

In France, Norman waited for the publication of his first book with something like serenity, interrupted only by his successful fight to prevent his publisher (Rinehart) from removing "fug" and other bits of army profanity. ("Fug" was itself a compromise. That such objections existed at all now seems ridiculous.) He returned to New York in May 1948, only after the reviews for the book began to appear. Suppressing his impulse to straighten out the reviewers (even the many favorable critics, he thought, misrepresented what he was doing), he escaped to the New England countryside, spelled by periods of campaigning for Henry Wallace, who had been Roosevelt's vice president from 1940 to 1944. In 1948, Wallace ran a leftish third-party campaign for president—a candidacy, Mailer said, that offered the only hope of preventing still another world war, this time set off by the rivalry of the United States and the Soviet Union (Malaquais accused Norman of naivete). Wallace went nowhere, but by 1949, at the age of twenty-six, Mailer had become a figure among political intellectuals of New York.

He remained close to his family, going home for dinner on Fridays, but his marriage with Bea was in trouble. He was a slender, well-knit young man with blue eyes and a delicate long face suggestive of melancholy and amusement (that familiar gazing-into-the-apocalypse look, with its aura of potent calculation, came later). Young women openly flirted with him in front of Bea; he was available, he fooled around, and she undoubtedly knew it. Friends and family noticed that her speech, always brazen about sex, was actually becoming coarse, almost boastful, as if she could hold her husband with language as she was losing him in bed. In some ways, as a friend of Mailer noticed, she had become a caricature of her husband. The same fate would also envelope Adele Morales, his second wife.

In 1949, Mailer made his first trip to Hollywood—with Bea, who was pregnant, and also with Malaquais and his wife. Mailer wanted to sell *The Naked and the Dead* to the movies, and in general to make the scene. He and Malaquais (an unlikely Hollywood writer) met with producers, including the legendary Samuel Goldwyn, and they took money to draft what sounds like a very unpromising script. It went nowhere, and Mailer returned the money. In all, it was a futile time professionally, though Mailer the hot young novelist in town was much in demand. Charlie Chaplin came to his Christmas party; so did John Huston, John Ford, Humphrey Bogart, Marlon Brando, and the young Shelley Winters. And yet, as he later admitted in *Advertisements for Myself*, even as he enjoyed the attention, he was in deep trouble, unnerved by feelings of inauthenticity, even shame, and a gathering fear of failure. At the end of the Christmas party, according to Shelley Winters, Marlon Brando, heading for the door, stopped and said, "Norman, what the fuck are you doing here? You're not a screenwriter. Why aren't you on a farm in Vermont writing your next novel?"

Brando may have noticed Mailer's anxiety. But Norman was actually working hard, even in California, finishing his second novel, *Barbary Shore*, in 1951. All along he had severe doubts about it. He was right to have doubts: the book is set in a void and feels like it was composed in a void. The characters are a repentant American Communist (a Russian spy), a distraught and highly sexual Trotskyite woman, and a vicious government agent, all stewing in their own juices in a Brooklyn boardinghouse. The hero, who watches these three and stews quite a bit himself, is something of a cipher: wounded in the war, he has amnesia—an admission, perhaps, of Mailer's inability to find an identity and a voice for himself. *Barbary Shore* was Mailer's Malaquais novel, a bitter footnote to Mailer's interest in the Stalinist and Trotskyite factionalist struggles in the American Left. It baffled and bored a lot of people and was both a critical and commercial failure. In a twist of the knife, Malaquais disliked it.

Bea, depressed and casting around for a vocation, tried writing fiction and took up painting; she was also working on a proto-feminist text of her own (never finished). Mailer suggested she become a doctor, and she eventually did become a psychiatrist. The Mailers had a little girl, Susan, but Norman, restless, his freedom curtailed, was far too young to be a husband and father. In *Advertisements*, he tried to account for his mood after the failure of *Barbary Shore*.

> I suppose I might have learned to take my return ticket to the minor leagues without weeping too much into the beer, except I was plagued by an odd intuition: what I sensed (to my deep depression) was that I was working my way toward saying something unforgivable, enough so that most readers were already agitated—or what is worse—bored, by their quick uneasy sense that my vision—what little I had of it—was leading toward the violent and the orgiastic.

He wasn't just speaking of literary ambition; his life was running toward extremes. In 1951, Mailer was introduced to Adele Morales, a beautiful Latina often described as "fiery"—a kind of Brooklyn Carmen, an instinctively honest woman with ready judgment but not much education or social ability. She painted in an abstract expressionist style and worked as a papier-mâché artist for department store display windows. With Adele, Mailer said, sex was intense and even dangerous. "There was this feeling that it was never under her control. There was a power that took her over."

LIVING-ROOM BATTLEFIELD

He and Bea broke up (she needed to get away from him), and Mailer and Adele moved first to one and then another ungainly space on the Lower East Side—not to the fabled Jewish immigrant neighborhood of Delancey

Street but *way* downtown, in bad neighborhoods near the bridges across the East River. Mailer fixed each place up, installing new plumbing himself, and eventually threw a big party in his reconditioned apartment so Adele could meet his friends. Again, famous actors showed up, as well as artists, intellectuals, and journalists. Late in the party, some local thugs walked in, got into an argument with Mailer, and began attacking him with a hammer. Bloodied and dazed, he fought back until Adele and some of the guests pushed them out.

In the fifties, the hard-drinking party was as central to New York intellectual and artistic life as libraries, museums, little magazines, galleries, agents, and publishing houses. No matter how seriously one worked, there was, in the avant-garde, an almost ideological drive, or at least a psychological necessity, to act freely, even badly, as a strike against hated conformity. Yet violence was rare enough and particularly anathema to the postwar Jews, who had miserable feelings about bully boys in Nazi Germany and elsewhere. Rather than get into a fight, better to call the cops or a lawyer when challenged—exactly the kind of calculation that Mailer hated. He didn't invite the toughs into the party—they were looking for a woman they thought was there—but in general he liked a door open to the street, the possibility of surprise and trouble. Later he noted, "I took a tolerant compromising line and that was intolerable to them. They had to find out, destroy or be destroyed." He could have pressed charges (they were neighborhood guys), but he let it go. What mattered to him was that he had behaved honorably in the fight.

Living rooms became both theater and battlefield for Mailer, places in which he seduced, and conquered, confronted enemies or potential enemies. He would spy someone on the other side of the room and cross the intervening space to see what he was made of. He wanted to change everyone's reality. He was a genuinely serious man, but he needed (among other things) to violate the behavior expected of bourgeois intellectuals. The Jewish academics and critics who were his friends in the fifties and sixties, Diana and Lionel Trilling, Norman Podhoretz, Irving Howe, and Steven Marcus, considered him highly gifted but a little crazy, a Brooklyn D. H. Lawrence burning with the fires of life in the midst of the deadening forces of advanced consumerism. They certainly believed in intellectual combat but he butted heads; he had convinced himself that creativity was inextricably linked to violence.

He would speak publicly of body functions, of belly, cock, and anus; of fuck, cum, and the exaltations and depletions of sex. He was the most olfactory of writers, evoking odors that bourgeois society was committed to extinguishing. He loved the saying, *Inter faeces et urinam nascimur*, ascribed to one of the Church fathers: "Between piss and shit are we born," in his translation. This was the central fact of life, and you were a stiff if you couldn't admit it. In the next decade, during the era of protest against the Vietnam War, he was furious at Americans who would condemn a few words of public profanity while ignoring the immolation of Asian children.

TEA, GRANDIOSE PROJECTS, THE DESERT

In the summers, he and Adele, along with other New York artists and intellectuals, usually escaped to the northern end of Cape Cod—in Mailer's case, to Provincetown, a fishing village that had a Wild West, anything-goes feeling that Mailer relished. In Provincetown, they were joined by bikers, tourists, and assorted hangers-on, all part of the seething local mix (Mailer did not disdain hangers-on if they could drink, tell stories, fill out an exciting evening). He eventually bought a big redbrick house on Commercial Street facing Cape Cod Bay, a house in which he wrote, partied, and raised children; a house in which, decades later, he wanted to die.

As he struggled to finish a new novel, *The Deer Park*, he kept a journal (in 1954 and 1955), known as the "Lipton Journal," in honor of the sizable amounts of "tea" (marijuana) he was doing. (The journal was published in 2024.) Apart from some misadventures with mescaline, Mailer did not do hard drugs, though he had miserable periods in the fifties when he was consuming, in a single day, Benzedrine to speed up, Seconal to calm down, as well as serious amounts of marijuana, coffee, booze, and unfiltered cigarettes (two packs a day). J. Michael Lennon, in his extraordinary biography *Norman Mailer: A Double Life* (2013), says that Norman was looking for some middling range between excitement and calm in which he could write prose. Was this witch's brew of any use? It's hard to say that it liberated his creative abilities; it certainly liberated his belligerence and his unrealizable ambitions. In *Advertisements*, he wrote fantastically of planning a Balzacian or Zolaesque sequence of eight novels devoted to "pleasure, business, communism, church, working class, crime, homosexuality and mysticism." At other times the grand project was a monster novel about "the mysteries of murder, suicide, incest, orgy, and Time." Yet the spark, no matter how many times he blew on it, never caught fire. The series was finally abandoned.

Perhaps no other writer suffered as many public failures of his grandest ambitions yet still composed great works—hybrids, many of them, journalism shaped by fictional techniques, or fiction inspired and enlarged by interviews and research, both forms a realization of time, place, and mood so detailed, pungent, and soul-defining that past standards of appropriateness and literary form retreated into silence. Mailer re-created the most sordid and exalted details of American life. Many of these projects fell into his view without plan; Mailer wrote them because he needed money, or because a certain event struck him as an opportunity. In the end, he *did* write his ambitious portraits of America, not as novels but as genre-busting explorations.

IN THE "LIPTON JOURNAL," he composed awed descriptions of Adele's naked beauty—and also aired his fear that sex was the only thing holding them together. Spontaneous, risk-taking people, they fought a lot and at times loved each other greatly. Yet even in this period of the early and mid-fifties, before they were married, one can see signs of the tragedy in the making. Mailer was irritated by Adele's ignorance, her lack of social sophistication, her bouts of self-contempt; on her side, she wanted to outdo him in daring, taking off her clothes at one party in order to silence his talk of orgy (nothing happened). They knew each other only too well and worked on each other's nerves, like the hyperconscious couples in D. H. Lawrence's *Women in Love*.

Some of this found its way into *The Deer Park*, which finally came out in 1955, after being rejected by Mailer's publisher, Rinehart, and by six other publishers (Putnam's took it on). The grounds were obscenity, which, again, seems absurd now, especially since this novel about failures and lowlifes is shaded by a stern Jewish sense of disapproval. *The Deer Park* is set in Desert D'Or (i.e., Palm Springs), an alternatingly sunshiny and grotto-bar province of Hollywood, inhabited by sexual adventurers, drunks, and layabouts, and ruled by two visitors from Los Angeles, the studio boss Herman Teppis and his intelligent, manipulative son-in-law,

Collie Munshin, a producer. Mailer's satire of the two power types—bullying, maudlin, sanctimonious men—is easily the funniest thing he ever wrote and is also the main source of energy in *The Deer Park*, which, apart from the devastating portrait of movie-business manners, molders in a depressed state.

The nominal hero, Charles Eitel, is a blacklisted director, an intelligent, guilty man who winds up betraying his honor and his art; he almost loves his on-again, off-again mistress, Elena (passionate, self-hating, and clearly based on Adele). Mailer portrays sex rather grimly as an existential undertaking in which lovers draw forces and experiences from themselves and each other and either ascend into greater daring or sink back into dread. His writing about sex at this point is less sensual than moral; he's an anxious Jewish writer about sex, seeking spiritual improvement, warding off the grievous suspicion that sex cannot provide all the meaning that he wants from it. Afterward, he admitted that there was a certain muddle in the novel's purpose.

> *The Deer Park* is a parade of psychopaths. I pretend to be condemning, but what repels most people from the book is that I am really saying Rejoice in these people—they are marvelous, they are helping us to destroy the world [i.e., repressive society]. *The Deer Park* is perhaps the first successful and almost-honest expression of myself as a saint writing about psychopaths and loving them. But the neurotic little boy clouded the issue and tried to make people think he was condemning.

Whatever Mailer may say, he made his characters unappealing, a confusion that suggests that his desire to shock and his desire to make moral sense out of his story were at war with each other. The neurotic little boy (i.e., the Jewish little boy) won the battle but lost the novel: the book is no more than languidly wicked.

IF HE WAS a little muffled in his sexual writing at this point, he was more than muffled about the Jewish identity of several of his characters. In America, many of the actual Communists—both Stalinist and Trotskyite varieties—were Jewish, but in *Barbary Shore* Mailer doesn't make them Jewish. The two studio types in *The Deer Park* are clearly Jewish, though

Mailer doesn't say so. In a famous 1974 essay, "Writing about Jews" (republished in *Reading Myself and Others*, 1975), Philip Roth complained that Mailer was disguising his characters, giving them odd names, unwilling, in other words, to allow men who fornicate endlessly or push people around to be identified as Jews. Roth certainly has a point. The nominal hero of *The Deer Park* is another narrating cipher—this time a former air force flier named Sergius O'Shaugnessy, tall, blond, and good-looking, a would-be writer but vaguely guilty, a Jew wrapped in a fantasy of WASP beauty.

This name switching had happened before. In 1951, Mailer had written an autobiographical story about an army cook, "The Language of Men," but had changed the name of the protagonist from Sanford Cohn to Sanford Carter. "I regret that to this day," he told J. Michael Lennon in 2006, "because it was a simple Jewish name." Mailer's uneasy half-suppression of the Jewish nature of his settings and characters may have been part of the reason the two novels after *The Naked and the Dead* stalled out. His characters have no particular flavor, no native self-expression. Except for the Teppis-Munshin scenes in *The Deer Park*, the books lack exuberance, appeal, life.

His identity as a Jew was nevertheless gnawing at him. In this early-fifties period, he began a novel about a Jewish couple working in Europe administering the Marshall Plan. He abandoned it—but then it sounds like a rum subject for a novel. In 1956, he and Adele were in Munich to speak to his publisher there, and they visited Buchenwald, the concentration camp in central Germany. He had to see it, and when he was struggling to get *The Deer Park* in print, he made a pass at writing a novel called "The City of God," in which, in the words of Mailer's agent, Scott Meredith, "An American Jewish doctor and German doctor . . . confront each other and clash over contending philosophies." But the project never went very far. That makes two unwritten novels with Jews at the center. There would be other attempts later on.

IMPRISONED AND FREE: A NEW KIND OF JEW

In the fifties, he was all over the city, widely courted and mocked, a figure in the newspapers and the fantasies of many men and women. To his great good fortune, Norman discovered the jazz creators Sonny Rollins, Miles

Davis, Thelonious Monk, and Dizzy Gillespie as they performed in Harlem and Midtown clubs. With several friends, he founded, in 1955, the *Village Voice*, the first and greatest of the many alternative newspapers that flourished for decades (until the Internet killed them off). He wrote a weekly column for the paper, "The Hip and the Square," taunting his bohemian readers for the alleged inadequacy of their sexual and spiritual lives. Pugnacious and unstable, the column was short-lived. Throughout the fifties, he was belligerent and self-dissatisfied, surging and collapsing in alternation.

Early in *Advertisements*, he famously writes, "I am imprisoned with a perception that will settle for nothing less than making a revolution in the consciousness of our time." Notice that he says "imprisoned," not "inspired," for there was no escaping the long sentence of his character. Nor did he want to escape it. In the same "advertisement," Mailer speaks of "the hard price of full consciousness," which is an extraordinary phrase. You pay for seeing everything, knowing everything, feeling everything. What, however, was the *gain*—the "perception" that could change everyone *else's* consciousness?

It has many aspects, but it begins with his creation of himself. If he noticed some flickering element in his nature—an impulse, a hidden desire, a semiconscious thought—he was sure he needed to acknowledge it and act on it. Whatever emerged from the deep had to be authentic and could be ignored only at the cost of spiritual failure. "I, who am timid, cowardly, and wish only friendship and security," he wrote in his journal, "am the one who must take on the whole world." Like the existentialists in Paris, he demanded freedom, and exacted the same penalty for failing to exercise it—annihilation of any kind of authentic self. The existentialists insisted on choosing to act, but Mailer's acts, by his definition, were compelled by his very nature. Living as a respectable middle-class Jew was not possible for him. And accepting the protector of that life, Sigmund Freud, the most significant guide for American Jews at midcentury, was also not possible.

In *Civilization and Its Discontents* (1930), Freud wrote that peace, order, and creativity were made possible by men renouncing sexual and violent instincts. In the Freudian economy of the inner life, those renunciations turn inward, reemerging as anxiety or even guilt, though in lucky and talented individuals, unruly instinct could be sublimated into work and creative effort. But Mailer thought psychoanalysis was a mistake: it drained people of their vitality, their most interesting ambitions and perversities; they became shadows of their most creative selves. He reversed the diagnosis and the process of psychic repair: You don't reconstruct your infantile desires in analysis in order to cleanse the unconscious of its power; nor do you transform—sublimate—forbidden or offensive drives. You acknowledge their power and, as much as you can, act them out— *that* is the source of creative labor and the way to eliminate anxiety. "Act stronger than you feel," he told his sister Barbara, "and you will soon feel as strong as you act."

He had the most energy, he insisted, when his best and worst instincts were working together. In those situations, he demanded of himself a continuous performance with phallus, fists, skis, sailboats, booze, sustained ass-in-chair writing sessions—viciously concentrated sessions, seven hours a day. That kind of acting was, in fact, his own version of sublimation, but sublimation cleansed of the spiritless "adjustment" required in so many fifties psychoanalytic sessions. Most people pride themselves on resisting temptation; he was proud of giving in to it. He assumed that violence, including his own, was as natural a human characteristic as any other. In the end, he paid "a hard price" in damage to himself and sometimes to other people, but the effort was heroic nonetheless. Freud's view is tragic: man in civilization is unhappy. Mailer's view is romantic: man transcends himself through activity.

Diana Trilling noted that Mailer couldn't distinguish between his metaphors and physical reality. But he needed to ignore those distinctions. He needed to believe that timidity led to cancer (the frustrated cells turned in on themselves), for without such belief he could not climb the ropes of his ambition, which required that he never turn away from a challenge. He wanted to be a new kind of Jew, unhampered by fear and guilt— although not unvisited by shame (which is different from guilt), an emotion he felt strongly, like some ancient noble Greek who had not lived up to his standards of courage. The Greeks had believed that intellectual courage and physical hardihood and grace could go together. Why couldn't a Jew demand the same? It was necessary to face shame and annihilate it.

He exercised ferocious rule over his own body and spirit without employing such formal disciplines as meditation, yoga, karate, or any other ritualized self-administration. He mostly abjured weight lifting (which doesn't involve much risk), in favor of boxing, which he studied and practiced, sparring with friendly professionals as well as with buddies and eventually with his sons. He dallied for a while with the orgone box, which was created by renegade psychoanalyst Wilhelm Reich—a constructed wooden cabinet in which a man or a woman, sitting inside the box, gathered extra sexual energy from the box's magical panels. But extra sexual energy was not something Norman Mailer had need of.

WHITE NEGROES, JEWS, AND GOD

He pulled together his most radical thoughts in a famous philosophical essay, "The White Negro: Superficial Reflections on the Hipster," which appeared in *Dissent* magazine (summer 1957), an earnest outlet (mostly written by Jews) for socialist analysis of the economy and the culture. *Dissent* had no more than a tiny circulation, but the piece quickly became notorious, and Mailer made it the centerpiece of *Advertisements for Myself*. It begins as follows: "Probably, we will never be able to determine the psychic havoc of the concentration camps and the atom bomb upon the unconscious mind of almost everyone alive in these years."

In opposition, Mailer posits a rebel, the hipster (not to be confused with the gentle, flower-strewing hippies of a few years later). Mailer describes an utterly selfish man, nearly a psychopath, who exorcises the horror of the atomic age by living for the intensity and immediacy of his pleasure. Black men—"the Negroes," in fifties parlance—had lived with violence their entire lives and had developed a proud indifference to respectability. The great jazz musicians and their followers were certainly hipsters. Some whites could experience the same state of being—some actors, writers, artists, politicians, highly conscious drifters, addicts, mystics, both the intuitive inside-dopesters and the bitterly maladjusted losers. Mailer was done with his forties interest in left-wing politics; his cooled-out hipsters could never have served as the vanguard of a new proletariat. What mattered was individual salvation, which then might lead to cultural change. For himself, he was trying to enter into the mind of a violent young man, the ultimate rebel against conformity.

The essay praised violence as a method of release; it solemnly proposed "the search for an orgasm more apocalyptic than the one that preceded it." Which is quite an idea, since one wonders how apocalyptic an orgasm can get without rending the liver from the gallbladder. At the time, "The White Negro" was widely read (with amazement) and widely attacked. The Beats admired Mailer's spiritual ambition but found the essay square and wrongheaded (they wanted openness, not cool, and certainly not violence); the New York intellectuals gazed at it nervously through their fingers (it was fascinating but irresponsible); and African Americans found it condescending—a celebration of Blacks as instinctual rather than as intellectual or spiritual beings. "Why malign the sorely menaced sexuality of Negroes," James Baldwin asked, "in order to justify the white man's own sexual panic?" As Baldwin and others pointed out, Mailer was no hipster himself; he was far too earnest and explanatory to be cool, or even to lose himself in hedonism. He could be aggressive, but he lacked the superb insolence that united the Black jazz musicians he so admired.

In later years, Mailer called the piece "naïve." As he told me in 1998, "I didn't understand that there were two things vastly more important than orgasm to most people, and that's power and its handmaiden, money." Still, "The White Negro" sets up a spiritual hierarchy of acts, ranked by danger and risk; even now, it has a discomforting effect on anyone who reads it.

It is particularly discomforting for Jews. "The White Negro" marks, among many other things, an almost complete negation of everything Jews had fought to achieve in America—safety, professional success, intellectual distinction, family happiness, property ownership, law abidingness, and the rest. The piece's most notorious passage touches on Jews in a demeaning way.

> The psychopath murders—if he has the courage—out of the necessity to purge his violence, for if he cannot empty his hatred then he cannot love, his being is frozen with implacable self-hatred for his cowardice. (It can of course be suggested that it takes little courage for two strong eighteen-year-old hoodlums, let us say, to beat in the brains of a candy-store keeper, and indeed the act—even by the logic of the psychopath—is not likely to prove very therapeutic, for the victim is not an immediate equal. Still, courage of a sort is necessary, for one murders not only a weak fifty-year-old man but an institution as well, one violates private property, one enters

into a new relation with the police and introduces a dangerous element into one's life. The hoodlum is therefore daring the unknown, and so no matter how brutal the act, it is not altogether cowardly.)

The paragraph, as many have said, is a moral disaster: the psychopath cures himself by destroying another. But leave the moral issue aside for a moment. Notice the uncharacteristic coyness. The location of this scenario, and the ethnic identity of the players, could not have been unknown to many readers of the essay. The place is almost certainly Harlem, and in Harlem, as James Baldwin wrote, the landlords and store owners when he was growing up in the thirties and forties (at the same time as Mailer) were mostly Jewish. Mailer allows for the possible heroism of the young men but not for the possibility that the candy-store owner might fight back, as some did in such situations, wielding a baseball bat or even a gun hidden beneath the front counter. Some of those store owners in Harlem, even as they exploited the neighborhood, were tough old birds in their own defense. Even in Mailer's limited macho terms, then, the passage is obtuse and doubly hostile to Jews, who are both the objects of violence and passive in the face of it.

IN THE FIFTIES, he put into practice his idiosyncratic version of the Reform Jewish mandate *tikkun olam* (to repair the world): he became responsible in his own eyes (though not always in the eyes of others) for the spiritual well-being of the nation. He thought of himself as a kind of disreputable prophet, both psychopath and saint, and he held forth eloquently and disruptively in magazines, on television, and at universities.

His religious views were idiosyncratic, mostly self-created: he diminished the Judeo-Christian God, telling novelist Richard G. Stern in a 1958 interview that "God is in danger of dying." In 2000, looking back at how he came to that view, he told the German magazine *Der Spiegel*, "My religious feelings . . . came from the Holocaust. Since then, it has been impossible to believe in an all-good and all-powerful God." The moral consequences of his new understanding, he told Stern in 1958, "are not only staggering, but they're thrilling; because moral experience is intensified rather than diminished," by which he meant that man must be responsible for the earth and for himself rather than leave it to a semi-impotent deity. His view could be called Jewish Manichaeism: God had created life but was locked in an endless struggle with the Devil. And this embattled God, he insisted, is a more interesting being than the standard all-powerful deity who is given to mysterious absences. Mailer thought man, at the least, must fill those absences. In 1846, Karl Marx wrote that religious man, by giving more to God, took away more from himself. Mailer was trying to reverse the flow.

The "perception" he was imprisoned with, which vibrates throughout *Advertisements for Myself*, was the danger of repression of body and soul, the fear of life itself, vital, messy, violent, conscious and unconscious together—the fear of life, which, in the security-conscious era after the war, Mailer thought of as an American disease. What he wanted was a change in consciousness, which meant an individual embrace of authenticity, beginning with an acknowledgment of the unappeasable impressions flowing in from one's senses. Greater authenticity would lead to a sexual and moral revolution.

Parts of what he called for actually happened, for good and for ill, in the sixties. In the beginning, however, a good part of his revolt was produced by his determination to flee from what he took to be Jewish middle-class mediocrity. He dramatized his unhappiness with that life in a remarkable short story from 1952, "The Man Who Studied Yoga," in which three Jewish couples watch a pornographic movie at home but are too timid and inert to give themselves afterward to the appropriate orgy.

TERRIBLE NIGHT

He and Adele had two daughters, Danielle and Betsy, and in the late fifties the family moved for a while to rural Connecticut, where Mailer lived close to his novel-writing friends William Styron and James Jones. The three ambitious, relentless, and quick-tempered men were combative and also easily hurt; they read and criticized each other's work, and, inevitably, the friendships fell apart. Mailer was sure, at one point, that Styron and his wife, the socially ambitious Rose Styron, were condescending to Adele. Their criticisms mirrored some of his own feelings, which was painful for him (as it certainly was for Adele). In this period, Mailer quarreled with people of substance and hung out more and more with men feeding back to him his own temperament and ideas, including the actor

Mickey Knox, a friend for decades. He lost a great friend, psychologist Robert Lindner, in 1956, but apart from Lindner, an inventive renegade therapist, he didn't get from his friends the toughest, most imaginative, most engaged and devastating reflection of himself that he needed.

In 1960, he told people close to him that he was going to run for mayor of New York—on the Existentialist ticket. A few of his friends supported him, but his family, including Adele, thought he was crazy. He became furious with all of them, even slapping his sister, Barbara, who adored him. How much of his behavior was chosen recklessness and how much actual madness? He had genuine troubles: he was obsessed with the gigantic, multipart novel that he could not write; he was quarreling with the publisher (Arnold Gingrich) and the editor (Harold Hayes) of *Esquire*, which had printed many of his most provocative essays. Simultaneously wired and sodden, he would go out for a walk with his dog, or encounter a police car passing on the street, or contend with a bartender collecting a check—and in each case get into a fight that would land him in jail for the night. He was paying more than a hard price for full consciousness; spiritually, he was spending himself into bankruptcy.

He and Adele moved uptown to West Ninety-Fourth Street. On the night of November 19, 1960, he threw a big party in his apartment for his friend Roger Donoghue, a former middleweight who had given him a few boxing lessons. Mailer planned to announce the mayoral run at the party, but the event was chaotic from the beginning: strangers again barged in, writers screamed insults at one another, and Mailer, wearing a bullfighter's tunic, paced about restlessly and challenged various men to fight him. Around 3 a.m., he demanded to know which of the remaining guests supported his run for mayor. Unanswered, he departed, returning ninety minutes later after several scraps on the street. "His face and bullfighter's shirt were bloody," in J. Michael Lennon's account, "and he had a black eye." According to Adele, who wrote a memoir about her marriage to Mailer, *The Last Party* (1997), she taunted him when he came back to the apartment: "*Aja, toro, aja,* come on you little faggot, where's your *cojones,* did your ugly whore of a mistress cut them off, you son of a bitch." Mailer then thrust his three-inch penknife, which he was carrying in his pocket, into Adele's body; he just missed her heart with the second thrust.

If Mailer had left his penknife on the dresser table, or if Adele had insulted him in a different way, there might have been a fight and nothing worse. But any such thoughts cravenly dodge the issue. The entire decade, with its cultivated turmoil, its spiritual need to behave badly, and its increasingly violent arguments between husband and wife—an erotic dance of death—led up to that moment in which Mailer assaulted the mother of his children. When you read *Advertisements for Myself* now, you have to read it ironically—or perhaps sardonically. It's a convulsively brilliant book, but you have to think that some of Mailer's turmoil was leading to *this*; and that no matter how much he theorized, fantasized, and boasted of his attraction to violence as a mode of authenticity, he little imagined a violent act that would cover him in shame.

Adele Morales was saved by a good surgeon; Mailer was saved by his family and friends, who gathered around him and took the line that Adele had goaded him into it. (Fanny advised her to say that she had fallen and hurt herself.) He was sent to Bellevue Hospital for observation, and, after seventeen days, went home, where Adele, in a weakened state, was waiting for him with their two little girls. However unlikely it seems, she wanted to continue the marriage. A few months later, even though Adele refused to press charges, Mailer was indicted for the stabbing. In the end, he pled guilty to felonious assault ("I feel I did a lousy, dirty, cowardly thing," he told the court). He was eventually given a suspended sentence and three years' probation. The marriage, putting it mildly, was over.

HE WAS A famous writer, and he got away with it, though not without remorse. Years later, looking back, he wrote that "the damage to our two daughters would be incalculable." On the whole, however, he suffered less than Adele, who spent the rest of her life bitterly obsessed with him. At the end of her memoir, published thirty-seven years after the event, she writes, "I was trapped in my purgatory of hatred." Going back to the assault, she recalled that someone tried to help her as she lay on the floor, but Mailer said, "Get away from her, let the bitch die."

This line has been repeated by cultural historian Louis Menand in a *New Yorker* article (October 14, 2013) and in his book *The Free World* (2021). At the time, however, Adele told the police that "He just looked at me. He didn't say a word. He stabbed me." Was she lying to the police in 1960 to protect her husband? Or herself? Or did she make up the line "let the bitch die" when she was writing her book decades later? (Mailer, preferring to let the matter drop, was silent on the issue.) As she was writing her memoir, Adele was trying to get more alimony out of him; she had written a play about their marriage, which, she says, she read to him. The truth can't be known, but it may matter that Adele's book, composed from memory, is inaccurate in many of its dates and details.

Throughout this period, Mailer refused to believe that in the months before the stabbing he had been walking around in a semipsychotic state. He later remembered telling the doctors at Bellevue, "'Didn't you guys ever hear of a crime of passion?' From their point of view, there I was a Jewish intellectual. Jewish intellectuals don't have crimes of passion, they just go crazy." He wanted the dignity, the *authority* of such a crime. He was trying to make a romantic myth out of a sordid act and hoping, in this perverse way, to liberate the Jews from what he took to be their bondage of weakness.

Admiration for Mailer as a writer and man has to be retrieved from periods of mourning. It is that way with many artists, though not always to the same degree. Shakespeare left his wife and children in Stratford-upon-Avon and headed for the literary and sexual excitements of the London theater. Dickens ignored *his* children, set up his chorus-girl mistress in the country, and attacked his wife in the press as a terrible mother. The elderly Tolstoy disdained his Sophia, who had borne him thirteen children and had copied *War and Peace* several times, in favor of his sinister religious followers and various hangers-on. Pablo Picasso treated women badly and joined the Communist Party in 1944, well after the Stalinist purges were known to anyone who cared to know. Igor Stravinsky was an anti-Semite. So were T. S. Eliot and his friend and fellow American poet Ezra Pound, a broadcasting fascist. Yet art would be poorer without their work—and without their faces, bodies, and temperaments, too. Mailer performed some terrible acts and wrote some foolish texts, and only appreciation and discrimination combined can do him justice.

REBIRTH: CONVENTIONS, KENNEDYS, JOURNALISM

However you classify the assault, you might have concluded in 1960 that Mailer, at thirty-seven, was through—finished as a man, as a writer, as a Jew. At the time, some of his literary friends feared as much. In December 1960, a group of supporters, including James Baldwin, Lionel Trilling, Lillian Hellman, Robert Lowell, and Alfred Kazin, wrote a letter to *Time* magazine attesting to his brilliance. But they need not have worried. His life was not yet half over, and the truth is he recovered in almost every way. After Adele Morales, four women accepted him as their husband. (Young women don't believe this when I tell them.) He wrote most of his books and had most of his adventures, good and bad, after the event. Most astoundingly, just months before the assault, in the middle of the summer of 1960—a Provincetown summer filled with fights and revelry—he wrote an article that revolutionized political reporting and, as it turned out, revived his career.

It was called "Superman Comes to the Supermarket," an account of the 1960 Democratic Party National Convention in Los Angeles (the Kennedy convention). It appeared in *Esquire* in October, just weeks before the election, and caused a sensation. No one since H. L. Mencken had written about American electoral politics with such brio and malice, no one had evoked in such sweet detail the bodies and faces, the clothes and manners of the people who gathered around a noisy national carnival—an event meaningless in much of its ritual until Mailer captured its spiritual essence. Political journalists count up delegates, recite polls, and parse the words of the candidates' statements; they display acumen. Mailer quoted speeches, but he also wrote about the noxious pall of cigarette smoke in public rooms, the mentality of ward heelers, the looks of the young women hired by each candidate to cheer on their man ("the Kennedy ladies were the handsomest; healthy, attractive, tough, a little spoiled— they looked like the kind of girls who had gotten all the dances in high school and/or worked for a year as an airline hostess before marrying well"). "Superman" was a New York Jew's amused rendering of the square but threatening Christian world of power, the first of many such accounts, rueful, knowing, and unanswerable.

Portraiture—a novelist's belief in faces as revelation—became central to his writing. John F. Kennedy, magnetically handsome, intelligent, witty, and calculating, had mysterious qualities and the surprising gift of metamorphosis.

> His personal quality had a subtle, not quite describable intensity, a suggestion of dry pent heat perhaps, his eyes large, the pupils grey, the whites prominent, almost shocking, his most forceful feature; he had the eyes of a mountaineer. His appearance changed with his mood, strikingly so,

and this made him more interesting than what he was saying. He would seem at one moment older than his age, forty-eight or fifty, a tall, slim, sunburned professor with a pleasant weathered face, not even particularly handsome; five minutes later, talking to a press conference on his lawn, three microphones before him, a television camera turning, his appearance would have gone through a metamorphosis, he would again look like a movie star, his coloring vivid, his manner rich, his gestures strong and quick, alive with that concentration of vitality a successful actor always seems to radiate.

Mailer had found his hipster (aboveground division), his existential hero, and he aired the possible psychic and moral consequences for the nation (dangerous but exciting) of choosing anyone so young and little-known. He found his own public voice, too—three-dimensional, poetically rich, self-aware, the voice that he hadn't quite achieved in *Advertisements*, for all its arrogant and self-punishing brilliance. He wrote journalism as literature, and for the rest of his life he wrote it for the monthly magazines that had a taste for experimental forms and risk-taking prose, *Esquire*, *Harper's*, and *Playboy*; and a bit later, he wrote it for *Life*, *Look*, and *Parade*, each of them a national calendar of down-the-middle patriotism. His mode was disaffection mixed with irrepressible love of America.

Since the First World War Americans have been leading a double life, and our history has moved on two rivers, one visible, the other underground; there has been the history of politics which is concrete, factual, practical and unbelievably dull if not for the consequences of the actions of some of these men; and there is a subterranean river of untapped, ferocious, lonely and romantic desires, that concentration of ecstasy and violence which is the dream life of the nation.

He joined the unyielding facades of public occasions—conventions, boxing matches, protest marches, feminist polemics, space flight—to the hidden being of the country, all seen with an urban Jew's skeptical descriptive ardor mixed with metaphysical speculation. He had initially thought of journalism as a way of staying in shape for writing fiction; in the end, he gave all of himself to it.

Covering the Republican National Convention of 1964, he wrote that the teenage boys who turned out for Goldwater "tended to have a little acne, an introspective pimple or two by the corner of the mouth or the side of the chin, a lot of the boys looked solemn and serious, dedicated but slightly blank—they could fix a transistor radio, but a word like 'Renaissance' would lay a soft wound of silence, stupefaction in their brain." The girls supporting Governor William Scranton were "good-looking most of them, slightly spoiled, saucy, full of peeves, junior debs doing their best to be cool and so wearing their hair long with a part down the center in such a way that the face, sexy, stripped of makeup (except for some sort of white libidinous wax on the lips), was half-concealed by a Gothic arch of falling tresses." Neither Henry James nor F. Scott Fitzgerald ever wrote more extraordinary sentences. His reports on the Democratic Convention of 1960 (reprinted in *Presidential Papers*), the Republican Convention of 1964 (*Cannibals and Christians*), and the conventions of both parties in 1968 (*Miami and the Siege of Chicago*) are both superlative political entertainments and classic evocations of mood and place. Sweaty Miami, vegetation bursting through the sidewalks, and stockyard-reeking Chicago were "done" in ways that any poet or writer of fiction might envy.

Mailer told an interviewer in the early sixties that he wrote for men and women who had "no tradition by which to measure their experience but the intensity and clarity of their inner lives." The writing had a stunning, creative effect on young readers—on me and my friends, certainly, hidden as some of us were. At Columbia, we read the essays aloud to each other, trying to fathom the syntax, so potently "wrong," like irregular phrases from advanced music. For all of us, writing like that asserted very plainly that the world could be conquered. The stone-hard American blankness—the America of business and politics and technology, of dreadful architecture, dull kids, and stolid men, the America that left one depressed and defeated—all of it could be described, and thus in some way mastered.

CLIMBING TO NOWHERE

In 1961, at a party in Gore Vidal's East Side apartment, Mailer met Lady Jeanne Campbell, the daughter of the Duke of Argyll and the granddaughter of Lord Beaverbrook, the powerful British press lord and intimate of

Winston Churchill. Jeanne Campbell was a journalist employed by one of the many papers in Britain controlled by Beaverbrook. She was tall with tousled hair and green eyes; she was perceptive and funny—a journalist who was curious about everyone she met. For years she had been the mistress of Henry Luce, the founder of the Time Life empire, a magazine group always ready to torment Mailer in print. Norman and Jeanne glared at each other (Mailer was big on staring contests) and fell in love.

"I had never gone to bed with a Jew before," Lady Jeanne later told Vidal. And Mailer had never gone to bed with an upper-class Brit. She was slumming, and he was social climbing, going where few (if any) middle-class Brooklyn Jews had gone before him. It was sex tourism on both sides, and for a while they were good together. He drove her around the country in his (very British) Triumph sports car with his poodle Tibo in the back, a large, thickly curled creature that Norman was convinced had great intelligence. After he and Adele finalized their divorce in 1962, he and Jeanne, who was pregnant, got married and moved to his new place in Brooklyn Heights.

The beautiful old neighborhood, with its row houses from the nineteenth century and its blessed absence of traffic, offered a rare bit of quiet amid the New York tumult. Mailer's house had a glorious view from the rear windows—the East River, the Brooklyn Bridge, the peaks of Lower Manhattan, a panorama that combined both old New York and the financial engine of the corporations that Mailer was beginning to hate. He kept the house for the rest of his life. The top floor was fitted out as a ship, with a rope ladder, a deck, and catwalks—everything but barnacles. Mailer said the climb to his writing room at the top was tonic for him because "Jews have a bad head for heights." It's more likely the climb cleared his head from the previous night of drinking.

It's amusing to think of Lady Jeanne on a catwalk, but Mailer, acting sensibly for once, installed her and the baby in a garden apartment at the base of the house. Still, she was in the wrong place, and so, in some ways, was he. Mailer was accustomed to the tough bohemian women hanging around such New York bars as the San Remo and the White Horse Tavern. But the upper-class British were different; they were real killers. He admired their poise, their social acumen, the precision of their phrasing—tight and definitive, so unlike his own warm-spirited, all-encompassing flow.

There was at least one shaft of killing wit directed at him, though J.

Michael Lennon says Mailer didn't know about it until later. Novelist Evelyn Waugh enjoyed lounging at other people's country houses, including the estate of Jeanne Campbell's mother in Somerset. At a large party there, in which the stables were open for guests to explore, Waugh spied an alien. One of the horses, he wrote a friend, "bit an American pornographer who tried to give it vodka"—a nonsensical reference to Mailer. "The horse did bite me on the finger," Mailer later wrote a friend, "but I was not feeding him vodka, just petting him on the nose. Maybe it was my breath that enflamed the animal, or maybe he was fond of Evelyn Waugh." Like most American celebrities in Britain, Mailer was both fussed over and, whenever possible, kicked in the shins.

In a way, of course, Waugh got it right. Jeanne Campbell would have known how to pet a horse. Mailer always said she was fun to be around but too abrupt and imperious in her habits, and he, for all his drinking and socializing, needed to work steadily. They both knew it wouldn't last. In early 1963, she left Brooklyn and returned to her apartment in Manhattan. They were quickly divorced.

BUT MAILER'S ATTEMPT to storm the upper classes was not over. In "Superman Comes to the Supermarket," he had written that Kennedy's election would open possibilities of spiritual, aesthetic, and sexual renewal in America, an acceptance of risk and experiment. "Use your popularity to be difficult and intellectually dangerous," he advised the new president. "There is more to greatness than liberal legislation." This is high-flown flattery indeed. Norman was also impressed with Jacqueline Kennedy, whom he met just before the election at the Kennedy compound in Hyannis. She was merry, she was intelligent, she had admired his article on the convention. "She did not sit there like a movie star with a ripe olive in each eye for the brain, but in fact gave conversation back, made some of it, laughed often."

The love affair with the Kennedys didn't last very long. In April 1961, Kennedy green-lit the CIA-led invasion of the new Communist regime in Cuba, leading to the debacle at the Bay of Pigs. Mailer published an angry open letter to the president and later wrote that "Nothing could ever convince me the invasion of Cuba was not one of the meanest blunders in our history." His sense of betrayal was severe and only grew worse. On the evening of February 14, 1962, with something like fifty-six million Americans watching, Mrs. Kennedy, accompanied by CBS's Charles Collingwood, walked around the White House celebrating the Red Room, the Green Room, Dolley Madison's sofa, President Madison's clock, and so on. Mailer was shocked by what he saw and expressed himself at length in *Esquire*. Her voice, he said, was soft and breathy, like that of a sexy weather girl on local news. "She had that lack of comprehension for each word offered up which one finds only in a few of those curious movie stars who are huge box office. Jane Russell comes to mind." Jane Russell was large and thick; it was a terrible insult.

He had been tempted into . . . into *what*, exactly? The Kennedys were Catholics, not WASPs, but they were certainly American aristocrats. He longed to be taken seriously by them, to advise them on cultural matters. Why couldn't Beat poet Allen Ginsberg be invited to the White House? Mailer fantasized about sitting in cabinet meetings that would lead America to an audacious future. He was tempted into relinquishing his sovereign role as outside observer. Yet this project of breaching the upper-class ruling circles was doomed from the start—fraught with Jewish ambition and stubbornness. He wanted status and praise and power, but he also needed to assert who he was and what he believed. He was determined not to genuflect before The Great; it was better to offend them, thereby rejecting them before they could reject him, the classic self-defeating strategy of the outsider. In any case, it was an honorable defeat, and he went back to his proper role as observer, which for him (and for us) was an actual victory.

LOOKING BACK AT THE TERRIBLE NIGHT

Mailer continued to make attempts in the early sixties to write his enormous eight-part Balzacian novel, but he never got very far with it. The unworkable project bedeviled him, and there was another problem: he had ex-wives and children to support and secretaries to pay. He took on magazine assignments for cash—and turned them into astonishing flights of poetically realized atmosphere, intricate creation of character, and philosophical speculation. The political pieces were only one part of his granular yet soul-enlarging journalism. In his *Esquire* article ("Ten Thousand Words a Minute," February 1963) devoted to the first heavyweight championship fight between Floyd Patterson and Sonny Liston (September 25, 1962), Mailer recapitulated his "Superman" strategy: he wrote about the fight itself but also about such things as the grubbiness of the freeloading fight press ("a reporter has a stomach like a shaving mug and a throat like a hog's trough") and the power structure of championship events, with its Mafia meatheads everywhere at the Chicago hotels—"the strong-arm men, the head kickers, the limb-breakers, the groin stompers. If a clam had a muscle as large as a man, and the muscle grew eyes, you would get the mood." The urban Jew was not an outsider at the fights the way he was at the political conventions; he was more like a consummately wised-up insider, a purveyor of barroom gossip laced with moral and metaphysical conjuration. Mailer's boxing pieces become enormous prose poems on a corrupt and fallen world, yet a world ennobled by courage and haunted by death.

Midway through the *Esquire* piece, there is a startling digression, a passage that may say more than Mailer intended about events in his own life. Earlier that year, in March 1962, Emile Griffith III and Benny Paret had met in New York for the welterweight championship. Before the fight, rumors were circulating that Griffith was bisexual. This made Paret angry ("I hate that kind of guy," he told journalist Pete Hamill). Mailer continues: "Now, at the weigh-in that morning, Paret had insulted Griffith irrevocably, touching him on the buttocks, while making a few more remarks about his manhood." (The insults have been recapitulated and enlarged in Terence Blanchard's exciting 2013 opera about Griffith, *Champion*.) In the fight itself, Griffith retaliated. He trapped Paret in a corner and pounded him again and again before the referee at last interfered. Paret went into a coma and died in a hospital ten days later. Mailer interprets:

> The accusation of homosexuality arouses a major passion in many men; they spend their lives resisting it with a biological force. There is a kind of man who spends every night of his life getting drunk in a bar, he rants, he brawls, he ends in a small rumble on the street; women say, "For God's sake, he's homosexual. Why doesn't he just turn queer and get his suffering over with." Yet men protect him. It is because he is choosing not to become homosexual.

It's a sweetly written paragraph. But notice what set off the uncontrolled explosion in Griffith—the accusation, or the fear, of homosexuality. On the night of November 19, 1960, when Mailer returned to his apartment, drunk and bloodied, Adele taunted him, as you have heard: "*Aja, toro, aja,* come on you little faggot, where's your *cojones*, did your ugly whore of a mistress cut them off, you son of a bitch." Mailer, I'm quite sure, was not fighting homosexuality, but the taunt, in macho circles in 1960, was a grievous one, and he pulled out his knife. In his fight essay, Mailer doesn't make any connection between Griffith's rage and his own. Nothing can excuse—and certainly nothing can justify—what Mailer did that night, but his account of Griffith's homicidal anger may partly explain it.

FAMILY MAN

In March 1963, Mailer dropped into P. J. Clarke's, a steak-and-whiskey pub on East Fifty-Fifth Street. The place was frequented by celebrities, locals, and wealthy bums. Beverly Bentley, a theater and television actress, hailed Norman from a table. She was sitting with the former middleweight champ Jake LaMotta, not exactly an easygoing guy (Martin Scorsese made *Raging Bull* about him). Yet Mailer took Beverly home that night. Each of his wives came from a distinct background, and each had a distinct temperament—Jewish/feminist lefty (Beatrice); passionate Latina painter (Adele); witty Brit aristocrat-journalist (Jeanne). And now he settled down with a blond Gentile actress from Georgia, a woman who wanted family and children. Beverly Bentley became his fourth wife.

Why this need to marry all the time? Mailer taking Beverly Bentley away from Jake LaMotta at their first meeting has an almost mythical feeling to it—a dragon slain, a princess liberated. He did many venturesome things in the middle 1960s. He engaged in multiple debates with William F. Buckley, the deep-baritonal, formidably articulate conservative writer and editor; he appeared on television, made anti-war speeches, participated in literary symposia, gave many interviews, and geared up to run for mayor (this time seriously). He grabbed at every chance to thrust himself into public view, often embarrassing himself—on television, for instance, where he was usually awful, a man so obsessed with his ideas and emotions that he overloaded the cool medium in which svelte performers like Gore Vidal could flourish. Some of his campus appearances turned into profane revels, curses lobbed back and forth like water bombs. He didn't always know how to handle an audience, especially when he was drunk. He became the designated miscreant of *People* and other magazines.

But after each adventure, he needed to return home. For all his insistence on instinct and freedom, his railing against the suffocations of conventional existence, he did nothing comparable to, say, Lord Byron's hurling himself into other people's revolutions; nor was he endlessly itinerant like the tormented D. H. Lawrence, who was certainly married (to his Frieda) but journeyed in search of sunshine and health to Italy, Sardinia, and New Mexico. Mailer got around but always returned to Brooklyn and Provincetown—and to marriage, six times before he was through, and all of them, apart from the flirtatious romp with Lady Jeanne, unions of some length. In 1975, during his first night with Norris Church, who would become his sixth wife, he told her that he was responsible for the support of fourteen people—the boast of a Jewish stud-husband in the act of committing adultery with a new woman.

There's no mystery here. Like millions of other Americans, he wanted the status and the comforts of married life. He needed a woman faithful to him (without recognizing the same obligation in himself). He liked dinner on the table, children playing downstairs, a decent party space when he required it (his parties became less fraught as he got older). A Jewish patriarch, then, the leader of a large brood, King David almost, richly propertied and multiplied. And also a man who needed someone to love him as much as his mother did. Both things are true, and women will say, "Marriage worked much better for him than it did for his wives." That's true, too, though it may be notable that only two of his marriages, to Bea Silverman and Jeanne Campbell, broke up because the women wanted to leave. Mailer's greatest need, apart from sex and companionship and children, was to continue working, and the family setting enabled the long days at his desk. For all his brain-and-body-busting restlessness, he could always draw on reserves of *sitzfleisch*—the ability to sit still and keep at it. Lord Byron wrote a great deal of poetry, but he did not possess *sitzfleisch*.

MAILER BELIEVED PARENTS and children were held together by the most powerful of bonds. That comes through very clearly in the bizarre text he began composing in 1962, "The Book of the First-Born," a novel about an immigrant Lithuanian Jewish family (i.e., his own family) and the birth of a hero (himself). "I've been waiting to write an autobiographical novel all these years," Mailer told me much later, in 1998, "but I've been waiting to become the hero of my own life in order to write it. I have never become the hero of my own life." By which he meant, I suppose, that he had never successfully pulled off his big novel. But perhaps at that moment he had forgotten an abandoned text from years earlier.

"The Book of the First-Born" begins in facetious mock-grandiose style with the birth of a boy named Merrill, who can only be Mailer. J. Michael Lennon has pointed out similarities to the beginning of Laurence Sterne's eighteenth-century classic *Tristram Shandy*: in both cases the male child is breach-born and delivered by a clumsy doctor wielding forceps. The style of the two books is jaunty, knowing, poised between outrage and mockery.

The newborn baby is highly conscious. Not for him the "blooming, buzzing confusion" that William James described as an infant's first experience of reality. No, Mailer creates his own emergence as a myth of mindfulness. Merrill's mother, Jenny (who is definitely meant to be Fanny), is lauded as an iron-strong peasant ("proud, timid, and fierce"), but her baby boy is more like a natural aristocrat. He confronts a world that exists for his pleasure or pain.

> He learned early to gag and spit out his own cocktail of synthetic protein, synthetic carbohydrate, pasteurized milk powder and wax paper, an odor which would attack him in later years when he entered a drug store.

The baby has Mailer's hatred of technological products: formula, we gather, is not fit for a hero. Merrill then comes close to dying from the disinfecting zeal and overheated rooms of the New Jersey hospital (Mailer could never accept that doctors knew what they were doing). He longs for his mother's breast, but suddenly the barbarians attack.

> He was taken up from the cage, brought to the breast, and before he could even suck was lifted again, and smelled new odors, small-town odors of small-town hardworking Jews, which of course he was not in a position to classify, and then a smell of black cloth, a smell of an odd being, a *mohel* (pronounced moil) redolent of cigar smoke, of grease spots, of synagogue incense, and the smell of metal which came over him like an omen for

it was close to the smell of the forceps. . . . He discovered the tip of that appendage in the indescribable cruelty of those two fingers which pinched. They said to the unmarked meanings of his nerves, "You, son of Israel, will never go where you want to go," and then the sword of the Assyrian came down, and Merrill found his first real voice, and gave a barbaric shriek at the treachery worked upon him.

The Jewish hero receives his wound just after birth. Yet this hero, as we know, will spend the rest of his life ignoring the blade and going exactly where he wants to go. But first he must get back to his mother's breast. When the teenage Mailer was writing fiction in the family's Long Branch hotel, Fanny wrote him, "When you were a tiny infant, every time I nursed you, I would whisper a little prayer in your ear, 'Please God, make him a great man someday.'" So now Mailer/Merrill returns to that position, drawing strength and character from his mother's milk. She, in turn, is irradiated with love. "Something seemed to come to her then from the infant, some echo of ecstasy into the sores of her center, and she knew happiness as she had never known it with her husband."

What a stud! He cuckolds his father even as he is feeding at his mother's breast. The circumcision, as he presents it, is a violent act more like castration—the fear of which, Freud said, in his account of the Oedipal drama, a boy experienced when he felt the stirrings of erotic attraction to his mother. Well, Norman seems to have beaten that fear; he has an erotic relationship with his mother and escapes any punishment.

THERE'S A BIT more. Mailer re-creates his grandfather the Lithuanian rabbi and writes for the rabbi a tough cross-examination of God—the God, in Mailer's estimation, who needs man's help. Mailer then produces some exasperated humor, in the manner of Sholem Aleichem's tales of Tevye the dairyman, humor devoted to the difficulties of getting one's daughters married. He was trying, for a minute, to write classic Yiddish-language fiction. But the writing stops there. He knew he wasn't equipped to go any further.

Cynthia Ozick, the high-powered novelist and essayist, wrote a complicated essay in 1970 called "Toward a New Yiddish" (reprinted in her collection *Art and Ardor*, 1983). The new Yiddish turns out to be English as written by diaspora Jews in America, saturated in the sensibility of the old Yiddish but stern and "liturgical," devoted to life's fundamental questions. Ozick insists a great writer begins with the particulars of his tribe; in so doing, he is blowing through the small opening of the shofar, and, if he is good enough, everyone will hear it. But Mailer, by rejecting the ethos of his shtetl, Brooklyn, and trying to write for all Americans, was "blowing out of the wrong end of the shofar." I doubt that Mailer would agree with Ozick's prescription for writing, but in this autobiographical composition he was certainly holding the instrument in the way Ozick wanted. He just didn't have enough air to keep going, and he acknowledged, as a reason for quitting, the supremacy of Isaac Bashevis Singer, whose stories of shtetl and city life in Poland and immigrant life in America are incomparably knowledgeable, perverse, and funny.

"Being a major novelist is not a natural activity for a Jew," he told Diana Trilling, by which he meant that Jewish American novelists were cut off from the past; they had no heroic roots to draw on. He may be wrong about that. In the case of his aborted manuscript, he tried to find something of the past and faltered. It was a failure of knowledge, not of will.

A NEW YORK JEW IN WASHINGTON

Mailer wrote angrily against the Vietnam War and marched against it more than once. During one of those marches, in the spring of 1966, early in the war, I unexpectedly ran into him. With thousands of others, he was walking down Fifth Avenue on a gray Sunday afternoon. Not a tall man, I thought; in fact, surprisingly short, but with a big head, a noble head like Richard Burton's. He was forty-four, a famous writer in a trench coat, walking arm in arm with his wife and friends, an entire entourage with linked arms, all of them moving forward steadily, a genial line of force. My second thought: the big head was not an actor's head; it belonged on the shoulders of a general. He looked like a leader.

I was a student holding a little Bell and Howell 16-millimeter camera. I was "covering" the march. Out in front of him, I stumbled backward with my camera, and he nodded, smiled, and stopped walking for a minute. He was not going to miss an opportunity to be photographed, even by a student. Beverly Bentley also smiled. An actress, she liked to be photographed, too, and I shot a few feet of film and moved out of the way, pulling off to the side as they moved on.

Mailer looked very benevolent on that day, but he published a novel in this period so furiously written that it felt like a burning log cast out of a fire. You touched it at your peril. In *An American Dream* (1965), a half-Jewish war hero, professor, and TV celebrity named Stephen Rojack strangles his nasty rich wife, an American aristocrat (so much for remorse over Adele; so much for regret over Jeanne). He then throws her body onto the East River Drive and sleeps with her maid. *An American Dream* is a highbrow pop fantasia; no human being could have kept Rojack's thirty-two-hour schedule of suffering, risk, sex, and spiritual recovery. But in its lush, damp, flowing way—in its gaudy sensual effulgence and its exploration of states beyond exhaustion—*An American Dream* is a sustained piece of fiction writing.

An angry rhythm of revolt churns through the book. I don't like it much, but I'm willing to be seared by a few pages of intense pleasure. No other Mailer text had so thoroughly vanquished such Jewish middle-class virtues as rationality, responsibility, and lucidity. His mood of revolt, however, would soon be combined with his own version of those virtues, doused for a while in bourbon, but in the end triumphant in their clarity. It was a book Mailer didn't plan to write, didn't want to write, but was born to write. Another protest march was the launching pad for a masterpiece.

IN VIETNAM, IN the fall of 1967, the United States was still waging technological war—including the use of napalm, a flesh-burning compound—against Asian peasants and political cadres struggling to rid their country of foreigners. Few Americans had the wit and historical savvy in the sixties to understand that the specter haunting Southeast Asia was not so much communism (which we fought against) as it was capitalism (which would eventually triumph in much of the area). It was a large error. Almost 450,000 Americans were in Vietnam in the fall of 1967, and opposition at home was fierce. The protests had little discernible effect on policy, but in October, the anti-war forces tried yet again. Some 50,000 people prepared to approach the Pentagon, the seemingly impregnable fortress of American militarism, in order to "invest" it—surround it, shame it, and maybe break into it.

When asked to participate, Mailer refused. He had had enough of marches. They were good people, the anti-war crowd, but he wasn't much attracted to virtue; he was attracted to power. A march with losers? Doing one's own work was the best way to fight the war. In the end, however, he was charmed by the brave oddity of the event and by some of the prospective company among the crowd, including the poet Robert Lowell and the critic Dwight Macdonald, who was a good friend. Pediatrician Benjamin Spock would be there, and also the redoubtable William Sloane Coffin, anti-war chaplain at Yale. Mailer would be a Jew among distinguished WASPs. He went to Washington, engaged with all kinds of Americans, and got himself arrested. He used this minor adventure as a way of interrogating both his own courage and the moral destiny of the nation, producing the best portrait we have of both the ethically ambitious and the sensational aspects of "the sixties"—its earnest indignation, its wild desperation and humor, its lyricism and fantasy.

Until he got home, he had no intention of writing up the events. But his agent, Scott Meredith, negotiated a then-munificent fee of $10,000 with *Harper's Magazine*, and Mailer sat down in Provincetown, accompanied by Beverly Bentley and a typist. Eschewing drink, he wrote almost ninety thousand words in seven weeks. He had to work without notes—he hadn't taken any. He made lists of the scenes he wanted to cover, numbered in a rough sequence. Trying out different strategies, he had trouble getting underway, but when he found his voice, he wrote the first draft by hand in pencil, covering page after page of unlined paper, sometimes thirty-two or thirty-three lines a page, sometimes more. A lot of this work was done on a full-sized pad, the pages still pasted at the top, which suggests Mailer's longing for continuity. As his secretary typed the manuscript, he did serious rewriting.

All ninety thousand words went into the January 1968 issue of *Harper's*; at the time, it was the longest article ever published in an American magazine. To his highly subjective, minute-by-minute account, he added a more orderly and top-down relation of the events, which was published in the April issue of *Commentary*. The two pieces together make up the book *The Armies of the Night*, which won both the Pulitzer Prize and the National Book Award for 1968. It is a great garrulous American work, joyous and grief-struck, a book that comes within hailing distance of Whitman's poetry and James Agee's text for *Let Us Now Praise Famous Men*. And through it all runs an inquiry into Mailer's status as an American Jew.

MAILER CALLED IT "history as a novel, the novel as history." He certainly uses the resources of fiction, re-creating atmosphere, testy and companionable exchanges, interior thoughts, the play of bodies and temperaments. In an unpublished note for the book, he wrote, "Some of the dialogue is recollected exactly, about a full share has been re-created. This novelist does not pretend to an accurate memory of words and the sequence of motions—he does claim a reasonably inviolable sense of the shifting mood of each event within the sequence of events." So partly fiction, mostly not. Hemingway had put himself into his nonfiction books *Death in the Afternoon* (bullfighting) and *The Green Hills of Africa* (hunting), but without Mailer's portrait of changing consciousness or his habit of lacerating self-exposure. Who was doing the observing and writing here? What was the author's relation to the events? Mailer made himself the center of the story—terrible intellectual manners in general but, in his hands, a strategic and expressive coup. As he explains, this protagonist has his uses.

> [He] serves willy-nilly as the bridge—as many will say the *pons asinorum*— into the crazy house, the crazy mansion, of that historic moment when a mass of the citizenry—not much more than a mob—marched on a bastion which symbolized the military might of the Republic, marching not to capture it but to wound it *symbolically* . . . It is fitting that any ambiguous comic hero of such a history should not only be very much to the side of the history, but that he should be an egotist of the most startling disproportions, outrageously and often unhappily self-assertive, yet in command of a detachment classic in severity (for he was a novelist and so in need of studying every last lineament of the fine, the noble, the frantic, and the foolish in others and in himself).

As J. Michael Lennon has pointed out, Mailer in his early books had difficulties with narrative point of view. *Armies* can only be called a double-barreled third-person work. Mailer, the narrator of the drama, dramatizes "Mailer," the actor in the drama. This "Mailer" has a complicated temper formed by history, politics, and love of country. He has complicated needs, too; he's forty-four years old, married, with three ex-wives and six children, a man with a belly. In the middle of the tumultuous events, he longs for the downy comforts of Washington's Hay-Adams hotel. As Mailer the author observes, makes his assessments, and relates one thing to another, "Mailer" stumbles around and longs for grace, a comic hero who may be no more than a fool. For Jews there is always some danger in looking like a fool. Mailer exults in the danger.

"Mailer" behaves rudely at a party given by liberal Washington academics, drinks too much, and later urinates on the floor of a darkened movie-theater bathroom. He then gives an excruciating speech in mock-redneck tones (his LBJ imitation), dismaying the earnest political youths who have gathered for a pep talk the night before the march. It is an embarrassing beginning to an epic narrative, even a mock-epic narrative. But then consider the shame-ridden episodes in the great confessional works of Saint Augustine and Rousseau. The author rides down to the bottom of his soul, airing (showing off?) his misdeeds, humiliations, and ill thoughts. This experiment may lead to what every writer wants—authenticity, and perhaps authority. For Mailer, what begins in drunkenness and piss will end in history, philosophy, and moral speculation.

IN 1965, FIVE years after assaulting Adele Morales, Mailer told the magazine writer Brock Brower that the act had destroyed forever "the possibility of being the Jeremiah of our time." However scandalous his life, however skeptical of the Hebrew Bible's God, Mailer very much longed for the power of Jewish prophecy—longed for it as much as he desired his promised land of the big novel. As critic George Steiner put it in his review of *Advertisements for Myself*, "To the Jewish tenor of mind fiction does not come easily. The Judaic tradition is narrowed and ennobled by the predominance of argument and verity."

In 1967, in Washington, Jeremiah was reborn in argument and verity. How was it possible that America was waging war against Asian peasants? How could the war be accepted by so many of our countrymen? What did it say about the country's future? The Americans who supported the war are very much present in the book—in the military and local police guarding the Pentagon and in Mailer's speculations about them and about the more than half the country they represent.

Mailer was obsessed with concentrated and possibly corrupt power—the Mafia, the CIA, the FBI, the media networks. But corruption of a more pervasive sort, he thought, was built into American postwar culture, and it was spilling out in extreme militarism and moral apathy. As he said many times, building his critique through earlier essays, the evil lay in the encompassing role of technology and corporate domination, the bland authoritarianism of the repetitive exercise of control through "enormous banks of coded knowledge." (This was written in 1967, way before the Internet, social media, and big data.) He pointed as well to the replacement of such organic materials as wood, iron, and stone with plastic, the baked chemicals spreading into every corner of American life. He attacked the routine functional architecture in which a school, a prison, and a small office building all looked alike, and the massification of popular culture in TV sitcoms—all of it taken together, he thought, induced a creeping demoralization, literally a dulling of the moral sense, an indifference to distinction and reasoning. In his specialized use of the word, we lived in a "totalitarian" culture.

Some of Mailer's cultural criticism has been dismissed as passé or futile. Why fret over all this? After all, the argument goes, we who benefit from Tupperware, computers, and efficiency (and now the Internet, AI, and instant delivery of whatever we want)—we are not in the best position to criticize what has made our lives easier and more prosperous. But this kind of critique is beside the point. Mailer was registering the way many Americans were assaulted by the hurtling postwar material and technological change—just as many more of us are now jostled, harassed, frightened, even depressed by even more rapid changes (AI spreading through us like a virus). Yes, depressed, even though these "advances" again make our lives easier and more prosperous. Cultural criticism of great eloquence does not become obsolete, easily dismissed as if it were itself a piece of technology. John Ruskin's tirades against the soul-destroying nature of factory work and D. H. Lawrence's hatred of what English industry was doing to landscape and spirit have only gained in flavor and consequence over time. Maureen Corrigan, professor of English at Georgetown University and longtime book reviewer for NPR's *Fresh Air* program, has described Mailer as "one of the Victorian sages' great inheritors [she mentions Thomas Carlyle, William Morris, and Ruskin] but, frankly, better than them, more alive on the page, because Mailer wrote as an American and that meant he wrote with explosive humor."

From our point of view, Mailer's analysis is more interesting than the standard Vietnam-era liberal attacks on imperialism, militarism, obsessive anti-Communism (though he wrote some of that, too). He wanted to identify the background of moral stupidity—the failure in so many parts of America to see the cruelty and absurdity of what we were doing in Southeast Asia. Separated in its daily routines from meaning and accountability, the country had slipped into waking madness and had lost its moral grounding.

HE TAGGED ALONG as hundreds of young men turned in their draft cards at the Department of Justice. Watching the draft resisters, whom he knew would be beaten the next day, Mailer felt abashed; he felt a sense of modesty, which alarmed him. "He had been born to a modest family, had been a modest boy, a modest young man, and he hated that, he loved the pride and arrogance and the confidence and egocentricity he had acquired over the years." But Mailer was alarmed by more than a possible return to modesty; he was simply outclassed. Crossing the Arlington Memorial Bridge to the Pentagon, he walked alongside Robert Lowell—a great poet, a Boston Brahmin (despite his brief conversion to Catholicism), tall, handsome, with a melancholy high forehead and a demeanor so elegantly undemonstrative that it made Mailer, always grasping for attention, feel like a noisy buffoon.

There's a passage in the manuscript that didn't make it into the printed text: "Secretly, Mailer adored Lowell. The elegant makes great difficulty look simple. What is admirable about it, is that it can't easily be copied. And no one could copy Lowell." In the published version, however, the Jew from Brooklyn grows rebellious.

You, Lowell, beloved poet of many, what do you know of the dirt and the dark deliveries of the necessary? What do you know of dignity hard-won? And dignity lost through innocence. And dignity lost for a cause one cannot name. What do you know about getting fat against your will, and turning into a clown of an arriviste baron when you would rather be an eagle or a count, or rarest of all, some natural aristocrat from these damned democratic states?

Could there be any kind of redemption for this envious boor? Well, he was at least able to praise. The draft resisters were brave, and he gloried in the troops, a ragtag army of academics and students, yippies "gotten up like Arab sheiks, or in Park Avenue doorman's greatcoats." The yippies perform an exorcism of the Pentagon, an attempt, that is, to encircle the building, levitate it three hundred feet in the air, and chase away its bad spirits. "Out, demons, out!" the crowd cried. The sixties! The yippies were arrested and some were beaten; so were the draft resisters. Mailer had to equal their courage. He startled the military police by abruptly rushing forward, a bourgeois projectile alarmingly in motion: "Dark pinstripe suit, his vest, the maroon and blue regimental tie, the part in his hair, the barrel chest, the early paunch. He must have looked like a banker himself, a banker gone ape!"

MAILER IDENTIFIED A cultural divide in America but, as he portrayed it, the divide was no simple matter—certainly not a clear-cut case of righteously hip (anti-war) and compliantly square (pro-war). Of the military police and US marshals facing the demonstrators he writes, "Their eyes were blank and dull, that familiar small-town cast of eye which speaks of apathy rising to fanaticism only to subside in apathy again." But this judgment of rural America in authority gets qualified in extraordinary ways. Mailer develops the confrontation between protesting, middle-class students and working-class policemen with great psychological acuteness.

It is the urban middle class in America who always feel most uprooted, most alienated from America itself, and so instinctively most critical of America, for neither do they work with their hands nor wield real power, so it is never their lathe nor their sixty acres, and certainly never is it their command which is accepted because they are simply American and there, no, the urban middle class was the last to arrive at respectable status and it has been the most unprotected (for its dollars are the great nourishing mother of all consumer goods) yet the most spiritually undefended since even the concept of a crisis in identity seems most exclusively their own.

The sons and daughters of that urban middle class, forever alienated in childhood from all the good simple funky nitty-gritty American joys of the working class like winning a truly dangerous fist fight at the age of eight or getting sex before fourteen, dead drunk by sixteen, whipped half to death by your father, making it in rumbles with a proud street gang, living at war with the educational system, knowing how to snicker at the employer from one side of the mouth, riding a bike with no hands, entering the Golden Gloves, doing a hitch in the Navy, or a stretch in the stockade, and with it all, their sense of élan, of morale, for buddies are the manna of the working class: there is a God-given cynical indifference to school, morality, and job. The working class is loyal to friends, not ideas.

"The urban middle class," with their late-arriving status and their identity crises, are unmistakably Jews, including Mailer himself, who experienced none of those "nitty-gritty American joys" as a teenager and had to contrive such artificial devices as pretending to be a hobo in order to gain experience. But his celebration of tough American rural and small-town boys has an element of despair built into it. Mailer admired the American working class in many ways, but he knew the youthful joys might dissipate, that the indifference to school, morality, and job would likely lead to income stasis, bitter resentment, even early death. The blank-eyed military police and marshals at the Pentagon could be some of those courageous boys grown older.

In 1967, Mailer wrote that "the two halves of America were not coming together, and when they failed to touch, all of history might be lost in the divide." He anticipated the contempt now shooting across class, racial, and cultural lines—especially the rural and small-town whites despising the educated elites. He foresaw the crowds gathering at Donald Trump's rallies, harsh, derisive, glorying in the vengeful release of self-pity. The Jeremiah in him saw it and warned against it more than a half century ago.

URBAN POL, SPACE WALKER, MOVIE DIRECTOR

Norman was sure he loved and understood New York City better than anyone else. His first attempt to run for mayor had collapsed at the chaotic party of November 19, 1960. But in 1969, at the suggestion of Gloria

Steinem and other friends, he entered the Democratic primary, and this time he was serious: he got beloved New York journalist Jimmy Breslin to accompany him, as candidate for city council president; he hired a staff, put on a three-piece suit, and made hundreds of speeches. He wanted to "have his hand on the rump of history," as he later said. Serious as it was, the campaign was also marked by merry invention and easy spontaneity. The favored slogans were No More Bullshit and Vote the Rascals In. Its principal platform item was that the city should detach itself from the dour conservative hinterlands north of town and become the fifty-first state. Free bicycles should be available at city parks, a central fruit-and-vegetable market set up. Those last two perfectly reasonable ideas, in altered form, went into effect a few decades later.

The campaign was over in June (he finished fourth in the Democratic primary), and Mailer went off to Houston to do early work for a report on the Apollo 11 flight to the moon. He was working for *Life* magazine, and you couldn't swim down any stream more main than that—or get better paid for it. Yet a trip to the moon made him uneasy. He wondered if we were not profaning the natural order by invading another celestial body—invading the *moon*, a body with its pull on the tides, its pull on the moods of men and women. Metaphysical speculation runs riot in his prose but gives way after a while to a remarkably detailed exposition of the nuts-and-bolts technology involved in getting an enormous rocket off the ground. What nuts! What bolts! Mailer, the Harvard engineering major, produced pages of data enlarged by an ambition to explain the science of rocketry to America.

Unease returned to him, but in a different way. Here was his dreaded technology in one of its greatest triumphs, and it made him, a mere literary man, feel small. At length, he tried to understand the hyper-straight culture of NASA's Manned Spacecraft Center in Houston. He devoted pages to the imagined psychology of the astronauts—fascinating, guarded men who speak in the blandest tones possible. Could he observe this high-tech scene impartially—"observe without ego"? He could not. He was an outsider, an urban Jew in a very strange land. The people who worked for NASA "were also by every evidence part of that vast convocation of Americans, probably a majority, whom one saw in New York only on television. They were, in short, WASPs, and it was part of the folklore of New York that WASPs were without odor"—that is, without the smells of youth or age that suggested a connection with life's processes. In actuality, there were (and are) plenty of WASPs in New York, and they smell great, but for him "Wasps were already halfway to the moon"—that is, overcontrolled, impersonal, abnormally neutral. In all, the space culture, however impressive, was too clean for him, too mechanical and altogether too spooky. We feel relief at the end of the long report (published in 1970 as a book, *Of a Fire on the Moon*) when the trip is over. Life ruled by bland officials and somber space athletes was not his thing.

WHEN MAILER WENT to Houston, Beverly Bentley stayed behind. The couple had two boys in the sixties, Michael and Stephen, which greatly pleased Mailer, who had fathered four daughters earlier. Beverly, however, was often frazzled by taking care of an expanding and contracting brood. Children from Norman's earlier marriages would show up for a while and then leave. Like his earlier wives, Beverly drank and fought with him, often in front of friends; the marriage was vital but fraught from the beginning, and by the time Mailer went to Houston, it was all but finished. In one way, Beverly suffered the same fate as Bea and Adele, all three women trying to keep up with Mailer, drinking heavily and getting into terrible fights. Mailer later said of Beverly, "She gave up acting too soon. It ate at her, it ate at her, it ate at her," which suggests that he had understood (at last) how a woman's vocation might be as important as a man's. (Beverly Bentley actually continued acting for years, mainly in theater.) They wouldn't officially divorce until 1980. When Mailer wrote the *Life* pieces after returning from Houston, he was living in Provincetown not with Beverly but with Carol Stevens, a sultry and talented jazz singer he had met years earlier. The imperious Fanny Mailer told her that her son "needed more love than other men."

At the end of the decade, he also spent many hours editing *Maidstone*, a movie he shot from 1968 to 1970 on various estates in the Hamptons. Earlier he had made *Wild 90* (1968) and then *Beyond the Law* (1968), semi-improvised fiction films shot in documentary style with handheld cameras—Mailer's idea of "existential" cinema. Without preparation or much of a script, Mailer and his actor friends (Mickey Knox, Rip Torn) would make a pass at playing gangsters, cops, pols, the denizens of corrupt urban life. Occasionally, sparks flew (an off-center revelation of character, a potent inadvertence), but much of the finished films are messy, fragmentary, almost indecipherable, and they produced intense audience misery.

For *Maidstone*, the performing group included Mailer's pals and ex-wives and a few professional actors. They all got boozed and laid—it was a wild enough scene—while Mailer paced around, barrel-chested and shirtless, working everybody up into meaningless rages. The picture is remembered now mainly for the moment in which actor Rip Torn, playing an assassin, attacks Mailer, who is playing a presidential candidate—attacks him with a hammer, whereupon Mailer, wrestling with Torn on the ground, bites the actor's ear. Mailer's children, who were on the scene, screamed in terror. Norman wanted fiction that had the spontaneous feeling of real life, but in this case real life charged into fiction and almost destroyed the fiction makers.

THE JEWISH PATRIARCH I

During the summer of 1970, Henry Grunwald, the editor of *Time*, reached Mailer on the telephone. Did he realize that he had become the principal target of the women's liberation movement? Mailer claimed he knew nothing of his notoriety and refused to take the bait. But five weeks later *Time* put Kate Millett, the author of *Sexual Politics*, on the cover of the magazine. *Sexual Politics*, adapted from a Columbia PhD thesis, was the hot nonfiction book of the season, a feminist polemic, theoretical (in a haphazard way), bristling with contempt for villains. Without more than a nod to Simone de Beauvoir, whose ideas it lifts, the book lays out the case against patriarchal oppression and the myths of romantic love and family security—mere ideological entrapments for women, who, it seems, have been oppressed at all times and everywhere, robbed of dignity throughout history. In the section of the book that deals with literature, Millett's targets were D. H. Lawrence, Henry Miller, and Norman Mailer, proponents of sex as male power.

Norman could no longer hide. In response, he wrote not a comment or two but an entire book—*The Prisoner of Sex*, a work astonishing for its combined rhetorical brilliance and moral stupidity. (The text first appeared in *Harper's*, which devoted its entire issue of March 1971 to it.) He was a prisoner because he always needed women; a prisoner as well because no sexual act arrived without meaning, and he was doomed to provide that meaning.

He studied liberationist polemics, praising some writers, angrily attacking others, especially Millett, a leaden-toned prosecutor and—even worse—a literary swindler who quoted passages from Miller, Lawrence, and himself by snipping the surrounding context in ways that make the novelists seem like heartless brutes. (Mailer's forty pages on Lawrence in *The Prisoner of Sex* may be the best criticism ever written about him.) At the personal level, Millett's threat to Mailer is clear enough: "She had all the technological power of the century in her veins, she was the point of advance for those intellectual forces vastly larger than herself which might look to the liberation of women in the ongoing incarceration of the romantic idea of man." Mailer's entire text is a poetic defense of the romantic idea of man. Yet few people, I've discovered, know that Mailer throws in the towel in the end: you win, I lose. The romantic idea of man has been vanquished, though not without an epic struggle. The eloquence of this text, as journalist Pete Hamill said, feels improvisational, as free as a great theme-and-variation jazz piece developed by Charlie Parker or John Coltrane. It may be a foolish book, but only a great writer could have written it.

Like many chauvinists before him, Mailer depresses women by elevating them. Women, he writes, were "a step, or a stage, or a move or a leap nearer the creation of existence, they were—given man's powerful sense of the present—his indispensable and only connection to the future." He rhapsodizes over women's power of conception, a direct link to the sources of life in the universe, the primal forces flowing beneath everyday existence. But he speaks narrowly of women's needs. His notion is that women's "prime responsibility" on earth is "to find the best mate possible for herself, and conceive children who will improve the species."

Now, before going any further, I need to point out that Mailer had no quarrel with mainstream feminism. Gloria Steinem was a friend, and he regarded Bella Abzug, as you may recall, with admiration and (amused) affection. In *Prisoner* he lists with approval the principal objectives of Betty Friedan's organization, the National Organization for Women— equal pay, the right to abortion, and the rest. But he takes on the radicals, and he demands clean combat, no hitting below the belt. "If he had begun this remedial reading with the firmest male prejudice of them all, which is that women might possess the better half of life, he was never to encounter any comprehension among female writers that a firm erection on a delicate fellow was the adventurous juncture of ego and courage." Which comes as something of a surprise. How could a supposed macho jerk have described an erection as a risk, a partway con job? Mailer insists that women need to understand that sexual satisfaction for men may be as complicated and as difficult as it is for women.

He likes some of what he reads. He absorbs Meredith Tax on what it feels like for a woman to be mentally undressed by lounging hardhats. He quotes at length the candid and witty Australian disrupter Germaine Greer, whose book *The Female Eunuch* was also much discussed in 1970. He relishes such anonymous sallies as "The sex life of spiders is very interesting. He fucks her. She bites off his head." The new writers wanted to shock, which was all to the good. "A few of the women were writing in no way women had ever written before. . . . Every point was made with a minimum of words, a mean style, no question of that." The base of male conceit was the notion that "men could live with truths too unsentimental for women to support," but that belief had been overturned. Blood and anger had surged into women's writing.

BETTY FRIEDAN HATED the radical-feminist attack on the nuclear family; Mailer felt the same way, but he knew that "orgasm talk," which Betty huffily dismissed, was in fact the heart of the matter. He is enraged by women who want to replace the penis with battery-driven stimulation and the splendors of ordinary conception with an implanted egg or a surrogate mother—and everything else that follows from the introduction of technology into the creation of life. The difficulty that some couples have in conceiving is lost on him. And he is, it seems, late in registering the news that the clitoris is central to a woman's pleasure. He now responds with fear and contempt, for the shift away from the vagina threatened to make men feel clueless or, in extreme feminist polemics, expendable, little more than walking sperm banks. He is not ready to give up on husbands and lovers. And certainly not on the penis.

Jump forward for a second: after the *Harper's* article came out in March 1971, Mailer, on the night of April 30, 1971, confronted prominent feminists and a great many angry women (as well as abashed men) in a noisy public debate at New York's Town Hall. The event, as recorded by D. A. Pennebaker and Chris Hegedus in their documentary film *Town Bloody Hall*, was raucous, hypercharged, emotionally dangerous. A number of people said that middle-class feminism (i.e., Betty Friedan's feminism) was played out, and it was time for revolution. Members of the audience seemed, at different moments, furious, stricken, exhilarated.

The women on the panel, including Germaine Greer and Diana Trilling, all advocated for a new society in which women would no longer be under the thumb of men, and Mailer, increasingly angry, a wounded king, or perhaps a wounded harem master unable to corral his brood, was by turns gracious, sore, and insulting. As the evening went on, it became clear that women's liberation demanded him as a sacrifice. Freud had to be killed, and so did Mailer. Some women in the audience hurled flirtatious taunts at him, others shouted epithets. Exasperated by some of the taunts, Mailer finally said, "If you wish me to act the clown, I'll take out my modest little Jewish dick and put it on the table. You can all spit at it and laugh at it, and then I'll walk away, and you'll find it was just a dildo I left there. I hadn't shown you the real one."

THE MOVIE IS nerve-racking entertainment; the text is serious. In *The Prisoner of Sex*, the Jewish husband and lover strikes back. Who says that pleasure for women depends entirely on friction upon the clitoris? He calls to his side Germaine Greer, who insists that such obsessive manual stimulation is a betrayal of the potentially sexualized body. ("If we localize female response in the clitoris," Greer writes, "we impose upon women the same limitation of sex which has stunted the male response.") With that issue solved to his satisfaction, Mailer offers a prose poem devoted to the varieties of female orgasm, all of them produced, one assumes, vaginally and with the collaboration of Norman. "If there were women who came as if lightning bolts had flung their bodies across a bed, were there not women who came with the gentlest squeeze of the deepest walls of the vagina . . . yes, women who purred as they came and women who screamed . . ."

And so on. It doesn't seem to have occurred to him that some of these women might have been faking. But the passage is no more than a gateway to a larger event, the generation of splendid children who, in Mailer's fancy, are produced by splendid sex.

He preferred to believe that the Lord, Master of Existential Reason, was not thus devoted to the absurd as to put the orgasm in the midst of the act of creation without cause of the profoundest sort, for when a man and a woman conceive, would it not be best that they be able to see one another for a transcendent instant, as if the soul of what would then be conceived might live with more light later?

For an intellectual, it's the ultimate romantic idea: creation occurs at the moment of highest consciousness. Such an experience was much more powerful than mere lust, which Mailer, like his mentor in sexual matters, D. H. Lawrence, thought was actually trivial. Sex must come up from the earth, in magnificence; or, at its peak, from God. He was disdainful of masturbation (years earlier he had written that "everything that's beautiful and good in one, goes up the hand, goes into the air, is lost"), and he was vociferously against birth control. Sex should place one's entire being at risk: one either has an extraordinary illumination or not, one grows or not, and central to the experience is the risk of conceiving a child. Which, the entire world now responds, is a cruel and foolish idea. Men will experience bad sex as a defeat, good sex as a blessing; women, whatever their experience, may be left with diapers to buy, schools to engage, a life turned upside down.

WHY, ONE WONDERS, does Mailer insist on *learning* something in sex? Critic Alfred Kazin wrote Mailer that he was "the rabbi of screwing, the Talmudist of fucking." Isn't pleasure enough? Or closeness to one's mate? This mania for knowledge is some sort of buried Jewish compulsion, such that no given act, not even sex, can be regarded as sufficient in itself without some gain of understanding. Jews look for self-improvement in the strangest places.

In his role as moralist and prophet, Mailer tried to slow down or at least lament a shift in reproductive behavior—slow it down not only because he thought technology was a violation of the sacred but because he was upset that Jews had played a major role in the new developments. The nineteenth- and early-twentieth-century suffragists were largely Protestant (Elizabeth Cady Stanton, Susan. B. Anthony, et al.), but the Jews were central, as we have seen, to American feminism of the sixties and seventies. It proceeded from a general liberation.

Yes, the Jews emancipated at last from being Jews [i.e., subservient to the Law, orthodoxy, etc.], able to learn the skills of sciences and professions closed to them for centuries, had of course become the very principle of emancipation. . . . The modern Jew, whip-slick free of taboo, had acquired influence in every field of science, medicine, law and finance.

All very well, but there's something mysterious and perverse in Mailer's assessment of the Jews and sex, a rare failure of consciousness, perhaps. One wonders if Mailer in 1971 was familiar with the mystical sections of the Talmud, with its erotic rabbinical fantasies; or whether he knew some of the more extreme theorists of the Kabbalah, written in the twelfth and thirteenth centuries by mystics who hinted that ecstasy was a communion with God, that sexual and spiritual ecstasy were not opposites but were intimately linked. These are minority strains in Judaism, certainly nothing demanding obedience. Mailer definitely knew these texts later in life, but not, I believe, in 1971. His reproduction of their ideas was unconscious—tribal, if you like.

Ecstasy was one part of a possible Jewish inheritance. The other side was negative, the disapproval of sexual pleasure outside of marriage and procreation. Mailer's contempt for masturbation may have sprung, without his realizing it, from the Hebrew Bible. In Genesis 38, Onan's act was *coitus interruptus*, but over time, in a slippage of reference, "onanism" came to stand as a general term for masturbation. Norman's hatred of contraception may also have had antecedents in rabbinical texts. The men generating Jewish law from the third to the sixth centuries of the Common Era were not in favor of anything that interrupted the flow of semen into the birth canal. Jewish tradition insisted that women had to have children; that was their blessed function, and seminal emissions should not go for naught. So Mailer's loathing of both masturbation and contraception, which he defends with lofty existential demands for courage, may have been based as well on a kind of tribal memory, a prohibition that had slipped into his unconscious, like one of Freud's dawn-of-man taboos.

J. Michael Lennon tells me that Mailer arrived at his personal refusal of masturbation in the following way. In 1946, he was a twenty-three-year-old soldier in the American force occupying Japan. He found himself alone in the woods (he liked going for long walks), masturbated, and was so disgusted with himself that he vowed never to do it again. Throughout his life, and in many matters, shame gutted Mailer when he was displeased with himself. Masturbation was dishonorable; nothing was at stake in the act. But was that shame not inspired by ancient contempt?

Running away from Judaism and toward it at the same time, Mailer almost helplessly contradicts himself: he celebrates the suppression of the Law among modern Jews while succumbing to some of its oldest prohibitions. He may have been too deep within fear and desire to see how balled up he was.

Exhausted, Mailer gives up on male supremacy at the end of *The Prisoner of Sex*. He can no longer fight against history, against technology, against women's anger. The wounded king lets go and blesses the liberated woman, let's go but for one element.

> Let her travel to the moon, write the great American novel, and allow her husband to send her off to work with her lunch pail and a cigar; she could kiss the cooze of forty-one Rockettes in Macy's store window; she could legislate, incarcerate, and wear a uniform; she could die of every male disease, and years of burden was the first, for she might learn that women worked at onerous duties and men worked for egos which were worse than onerous and often insane. So women could have the right to die of men's diseases, yes, and might try to live with men's egos in their own skull case and he would cheer them on their way—would he? Yes, he thought that perhaps they may as well do what they desired if the anger of the centuries was having its say. Finally, he would agree with everything they asked but to quit the womb, for finally a day had to come when women shattered the pearl of their love for pristine and feminine will and found the man, yes the man in the million who could become the point of the seed which would give an egg back to nature, and let the woman return with a babe who came from the root of God's desire to go all the way, wherever was that way.

THE JEWISH PATRIARCH II

If your philosophy and temperament require that you gratify your senses as often as possible, how do you function as a family man? In the summer of 1970, just before his encounter with radical feminism, Norman rented a house on the Maine coast (the Provincetown house wasn't big enough). He was joined by a mysterious mistress—"an old love, his dearest old love"—and five of his six children. His oldest daughter, Susan, stayed for two weeks and left; Barbara, Norman's sister, also helped out; and a local Maine woman did the cleaning and laundry. Mailer and his girls (thirteen, eleven, and eight) took care of the little boys (six and four); together they shopped and cooked. Mailer says he "knew at last what a woman meant when she said her hair smelled of grease."

> It was not an unhappy summer, and he ended with the knowledge that he could run a decent home and sleep without screaming at children and be as a result thus empty-minded at night that solitaire pleased him, knew he could immerse himself in unintriguing subtleties of the thousand acts of order and timing which made the difference between efficient and catastrophic keeping of house—could do all this for year after year and never write another word, be content, honorably fatigued, free of dread, all credit deposited to his moral foundations, but in no uncertainty that the most interesting part of his mind and heart was condemned to dry on the vine . . .

Most women would say that Mailer had quite a lot of female help in this brave adventure. But at least he got partway to what many women experience—childcare as a life's occupation—and he was honest enough to admit that it would kill his writing career. In all, Mailer helped raise nine children, eight of his own, one adopted (Matthew, Norris Church's son from her first marriage). John Buffalo Mailer, the son of Mailer and Norris, had two parents throughout his childhood; all the others were raised by both parents for a while—until Mailer found a new wife, at which point they were raised mainly by their mothers.

"He wanted to be the architect of his family," Susan Mailer said to me. "We had to see him in the summer. Bring no friends. We had to be intelligent. He got the idea of family from his mother. A Jewish family."

They saw him at Christmas, too. An occasional father, then, but always, for good and for ill, a demanding one. He put his girls on ski slopes when they were little children, launched them into shaky boats off the Maine coast; he insisted that Kate (Jeanne Campbell's daughter) get in the water even though she hated water. He wanted them to grow up unafraid of physical challenges—reacting again to his own sense of himself as an overprotected child. "I had a lot of phobias when I was a kid," Michael Mailer (Norman's firstborn son) told me. "I was usually the last person to do something, and I felt ashamed relative to my brothers and sisters. I just wanted to please him." Mailer taught him to box, and later, Michael said, "Boxing was the way we related to each other." His fears vanquished, he boxed at Harvard and in the Golden Gloves in Boston—Michael Mailer became a real boxer. "But I went too far," he told me. "I went sky-diving, I hung out with the Kennedy kids, who were wild." Michael survived as a New York movie producer.

Mailer's wives did most of the childcare, but it says something for this celebrity father that his children were nothing like the children of Hollywood stars, so many of whom wind up as alcoholics, addicts, suicides, victims of car accidents, lifetime partygoers. In some ways, Mailer was a conventional upper-middle-class Jewish parent. He insisted that his kids study; he made them swear off marijuana until they had graduated from college. In the summer vacations, when the children were a little older, they made short movies with 8-millimeter cameras that he provided, and they acted out scenes from Tennessee Williams's *A Streetcar Named Desire* and Eugene O'Neill's *Long Day's Journey into Night*. For decades, American Jews have had a thing about summer camp. At Norman's camp, the activities were more demanding than color wars and scavenger hunts.

The children went to good schools, including NYU, Bowdoin, Princeton, Barnard, Wesleyan, and Harvard; they have productive lives in such professions as actor, painter, writer, producer, director. In interviews, they speak of their father with love and regret mixed together. What they got from him was a kind of radiant soulfulness, the men as well as the women. When I saw five of them together (at a 2023 conference of Mailer scholars in Austin, Texas), they teased one another, rehashed old scenes, told old jokes, carried on like any large happy family. No doubt they became skilled at managing diminished expectations of their father. Maggie Mailer, an artist, told me, "We survived by staying together."

A NEW YORK JEW IN AFRICA

This time he was not reporting from, say, Madison Square Garden, interpreting the familiar sweet-bitter mingling of perfume and beer emanating from the crowd of hoods, fight-crowd women, and big-time celebrities.

He was in Zaire for the world-historical "Rumble in the Jungle," the heavyweight title bout on October 30, 1974, between Muhammad Ali and George Foreman. Momentarily, Kinshasa, the old river port on the south bank of the Congo, had moved to the center of the world, and in this world, Norman Mailer, though a member of the media elite, was an outsider, even a nonentity. On the boulevards of Kinshasa, the surging crowds shouted, "*Ali, boma yé!*" ("Ali, will kill him!"). They ignored the New York Jew, the famous American writer. For Mailer, it was a humbling experience—and instructive, too.

As he knew, the Congo's history was more than sinister. After 1885, the Congo territory, under the domination of King Leopold II of Belgium, had become the Congo Free State and then the Belgian Congo, the private garden of the King. For decades, Leopold's operatives and private companies had robbed the land and killed many Africans. Their savage depredations had inspired Joseph Conrad's great novella *Heart of Darkness* (1899), from which Mailer quotes a famous passage, the description of exhausted African workers left to die. "Brought from all the recesses of the coast in all the legality of time contracts, lost in uncongenial surroundings, fed on unfamiliar food, they sickened, became inefficient, and then were allowed to crawl away and rest." They were mere shadows of men.

In 1960, the Belgians finally departed, and the country renamed itself the Democratic Republic of the Congo, then Zaire. *The Fight*, among many other things, is a portrait of a newly born country led by African men, or at least one African man, the vicious dictator Mobutu Sese Seko Koko Ngbendu Wa Za Banga. Mobutu, eager for fame, allowed the fight promoter Don King to set up a match, shown everywhere in closed-circuit TV, between two of the most physically powerful Black men in the world. Ali and Foreman both stood six feet three inches and weighed about 220 pounds. The match was a kind of answer to Leopold and the grove of death, an assertion of postcolonial Africa's importance in the world. The prefight atmosphere, as Mailer creates it, is richly textured, suggestive, an anticipation of finality of some sort. Particularly at night, the air is full of intimations whose presence he could sense without quite defining. He was in Hemingway country at last, the vast, quivering landscape, but Hemingway was no longer master in the new Africa, and Mailer, his disciple, was both awed and diminished.

The report he made, which appeared in *Playboy* in May and June of

1974, was then published (with some rewriting and additions) as *The Fight* in 1975. It is one of Mailer's best books, a text whose relationship to most fight journalism is like that of *Huckleberry Finn* to a boys' adventure book snatched from an old drugstore. Apart from its evocation of physical courage and its enormous zest for the craft and danger of boxing, *The Fight* is written with a ready candor about race that would likely be impossible today. And Mailer's newfound humility—his willingness to learn things—is part of its charm and its eloquence.

IN PREPARATION FOR his visit, he read up on Bantu philosophy. He was much taken with the idea that the Zaireans believed in *n'golo*, "a Congolese word for force, for vital force." *N'golo* included everything that was active in one's life, in one's past as well as one's present.

> Without putting it into words, he had always believed that. It gave a powerful shift to his thoughts. By such logic, men or women were more than the parts of themselves, which is to say more than the result of their heredity and experiences. Man was not only what he contained, not only his desires, his memory, and his personality, but also the forces that came to inhabit him at any moment from all things living and dead.

N'golo could be another name for his lifelong writerly instincts. He had always abundantly evoked the spirit of place (Miami, Chicago, Washington, Los Angeles), combining what he saw and felt with shafts from his unconscious, with the ensemble of the past, present, and future—his work, his clashes, his loves—that he carried around with him. He was closer to *n'golo* than any other American writer one could think of.

And there was something else: his interest in Bantu philosophy reinforced what he had recently been obsessed with. Since the beginning of the seventies, he had been working on a big novel set in the Egyptian past, in the reign of the Pharaoh Ramses IX, from 1123 to 1104 BCE, a time rich in military glory. Pharaonic Egypt had its highly developed erotic culture, its complicated funerary practices, its animal gods eating the hearts of the wicked—all of that mysterious, scary, hieratic stuff, established before the Judeo-Christian vision took hold. Both Egyptian mythology and Bantu philosophy, different as they were, answered to a common impulse in Mailer—the desire to get away from the solid-as-wood middle-class Jewish story of rational enterprise in business and in marriage. *N'golo* offered a kind of working metaphysics, speculative but also a way of living in the world.

What he observed of the fight impressed and frightened him. In 1957, in "The White Negro," Mailer had praised Black physical ability and grace. At home on the streets, where the police were a menace, Blacks had developed an awareness of danger unknown to most whites. He placed his observations in a complicated theory about humanity living with the bomb, apocalyptic orgasms, and all the rest of that. But now he leaves theory behind and liberates his skills as a novelist and journalist, a man uninhibited in his appreciation of actual bodies and minds. Tom Wolfe, in some of his nasty satirical journalism of the period ("Mau-Mauing the Flak Catchers"), had made fun of hyperaggressive African Americans. Wolfe turned them into hustling clowns, menacing and merrily dishonest. But Mailer writes with both amusement and love. *The Fight* has a forward-moving lilt, much of it produced by African American men holding forth in liberated Africa.

Each fighter has his entourage of trainers, sparring partners, mojo enhancers—the two camps stinging each other in Kinshasa's hotel lobbies like rival swarms of hornets. "My man will dance. My man will know how to prance. He's a genius, he's a god, your man's a pug." They were doing the dozens, right there in Kinshasa. By contrast, Don King, the fight promoter with a stand-up mass of dark hair—Don King, who put this monster event together—speaks in stately beatitudes, greeting Mailer with this extraordinary sentence: "You are a genius in tune with the higher consciousness yet an instinctive component of the untiring search for aspiration in the warm earth-embracing potential of exploited people." Even Mailer is floored.

Muhammad Ali himself is a compound of needling patter and bravado; some of his rants are almost majestic in their exalted summoning of his own beauty and power. The mere sight of him is enthralling.

There is always a shock in seeing him again. Not *live* as in television but standing before you, looking his best. Then the World's Greatest Athlete is in danger of being our most beautiful man, and the vocabulary of camp is doomed to appear. Women draw an *audible* breath. Men look down. They are reminded again of their lack of worth. If Ali never opened his mouth to quiver the jellies of public opinion, he would still inspire love and hate. For he is the Prince of Heaven—so says the silence around his body when he was luminous.

He is smart, too, but can he triumph? For all his skill, he seems over-matched by the champion. George Foreman, thickly muscled, polite, largely silent but for an occasional flash of deadpan wit—Foreman has the strongest punch in boxing. Seven years younger than Ali, he is heavily favored to win.

Ali initially takes endless punishment to his belly and sides as he leans back against the ropes. He doesn't dance (as he had everywhere prom-ised), he does rope-a-dope, but in that strategy all of nature is in play. "Ali, gloves to his head, elbows to his ribs, stood and swayed and was rat-tled and banged and shaken like a grasshopper at the top of a reed when the wind whips, and the ropes shook and swung like sheets in a storm." But he comes out of his defensive position in the eighth round and fells the champion with "six good punches, lefts and rights." The knockout is Homeric in its grandeur.

> Vertigo took George Foreman and revolved him. Still bowing from the waist in this uncomprehending position, eyes on Mohammad Ali all the way, he started to tumble and topple and fall even as he did not wish to go down. His mind was held with magnets high as his championship and his body was seeking the ground. He bent over like a six-foot sixty-year old butler who has just heard tragic news, yes, fell over all of a long collapsing two seconds, down came the Champion in sections and Ali revolved with him in a close circle, hand primed to hit him one more time, and never the need, a wholly intimate escort to the floor.

In the end, Ali's unexpected triumph is as much intellectual as physical, and, as such, it is apparently a Jewish triumph. Earlier in the book, Mailer had claimed the victory (in advance, so to speak) for the Jews. "It is striking how many of the Jewish writers at Nsele"—Ali's training camp—"had affec-tion for Ali, a veritable tropism of affection, as if, ultimately, he was one of them, a Jew in the sense of being his own creation. Few things would inspire more love among Jews than the genius to be without comparison." Since Ali was very publicly a Muslim, and not only a Muslim but a member of the Nation of Islam (whose leader Elijah Muhammad breathed anti-Semitism), Norman's claiming the champ for Judaism is downright perverse. I loathe the word *chutzpah*, but that is what it looks like. At least, at first.

In the past, Mailer came close to glorifying African Americans as primitives, closer to their bodies and the earth than white men—what Black intellectuals like James Baldwin disliked about "The White Negro." But he now prizes above everything else an athlete with terrific mind, an athlete who is spontaneous and inventive. *The Fight* is a momentous little book. The overall suggestion, offered in different ways, is that power is passing out of white hands, which means out of Jewish hands, too. Buried in Mailer's notes, I found this sentence, "black thought he was the chosen of God," an observation that suggests the possibility of God transferring His favor from Jews to African Americans. Mailer may have believed that the Jews had reached their apogee in American culture and needed to move out of the way. Reasoning creatures, many of them, they lacked *n'golo*.

THE EXPERIENCE OF seeing these two great men in the ring forced Mailer to make a serious accounting of his own situation. His self-dissatisfaction in this period was considerable. He tells a funny story against himself. He went for a jog with Muhammad Ali at three in the morning and gave up, winded, after a mile and a half. Walking back to Ali's training camp (it was still dark), he was terrified by the sound of a lion roaring in the trees. The raging beast, it turned out, was safely lodged in a nearby zoo. There was more of self-abnegation. Before the fight, he ventured onto the balcony attached to his hotel room. There was no guardrail (the hotel was a work in progress); the balcony was just a shelf. Mailer had to pass to the adjoining shelf by grappling his way across a partition, and he might have fallen seven stories. As always, he believed in tests. The murdering hero of *An American Dream* traverses a perilous ledge high in the Waldorf Towers, and Mailer himself had, at choice moments, advanced across parapets, climbed the pyramids, thrown himself into bodies of freezing water. But he admits in *The Fight* that the balcony walk was nothing more than a stunt. How could it help Ali? His small act of daring would not bring strength to the fighter he loved.

Mailer's self-dissatisfaction moves to a more practical question: What should he name himself in this latest essay in participatory journalism? In the past, he had used "Mailer" and, in his moon book, "Aquarius." He settles on "Norman," but the literary problem is an indication of something more serious.

> He had already had a love affair with himself, and it used up a good deal of love. He was no longer so pleased with his presence. His daily reactions bored him. They were becoming like everyone else's. His mind, he noticed, was beginning to spin its wheels, sometimes seeming to repeat itself for the sheer slavishness of supporting mediocre habits.

He was done with "Norman" and all the other ways of splitting the point of view between writer and actor, thereby relinquishing a mode of self-acknowledgment that had brought both renown and commercial success in seven books. And the boredom with himself? That kind of boredom has brought many men and women to the point of despair. A few years down the road, however, he found a way out. He solved his compositional problems and boredom itself in one of the most astonishing stylistic shifts in all of American literature.

A TRIGAMIST AND MORE

In 1975, when Mailer finished *The Fight*, he was still married to Beverly Bentley but was living with Carol Stevens. At a party in Arkansas (his best army friend lived there), he met a divorced teacher named Barbara Davis and spent the night with her. She eventually changed her name, at Mailer's suggestion, to Norris Church. (Norris was her former husband's last name, Church her own middle name.) In 2010, three years after Mailer died, Norris Church Mailer published a memoir, *A Ticket to the Circus*, a good book, funny and fluent and three-dimensional—a story of roots and self-transformation. Barbara Davis grew up in a religious family in the South. She adored her father, a strong and generous guy. In high school, she first attracted the attention of boys when her glasses broke in an accident; suddenly, they noticed she was beautiful, and they began falling out of trees. She went to Arkansas Tech, had a number of boyfriends (including the young Bill Clinton), became a teacher, married young, and had a son, Matthew. She divorced her husband when she was twenty-four and met Mailer a year later, in April 1975.

In order to get together for more than a night here and there, they had to tear through the bramblebush of Norman's affairs. In the summers, when he was living in the country with Carol Stevens and his children, he would rush out of the house and call Norris from a telephone booth. Later he set her up in a Brooklyn Heights apartment near his own place; they wrote each other passionate letters, and he took the fateful step of introducing her to his mother. According to the French proverb, "He who has two women loses his soul. He who has two houses loses his *mind*." But what if you have more of each?

As he and Beverly Bentley began divorce proceedings in 1977, one of the Boston papers called Mailer "a trigamist," which considerably under-counts the number. As well as Beverly Bentley, Carol Stevens, and Norris Church, there were longtime mistresses in San Francisco and Chicago and then, later on, several new liaisons and occasional one-night stands. He had two or three houses, depending on which summer we are talking about. (Norris describes a continuous traveling circus of people moving with children from property to property.) No man in his early fifties ever fought harder against being a man in his early fifties. I leave it to others to say whether Mailer lost his soul. He certainly did not lose his mind. In this mid-seventies period, he wrote *The Fight* and *The Executioner's Song*.

His divorce from Beverly Bentley came though, after a contentious three-year battle, in 1980. He and Carol Stevens wanted to legitimize their daughter, Maggie, so he married Carol for one day. (Norman figured he "owed" that much to Carol.) A few days later, on November 11, 1980, he and Norris got married, which means that Norman Mailer attended two of his own weddings in four days. By this time, he and Norris had a little boy, John Buffalo Mailer, or Buffalo, the only Mailer child, as I've said, to be raised by two parents all the way to adulthood.

He and Norris stayed married for twenty-seven years, until Mailer's death in 2007. Norris took on the children in odd lots, according to the season. Funny and startlingly beautiful, she was also kindly and sympathetic, a remarkably gentle person to show up in New York. She had considerable success there—as a Wilhelmina model for a while, as a painter and novelist (*Windchill Summer* and *Cheap Diamonds*), and later as a socialite. She did not take on Mailer's temperament or language; she was her own person. In public, they had a habit of one-upping each other, which made other people nervous, but the competition may have helped keep them together. When they argued at home, she slugged him several times but, she says, he never hit back.

In the mid- and late seventies, as Mailer was working on his Egyptian novel, he gave gloomy speeches about the impossibility of comprehending American culture. His disgust may have been produced by a diminishing sense of his own possible effect on the national mood. The voice that had so electrified young people fifteen years earlier had been produced by Mailer's war with America and with himself. But by the seventies it may have become clear to him that rebellion was no longer possible in the way he had imagined. He had underestimated the perverse wit, the encompassing and flattening power of American capitalism. Armed with its media spear of advertising, capitalism was fully capable of conquering and incorporating into itself rebellion as a lifestyle; it could sell Black consciousness as a consumer fashion and hipsterism as a joking irony that ridiculed the act of selling even as it sold everything to everybody. He wanted America to succeed, but only by getting braver and bolder, and that was not the way things were going. American subservience to "totalitarianism" and mediocrity would continue; he was not going to end either of them. Still, he was obsessed with the mind and spirit of the rebel, the outsider—the man who escaped the socializing steamroller, who ran so far from its tread that he became a criminal.

TWO NEW YORK JEWS IN UTAH

On January 19, 1977, Mailer received a telephone call from Lawrence J. Schiller—Larry Schiller, whom Mailer knew very well, an enterprising guy who had a habit of turning up at the scene of some hot-wired subject (say, the Manson murders). Schiller would gather interviews and photographs, and then turn his work over to a man who could write the words that he couldn't write himself. He was a "producer" of books—a hustler, some would say, a deal maker, spreading cash for information, but definitely a man who knew a good story. Mailer had worked with him on *Marilyn* (1973), his heavily speculative, often brilliant biography of the American beauty and movie star, a project that had begun as a gallery exhibition of Marilyn pictures organized by Schiller. Now Schiller was trying to interest Mailer in Gary Gilmore, the convict who had been executed, amid great publicity, two days earlier in Utah. Schiller had been on the case for five months. In February 1977, he sent Mailer the galleys of a *Playboy* interview he and writer Barry Farrell had done with Gilmore.

The convict was fascinating. He had spent most of his life in penal institutions of one sort or another. Released from federal prison in April 1976, he was taken in by relatives in Provo, Utah, but he was so estranged from ordinary life that he hardly knew how to enter a room or sit at a table and make conversation. Handsome in a lean, lone-wolf way, Gilmore was intelligent, observant, but preternaturally wary, and he flared up easily. He became the lover of a beautiful and lively young woman, Nicole Baker Barrett, who was in her third marriage (she had two small children from earlier marriages). But Gilmore was erratic and violent, and he lost her.

A few days later, he murdered, execution-style, a gas station employee in nearby Orem and a motel manager in Provo. Both men were married fathers and students at Brigham Young University, though Gilmore knew nothing of this—the men were strangers to him. He came away with $125 from the two crimes. When he shot the first man twice, he said, "This one is for me. This one is for Nicole." His cousin Brenda turned him in, and he was convicted of first-degree murder and sentenced to death.

As the date of execution approached, the ACLU and other anti-death-penalty lawyers petitioned courts to have the execution overturned or at least delayed. The situation developed into a grim sort of comedy. Liberal America was trying to save Gilmore, but he believed he deserved to die, and by firing squad, too. At one and the same time, Gilmore was a menacing, ice-cold punk and a severe moral agent of his own will. His perversely logical nature mocked the entire liberal temperament—not just its earnest legal efforts, but its educated desire to *understand*. Gary Gilmore was too proud to be understood. Nothing he said about murdering the two men made any sense.

A mob of reporters, TV personalities, and camera crews descended on Utah State Prison in Draper. For the press, Gary's value was greatest as a man determined to die. He came through for them. On the morning of January 17, 1977, all attempts to save him having failed, he said, "Let's do it." Four riflemen fired at him through slits in a black canvas blind. He had been released from federal prison only nine months and nine days earlier.

Larry Schiller was unwilling to read at any great length (he was dyslexic), but he was a remarkably patient interviewer, and after spreading some money around (a lot less than other people offered), he had sewn up exclusive rights to the stories of the principal players. He was prepared to turn over the entire lot to Mailer. Norman's hardcover publisher Little, Brown offered virtually nothing as an advance—$25,000, Schiller remembers—but Warner Books offered $500,000 for the paperback rights, which Mailer and Schiller split. The book was supposed to be around eighty thousand words long.

Gary Gilmore was everything that Mailer had been obsessed with—a young man violent yet undeniably lucid in many ways, a man who committed crimes (in his own eyes) as a way of surviving and expressing himself. He was a convict with sardonic insight into everyone he knew and the system he was trapped in. Like Julien Sorel, the hero of Stendhal's *The Red and the Black*, one of Mailer's favorite books, he commanded his own death. Caught, Mailer made multiple trips to south central Utah, "a place whose inhabitants have hardly heard of New York and where they certainly have never heard of me." He spent eight months (on and off) interviewing lawyers, court officers, and everyone in Gary's circle, sometimes side by side with Schiller, sometimes alone, gently and patiently drawing out the smallest details, the ambience, the attitudes that revealed a way of life that was touching in its loyalties but more than frightening in its purposelessness. Gary, Nicole, and their friends drive broken-down cars hundreds of miles, crossing state lines, to have a beer; they crash in different people's houses on the floor, drop their children off somewhere like gym bags. In an extraordinary *Times* review of the book that Mailer eventually produced, *The Executioner's Song*, Joan Didion wrote, "I think no one but Mailer could have dared this book. The authentic Western voice, the voice heard in *The Executioner's Song*, is one heard often in life but only rarely in literature, the reason being that to truly know the West is to lack all will to write it down."

MAILER BEGAN *THE EXECUTIONER'S SONG* in Provincetown in the summer of 1977 and continued it in Brooklyn Heights in a small rented room one flight below the family apartment (he had sold off the lower floors). He worked in that room through the winter of 1978 and, giving up Cape Cod, through the summer, too, as Norris painted and taught art classes in the city. The room, Lennon says, was irritated by the sound of a hissing steam heater and by the rumble and swish of trucks on the Brooklyn-Queens Expressway below. Piles of notes lay everywhere on the floor. The office was like Gary's cell, though this cell was blessed with the enthralling view of Lower Manhattan and the Statue of Liberty out in the bay. "I work six or seven days a week, don't go out," he wrote a friend, "and curse my primal verbosity of mind." Six different typists worked on the manuscript.

Mailer's earlier books are richly composed, sometimes overcomposed, as if he wanted to pass the entire world through the vibrating prism of his own senses. But in order to get Utah right, Mailer performed an amazing feat: he took his own voice out of the text. He extrapolates here and there, creating a connection, say, between two small moments, but the book is entirely composed in Gary's voice, Nicole's voice, the voices of their friends and families, scene after scene reconstructed out of letters, interviews, and documents, including Gary's extraordinary erotic letters to Nicole, a woman he possessed in his mind (in jail) after letting her slip through his fingers in real life. Some of the words are direct quotations, some of them Mailer's paraphrase in the voice of the speaker. As he wrote a friend, "There's no attempt to decorate, to amplify, to underline, to develop, to exaggerate." He called the book "a true-life novel" because it was shaped with a mounting pressure of suspense and dread leading up to the murders, and then another, even more alarming pressure leading up to the execution.

He finally asked her what she'd been doing. I, Nicole said, have been sitting on my ass over at my mother's. I didn't have enough gas to come back, so I had to stay there all the goddamn day. "Yes," she told him, "I've been sitting on my ass." Well, he told her, something feels different in the house than when I left this morning. Were you back here today?

Yeah, I got back here today, she answered. I thought you were sitting on your ass over at your mother's all day, he said. She gave a smile and said, That's exactly what I said.

Gary walked over from the car, looking as casual as if he was going into the house, and when he passed, he slapped her front-handed across the face. Pretty sneaky. Her head was ringing like an alarm clock.

Clockwise: Betty, college graduate (1942); Norman, soldier (1944); Mel, in "the Mountains" with Sid Caesar (early 1940s); Lenny, rehearsing (1949).

Clockwise: Lenny with Aaron Copland, his only composition teacher. The two were friends and occasional lovers for years (1945); Bernstein's success in New York was social as well as musical: Felicia instructing her husband on an important point of conduct (1960); Leonard Bernstein conducting the Vienna Philharmonic for the last time—in Bruckner's transcendent Ninth Symphony, at Carnegie Hall (1990).

Laughter defeats death. Clockwise:
Mel and Anne before getting married
(1963); Mel in old age reviving Hitler
once again in order
to kill him once again
(2014); Mel confronting
a bust of Peter Boyle as
Young Frankenstein's
monster—a human
reborn (1974).

Gary Gilmore

Jack Henry Abbott

Lee Harvey Oswald

Mailer never met Gary Gilmore, but he researched his life and the life of south central Utah for his masterpiece *The Executioner's Song*. He championed the release from prison of lifetime convict and murderer Jack Henry Abbott, and then was shamed when Abbott committed another murder. Lee Harvey Oswald—a nobody felling the most powerful man in the world—obsessed him, and he went to Russia to understand Oswald's life there, which he re-created in the half-masterpiece *Oswald's Tale*.

Clockwise: In a New York march celebrating the fiftieth anniversary of women's suffrage, Betty is surrounded by future generations of women (1970); Betty and Carl Friedan at the happy beginning of their violent marriage (1947); Betty speaks, Gloria Steinem claps dutifully, Bella Abzug looks bored at the Democratic National Convention in Miami (1972).

Adele Morales with Norman outside of Criminal Court, New York, December 1960, a month after the stabbing.

Norris Church and Norman: they dressed up, ate, and drank with the swells, becoming part of high society in New York (1977).

Lenny held aloft by Israeli soldiers (1977).

Leaping on tables again: Mel expounds his ideas to Sid Caesar, Mel Tolkin, and a very young Woody Allen.

Clockwise: Betty (1995); Norman (2000);
Mel (2015); Lenny (1990).

The sinister breaks Mailer inserts between paragraphs evoke the indifferent silence of the landscape, the nowhere towns, the characters' distance from any goal or structure. I say "evoke" because Mailer doesn't tell us what he made of the physically wide-open but spiritually confining helter-skelter of south central Utah. He doesn't explicitly tell us *anything*. But we know this: for all his rebellion against the values of middle-class Jewish family life, he was very much the product of that life—a family man and a relentless worker, too, producing book after book, article after article. In *The Executioner's Song*, he created a portrait of a peculiarly American emptiness, an entirely mobile yet aimless existence that (unintentionally) ignores the two greatest values held by American Jewish families—devotion to work and to children.

There are many ways of interpreting his silence, and I certainly don't mean to turn him into a goody-good; the book could only have been written by someone with an attraction to violence, someone with a profound curiosity about the void—and an equally profound detestation of it. Mailer did not condescend to the people he wrote about. Gary is three-dimensional, an intelligent man, sometimes eloquent, a killer both logical and mad. But we can infer from Mailer's own life that he viewed Gary's circle in Utah with astonishment. The many Mormons passing through the narrative—the two murdered fathers, various lawyers and court officers—live by severe moral codes, but Gary and his family and friends exist at the feckless, exhausted outer edge of Mormon culture. The book is an incomparable re-creation of a life Mailer could never have lived.

One person on the scene has purpose, and that is Brooklyn-born Lawrence Schiller, the only Jew present in the book, and not only a Jew but the epitome of the Jew as characterized by centuries of scorn—noisy, manipulative, and money conscious; a middleman, a fixer. Yet Larry Schiller is the hero of the second half of *The Executioner's Song*. Mailer records in astounding detail the extent of Schiller's duplicities and manipulations. Some of the horse trading makes one wince but, in the end, Schiller admires and protects both Gary and Nicole, and he brings the project home, delivering the goods to Mailer. Without Schiller the overinsistent Jew, we would not have *The Executioner's Song*, a masterpiece of almost four hundred thousand words (1,048 pages) that is devoted in part to the story of its own making.

It's an improbable work, and I want to suggest that it was partly produced by two improbable narratives. Remember that in central Mormon doctrine, the faithful are descended from the biblical Joseph. In one version of literal descent, the tribes of Ephraim and Manasseh, Joseph's sons, under the guidance of divine providence, crossed the Atlantic in perhaps the sixth century BCE and moved into the American territory. The Book of Mormon is a translation of ancient prophetic writings composed in "reformed Egyptian." In the 1820s, in upstate New York, Joseph Smith was granted revelation and received the gold plates (the basis of the Book), and in the 1840s Brigham Young led the Church of Jesus Christ of Latter-day Saints westward, where they created the new Zion in the mountains and deserts of the Utah Territory. That is one narrative. Now consider another: the Jews of Europe and Russia, disdained and persecuted, came across the Atlantic, first in the 1830s (the Germans) and then after 1880 (the Russians and Eastern Europeans), settling mostly on the East Coast and then spreading west. The two narratives overlap, and there is an astonishing coda. In the 1970s, two East Coast Jews came out to Utah and devoted themselves with utmost fidelity to the task of creating the life of descendants of the pioneering Mormons—not a distinguished life, but life as it is lived. Gary lives, Nicole lives, the victims and lawyers live. Consider Schiller and Mailer as two men performing an act of rescue, summoning an entire existence back from oblivion.

THE WORST STORY IN THE WORLD

A few years later, in the wake of *The Executioner's Song*, Mailer's Judaism would again combat disorder and murder, but in an entirely unexpected way. What follows is a strange story—no, it's the worst story—and nothing is stranger than Judaism's role in it.

In 1978, when Mailer was working on *Executioner*, he received a letter from a thirty-seven-year-old convict named Jack Henry Abbott, who was serving time in Marion, the same federal prison in Illinois that Gary had served in. Abbott was a convicted forger, bank robber, and murderer; he had killed another prisoner in a quarrel. Like Gilmore, he had had a miserable childhood; in prison, he had spent years in solitary and was repeatedly beaten by guards. Both men were paranoid and hair-trigger violent, but in other ways they were quite different. Gary Gilmore was given to romantic fantasy; he believed, as Mailer did, in reincarnation, and he had assured Nicole that they would be together in some future existence. But Abbott, in prison, was a reader of worldly texts. He studied Hegel, Marx, and Nietzsche (his sister brought him books); he became a Marxist-Leninist intellectual, theoretical and doctrinaire, ferocious in argument.

Mailer encouraged Abbott to write detailed descriptions of life in federal prison, which Abbott did, in letters bristling with psychological and political insight. "At his best, when he knew exactly what he was writing about," Mailer wrote, "he had an eye for the continuation of his thought that was like the line a racing-car driver takes around a turn. . . . He wrote like a devil." Abbott might have been Sergeant Croft from *The Naked and the Dead* reborn as a fluent left-wing convict intellectual. Some of the letters were reprinted in the *New York Review of Books*, and the entire batch was submitted to Random House, where a young editor, Erroll McDonald, turned them into a book. At the same time, Mailer, McDonald, and Robert Silvers, one of the editors of the *Review*, wrote letters to Abbott's parole board attesting to his extraordinary literary abilities and urging his release.

Abbott was paroled on June 5, 1981. Mailer picked him up at the airport and took him home for dinner with Norris and two of the boys. He was partly of Chinese descent, tall and lean, with dark eyes and high cheekbones. (Norris recalled that "he was much more attractive than I had anticipated.") In the summer, the Mailers invited him to Provincetown; he sat for hours on a porch staring at the sea; he took Mailer's daughter Danielle, then twenty-four, to the movies. He quarreled over politics with Jean Malaquais, who was still hanging around after decades as the house scold. In this period, in the early summer of 1981, Mailer learned that Abbott had been paroled not principally because of the supporting letters from literary gents but because he had snitched on two groups—the prisoners who were leading a prison revolt and some lawyers who were sneaking in drugs to their clients. Mailer, reasoning that he knew nothing about a life in prison, refused to judge him.

In June 1981, Abbott's letters were published as a book, *In the Belly of the Beast*, and received a great review in the *Times* from the Holocaust scholar Terrence Des Pres. A man who wrote literate, incendiary prose, a glamorously violent man, was about to become a celebrity. Abbott projected an aura of menace that made literary people want to gain his friendship; they may have thought (as Mailer certainly did) that their flattering attention would end his savagery. They were excited by him, gratified by their own interest in him.

On the night of July 17, 1981, Abbott got into argument in an East Village restaurant with Richard Adan, a twenty-two-year-old Cuban-born playwright and actor working as a waiter. In the alley behind the restaurant, Abbott killed Adan with a knife. He fled the city the next day and remained on the lam until he was captured, on September 23, in Louisiana, where he was working in an oil field. Released from prison after years of incarceration, Abbott had, like Gilmore, quickly killed for no apparent reason. He was convicted of manslaughter and given a fifteen-year sentence.

Mailer was in anguish. He faced the New York press, which taunted and goaded him, and he cried out, "Haven't you ever tried to help someone?" In the end, he seems to have suffered more over Jack Henry Abbott's tragedy and his own involvement in it than he did over his stabbing Adele Morales twenty-one years earlier. Or perhaps, as a psychotherapist friend said to me, he poured his shame over stabbing Adele with a knife into his grief over Abbott stabbing a stranger with a knife. His youngest son, John Buffalo Mailer, speaking in the documentary *How to Come Alive* (2023), saw Mailer's efforts on behalf of Abbott as an attempt at redemption: "If Abbott could be redeemed, he could forgive himself in some way." If so, that attempt failed in both ways; neither man was forgiven, neither redeemed. Mailer had been so convinced of Abbott's literary talent that he hadn't imagined he might blow up like Gilmore when he got out of prison. What illusions, what romantic infatuation! He admired these men for their fortitude in prison while not taking seriously what a lifetime behind bars might have done to them. "You have to take risks for culture," he told people at the time, which is a heartbreaking remark. What kind of risks? Risks with other people's lives as well as one's own?

Why is this a Jewish story? The strangest part is yet to come. Abbott went back to prison in 1982, and Mailer, still fascinated, still committed to Abbott's intellectual destiny, took up the correspondence once again. Abbott's doctrinaire Marxism-Leninism, however, was beginning to grate on him. Something else grated: Abbott, among his other cultivated hatreds, was a rank anti-Semite. Back in 1979, before Abbott's parole, Mailer had turned on him.

Just as I don't know what it is to be a convict, you the fuck don't know what it is to be a Jew. You don't know what it is to have six million of your people killed when there are only twelve million of them on earth [the worldwide population of Jews in 1939, when the Nazi slaughter began, was actually about seventeen million—DD]. You don't know the profound and fundamental stunting of existence that got into the blood cells of every Jew after Hitler had done its work . . .

In 1979, Abbott absorbed this rebuke, and, early in 1984, back in prison, he was taking an interest in . . . Jewish sacred texts. He even asked about getting a cassette player and tapes so he could study Hebrew, and Mailer advised him on the difference between modern and classical Hebrew, praising the latter as a "very masculine language full of harsh, strong, powerful tones, sounds of rocks against one another, rocks breaking." A macho language, as it were, spoken by tough Jews. Did he imagine that ancient Hebrew, the language of conscience, ethics, and the covenant, would cause Abbott to respect his fellow human beings? He tried to feed Abbott's contentiousness through an immersion in Jewish law (Halakhah instead of Hegel), and he volunteered to send him a volume of the Talmud, the monumental collection of Jewish laws and rabbinical commentary, citing such passages as a debate over what to do with a sacrificial goat that defecated on the way to the altar. Should the beast be killed? "If it was killed," Mailer wrote Abbott, "was the meat to be brought back to the man who brought it in?"

Well, should it have been? The Talmud insists that its readers become thinking, reasoning creatures but, still, there's more than an element of comedy here; I doubt Rabelais or Dickens could have created anything as strange. Leaving aside the sacrificial goat, Mailer was trying to inspire Abbott with the intellectual excitement of being a Jew. At the same time he was laboring over his own identity. "I don't believe that anyone has ever understood my relation to being a Jew," he wrote Abbott. "Someday if I get to it, I must write my novel about just that. It's very hard to explain, and it goes very deep, and in terms of [Jean-Paul] Sartre's two categories, I think I straddle both."

The two categories Mailer refers to were developed by Sartre in the momentous little book he wrote in 1946, *Anti-Semite and Jew*. The "authentic" Jew, in Sartre's existential terms, proclaims his identity and faces down the disdain of others; the "inauthentic" Jew tries to hide or run away from his Jewishness. Mailer did not often proclaim his identity (unless asked or challenged), but he didn't deny it either; and he had a rueful respect for the specialness of Judaism. "Jews, with some justice, see the world as very tough, very unforgiving," he told an interviewer in 1997. "Whatever you get, you pay for. We don't have this [Christian] idea of grace, or an extra forgiveness that you don't quite deserve."

As for Abbott, in 1984, he declared himself an Orthodox Jew and soon boasted that he knew more Jewish history and religion than his literary friends in New York. The year after, he somehow convinced a young Jewish woman named Naomi Zack, who had earned a PhD in philosophy at Columbia, to marry him; the two then collaborated on a fearsome-looking volume (*My Return*, 1987) in which Abbott claimed that the dead Cuban playwright and actor Richard Adan was the real aggressor in the restaurant. The book went nowhere.

Was Abbott actually Jewish? In 2022, Naomi Zack wrote me that she "could never determine if JA was sincere in his Jewishness or took it up to manipulate me or out of a deeply anti-Semitic 'if you can't beat them, join them.'" The latter suggestion is peculiar. When J. Michael Lennon was working on his biography of Mailer, Naomi Zack told him that Abbott converted in order to fatten his résumé: he imagined he would appear more distinguished in the eyes of his parole board if he were Jewish, a bizarre overestimation of Jewish prestige among parole boards. It didn't work, and his request for parole was denied. Naomi Zack divorced him after two years and went on to have a long career as a feminist writer, scholar, and teacher. Jack Henry Abbott, in 2002, at the age of fifty-eight, hanged himself in his cell, another dead Jew, mourned by a few, despised by many others.

IF LAUGHING WOULD do any good, we might laugh. If weeping would do any good, we might then weep. The entire string of events—the fierce intellectual ambition, the dreams of rescue, the vanities and delusions—leaves one exhausted. After Abbott's death, Mailer issued a statement: "I never knew a man who had a worse life." He wanted to save Abbott's mind and spirit even after Abbott had committed a second murder. Did he not, in fantasy, want to save Gary Gilmore, too—not from execution but from vulgar sensationalism and public ignorance? Gary Gilmore and his friends had given themselves over to what Joan Didion called "nihilism," but Mailer and Schiller could at least re-create what they did and how they felt about it and save them from obscurity. Judaism, for Mailer, fueled a devotion to work and child-rearing and large-scale intellectual effort, and then, later, at least partial devotion to intricate old laws that might rescue a vicious prison intellectual from hopeless political doctrines. He wanted to save two violent sociopaths even as he prized them for their violence. Judaism, not always acknowledged, had a kind of order-making and redemptive force for him, but he couldn't save anyone but himself—and then not even himself from regret and misery.

EGYPT, DUNES, THE CIA

He will have (as he would say) a not-unproductive quarter century yet to live.

In the period after *The Executioner's Song*, Mailer wrote sixteen books, including three enormous novels that I can't get through, *Ancient Evenings*, *Harlot's Ghost*, and *The Castle in the Forest*, as well as a nonfiction half-masterpiece, *Oswald's Tale*. He served for two years as the president of PEN American Center, fighting for the rights of suppressed writers all over the world. He put his children through college, ended long-lasting quarrels with Gore Vidal and William Styron, fought off the intellectual pest Jean Malaquais (on French television, Malaquais, after hanging onto Mailer for decades, called him a sellout). He wrote sympathetic letters to friends suffering from ill health or bad luck with publishers. He continued to show up in magazine interviews and talk shows, bursting with ideas. And from 1978 to 1982, on Saturday mornings, he would go to a decrepit gym on East Fourteenth Street in Manhattan, where he was joined by his friends, his sons, and actor Ryan O'Neal, a genuine roughneck (O'Neal broke two people's jaws in these sparring sessions). They referred to themselves as "the raging Jews." In many ways, Mailer in this late period was making a reckoning with his good and bad behavior and with death.

As always, he needed money. J. Michael Lennon noted, "In some years he earned $750,000, but after paying his agent, alimony, college tuitions (at one point six of his children were in college), mortgages on two homes, and rent for two studios, to name the major expenses, he needed every penny of it. He had no retirement fund." Scott Meredith died in 1993, and a new agent, Andrew Wylie, negotiated extraordinarily lucrative deals for him at Random House. But the charge, heard then and now, that Mailer had become some sort of mercenary opportunist is largely meaningless. Most of what he wrote was very serious.

All too serious, alas, in his devotion to "a world without Moses or Jesus"—his novel set in old Egypt. In *Ancient Evenings* (1983), Mailer enters and never leaves the realm of sorcery and magic, with its transmission of souls, its long day's millennium, with Meni and Menenhotet on the Boat of Ka into the Duad, or wherever, its exposition of the enhancing properties of beetle dung—of all dung, in fact, dung as repository of what is too strong for us as well as repository of our waste—and finally its zizzy Egypto-porn lyricism, importantly capitalized.

> "Would You like," I said to Her, my lips as thick as if they had been beaten, nay scourged, "would You like my obelisk in You, Queen Hat-shet-sup?"
>
> "In my *cunt*, yes, in My *weeping fish*, oh, speak to My *weeping fish*, enter My *mummy*, come into My *spell*, *work your oars*, work your *spell* . . . slaughter Me, shet, shet, shet . . ."

Ancient Evenings was received with both awe and amusement. The latter was sometimes expressed gently, sometimes not. I believe that Mailer's noble Egyptians have minds as complex as ours, but they are minds imbued with an impenetrable and uncommanding (for me) devotion to magic and to the certainties of afterlife and resurrection. Mailer the prophet, the transcendental conjurer! Some part of him, I suppose, was always an ancient Egyptian, bound for immortality, a man who would go on fighting and fucking in the next life. *Ancient Evenings* is a strange book for a Jew to have written, since mainstream Jewish monotheism is eager to dispel or at least ignore such fanciful goings-on—which, no doubt, is one reason Mailer was compelled to write it. I regret how little I respond to it, but I leave the exposition of it to others.

The book sold well, and Norman, now sixty, retreated to Provincetown, where he turned out *Tough Guys Don't Dance* (1984), a potboiler memorable not for its grisly story or its elaborately sin-burdened characters but for its evocation of the dunes and woods of the town he loved so much. He had become a local figure, much appreciated by the year-rounders (including many Portuguese fishermen) who gathered at one bar or another at night. At the big house on Commercial Street, a large glass window faced the bay and a sun deck; at high tide, water would lap against a masonry wall protecting the deck, a sound that Mailer loved to hear as he went to sleep. Both the Brooklyn and Provincetown houses offered a connection to the sea.

In the 1980s, he also worked on unproduced screenplays and took up with a new mistress, Carol Mallory, who had, before Mailer, bagged many Hollywood stars; later, she wrote about her conquests. I suppose it's stupid to ask, "How could a man with a beautiful, talented, and spirited wife like Norris Church have bothered with someone like Carol Mallory?" Still, I want to know. Was Mailer's philandering in late middle age a case of vitality or madness, or both? For the first eight years of his marriage to Norris Church, he was mostly faithful. The two of them wrote their own books and raised their many kids. Dressed to the nines, a celebrity couple, they dined with New York swells on rack of lamb and iced mounds of shrimp. (Mailer also liked foie gras. He thought it produced interesting digestive events.) But he was restless—heroically restless, some might say. A few lines from Blake's *The Marriage of Heaven and Hell* come close to an intimate truth.

> *Those who restrain desire, do so because theirs is weak enough to be*
> *   restrained; and the*
> *restrainer or reason usurps its place and governs the unwilling.*
> *And being restrained, it by degrees becomes passive, till it is only the*
> *   shadow of desire.*

Not feeling sexual desire would have been akin to death for Mailer. Intellectual desire, too. "Once you lose the power to experiment on yourself," he wrote a friend after he crossed sixty, "you lose half your ideas as well."

"Why was I consumed with this old, fat, bombastic, lying little dynamo?" Norris Church asked herself at the time. In 1991, when Mailer was almost seventy, she confronted him. "I don't want to end up a bitter wife," she wrote him, "searching phone bills and Visa receipts for clues of infidelity, dying inside when you take a trip; not believing you when you say in that flat voice, 'I love you.' I deserve better than that." She wrote the letter from Brooklyn; he was in Provincetown and returned to Brooklyn immediately. He held out for a while but then confessed everything, naming the mistresses in Chicago and San Francisco and the one-night stands, too. He couldn't stop confessing. She pummeled him with her fists while he leaned back and took all the blows, playing rope-a-dope like Muhammad Ali. At the end of it, according to Norris, they "fell into each other's arms, and had wild sex. Go figure."

THE CLANDESTINE ASSIGNATIONS with women, he later told Norris, helped him understand how secret agents worked, thereby helping him to write *Harlot's Ghost* (1991), another enormous book devoted to an exotic setting ruled by intricate rituals—the Central Intelligence Agency during the Cold War. Mailer threads through the plot both history and big-time celebrities—the Kennedys, Sinatra, the Mafia, J. Edgar Hoover, E. Howard Hunt, counterintelligence chief James Jesus Angleton—but he never unifies the history into a plot that matters emotionally. The work is held together (sort of) by Mailer's fascination with the vertical WASPs who ran American intelligence, stern yet jaunty fellows, Christ-loving and entirely duplicitous. These men have style. No Jew could have this kind of panache. The hero worship is a little embarrassing, and so is the facetious, high-WASP prose: "My dad had a serviceable stem turn, which was all you needed to claim a few yodeling privileges back in 1940. (People who could do a parallel Christie were as rare then as tightrope artists.)" Yes, I bet they were. This gibberish is Mailer's attempt to capture the blithe American ruling-class manner after the war, a knowing and allusive patter nurtured by St. Paul's and Yale and corrupted by power. Even if meant satirically, it's not a style that reads well.

LOST BOY

Once again, the opportunistic and propulsive Larry Schiller rescued Norman from the doldrums. They were an odd but productive couple, Schiller an unwilling reader but curious about everything, Mailer with his vast philosophical ambition.

After the collapse of the Soviet Union in 1991, KGB files were bursting

open, and Schiller reasoned that "the Organs" (as in the Organs of State
Security) had valuable property on their hands. In particular, property
regarding Lee Harvey Oswald. Back in 1959, Oswald, a twenty-year-old
discharged marine, had defected to the Soviet Union and had married a
young woman named Marina Prusakova. He and Marina lived together
in Minsk, where they were under constant surveillance (the KGB had no
idea what the young man was up to). Schiller inquired: Would Mailer be
interested in writing a book on Oswald in the years prior to the assassination of President Kennedy? Mailer was more than interested. He had been
obsessed with Kennedy for decades, and Lee Harvey Oswald had always
left him in despair. As he later wrote:

> It is virtually not assimilable to our reason that a small lonely man felled a
> giant in the midst of his limousines, his legions, his throng, and his secu-
> rity. If such a non-entity destroyed the leader of the most powerful nation
> on earth, then a world of disproportion engulfs us, and we live in a uni-
> verse that is absurd. So the question reduces itself to some degree: If we
> should decide that Oswald killed Kennedy by himself, let us at least try to
> comprehend whether he was an assassin with a vision or a killer without
> one.

He was trying not only to understand the unfathomable Oswald but
also to find some pattern, some hidden figure in the carpet that would
make America comprehensible to him, as it had been, in a negative way,
in the fifties and sixties. The Warren Commission report (1964) had
asserted that Oswald acted alone. But like millions of other Americans
(there were many, many theories, the obsessions of a generation), Mailer
had always suspected that Oswald was part of some larger plot, a plot,
perhaps, orchestrated by CIA or the Mafia. In pursuit of clues, Mailer and
Schiller wound up spending a total of six months in 1992 and 1993 in Russia and Belarus, existing through a cold Minsk winter on scrambled eggs
and borscht, interviewing people who had known Marina and Lee, and
reconstructing (as best they could) the cheerless atmosphere of Communist Russia thirty years earlier. The enormous book that Mailer produced
in 1995, *Oswald's Tale: An American Mystery*, is a fascinating hybrid, half
revelation, half intricately composed dud. Mailer's writing is factual and
sober, enhanced now and then by metaphor and authorial judgment. Apart

from his own sleuthing, he had access to extensive KGB files, which he, Schiller, and a collaborator (Schiller's translator and wife) spirited out of the country. Bugged conversations between Lee and Marina landed on Mailer's desk in Provincetown and Brooklyn.

What emerges is an incomparable portrait of Soviet life in the late fifties and early sixties, an existence pinched, shabby, and disillusioned, the citizens (except for intelligence agents) hardly "Communists" at all but very ordinary people obsessed with the good life (clothing, food, and culture) just beyond their reach. Mailer writes of them with the same lack of condescension he brought to Gary's friends and family in Utah. We learn that Oswald was chaotic and ambitious—a reader of world-historical texts (Marx et al.), a man who imagined himself a leader but who became, in Minsk, a loutish young husband parading around naked before his wife while demanding that she wash the floors. Even so, Mailer is sympathetic to the part of Lee that hungered for intellectual distinction, the part that longed to perform some extraordinary act.

Mailer's original plan was to write only about Lee and Marina in Russia, but he couldn't stop himself. Despite the pleading of both Schiller and Norman's publisher, Random House, he surged ahead, trying his hand at solving the mystery of the assassination. He brings Oswald and unhappy Marina to the United States in 1962 and then reconstructs with great narrative skill and extraordinary detail the lead-up to the assassination, and then the act itself, redacting and reshaping the Warren Commission's findings. Yet he offers little that is new. In the end, despite his many speculations, he apparently concludes that Oswald acted alone.

Has "absurdity" been overthrown? He believes it has. "If a figure as large as Kennedy is cheated abruptly of his life, we feel better, inexplicably better, if his killer is also not without size. Then, to some degree, we can also mourn the loss of possibility in the man who did the deed. Tragedy is vastly preferable to absurdity." But how much "size" did Oswald have? Oswald believed that killing Kennedy would make him a great man like Lenin, but he struggled to be any kind of man at all; he was grandiose and dishonest, and despite Mailer's detailed attention, he still comes off as a fantasizing punk who got appallingly lucky with his Carcano Model 38.

Absurdity has not been vanquished; and it is Mailer, I'm afraid, who is "tragic." He entertains many theories of the assassination without having reliable evidence for any of them. In the end, he gives up his search for some coherent American significance, a pattern that would merge public events to an underground of sentiment ("a subterranean river of untapped, ferocious, lonely and romantic desires"). *Oswald's Tale* is a muted, heartbreaking book, but a book, like *The Prisoner of Sex*, that only a great American writer could have produced. Against his will, following the logic of his scrupulous reporting, Mailer disenchants the world, dissolving the deep-lava currents and intrigues that he had long believed in. He had wanted to change the country, make history himself; he had to settle for making literary history.

What haunts one as well is Oswald's resemblance to Mailer as a very young man—both of them coddled by their mothers and grandly ambitious, both physically weak and inexperienced boys tested by tough military units. As a seventeen-year-old marine in San Diego, Oswald was slight, emotionally volatile, and, as far as the other recruits were concerned, "feminine." They brutally hazed him—until he slept with a bar girl in Japan.

> It must be repeated: In the mind-set of the 1950s, a century away from the prevailing concepts of the 1990s [when the book was written], to be weak among men was to perceive oneself as a woman, and that, by the male code of the time, was an intolerable condition for a man.

Oswald's marine buddies initially thought he was gay. So, once again, there's that "faggot" accusation, the word that may have set Mailer off when he assaulted Adele Morales in 1960. Both Mailer and Oswald struggled to attain manhood and conceived vast projects for themselves. One became a great writer.

Gary Gilmore, Jack Henry Abbott, Lee Harvey Oswald—all three are superfluous products of the American disorder, fatherless, culturally disinherited, self-educated men yearning for intellectual mastery, and all three became murderers. "There are evils and energies in America which will not speak at all unless they speak through Mailer," said critic Michael Wood in 1973 (*New York Review*, September 20), a sentence written before Mailer had composed enormous books about Gilmore and Oswald. The evils certainly "spoke." What we understand of such men was produced by Mailer's fascination with violence, his obsession with self-willed outsiders. He was lucky not to become a murderer himself. But that luck, joined to immense curiosity and unending hard work, opened the way for his endless exploration of a temperament he dramatized better than anyone since Dostoevsky. He couldn't write the story of a timid Jewish child, but he could write the story of the lost American boys.

MAILER AT SEVENTY-FIVE

When Mailer was seventy-five, in 1998, three years after the Oswald book, I spent some time with him in Provincetown for a *New Yorker* article. He greeted me in the landing area of the tiny Provincetown Municipal Airport; he was wearing a tight-fitting parka and a wool cap in the grim March weather, which he didn't seem to mind. He loved Provincetown in all kinds of weather. This time I was not backing away from him, as I had on Fifth Avenue in 1967. For two days, his gaze was direct, he listened, he responded, he poured scotch; he told me he had recently become interested in Mozart's *Don Giovanni*, a possible piece of flattery aimed at a music-loving magazine writer.

We left the airport, and I quickly got the tour: this is where the Pilgrims momentarily landed before going on to Plymouth; this, in centuries past, is where the whores worked; and this is where the painter Robert Motherwell had lived. An anecdote emerged from his love of the town. In February, the Crown & Anchor, a famous inn and tavern that was a longtime home to delirious Halloween revels, was badly damaged in a fire, and a good many feathers and tiaras as well as sections of the building went up in smoke. At a fundraising event for the place, Mailer read from *Tough Guys Don't Dance*, and the assembled mourners, including many cross-dressers from Boston and elsewhere, vigorously applauded. "Live and let live," Mailer said to me.

Considering how many hard days and hard day's nights had gone by, he looked rather well. His hearing had faded slightly, and he had some arthritic trouble with his knees. His hair was thinning but snowy white, his forearms strong, his voice hooded (as always) but urgent, his eyes a little paler than they had been but still Paul Newman blue. Using a cane, sometimes two canes, he swayed on Provincetown's streets, suggesting, alternately, a retired sea captain and Israeli pioneer David Ben-Gurion inspecting some brave kibbutz. In the house, Norris Church, tall and beautiful (she was forty-nine), showed me her paintings, some of them very good, and welcomed their son John Buffalo home from college.

When Norris fussed over Norman—buttoning him up on his way out the door on a cold day—he stamped and roared in mock protest. But he also told me, out of her hearing, "She's all right," with a rising inflection of approval, like Bogart offering tribute to Bacall. His philandering was apparently over. The days of challenging every man he met were over, too. It was on that occasion that he said, "I have never become the hero of my own life." He was not resigned; he considered himself incomplete. The article I later wrote was called "The Contender."

HE LIVED ANOTHER nine years, restless and impatient, and, always needing money, he took on new kinds of work. As a scriptwriter, he worked with the irrepressible Schiller on TV adaptations of *The Executioner's Song*, the O. J. Simpson trial (*American Tragedy*, 2000), and the life of the American spy Robert Hanssen (*Master Spy: The Robert Hanssen Story*, 2002). Schiller directed them all. He took up acting (not for money), something he had dabbled in years earlier in his scrappy "existential" films. He performed with Norris and writer George Plimpton (an old friend) in a touring stage production of *Zelda, Scott & Ernest*, a piece put together by Plimpton and Terry Quinn in which Norris played Zelda, Plimpton played Fitzgerald, and Mailer, in khaki pants and safari jacket, played Hemingway, his old idol and distant mentor, whom he had bested in some ways. Hemingway had a flawless lyric style (until it turned into sheer manner). He wrote about war, hunting, bullfighting, honor, and bravery, but his real subject, as novelist Don DeLillo pointed out, was his extraordinary sentences, particularly his way of overpowering us with pain and loss just hinted at. He was a master, but his range of interests was small, whereas Mailer, endlessly curious, took in and re-created much of the American world. Mailer reached for the American soul, as did DeLillo and Joan Didion after him.

FOUND BOY

In these late years, he tried yet again to come to terms with his identity as an American Jew and his response to the Holocaust. In silence, or near silence, I will pass over his last book, *The Castle in the Forest* (2007), a fantasia about the origins of Adolf Hitler, the world's most prolific Jew killer. The narrator is an SS agent, a certain Dieter, an operative for Satan who goes wherever he wants in time, entering people's minds and bodies. Back there in the nineteenth century, in the bestial muck of upper Austria, he recruits Hitler's ancestors into acts of incest, child molestation, and bad sex. Young Adolf masturbates among the leaves, which, apparently, tells you what you need to know about him. But I won't go there. The Devil did not create Adolf Hitler, and it means nothing to say that he did. Too many corpses lie in the wake of Mailer's whimsy.

But a decade earlier, in search of truth about an extremely famous Jew, or perhaps in search of himself, he had created a very earnest and gentle work. In 1995, he was in Paris, and it was a bad time for him. The monumental Oswald book had sold poorly. In his hotel room, unable to sleep, he pulled the Gideon Bible out of a drawer. He hadn't read the Gospels since college, and he found the Passion story awesome but unfathomable: Jesus was a stranger to him, and the progression of Jesus's life at the end was badly told (he thought) by the Gospel writers. There were too many absences, too many mysteries. Of course, as any local pastor could have told him, mystery was essential to the all-conquering fascination of the New Testament.

In Mailer's *The Gospel According to the Son* (1997), Jesus speaks in his own voice and relates his story from the beginning. When Joseph tells him who his real father is, at the age of twelve, he doesn't quite believe it. Some of the reviewers complained of sensationalism, but the book couldn't be quieter in tone. In somberly respectful words, Mailer creates an uncertain Jesus, not always sure that people will benefit from what he does for them. He's not only a good man, he's very much a Jewish good man—a "nice, middle-class Jewish boy from Nazareth," as critic Lee Siegel put it in the *New York Times* (January 21, 2007). He worries over everything; he finds his divine father too harsh; he rejects Satan's lustrous temptations but at considerable cost to his equanimity. An existential Jesus, he is never quite sure of his *being*. On the cross, he says "God, my father, was one god. But there were others. If I had failed Him, so had He failed me. . . . Had His efforts for me been so great that now He was exhausted?"

Why write a new Gospel? Jesus remains a doubting Jew, and I regret that I didn't take the chance to ask Mailer why a man who believed in karma and reincarnation should fret over Jesus's inability to bring humanity to goodness. If you were a brave man or woman in this life, you would, Norman believed, be rewarded with a stirring and useful life in the next. *The*

Gospel According to the Son is a tepid affair, muted in its despair, though Mailer cared enough about it to defend himself against attacks on it. After the *New Republic* published a derisive review of the book (by James Wood), Mailer encountered Martin Peretz, the magazine's publisher, in front of a Provincetown chowder house. He gave Peretz two solid punches to the gut.

ONE CAN SUM up the failures while proclaiming the overall splendid success. Mailer was an intermittent father but also a loving father with stout-hearted and soulful children. He abandoned the search for a unifying pattern to American life; he lost the plot of what he wanted to say in fiction, lost the connection between American politics and the underlying stream of fantasy and desire. He was better at supreme journalistic evocations of American reality than at devising stories that embodied it. He never created a convincing Jewish protagonist, or, apart from a story or two, a convincing Jewish milieu, but he was a New York Jew in everything he wrote, his style a mix of rapture and scorn, advocacy and doubt, analysis and evocation, all of it suffused with echoes of the city's dinner parties, bars, newspapers, literary magazines, boxing gyms, and bedrooms, and all of *that* mixed with his own unending ambition. He was a secular prophet, warning of technology's grip on our souls, of technology laying waste to "the substratum, the marrow of human existence." Here is the Mailer canon: *The Naked and the Dead, Advertisements for Myself*, the reports on the national political conventions (gathered in the volumes *The Presidential Papers, Cannibals and Christians*, and *Miami and the Siege of Chicago*), *The Armies of the Night, The Executioner's Song, The Fight*, the first half of *Oswald's Tale*, and half a hundred essays and provocations. Like other Jews, he was put on earth, as he would say, to do serious thinking about many things. Judaism, however much he escaped its middle-class way of life (while embracing it at the same time), laid on him that obligation, and he fulfilled it.

KADDISH

As he passed eighty in 2003, Norman Mailer relished time with his children, talking to them on the telephone, acting with his actor son, Stephen, working with his oldest son, Michael, a movie producer, on a script about a boxer. With his youngest son, John Buffalo, he did a book of conversation (*The Big Empty*) about favorite Mailer topics, including war, politics, sex, and boxing; and he wrote another book, devoted to religion (*On God*), with his friend and future biographer J. Michael Lennon. George W. Bush's war on Iraq in 2003 revived his polemical energies. In the *New York Review of Books* (July 17, 2003), he lit into Bush and asked, "Why did we go to War?" Part of the answer was the white American male's need to assert himself. At the end of *The Prisoner of Sex*, he had saluted (ruefully) the passing of power from men to women, and now, thirty years later, he wrote that "For better or worse, the women's movement has had its breakthrough successes and the old, easy white male ego has withered in the glare." And more: at the end of *The Fight*, he had imagined the passing of power from whites to Blacks, and now, he wrote, "the Black dominance of sports was obvious, and white men were suffering so badly they needed an easy military victory to cheer themselves up."

In the early aughts, Norris was often in Brooklyn with her two sons, Matthew and John Buffalo. She was in the early stages of battling the cancer that would claim her life in 2010, three years after Mailer's death. She tried to convince Norman to live in the city, where it would be easy to get him to a good hospital, but he loved Provincetown—his house, the sea air, the food. Norris drove up for periods to stay with him.

Like anyone of great energy who gets much older, he knew exhaustion and decay with bitter intimacy. The price of full consciousness now meant he had little recourse to denial. "The feet can go," he wrote a friend, "the knees, the hips—not that they're all gone yet, but they are going—the eyesight, the hearing, the sense of taste, the screwing." He took leave of his body organ by organ, limb by limb. When he was still able to travel, he said goodbye in person to Lois Mayfield Wilson, his longtime lover in San Francisco, and, while Norris was in Brooklyn, his Chicago mistress, Eileen Fredrickson, visited him for two days on the Cape. Friends came to see him; all scores were settled, all regrets vanquished. The children gathered around when they could.

Near the end, he had trouble eating much of anything, and he subsisted in Provincetown on oysters, ice cream sandwiches, and red wine mixed with orange juice. With friends, he asserted that the best way to die would be in the woods, alone, fighting wild animals. But he at last returned to Brooklyn: one of his sons-in-law carried him up to the fourth floor of his brownstone, with its great view of the river, the bridges, the Wall Street towers. He checked into Mount Sinai in Manhattan in early October, and he died in the hospital five weeks later of acute renal failure. Standing around his bed on the morning of November 10, 2007, three of the children read the kaddish prayer of mourning.

4

LEONARD BERNSTEIN AND THE END OF APPRENTICESHIP

NEW YORK SPEAKS TO VIENNA

Leonard Bernstein's way with orchestras was mostly genial and imploring, but on one occasion at least, working with the Vienna Philharmonic, he grew very testy indeed. In 1972, he became angry with the way the Philharmonic played its own composer, Gustav Mahler, who had been head of the Vienna Court Opera and conductor of the Philharmonic from 1898 to 1907. Bernstein was rehearsing the stormy first movement of the Fifth Symphony. In his own score of the Fifth, lodged at the New

York Philharmonic Archives, he had written, under the staves of the first movement, "Rage—hostility—sublimation by Mahler. And with heaven." And then, "Angry, bitter sorrow mixed with sad comforting lullabies—rocking a corpse." But he was getting neither rage nor consolation from the Vienna Philharmonic.

Sighing and shrugging, irritably flipping pages of the score back and forth, he finally burst out (in German): "I know you can play the notes. I know that. But it's *Mahler* that's missing." They had arrived at the great anguished climax near the end of the movement, and the strings weren't playing as if anything were at stake. "Why do we rehearse? Just to get the idea? Either we work or we don't. Or there isn't going to be any Mahler," which was a semi-explicit threat to walk out. Bernstein later reported hearing grumbling from the ranks. "*Scheisse Musik.*" Shit music. *Scheisse Musik* was Jewish music. "They thought it was long and blustering and needlessly complicated and overemotional," he said. The Philharmonic, after banning Mahler during the Nazi period, had played the great, tangled, tormented later symphonies only a few times. They didn't know the music; they didn't love it.

The moment is startling, since this was hardly Bernstein's initial encounter with the orchestra. He had first conducted the great Vienna Philharmonic in 1966, and with enormous success, too (bouquets were flung, champagne was poured), so his wrath carried a hint of betrayal, as if to say, "We are squandering a lot of hard work." Turning Mahler into a universal classic—not just a long-winded composer of emotionally extreme symphonies—was part of Bernstein's mission, part of his understanding of the twentieth century, and essential to his identity as an American Jew. In its prejudice against Mahler, which was both racial and musical, the Germans and Austrians at the heart of classical tradition had torn out of themselves an essential source of self-knowledge and emotional understanding as well as musical glory. Destroying Mahler made it easier for them to become Nazis. Bernstein was determined to restore what they had rejected.

He was proud of America's musical achievements—proud of the work of composers Charles Ives and Aaron Copland, and perhaps even prouder of the enduring native talent for popular Broadway entertainment, which, in 1972, was largely a Jewish creation. He had ennobled that tradition himself with the brilliant potpourri that is *Candide* and the galvanizing

West Side Story. Ever eager to break down the barriers between classical and popular music, he put elements of jazz, the great American invention, into his own work. In the twenties, Europeans had certainly become conscious of American jazz, but Bernstein wanted to enlarge that recognition; he wanted to join America to world culture, even world history. It turned out that he needed the Vienna Philharmonic, and they needed him, too; in fact, after the war, the orchestra needed him desperately. That angry rehearsal was a cultural turning point. Bernstein demanded that Vienna, and the European world in general, acknowledge what both America and Mahler meant to the twentieth century—the century that the Europeans were so dreadfully part of and that the Americans had helped liberate from infamy. An American Jew had become the necessary instrument in the New World's reforming embrace of the disgraced Old.

BERNSTEIN WAS IN a powerful position. After the Second World War, as American military and economic might dominated much of the globe, the federal government poured millions into support of the arts. By the 1950s, television and the long-playing record—the new mass media— expanded that dominance, and Bernstein, enormously ambitious, fluent in every medium, positioned himself centrally as music's herald and savior. For here was not a mythical Janus with two faces (conducting and composing) but a very real, hyperactive, and inescapable Lenny with six faces—conducting, classical composing, composing for the theater, playing the piano, writing books and TV scripts, teaching in every way imaginable. From the forties through the eighties, he was everywhere, making music, talking in his plummy Harvard accent, dear Lenny, *our* Lenny, very handsome, too aggressive to be simply a nice Jewish boy, pleasing many but infuriating others with his insistence.

In the first of Bernstein's *Young People's Concerts*, broadcast nationally in 1958 on CBS, he asked, "What Does Music Mean?" He sat at the piano and played a passage from the first movement of Tchaikovsky's Fourth Symphony. The same phrase is repeated with greater and greater insistence, and Lenny sang along with it, "I want it! *I want it!* I WANT IT!" That wasn't Tchaikovsky talking, it was Leonard Bernstein. In the past, Jews were not supposed to make such demands, certainly not in public. He wrote a number called "Cool" for *West Side Story*, but he was anything but cool. His shoulder-shaking groans as he sat at a piano playing jazz could have shamed the label off a bottle of bourbon. Trying to reach everybody, he didn't spread himself too thin (a frequent complaint when he was young); he spread himself too thick, giving everything he had to each activity, and often with an expense of sensual joy that alarmed some people very much.

A man of unending appetite, Bernstein was addicted to music, words, food, sex, applause. Again and again, he stayed up half the night, partying, working, making love, reading scores, reading poetry. In the morning, his assistants struggled to get him to rehearsal. Charlie Harmon, one of the young men who worked for him, told me that the only way to get him out of bed in some foreign city was to sit at the piano and play something badly—at which point Lenny would rise like Proteus from the sea and elbow his assistant off the piano bench. Until the end, when his body gave out (his musicianship never did), he rested only when he had reached some dreadful state beyond exhaustion. And even then, he couldn't always rest. Some hurt or perhaps guilt was gnawing at him.

From the beginning, the profusion of his talents carried within its abundance an almost tragic liability: he was fated to disappoint people from one part of his life or another who wanted more of him, more of what they wanted (more shows, more TV concerts); he was fated, perhaps, to disappoint himself as well. Bradley Cooper and screenwriter Josh Singer understood this when they made *Maestro*. Their Lenny tries to be everything for everyone, and he can't do it. Few stories of staggering success have carried within their triumphs so palpable a danger of failure. Yet as I read Bernstein's moods, it was the failure of individual projects (a bad show, a bad opera) that plagued him, not the profusion of his gifts, which he experienced as a blessing and was central to his strength. From the outside, the totality of his success astounds us—and the way the different parts of him nurtured each other. As for his guilt, it can be sometimes understood, sometimes not.

He seems a phenomenon mysteriously planted in America by God, or maybe by three or four of the muses working together, a Jewish demiurge of some sort, a freak almost. But no mythical or supernatural blessings attended the hero's birth. His essential strength came out of the most ordinary beginnings, the stresses and satisfactions of Jewish American immigrant family life.

BOSTON JEWISH BOY

His mother, Jennie, tends to fall into the background of the family story, and that is probably unfair to her. Her son Burton, Lenny's younger brother, tried to revive her in a series of *New Yorker* articles about the Bernsteins, collected later as *Family Matters: Sam, Jennie, and the Kids* (1982), but we still have no more than hints of who she was and what she felt. She was born in 1898, as Charna Resnick, in Shepetovka, Ukraine. Her father, Simcha, left for America when she was five; two years later, she and her mother also left, departing by sea from Riga, in Latvia, and arriving in New York after an uncomfortable trip. And then, at Ellis Island, mother and daughter were stranded for two days—Simcha was late to meet them. The family, once reunited, settled in Lawrence, Massachusetts, and Charna—renamed Jennie by immigration officials at Ellis—learned English rapidly. A good student, she wanted to be a teacher. But that was not possible; the family needed money, and, at the age of thirteen, she went to work in a textile mill. The place was noisy and dangerous, the working day lasted ten and a half hours, and the pay was ten dollars a week, of which Jennie kept fifty cents for herself. She took courses at night school, but she had to give that up, too.

From all accounts, she was bright, lively, high-spirited; the photographs of her as a young woman reveal a helmet of dark hair, dark eyes, a smile that mixes hunger and apprehension—in some photos she looks like a silent movie star. We can't divine what was there in that face—longing, maybe. Much later, fully armored in bouffant hair and harlequin glasses, she was the very public mother of the famous Lenny, a lovable and quotable Jewish sage. But as a girl, she was forced to play the cards she was dealt in a society offering a limited draw to poor immigrant women. At age nineteen, she married Samuel Bernstein, then twenty-five, a determined and serious young man in a high collar that stuck up into his neck. Sam was living in nearby Boston; just as important, his family came from the same part of Ukraine as Jennie's. When they were introduced, she didn't care for him and giggled in his face. But Sam was rising in the world, and Jennie's family pressed the union, going so far (in one family account) as to slip an engagement ring onto her finger as she slept. If true, it was a half joke that worked.

Sam brought her out of the textile mills (and never let her forget it), but the marriage was unhappy, even at times miserable. Sam and Jennie's daughter Shirley—Lenny's sister—said that her parents were never in love. But immigrant marriages did not easily break up, and Sam and Jennie remained together until Sam's death in 1969 at the age of seventy-seven. Jennie outlived him; she outlived Lenny, too, dying at the age of ninety-four in 1992.

IT WAS SAM who dominated Leonard's early life, loving, demanding, and foolish Sam, born Shmuel Josef, in Beresdiv, near Korets, Ukraine, in 1892. Sam was enraging in many ways; he was also a hero. In Beresdiv, he was disgusted with his own father, who did little but read religious texts as his wife worked all day. When he was sixteen, Sam walked out in the middle of the night, hiked across Ukraine, and then hitched a ride with a Jewish teamster going north through Poland to Danzig (now Gdańsk). He took a ship to Liverpool and then to New York, where he initially lived in a curtained-off portion of a room on the Lower East Side. He worked at the Fulton Fish Market for twelve hours a day gutting fish.

In 1912, he took a job in a barbershop run by an uncle in Hartford, Connecticut. He learned the wig and beauty trade, moved fast, and eventually opened a beauty supply house (the Samuel Bernstein Hair Company), getting rich in the late twenties by securing the New England franchise for a new invention, the Frederics permanent wave machine. It was a frightening apparatus right out of a thirties horror movie, with electric wires trailing down to a metal skull cap fitted onto the client's head. In the late twenties, Sam was smart enough to stay away from stocks, so the Great Crash didn't hurt him. In 1931, he was able to build a ten-room redbrick family house in Newton and a country cottage in Sharon, Massachusetts. Sam and his family had made it in America.

Sam knew the Torah, and he studied the vast Talmud (the rabbinic commentaries on the Torah). He knew about Jewish affairs in the Boston area—the synagogues, the business community, the social groups. He knew these things, but he knew little else. Burton Bernstein recalls the Sunday afternoon dinners: cooked-out roasts, stuffed cabbage, lima beans, potatoes, and Jell-O. Has there ever been a worse meal? It's no wonder that Lenny, traveling many years later from Milan to Paris to Vienna, grew fat from the best restaurants in each city. Burton also recalls the earnest discussions lasting for hours. Sam would hold forth on the New Deal, on agriculture, and, mostly, on Judaism. He was a proud man, insistent, formidable, but melancholy—haunted by the memory of pogroms and drunken peasant rampages; by his boyhood fear of being kidnapped into the czar's army; by the odors of the Fulton Fish Market.

His sadness would disappear on the Jewish holidays, when he would join with the Boston Hasidim in ecstatic dancing and celebration. For a day or two, he was free, even wild. It is not fanciful to locate the origins of Lenny's full-body conducting style—back, hips, pelvis in motion, the air agitated beneath his feet as he leaped—in Sam's jubilant release. Lenny insisted on the emotive kinship himself. He was in Israel just after the country's victory in the Six-Day War in 1967, and he saw some religious Jews dancing in front of the Western Wall. "I saw you there dancing with them," he wrote his father. "You would have been in ecstasy, but I experienced it for you." Like father, like son, but with this difference: Sam danced only on High Holidays, but for Leonard Bernstein every day was a high holiday.

HE WAS BORN on August 25, 1918, and was originally named Louis, which was rapidly changed to Leonard. The family was then living in Revere, Massachusetts, and he would bang on the door of a neighbor's house, crying "*moynik, moynik!*"—probably his version of the Yiddish "*muzik!*" He listened to the radio constantly and fell in love with jingles and popular songs, pounding out rhythms on the windowsill. Yet as far as we know, there was no blinding flash, no visionary gleam. If you had met him at seven or eight, you might have thought he was just another talented and eager middle-class Boston boy—a future stockbroker or furniture manufacturer, or perhaps a history professor who loved music.

Let me make the obvious comparison: in 1908, ten years earlier, Herbert von Karajan was born in Salzburg, Mozart's birthplace. There were two pianos at home, and Herbert played through Haydn and Beethoven symphonies with his family. On special evenings, string and woodwind players among the family's Salzburg friends would assemble at the house for chamber music. From Richard Osborne's biography (*Herbert von Karajan: A Life in Music*, 1999), we learn that "Karajan's great-great-grandfather Georg Johann Karajonne, a cloth manufacturer of Greek-Macedonian origin, had been raised to the nobility by Friedrich August, Duke of Saxony, on June 1, 1792." In truth, this doesn't much sound like an aristocratic lineage. Karajonne the cloth manufacturer is what folks in the Bernstein circle (and in my family, too) would have called "a man in the *shmatte* trade." But never mind: the Karajans were impressive. When he was six, Herbert began classes at the Mozarteum, the school that preserved the Austro-German musical legacy, and he soon became a protégé of Bernhard Paumgartner, the conductor and music scholar who took over the school a few years later. He spent his summers with his family on a stunning mountain lake, the Grundlsee, sixty kilometers east of Salzburg.

When Lenny was a child, he didn't *have* a piano—not until he was ten, when his neurotic Aunt Sally, disburdening herself of many possessions, sent the Bernsteins a robust-looking upright. From all accounts, Lenny couldn't stop picking out tunes. And then, within a year or two, like a foal breaking out of the pen and somehow racing across open spaces as a stallion, he accelerated to full speed, working with the best teachers in the Boston area, some of them European refugees. At the same age that Karajan was summering at Grundlsee, Bernstein stayed in the family cottage in Sharon, Massachusetts. As a teenager, he worked at summer camps in Massachusetts, where he presided over campfire sings and put on a drag *Carmen* and ramshackle productions of Gilbert and Sullivan.

The contrast with Karajan makes an American happy: on the one side, tradition, formality, serious public performance; on the other, amateur musicales, travesty, family shenanigans, émigré teachers. Yet what Boston had to offer in the 1920s and '30s, however scrappy, was enough to bring out Lenny's talent. Von Karajan was a prodigy; Leonard Bernstein was a genius.

JUST BEFORE THE piano arrived, he had his first serious musical experience, and it turned out to be central to the rest of his life.

In the 1920s, the Jewish community in the Boston area numbered about eighty thousand people. According to Jonathan D. Sarna, professor of American Jewish history at Brandeis, "Eastern European Jews in Boston who leaped from rags to riches in a single generation, as Sam Bernstein did, formed an elite group among the Jewish immigrants. Seeking to trumpet their achievement, these nouveaux riches Jews commonly joined Mish-kan Tefila, the most prestigious Eastern European synagogue in town." Then located in Roxbury, the temple had a Conservative congregation that emphasized ritual but also liberal politics and Zionism. These were the two foundations of Lenny's later political thinking.

He was, perhaps, eight, and he was excited by the rhapsodic cantorial singing at Mishkan Tefila. Many years later, he was very generous in his praise for the work of one particular cantor, Iszo Glickstein ("a great musi-cian and a beautiful man, very tall, very handsome") and the music direc-tor Solomon Gregory Braslavsky, an arranger and composer from Vienna. Braslavsky's work brought music-loving Jews to the synagogue, and not just on the High Holidays but on routine Friday evenings. His composi-tions and arrangements introduced Bernstein to the idea of counterpoint—multiple strands of a piece (solo voice, chorus, organ) at odds, in different rhythms, at different volumes, joining together. The rich harmonies of the chorus added to the organ went right through him, and he broke into tears. In 1964, he wrote a letter to Mishkan Tefila that included the lines, "I shall never forget that music, nor cease to be grateful for the power, conviction and atmosphere with which it was conveyed. I may have heard greater masterpieces performed since then, and under more impressive circumstances; but I have never been more deeply moved."

He had a piano, he was enthralled by music, and he had good teachers. But the rest isn't quite history. Sam dearly loved his effervescent son, but he displayed an almost comical inability to understand that Lenny could earn a living as a musician. Sam wanted him to become a rabbi or, best of all, to inherit his beauty-products business. He was afraid that Leon-ard would wind up a modern equivalent of a klezmer musician, wan-dering from one shtetl to another—in this case, playing at Boston bar mitzvahs and weddings or serving as a hotel-palm-court adornment, a mendicant in a tuxedo. At times, Sam withheld money for lessons, and when he did—the comedy here is satisfying—Lenny became exactly what his father feared, running around the neighborhood with pals, playing at "affairs" and weddings, earning what he needed. At times, Jennie had to intervene in the matter of the lessons, and the house was noisy with Sam and Jennie's quarrels.

In the end, Sam gave way. Lenny went to Boston Latin, the city's pre-mier public school, and Sam put Lenny into Harvard at seventeen. He believed in the Torah, and he believed in Harvard. He also allowed his son to major in music—though he may not have had much choice by that point, since you cannot argue with a tidal wave. In the end, Bernstein's temperament is unimaginable without Sam as his father—without Sam's sententiousness, his overbearingness, his he-wrote-the-book-on-every-subject pride. Lenny was the cultivated and gracious fruit of Sam's powerful ignorance.

On Sam's seventieth birthday celebration, in 1963, Lenny, who was then forty-seven, stood up before family and business friends and spoke of fathers, in a general way, as "authority, protector, provider, healer, comforter, law-giver, creator. . . . To the child, the father is God, the model to be followed, in whose image he was created. . . . Every son, at one point or another, defies his father, fights him, departs from him, only to return to him—if he is lucky—closer and more secure than before."

Filial emotion and religious emotion were mixed together for him. In 1943, when he was twenty-five, he dedicated his first symphony, subtitled *Jeremiah*, to Sam, the sour prophet of suburban Boston. The piece, drawing on Jeremiah's warnings to the Israelites, is a compound of awe, amazement, and propitiation. The first movement ("Prophecy") is built around a full-throated, deep-foundation melody; it gives way to high-pressured thunderous dance ("Profanation"), a representation of the sinful Hebrews. The last movement draws on texts from the book of Lamentations—a memorial for a fallen city, sung by a mezzo-soprano supported by gentle winds. It builds to a shattering climax and fades away.

Again and again, Bernstein would return to the Hebrew Bible and Jewish liturgy. In the preface to *Findings*, his 1982 collection of personal writings, he expresses his astonishment over how little he felt during the Holocaust, how little he *did*, and he suggests that thereafter he had felt the need to assert his own identity as a Jew as a way of overcoming that failure. He became obsessed with the new state of Israel, and, as his longtime assistant Jack Gottlieb pointed out in his book *Working with Bernstein* (2010), he drew repeatedly on the modes of traditional Jewish music, on religious texts, and even on Kabbalistic numerical schemes. Those sounds in Mishkan Tefila never left him. As Gottlieb and others have said, the abrupt opening notes of *West Side Story* imitate the shofar hailing the congregation gathered to celebrate Rosh Hashana.

"He was an intensely spiritual man," his daughter Jamie told me. It is something you can see just by looking at his face as he was conducting Brahms, Shostakovich, Mahler; he was so given over to the music that he was no longer quite in his own body even as his body was re-creating the current of sound. He was in the realm of spirit. Yet Bernstein wasn't observant in a conventional sense. He struggled to believe in God and, at the same time, often excoriated God for his disappearance from the modern world. In his powerful Symphony No. 3 (*"Kaddish"*), from 1963, an indignant speaker assaults God for his lack of faith . . . in *man* ("Are you listening, Father? You know who I am"). God the father was someone he had to assail, propitiate, and then forgive for His failures. In brief, he furiously engaged a God he didn't quite believe in, a tormenting paradox. Musically, he found release from this struggle in his later work—not once, but twice.

Lenny escaped Sam; he didn't want to escape him. He overthrew him; he *became* him. Largely homosexual in his sexual interests, he was nevertheless obsessed with fatherhood. In his early twenties, when he was much in demand and sleeping with both men and women, he told friends that he had to have a family. It was the Jewish paternal injunction: a man needs to have a family. And he did finally have a family, with both joyous and misery-inducing results. When Bradley Cooper and screenwriter Josh Singer made their 2023 biopic, *Maestro*, the marital story, and the family story, took over the narrative.

HARVARD

When Herbert von Karajan was an early teen, he was studying and playing the piano in Salzburg and attending rehearsals of orchestral music conducted by his mentor, Bernard Paumgartner. Then and in future years, the Karajan family journeyed to Vienna and heard concerts of the Vienna Philharmonic and performances at the Vienna State Opera directed by composer Richard Strauss and others. For a young musician growing up in the early years of the century, it was a treat without parallel.

Lenny did not hear his first orchestral concert until he was fourteen. He was knocked out by Ravel's *Bolero* at the Boston Pops—*Bolero*, the orchestral showpiece with its sinuous Spanish melody repeated over and over, almost to the point of madness. At the time, he was a student at Boston Latin, studying history and literature; later, at Harvard, he studied the

Greeks and Shakespeare as well as languages and philosophy, especially aesthetics. It was a period in which serious young people were not self-conscious about the desire for what they called, without irony, culture.

In his senior year, Lenny wrote a bitter letter to a friend, Kenneth Ehrman, who had already graduated the college: "I hate the Harvard Music Department . . . I hate it because it is stupid & high schoolish and 'disciplinary' and prim and foolish and academic and stolid and fussy." The music courses at Harvard were largely devoted to the academic staples of counterpoint, harmony, and music history. "There was no way you could learn to play an instrument or to sing," he later recalled. "That was beneath collegiate contempt. Why, you could spend hours wandering through the Music Building and never hear a note of actual music." On one occasion, he came into a class on seventeenth-century counterpoint, sat down at the piano, and banged his way through a dissonant piece of his own. "Well, *I* like it," he said when his professor reprimanded him.

There was another problem at Harvard: in the late 1930s, the university was operating in modified anti-Semitic mode. Jewish enrollment for years had been held to 15 percent. In 1935, the year before Bernstein entered, James B. Conant became president of the university, and the number of Jews in the college expanded. Though accepted into Harvard, Lenny was nevertheless kept out of various organizations, including the Hasty Pudding Club, which mounted musical revues. He was kept out of *what*? Was there an undergraduate *better* than Leonard Bernstein at mounting musical revues? He did write some chamber pieces at school, and he composed the incidental music for a campus production of Aristophanes's *The Birds*, music he later raided for the ballet *Fancy Free*. He also staged Marc Blitzstein's left-wing opera *The Cradle Will Rock*, which had only recently been performed in New York.

As far as we know, he simply shrugged off Harvard's anti-Semitism. Perhaps it was hard for him to conceive that anyone could denigrate his worth. He tore through his courses (when he bothered to attend classes) and played the piano a great deal, sometimes in university concerts, but more happily at parties, in dorm lounges, say, where every kind of music poured out of him—Chopin, Gershwin, Latin dance music, hit tunes on the radio, and Copland's demanding, modernist *Piano Variations* (1930), a piece, he boasted, that would clear the room in two minutes tops. He even accompanied screenings of Sergei Eisenstein's silent film classic

Battleship Potemkin. Musically, this teenager was functioning as a kind of pre-digital all-music website. He was beautiful, he was bisexual, he was showing off—but not simply showing off. Throughout his life, he didn't possess something until he had shared it with someone else—a seeming paradox essential to his nature. Generosity was built into his form of egotism. Learning, performing, and teaching were inextricably joined for him. Sex was often added to that triad.

Whatever Bernstein's irritations with Harvard, he got a great deal out of the place. Unlike the many musicians who are entirely conservatory trained, he wasn't cut off from the rest of the intellectual world. He read widely, took an interest in many things. Years later, in 1973, he came back to Harvard and gave the Norton Lectures ("The Unanswered Question"), a six-part history of tonality in music that is incomparable as instruction. Among other things, he picked up his swank accent at Harvard, a sound as rich as a Godiva Chocolatier Gift Box, and about as far as you could get from the Yiddish inflections of the Boston suburbs. The first time you heard it you wanted to laugh; after that, it seemed completely natural to him, an unmistakable accompaniment to his erudition, his smile, his abundant head of hair, his handsomeness and charm. He was a suburban Boston Jew who could match vowels with the fanciest of music commentators. In time, he would overthrow them.

MINISTERING ANGELS

After graduating from college in the spring of 1939, Bernstein moved to New York, excited but baffled. "You see, I still don't know quite what I want to do," he wrote his friend Ehrman. "Conduct, compose, piano, produce, arrange, etc. I'm all of these and none of them." He may have been anxious, but everyone could tell he was going somewhere. ("Doomed to success"— that was the phrase theater director and critic Harold Clurman used when meeting him.) Like so many talented and attractive young persons in the arts, he received help from people who wanted to do something for him, or sleep with him, or both. In brief, proprietary angels descended from the highest reaches of the music world and showered beatitudes upon his very willing head.

The first of the angels was Dimitri Mitropoulos, the extraordinary Greek conductor who was music director of the Minneapolis Orchestra in the thirties and who took over the New York Philharmonic in 1951. Mitropoulos had an odd, tense presence—he was bald, his eyes protruded slightly, and he made abrupt and violent movements before an orchestra with his hands and arms, pulling enormous sonorities out of the players (he specialized in big-bang composers like Mahler, Strauss, and Shosta-kovich). Bernstein, as a sophomore, met him at a Harvard social occasion in 1937 when Mitropoulos was doing a guest-conducting stint with the Boston Symphony.

Mitropoulos was gay, and from all accounts, including his own, a sad and lonely man. Their meeting was emotionally fraught. In 1937, Bern-stein fictionalized the meeting in a rather creepy erotic story submitted as an assignment in English composition class. Mitropoulos becomes "Eros Mavro," and Lenny has Eros say (about himself), "'The moment I set eyes on this boy I felt—something'—he struggled for expression—'a feeling of the presence of greatness; of something—genius.'" This presumptuous eval-uation may actually be close to what Mitropoulos felt. When Mitropou-los went back to Minneapolis, the two men exchanged ardent letters. But Mitropoulos also sounded a high-flown, almost Victorian note of concern. "I hope you are a clever boy and that you realize the great responsibility toward yourself, its importance." He spoke to Bernstein of purity and self-lessness, the duties of the artist, the greatness of the conductor's role.

Was this elevated palaver a way of forestalling any sexual relation? Despite the warmth of the letters, the two men don't seem to have been lovers. Yet Mitropoulos would be Lenny's lifeline to the great world, his way into the hard business of classical music. He helped Bernstein for years, sending him money at one point when he was still a student, and trying, without success, to get him hired as his assistant in Minneapolis. In 1958, twenty-one years after their first meeting, Mitropoulos gave way to the younger man as music director of the New York Philharmonic.

FROM THE 1920S on, Jews were an enormous presence in American clas-sical music, both as instrumentalists and as conductors. After the Nazis took over in 1933, something like 1,500 European musicians (many of them Jews) arrived before the Second World War ended. In Boston, Serge Koussevitzky, a Russian Jewish pretend aristocrat, had been music director of the Boston Symphony since 1924. In later decades, Hungarian Jews would become music directors in Philadelphia (Eugene Ormandy), Cleveland (George Szell), Chicago (Fritz Reiner), Minneapolis, Dallas, and Detroit (Antal Dorati), and Chicago again (Georg Solti). All Jewish, but not an American among them. As Europeans, they settled with few regrets into an American music culture prepared to be awed by their talent, their haughty manners, their beautifully severe authority.

Aaron Copland was a different kind of musician; he was as much an American product as Bernstein himself. Copland's people were from Lithuania, but he was born in Brooklyn in 1900 and lived above the family grocery store. He never went to college, but he gained musical training from significant teachers in New York, and then, in Paris, from the legendary French pedagogue Nadia Boulanger. Physically, Copland was a sort of Jewish Ichabod Crane—tall, gangly, careless about his clothes, with a face dominated by a large, curved beak and a receding chin. It was a face as homely, and as mesmerizingly photogenic, as that of Eleanor Roosevelt, with whom Copland shared certain qualities of resolve, independence, and decency.

Bernstein met him at a dance concert in New York in 1937 and was astonished. Knowing only Copland's spiky early modernist pieces, he had expected an iron-gray beard, a fierce pride. But here was a new kind of classical artist—an *American* artist, informal in style, practical and positive, a shrewdly sociable man making his way with good humor across the stony meadow of the country's general indifference to art. That same night Lenny went to Copland's loft—it was the composer's thirty-seventh birthday—and played for him and various distinguished friends the daunting *Piano Variations*, Bernstein's room-clearing party piece at school. Copland was impressed. After this great beginning, I think it can be said without exaggeration that the two men fell in love.

And then, in 1938, while still a student, Bernstein heard Copland's *El Salón México*, a twelve-minute, high-powered orchestral romp through Mexican folk materials. The piece would now be denounced as appropriation, but eighty years ago most people did not worry about such things—it was vitality that mattered, not ownership. *El Salón México* was the first of the "populist" compositions that were to make Copland famous. Lenny wrote to him as follows.

It's a secure feeling to know we have a master in America. I mean that too (don't pooh-pooh). I sat aghast at the solid sureness of that construction of yours. Timed to perfection. Not an extra beat. Just long enough for its material. Orchestral handling plus. Invention superb. And yet, with all that technique, it was a perfect rollercoaster ride.

The man writing these authoritative judgments had just turned twenty. A few months later, in his senior year, Bernstein wrote a thirty-thousand-word thesis, "The Absorption of Race Elements into American Music," calling for an American classical music that incorporated folk songs and jazz and other native elements. (Antonín Dvořák, visiting in the 1890s, had made comparable statements before writing the *New World* symphony.) In the next few years, Copland in effect did what Bernstein wanted. In such compositions as *Billy the Kid*, *Rodeo*, *Lincoln Portrait*, "Fanfare for the Common Man," and the Symphony No. 3, he moved popular materials (hoedowns, gunfights, Shaker hymns) into classical music as easily as Picasso moved guitars and newspapers into painting. Along the way, he established what most people thought of for years as the sound of American classical music—big-boned, clean-limbed, both rugged and touching, suggestive of both brutal cities and underpopulated open plains.

The letters back and forth between Copland and Bernstein are enlivened by sailors and soldiers on leave, men known only by their initials, or by a fleeting reference ("the charming boy in the Tanglewood box office last summer"). Comedy lurks in some of the brief encounters: during a blackout, Lenny had sex with a young soldier he met on his rooftop, which was fine until the lights came back on, and, as he wrote Copland, "he turned out to be so fat I could hardly stand it." In the early forties, the composers' scene in New York was heavily (though not exclusively) gay. Sex was naughty and fun, but the danger of exposure to disapproving eyes loomed everywhere. In 1940, Copland wrote,

What terrifying letters you write: fit for the flames is what they are. Just imagine how much you would have to pay to retrieve such a letter forty years from now when you are conductor of the Philharmonic. Well it all comes from the recklessness of youth, that's what it is. Of course I don't mean that you mustn't write such letters (to me, that is), but I mustn't forget to burn them.

Bernstein at that point had conducted no more than a couple of school productions and a student orchestra the previous summer at the Tanglewood Music Festival in Lenox, Massachusetts, so Copland's guess about his conducting the Philharmonic someday was remarkably prescient. But it would hardly take forty years. Bernstein made his Philharmonic debut exactly three years later, at the age of twenty-five. And Copland's grim joke about future blackmail, according to Bernstein's daughter Jamie, has never become an actual threat: no one has come forward to complain of Bernstein's attentions years earlier. Why not? Well, these were young men, not boys; and I would guess that Bernstein gave his many bed partners something of himself and something of music that was valuable and lasting. Leaving aside the encounter on the roof, the meetings were about sex but not only about sex.

The friendship with Copland went through periods both sexual and chaste, and this enduring bond became perhaps the most important line of influence in American music. Copland was the only composition teacher Bernstein ever had, and Copland's musical strengths played into Bernstein's sensibility. You can hear his influence in the ferocious pounding of the percussion and full-bodied lyricism of such Bernstein works as Symphony No. 1 (*Jeremiah*) and the turbulent score for the 1954 movie *On the Waterfront*.

IN 1939, BERNSTEIN graduated from Harvard's music program. After so much music theory and history, he wanted training as a conductor and a pianist. He applied too late for fall entry into the Juilliard School, so Copland advised him to seek out Fritz Reiner, the great conductor of the Pittsburgh Symphony Orchestra (and later the Chicago Symphony Orchestra). Reiner taught at the prestigious Curtis Institute in Philadelphia. Hearing that the young man in front of him wanted be a conductor, Reiner raised his arms and exclaimed "Bad!" Fritz Reiner was irascible, often contemptuous. "*Total unbegabt*"—"completely untalented"—was his phrase for students who faltered in his class. He agreed, however, to give Bernstein an entrance examination for Curtis. Showing up with a sneezy hay fever, Lenny suffered through a harrowing trial in which he had to sight-read at the piano a score he had never seen before, Brahms's "Academic Festival Overture." But Reiner accepted him, and, over the next two years, taught him, praised him, deplored him.

Reiner had a thick neck and a hawk's profile; he conducted with tiny movements of his stick, tiny turns of his head, and a baleful stare, puffing his cheeks or raising his eyebrows when he wanted greater volume from the winds and brass. The thought of this man as Bernstein's teacher is comically satisfying, since his prize pupil was a tumult of whirling arms and gyrating hips and shoulders. Reiner and Bernstein were both Jews, but the American Jew would conduct in a way that demonstrated his own emotion in the music as a signal to both orchestra and audience. Later on, Reiner was one of many conductors (as well as critics) who disapproved of Lenny's effusions. They thought he was vulgar, out of control. After seeing Lenny on television, Reiner said, "He didn't learn that from me."

But putting his body in motion was completely natural to Leonard Bernstein. At some point in his adolescence, he discovered that he could express with his body whatever he thought or felt, a discovery that was just as important as a sexual awakening, though in his case the two were obviously related. As in so many artists, his intellectual life and his sexual life were strongly developed, but for him, there was no essential difference between the two. If he knew something, he felt it in his body. There was no wall between intellect and sensuality, which is one reason he made so many people uncomfortable.

In his romantic life, in his conducting, in his entire manner, he became a prime liberator of the Jewish body (the earlier contributions of actresses Theda Bara and Hedy Lamarr are duly noted), freeing it from the constraints felt by the immigrant generation, many of whom were never sure that physical pleasure wasn't dangerous to the Jews in America—dangerous to them *personally*. Was it fear of punishment that made them think so? Fear of social disapproval, or—more seriously— self-disapproval? Certainly, it was not terror of hell, which is a habitation little imagined by Jews. Bernstein let loose, though hardly like some country-club drunk on Saturday night. When this Jewish body moved, it created excitement, emotion, even revelation.

LENNY'S FOURTH AND final angel, Serge Koussevitzky, offered not just musical training but something mysterious: the notion that a conductor needed to carry within himself the genius of music. The conductor had to sum up, in any given concert, everything that had happened in music up to that point. Koussevitzky offered power, showmanship, consequence. As music director of the Boston Symphony, he brought the orchestra to a state of virtuoso perfection, and he and his wealthy wife, Natalie Ushkova, directly commissioned or supported an astonishing amount of good new music—works by Bartók, Stravinsky, Ravel, Britten, and Hindemith. It was Koussevitzky who essentially nursed into being the Big American Symphony—works by Copland, Roy Harris, William Schuman. All of it was tonal; his taste was, so to speak, conservatively modern. A Russian Jew from the town of Vyshny Volochyok, north of Moscow, he converted to the Russian Orthodox Church to help his career. In America, he carried himself as an aristocrat, sporting magnificent shoes and capes, an attending valet, and an arrogantly raised chin, all of which awed and amused the young musicians drawn to him.

In 1938, Koussevitzky had set up, on the beautiful Tanglewood grounds near Lenox, Massachusetts, a summer home for the Boston Symphony. Two years later he began an annual six-week program in composition, conducting, and instrumental instruction for the most talented students from the music schools. In 1940, when Bernstein was still a student at Curtis, Koussevitzky accepted him as a conducting student. What followed was one of the great love affairs (nonsexual) in the history of music education. Koussevitzky, sixty-five when he met Bernstein, adored the eager twenty-one-year-old, fussed over him, praised him, advanced him rapidly, and Bernstein flattered the old man and absorbed everything he could. Quite early in their relationship, when Bernstein was still in his twenties, there was talk that he would replace Koussevitzky as conductor of the Boston Symphony.

In the summer of 1940, and in two subsequent summers, Bernstein studied scores, tramped around after his mentor, and conducted the student orchestra with great success. Recalling those summers more than thirty years later, he said, "It was so exciting: we were working all the time, or playing all the time, because it became the same thing; playing music and playing with each other, making love, making music was all one thing, and it was constant, and of constant intensity."

MITROPOULOS, COPLAND, REINER, and Koussevitzky all dealt with Lenny in a special way. They did not see him as a younger version of themselves. They saw him as unique, and in this respect his identity as a

Jewish American played a major role. By the late thirties, the immigrants and their descendants in this country began to feel something like relief. Europe was inexorably heading toward war, and America was a refuge—for art, for the Jews, for hope itself. And here was this American youth, a brazen and charming boy who talked big and who also had the stuff, a musician who saw life as an explosion of delight. Lenny's European teachers poured what they knew of tradition and skill into the temperament of an American musical genius. They knew what they were doing. There may have been many Jewish musicians in American orchestras, but a great Jewish American conductor!—that was something new. As his powerful friends were making plans for him, however, he was busy at the same time doing things that they could hardly approve of.

HELLUVA TOWN I

There is a startling photograph of Lenny from the early 1940s. He sits at a piano, his thick hair rumpled, a cigarette dangling from his lips. At that moment, he's a long way from Mitropoulos and Koussevitzky's exaltations of the divine role of the classical conductor. He appears to be a young man at home among the drinkers and sexual adventurers in an after-hours club, a man more like Ellington and Sinatra than a classical star.

As a small child, he had loved the pop tunes he heard on the radio. For his entire life, he listened to popular music, jazz, and show music, and he relished being among people who put something on a stage or on a nightclub floor. In the summer, at Bernstein family headquarters at Sharon, there was that drag *Carmen*, with the teenage Lenny as Carmen in a red wig and a black mantilla; and a tumultuous *Mikado*, in which Lenny sang Nanki-poo. The rehearsals took place in the house, and Sam, his routine disturbed, said, "This is *Shabbas*. Get to the *shul*." They did not go to the *shul*.

And then at Camp Onota, in the Berkshires, in the summer of 1937, Lenny mounted a production of *The Pirates of Penzance*. A Pirate King was needed, and, at the right time, a large, goofy person from New York presented himself. This was Adolph Green, then twenty-three years old. Judging by his photographs and screen appearances, Green was permanently exhilarated—for decades, his big happy smile could be that of a

stage juvenile eager to please. He was, however, one of the most sophisticated madcaps ever to work in movies and theater, a born satirist-buffoon,
amused by every kind of absurdity, and a verbose and encyclopedic young
man in the manner of culture-mad Jewish boys long ago. In particular, he
could sing through a classical piece after hearing it on the radio a few
times (try that with Sibelius). Singing and shouting symphonies in the
Massachusetts hills, Lenny and Adolph Green instantly became friends,
and they remained friends until Lenny's death, fifty-three years later.

In 1938, Green formed a satirical nightclub troupe called the Revuers
with Betty Comden, a dark-haired beauty with a grin equal to Green's and
a comparable satirist's gift. Betty Comden, born Basya Cohen in Brooklyn, teased wartime sex bombshells; she teased operatic pretension and
everything else. She had a flexible voice, capable of serious lyrical singing
and melodious horseplay. She and Green became a longtime performing-
and-writing team. They wrote the lyrics a few years later for Bernstein's
shows *On the Town* and *Wonderful Town*; they wrote the scripts for two of
the greatest Hollywood musicals, *Singin' in the Rain* and *The Band Wagon*.
Judy Holliday, then known as Judith Tuvim, was also a member of the
Revuers. The group did rapid-tempo skits with music; they mocked
Hollywood and the American provinces. There was a Jewish edge of big-
city knowingness to their routines (nothing took them in, including their
own smarts), but knowingness blessedly free of the sententious politi-
cized sourness of European cabaret.

When Lenny was at Curtis studying hard with Reiner, he would escape
his stern teacher and dull Philadelphia and slip into Manhattan, where
he would meet friends and lovers, talk with Aaron Copland, and—just as
productively—fool around with Comden and Green. He was soon performing with the Revuers at the Village Vanguard, a jazz club on lower
Seventh Avenue. From a number of accounts, he was never happier than
when he was in their company. On the album *Leonard Bernstein: Wunderkind*, one can hear an extended musical number entitled "The Girl
with the Two Left Feet," a spoof of Hollywood and media hype, 1940s
style, in which Bernstein plays the piano accompaniment, rapidly switching from one pastiche style to another with extraordinary delicacy and
pointed rhythm.

In the succeeding years, Lenny would spend long periods as a theater
person, a habitué of dingy rehearsal rooms and out-of-town tryouts, a

man familiar with stumbling rehearsals and last-minute rewrites. Beethoven, Mahler, and Stravinsky ran through his head, but so did Jerome Kern, George Gershwin, Richard Rodgers, Vincent Youmans, and songs he heard on the radio. This was disconcerting to many people, though not to him. Conducting an orchestra, he did what Reiner had instructed him to do: master every element of the score (which meant knowing every player's part) and master the men and women in front of him as well. But there were pleasures in collaboration equal to those of mastery—the joy of companionship, the give-and-take and never-satisfied aggressions of talented people working together, the fights, the endless cigarettes-at-dawn sessions, and the sudden bursts of exhilaration when something came together.

OVERNIGHT STAR

His success as a conductor came more quickly than anyone had expected. In 1943, Artur Rodzinski, the music director of the New York Philharmonic, approached Bernstein with a wonderful offer—to become assistant director of the orchestra. Since finishing Curtis, Lenny had been knocking around in Boston and New York, working with the Revuers, composing some, trying to make a living as a piano teacher and music arranger. He was almost twenty-five and at times, for all his activity, close to despair. *Maybe Sam was right. Maybe making a living as a musician was impossible.* He eagerly took the Philharmonic job, which required him to read new music submitted to the orchestra, attend rehearsals, learn the scores that had been programmed, and be ready to step in if a conductor got ill.

Miracles happen only once but are many times recounted. On the night of November 13, 1943, some of Lenny's own music—a jaunty little vocal piece called "I Hate Music"—was given its premiere at Town Hall. He went to a party afterward, returned home near dawn, and was awakened at 9 a.m. by a call from the Philharmonic: *You're on, kid.* He had to conduct the orchestra without rehearsal at three that afternoon. The concert would be broadcast on the CBS radio network. He knew the scores, and he was able to visit the scheduled conductor, the great Bruno Walter, who was down with the flu. In Walter's New York hotel room, the two men went over the music, particularly the difficult contrapuntal maze of Richard Strauss's tone poem *Don Quixote.*

Half-dazed from sleeplessness and excitement, he cast away some pills a pharmacist gave him. What followed is available on CD, and Lenny is sure-handed right from the start—the Schumann *Manfred* overture, with its difficult opening (it begins, so to speak, in the middle of a sentence). And he handles the romantic feeling of the rest of the piece with both intensity and discipline, and then holds together Strauss's complex web of motifs without evident trouble. The audience loved it, and the *Times*, having been tipped off by the Philharmonic's publicists, reported the story on the front page the next day; papers all over the country picked it up. Sam, who was there for the concert, was impressed at last. A few years later, he would utter his comic masterpiece: "How could I know my son would grow up to be Leonard Bernstein?" Meaning: *How could I know that he would surpass me? That he would be famous and loved?* Lenny's future as a symphonic conductor was brilliantly launched. And his future as a Broadway composer, at the same time, grew out of his nighttime prowls with the friends he adored, friends amusing themselves and a smart audience with music, with wit, with the serious business of having fun.

HELLUVA TOWN II

In the war years and just after, New York was bursting with talented people—both a newly conscious avant-garde and an audience eager for advanced art. Modern painters like Klee, Kandinsky, and Picasso were getting major shows, and the younger painters Mark Rothko, Barnett Newman, Jackson Pollock, and his wife, Lee Krasner, also Willem and Elaine de Kooning—the abstract expressionists—were living, working, and drinking in Greenwich Village. Art critic Harold Rosenberg spoke of "action painters," artists using the canvas with complete freedom. Heart-wrenching Italian neorealist imports and classic Soviet movies from the twenties, some with radical editing techniques, played the art houses. Bebop geniuses Charlie Parker and Dizzy Gillespie worked in after-hours Harlem clubs and then on West Fifty-Second Street. Rodgers and Hammerstein, Frank Loesser, Cole Porter, and Kurt Weill were writing for Broadway. Producer Max Liebman, beginning in 1950, was putting the best young talent in the country into his weekly TV show on NBC, *Your Show of Shows*. Martha Graham and other independent dance companies had their fervent audiences. In 1948, George Balanchine and Lincoln

Kirstein established the incomparable New York City Ballet. There was fresh, provocative work all over town if you knew where to look for it.

The American giant had arisen, fighting and winning a two-front war, and the economy was about to take off on a thirty-year boom. By the late forties, many people began to think that New York, not Paris, was the arts capital of the world. True or not, it was rapidly becoming the financial capital, with elites pouring in from South America and Europe. Yet cheap rents were still available, and young writers, painters, musicians, and theater people could live in Manhattan or Brooklyn if they were willing to ride the subway and eat at Nedick's (a hot dog and orange drink) or perhaps at the Automat with its little windows offering stewed chicken on a biscuit or grilled American cheese. Lenny lived in odd places, in hotel rooms, in shared apartments with friends, and, finally, in a studio set aside for artists in the tower above Carnegie Hall.

IN AUGUST 1943, a few months before Lenny's debut with the New York Philharmonic, a young choreographer and dancer named Jerome Robbins came to visit him in his apartment. At the time, Robbins was working with a major company, Ballet Theatre, a precursor of American Ballet Theatre. Robbins had an idea to share. He was sick of ballets with swans and princes, tired of fairy tales and myths. He wanted an explicitly American dance—and not rural Americana in the style of Martha Graham's work with Copland on the classic *Appalachian Spring*. He wanted a subject drawn from city life. Why couldn't the street life of an American city be as good a subject as any other? He was an exceptionally ambitious young man, tense and angry, and, later in his career, verbally abusive to dancers and actors ("We're doing our best." "That's what worries me"). But he was electricity itself and many people wanted to work with him.

His background was similar to Bernstein's. In 1918, he was born Jerome Wilson Rabinowitz on the Lower East Side of New York; his father, Harry Rabinowitz, was an immigrant from Poland who eventually opened a neighborhood delicatessen, and then moved it uptown on the East Side. After relocating the family to New Jersey, Harry opened the Comfort Corset Company in Weehawken. Jerry Robbins declined to work in the corset business. He entered and then dropped out of NYU (the family couldn't afford college during the Depression). He began dancing in 1936, when he was eighteen, and was certainly uncorseted when he moved. He did as much as Bernstein to free the Jewish body from constraints.

Robbins's idea: three sailors on leave in the city for a day, three sailors in the middle of the war who meet two girls. Bernstein responded to what Robbins said by playing a short theme he had written that afternoon on a napkin while having lunch downstairs, at the Russian Tea Room. Robbins, hearing the jazzy motif (it runs through the score), was thrilled, and Bernstein went to work as Robbins sat there, producing variations on the theme at the piano—and continued working as Robbins went on tour with Ballet Theatre.

On the road, Robbins choreographed different parts of the ballet, often without the music, working with friends in the company in rehearsal rooms, on trains, even on the streets of American cities, incorporating details of his observation into the plot of the ballet that came to be known as *Fancy Free*. Bernstein wrote him letters with very specific notes on the action, beat by beat, measure by measure, accompanied by such mood evocations as, "So you will have, in general, a slow, slightly tense, slightly serious section, but lyrical, perfumed by these little rhythmic urgings in the balls." The ballet, created by two urban Jewish bisexual men, was about three sailors bursting out of their pants.

Fancy Free premiered at the Metropolitan Opera House on April 18, 1944, with Bernstein conducting and Robbins dancing one of the sailors. It was an immediate smash hit, with standing-room-only crowds and extra performances. The ballet has a special wartime urgency—the fervency, excitement, and melancholy of an interlude in actual lives. I've seen it recently, in the version that Robbins created with his later company, the New York City Ballet, and even now, it seems a very *young* dance.

A lonely bartender hangs out, with Billie Holiday on the radio, and suddenly the Bernstein score takes off with rapid rim shots on a drum (*bop, bop, bop, bop!*), like the opening of a big-band number. The three sailors come somersaulting and jumping onto the stage, bouncing off each other with chest-up swagger. There's a steady pulse underneath the music, a Stravinskian neoclassical tread, with jazzy and melancholy interludes on top of it. If Copland and Stravinsky had borrowed from jazz for their compositions, now Broadway dancers learned to move to rhythms borrowed from *them*. The women enter, strutting, fighting off advances, and so on, through the entire realm of flirtation, engagement, abandonment—until they leave in a huff and the men run off, eager for the next adventure. Robbins's choreography mixes classical ballet (lifts and pirouettes) with such contemporary dance crazes as boogie-woogie and the Lindy Hop. Bernstein's music, which included waltzes and a Latin *danzón*, as well as jazz and swing, unifies the different episodes, and the mood, always, is pressing, hastening, urgent. The two Jewish children of Eastern European immigrants, working on the fly, created an all-American classic (you get to see some of it in *Maestro*).

Of course, the classically trained young men were not alone in their ambitions. A group of Russian and Eastern European furriers and glove makers who arrived before them, in the 1890s, crass, eager men, settled in Los Angeles, where they built movie studios and a sizable infrastructure in only a few years. In hundreds of films, the Hollywood moguls (the Warner brothers, Carl Laemmle, Louis B. Mayer, et al.) indulged their fantasies of WASP America—the moral struggles to purify the Old West, the scrubbed-clean contemporary small towns, the virtuous heroes and heroines. As Neil Gabler wrote in *An Empire of Their Own* (1989), the moguls imagined and literally projected what American ideals were. It was their way of paying an admission fee to enter a business elite they couldn't otherwise join and they wound up imposing those ideals on the public, creating a substantial portion of American national culture, just as the composer Irving Berlin did by writing "White Christmas" and "Easter Parade," two songs created by an immigrant Jew that eternally set the tone of Christian holidays.

Work like this goes beyond assimilation; it creates the culture that the artist is breaking into. Aaron Copland, a gay Jewish man of central European descent, wrote music so identified with America that some of it, as Alex Ross has pointed out, "was piped into Ronald Reagan's 'Morning in America' commercials." Robbins and Bernstein, two Jewish city boys, working feverishly in wartime, made their own distinctly American contribution. The forties had their noirish and pessimistic moods, but *Fancy Free* was pure American exhilaration—the desire to flirt, fight, make up, just *go*, and then forget it all.

A FEW MONTHS after the premiere, Oliver Smith, who had designed a simple barroom set for *Fancy Free*, came to Bernstein and Robbins with an idea—expand the ballet into a Broadway show. Smith was also a producer, and Bernstein took him to see Comden and Green perform at the Blue Angel nightclub. The Revuers had dissolved, and the two were doing comic songs and skits alone. Smith was happy, the project took off, and it was completed and mounted on stage as *On the Town* in New York by December of 1944, only eight months after the premiere of *Fancy Free*.

The ballet is devoted to moods of emerging, exploring, becoming; it's a male adventure with women as objects of the men's curiosity. Working together on *On the Town*, Comden, Green, Bernstein, and Robbins retained the concept of three sailors on leave for a day. But they added a high-pressure, up-tempo encounter with New York; and they added women who were idiosyncratic and aggressive—three women this time, not two: a tough taxi driver ("Come Up to My Place"), a libidinous anthropologist ("Carried Away," sung in mock-operatic style), and a beautiful subway poster girl who wants to be a dancer. All of them are a bit more than the men can handle. Every note of Bernstein's music was new, including a full thirty minutes of dance music, which Robbins choreographed and Bernstein later turned into a symphonic suite. Yet the mood of an urgent quest was the same. The show takes off with "New York, New York":

New York, New York, it's helluva town,
The Bronx is up and the Battery's down.
The people ride in a hole in the ground.

This ecstatic bouncing hymn, sung by the three men, is immediately turned into a round, the men's voices overlapping; later it is danced, jazzed, combined with other motifs from the score, gloriously reprised. It's the show's anthem, embodying the insistent love of the big city, a place that is always demanding, always exciting.

MANY MEN IN ONE MAN

Following a single line of Bernstein's work or life is rather like clinging to a single bush in a flourishing garden—inevitably, it misrepresents the blooming profusion. In the mid-forties, when he was working with his dance and theater collaborators, he was also conducting the New York Philharmonic and other orchestras, presenting his first symphony, *Jeremiah*, all over the country, and doing much else. "When I am with composers," he said later, "I say I am a conductor. When I am with conductors, I say I am a composer." He loved pleasing people, loved fulfilling and exceeding expectations, finding new audiences, new men and women whom he might conquer. In *Maestro*, Bradley Cooper and Josh Singer re-create how profoundly social a creature he was, a man moving through endless parties— chatty, gossipy, promiscuous parties, a scene friendly but also dangerous. Lenny is host, provocateur, and the best-looking and most available person in the room. Bradley Cooper's blue-gray eyes and rakish smile are almost startling in their candor: this is a man of immense avidity, overwhelming in his desire and need. He was generous to many people out of an abundance of self-pleasure. Why not give more? He had a bottomless well of giftedness to draw from.

Those who don't like *Maestro* complain that the movie left out this or that element of Bernstein's life (his Broadway career, his Jewishness)— complaints that demonstrate either naivete or possessiveness ("Why haven't you made a movie about *my* Lenny?"). But a biopic needs a centralized *plot*; otherwise you get a whirling mass of reference, a hapless inclusiveness. *Maestro* is a moving family story and the portrait of a complicated man. In the movie, as in life, Lenny's great kindness leaves everyone breathless; his eventual selfishness leaves everyone breathless, too.

In a *New Yorker* article from 1998, I described Bernstein as "split" between family life and sexual adventure, between Broadway and classical music, conducting and composing. But I now think this kind of writing is merely conventional. He wasn't *split*; on the contrary he desperately tried to make the parts of his life flow together, even if that attempt appalled many people, some of whom sounded almost hurt by his many talents. Shirley Gabis, a pianist who was Lenny's best friend—and for a while his girlfriend—at Curtis, wrote him in January 1944, some months after his Philharmonic debut.

And Lenny, believe me when I tell you that although you are headed for a brilliant career, it will never be a great one. Your driving ambition to be the most versatile creature on earth will kill any possibility of you becoming a truly great artist in any one of the talents that you possess.

Such sentiments were voiced in the music press again and again and with more than a taint of disapproval, sometimes outright sarcasm. Why couldn't he just stick to Broadway? Or to conducting? Or composing? In 2004, some years after Lenny died, his friend and collaborator Stephen Sondheim said, "Any gift has to be fully concentrated on to reach its fullest potential. And I don't think Lenny reached his fullest potential in any of the fields." But he *did* reach his fullest potential as conductor and teacher. The remark is peevish and inaccurate.

Bernstein didn't listen to the friends and critics lecturing him because he didn't need to. American life had actually changed in ways that enabled his temperament to flourish in many places at once. In a classic Victorian-era dilemma, people were forced to choose between duty and personal fulfillment, between work and pleasure. Duty was omnipresent and pleasure, for many, a scarce resource. But how do you choose among many things that give you satisfaction? That's a privileged, twentieth-century dilemma, available seventy years ago only to men, and only men in wealthy countries. By the fifties, America had become a media society and a restlessly mobile *business* society, including the arts business. After the war, such things as air travel, television, film, long-playing records, and tapes enabled a few men in the arts to reach out in many directions at once. In quiet support, there were pills that fought off depression and fatigue; psychoanalysis for the wealthy. Bernstein took advantage of all this and exercised all his gifts at once.

In any case, the people disapproving of him may simply have been wrong. Would he have become a greater artist if he had held to a single career? Maybe he needed the constant tumult of his life to be at his best in each of his different activities. I have said that disappointment was built into the multiplicity of his gifts. But what would his critics agree to give up among his work—what would I give up?—if he had limited his activities? His conducting of Stravinsky and Mahler? His wonderful *Serenade* for violin, strings, percussion, and harp? The *Young People's Concerts*? *On the Waterfront*? *Candide*?

But what of his own expectations? He deplored his inability to spend more time composing. In letters to friends in the early forties, and later, too, he would renounce something—conducting, usually—and insist that he had to go off somewhere to "get to know myself," by which he meant find the inner structure of his being, master his unconscious. But I believe these effusions of Lenny's were essentially rhetorical. If he had actually wanted to give up something, he would have given it up. As he got older, he did renounce playing Beethoven, Mozart, and Ravel piano concertos, but that was because he no longer played them very well. He seriously renounced only one thing—and then only for a time.

In 1944, Serge Koussevitzky had seen *On the Town* in a Boston tryout. He was amused but disapproving, and he severely lectured his Lenushka, summoning his soul to his sacred calling as a conductor. In his imperious way, Koussevitzky was repeating Sam's fear that Lenny would become a trivial klezmer musician. Koussevitzky didn't understand much of American culture—explicitly, he didn't understand that composing for the theater had become a highly developed way of making art in this country, that the best of the Broadway composers were not just stringing tunes together but through-composing an entire score. He was humorless, uninformed, and simply wrong about Bernstein's future, just as he was wrong when he suggested that Bernstein, in order to succeed in classical music, should change his name to Leonard S. Burns. This surrogate father wanted to take away his son's Jewish identity, which Sam wouldn't dream of doing. And, dear God, Koussevitzky's suggested name! Leonard S. Burns could be a hotel bandleader in suburban Milwaukee. Bernstein refused to make the change.

But he did give in on the theater issue. In 1944, he promised Koussevitzky he would write no more musicals. His debt to Koussevitzky was enormous, and Koussevitzky had promised to recommend him as the next music director of the Boston Symphony. For nine years, from 1944 to 1953 (from *On the Town* to *Wonderful Town*), Lenny conducted and composed classical music and stopped his ears to entreaties from collaborators like Comden and Green. In the end, however, his obedience was all for naught. In 1949, Koussevitzky retired after twenty-five years as Boston's music director, but the orchestra's board rejected his recommendation of Bernstein as his successor, opting instead for the Alsatian conductor Charles Munch. Bernstein waited a few more years before profaning himself in the commercial theater. Koussevitzky died, in 1951, at the age of seventy-seven, and Lenny's way to Broadway was open again.

OUTSIDERS

After *On the Town*, there were three more shows in the Bernstein canon, *Wonderful Town* (1953), *Candide* (an operetta, 1956), and the cataclysmic *West Side Story* (1957). Bernstein also worked on a number of aborted projects and one that was completed, *1600 Pennsylvania Avenue*, a collaboration with Alan Jay Lerner, that opened on Broadway in 1976 and lasted exactly seven performances. There were other attempts to create shows later, but Lenny's Broadway career was effectively over.

A structural and thematic strain runs right through all the successful shows. They were all created by Jewish Americans, and they are all about outsiders. I don't mean to say that the shows are devoted only to Jewish self-expression. On the contrary, they have musical, dramatic, and comic riches that make them widely popular, and much of what's wonderful in them has little to do at the explicit level with American Jews. But I think it's likely that Bernstein and his collaborators were suggesting something about the situation of Jews in America—in disguise, of course, and by implication.

Consider: In *On the Town*, three sailors come to New York and mix it up with the locals. Merry and blunt, the show runs helter-skelter all over the city, and its general tone is wised up but not cynical. It expresses the New York ethos of not being fooled by anything but not giving up on anything, either. It was formed by what Jews call *sechel*—knowingness, judgment—with a definite tinge of hope.

The musical comedy *Wonderful Town*, emerging in 1953, is another exuberant coming-to-New-York story, with many NYC-chauvinist blasts but with a certain bitterness as well. This time the outsiders are two sisters from Columbus, Ohio—would-be writer Ruth (Rosalind Russell in the original production) and her blonde kid sister, Eileen (Edie Adams), an aspiring actress. They rent a basement apartment in the Village and try to get ahead. Along the way, they fall into ridiculous tangles and seemingly meet everyone in town—Brazilian sailors, noble and scuzzy journalists, policemen, and jailors. The show would seem to be the ultimate New York romance, but it doesn't turn out that way.

Bernstein, Comden, and Green wanted to demonstrate the difficulty of early encounters, and they created one of the strangest songs in the history of Broadway, "Conversation Piece," in which, at a party, one character after another tries to launch a conversational gambit, only to stall. The song stalls, too, coming to a dead halt before taking off in an astonishing gallop to the end, complete with desperately flung high notes. "Conversation Piece" goes from musical deconstruction to Rossini in a few minutes. After the women's early setbacks, they sing a duet in thirds, "Ohio," filled with longing for home ("Why, O why, O why-o, why did I ever leave Ohio?"). It is one of Bernstein's gentlest creations, but even this dulcet bit of harmonizing gets jolted. An explosion goes off nearby (dynamiting for a subway tunnel), and the song jumps into a higher key, becoming an almost hysterical wail—before settling into wistfulness again. A bit later, a fellow, who had arrived from the sticks earlier and struck out, bellows at the women, "Go back! Go back where you came from!"

The show lurches (not very convincingly) toward romance at the end, but it makes New York a daunting place, where you can never be sure you are going to find work and love. It's about uncertainty, anxiety, dealing with what scares you, the predominant emotion of outsiders. The four American Jews who created these shows needed to keep the emotions of displacement before them even as they succeeded in the big town.

I WILL COME back to *Candide*, Bernstein's greatest theatrical score, but first, think about *West Side Story*. When you hear of the original conception, you have to laugh: the show, based on *Romeo and Juliet*, was to be called "East Side Story"; it was to be set in the East Side slums at the time of the Easter and Passover celebrations, when feelings run high between Catholics and Jews. Such was the idea that Jerome Robbins brought to Bernstein in January 1949—a kind of holiday-season passion play, with such scenes, outlined by Robbins, as "Act I, Scene II. Ball or Seder or Motza'ei Shabbat [Saturday evening after Sabbath]." The playwright and novelist Arthur Laurents joined them soon after, and the three men talked it over and worked on an outline.

The idea sounds about as exciting as an interfaith conference. And it was possibly embarrassing as well. Years later, Bernstein remembered "a strong feeling of staleness [in] the East Side situation and I didn't like the too-angry, too-bitchy, too-vulgar tone of it." If I may interpret his remark: he felt that the familiarity on the part of his Jewish collaborators with Jewish life would bring out something like derision or self-hatred, the self-deprecating whine of bad stand-up comedy routines. The idea lacked toughness, freshness, daring. Perhaps inanition simply overtook the project: all three men were busy with other work, and the idea faded away. In its core, however, it remained a Jewish musical project.

It was revived by a shift in the population of New York. Between 1949 and the middle 1950s, Puerto Ricans poured into the city, more than fifty thousand a year, often poor, low-skilled or unskilled, many arriving in loosely composed families. Whatever their difficulties, they were not generally violent people. But the young immigrants and their children often encountered hostility from the children of earlier immigrant groups (Poles, Italians, Irish)—something that the Puerto Ricans did not expect and that caused them to form gangs for neighborhood protection and as a way of belonging here.

In 1955, the gang wars chronicled in the Los Angeles and New York papers galvanized Arthur Laurents into reviving the project. He and Bernstein, in late August, had an epochal meeting in a suitably tough urban milieu—at the side of the swimming pool of the pink-stucco Beverly Hills Hotel. Within a few months, the two had developed the plot and stage action in considerable detail. The old premise was dropped; the new idea was gang warfare between recently arrived Puerto Ricans and "Americans" on the West Side (in the slum area soon to be torn down for Lincoln Center); and the music was to be infused with Latin rhythms and pulses throughout.

In October 1955, Jerome Robbins praised and deplored the outline, and insisted that everyone but the principals had to be dancers. Dance rather than words, he believed, would be the best way (also the most exciting way) for working-class kids to articulate what they felt. Robbins also insisted on a certain tone: "We're dead unless the audience feels that all the tragedy can and could be avoided, that there's *hope* and a wish for escape from the tragedy, and a tension built on that desire. . . . Let's not have anyone in the show feeling sorry for themselves."

Comden and Green were approached about writing the lyrics, but they were committed in Hollywood—which is just as well, since it's hard to imagine these two blithely talented satirists fitting into the tragic but earnestly hopeful mood that Robbins wanted. At one point, Bernstein was going to write the lyrics himself (a couple of lines survived), but even he was overwhelmed with work—as he said, there was a lot of music to write for the show, "ballet music, symphonic music, developmental music." In that same month, October 1955, Arthur Laurents met the twenty-five-year-old Stephen Sondheim at a party; Sondheim auditioned for Bernstein the next day, playing and singing some of his own material. The team was set. Consider that all four were abnormally ambitious, aggressive young men: Laurents cagy and irritable; Robbins frightening in his demands; Sondheim soon to be the most intelligent and articulate man in the New York theater world. Lenny, who overwhelmed people with his talent, was the gentlest of the four.

But there was more delay. *Candide* intervened, opening on December 1, 1956, a difficult time for Lenny and all his collaborators on that Broadway operetta. "Maybe it's all for the best," Lenny counseled himself. "By the time [*West Side Story*] emerges it ought to be deeply seasoned, cured, hung, aged in the wood." When they finally got going, the four men fed and challenged one another, meeting often at Bernstein's apartment as they juggled other commitments. Lenny worked on the songs directly with Sondheim, the two men meeting every few days with perhaps only a fragment—a musical idea or a few words of a lyric, each stimulating the other. The song would then be pushed along to completion by telephone.

When they had the material together, the four auditioned the show for potential backers. They took turns acting, singing, and even dancing for some of the best producers working on Broadway, and they were repeatedly turned down. The material was too upsetting, they were told, too dangerous, there was no audience for it, it should be more explanatory about racism, and so on. Producers Roger Stevens, Hal Prince, and Robert Griffith eventually came to the rescue, and, after many difficulties, *West Side Story* opened in New York on September 26, 1957, and in one sense it has never closed: some school or community group is always putting it on, in cities and towns all over the world—even preschoolers in Los Angeles have done it, as have innumerable groups in Japan. Two movies have been made from it, one directed by Robert Wise and Jerome Robbins in 1961 and one by Steven Spielberg in 2022. It is the closest Bernstein came to a universal classic.

THROUGH THE TWENTIES and thirties and the war period, the American Jews had placed their best hopes for their own acceptance on enlarging general tolerance for minorities. That's putting it bluntly and perhaps a little opportunistically. But certainly the Jews knew what it felt like to be outsiders, and certainly anti-prejudice became a central tenet of Jewish liberalism, as it still is today. Bernstein, Robbins, Laurents, and Sondheim were all descended from immigrants (German and Lithuanian Jews in Sondheim's case). They may have known of insults and humiliations heaped on their ancestors, freshly arrived in America. Jerome Robbins was born Jerome Wilson Rabinowitz; Arthur Laurents was born Arthur Levine. They were close enough to prejudice to change their names. Bernstein and Robbins were bisexual; Laurents and Sondheim were gay; all four creators were living half-closeted lives in the mid-fifties. Not even the relaxed atmosphere of the New York theater and music world could protect gay men from the silent or active distaste of so many people around them. So these four had many reasons to create a show about outsiders, race hatred, and prejudice. *West Side Story* has become "universal"; but only American Jews could have created it.

The Broadway musical scene in the mid-fifties was dominated by Rodgers and Hammerstein, by *My Fair Lady*, and by such amiable musical-comedy entertainments as *The Music Man*, *Damn Yankees*, and *Bells Are Ringing*. In this atmosphere, the racially conscious *West Side Story* became the hip show, the dangerous show. Yet what's remarkable is that *West Side Story* is not a liberal sermon. ("Avoid being 'messagy,'" Bernstein advised himself in 1956.) Everything in it, including insults and gang fights, is conceived lyrically. No matter how hard the reality of intolerance is dramatized, and no matter how much production styles vary in the latest versions, *West Side Story* is always a music-and-dance piece.

An imperishable image in music history: Lenny playing through parts of the score in 1956, and Jerome Robbins standing with his hands on Lenny's shoulders, demanding a beat or two more here, a beat less there, the two of them composing the score together. Robbins wanted the music to support not just good dancing, but good *narrative* dancing—he wanted it to be a story of anticipation, bravado, lust, violence, and, finally, sorrow, all told through dance. As the world knows, the choreography is thrilling. What many music lovers know as well is that the score is actually better *composed* than most classical music from the postwar period. There's Tony's eager, unstable, rhythmically off-center "Something's Coming," and there's "Maria," with its octave-leaping reach, and the beautiful "Tonight." When "Tonight" is reprised, with the lovers Tony and Maria singing together, and with the street gangs (in a different rhythm) joining the lovers, the crosscurrents coalesce and suddenly Bernstein is soaring with Mozart and Verdi in a five-part ensemble—sheer musical bliss.

He drew on such modern music techniques as dissonance and bitonality; he matched some of Stravinsky's and Copland's rhythmic complexities; he wrote melodies that came close to Puccini's. Yet it's a Broadway show through and through (and not an "opera," even though Bernstein treated it that way in a mistaken 1984 recording made with opera singers). *West Side Story*, as Bernstein said on a saner day, is a tragedy working within the frame and the preoccupations of a musical comedy. In "The Musical Theater," a 1956 episode of *Omnibus*, the most serious of network TV shows, he described the form as "an art that arises out of our American roots, out of our speech, our tempo, our moral attitudes, our timing, our kind of humor." In *West Side Story*, four gay American Jews, descended from immigrant families, enlarged both the music and the vernacular to embrace the timing and humor of a group of recent arrivals—and the native opposition to them. A later composer like Lin-Manuel Miranda may speak more authentically for Puerto Ricans, but Bernstein helped create the atmosphere in which Miranda could flourish.

The music written for the Sharks—charged-up variants of Latin dances enhanced by a percussion battery of cowbells, maracas, and castanets—gets under your skin. On his pencil-written first draft of "Dance at the Gym," under the staves, Bernstein wrote "Slow Mambo. Fast Mambo, Puerto Rico." And then, rather wonderfully: "Rock 'n' Sweat in Burst." Bernstein and Robbins now had forty kids—not three—bursting out of their pants. Lenny wanted the authentic Latin sound, he wanted to compose it symphonically, and he wanted it to have the power of rock.

The symphonic mambos in *West Side Story* now seem an early forecast of how important Latin music and culture would become in the States. Despite its tragic story, the show could be called a Pan-American celebration. It's also a summing up of Bernstein's New York theater and cabaret work. Earlier, in *On the Waterfront*, Elia Kazan's 1954 melodrama about union corruption on the Hoboken docks, Bernstein ignored the traditional mood-painting and space-filling conventions of American film music and composed a shockingly turbulent and lyrical symphonic score. The whirling figures and rattling fugue-like passages (for three sets of timpani) chase the vulnerable characters down alleys into disaster; a love theme that begins tentatively turns back on itself and gathers strength, soaring and soaring, illimitably it seems, into full-blown eloquence. A lot of this emotionally overpowering music (no one had ever heard anything like it in an American film) was reprised with equal emotion but greater subtlety and wit in *West Side Story*. The New York entertainer sitting at the piano, a debonair creature of the night, available and eager to please, and a parodist, too, with summer-camp shenanigans still in his fingertips—this young musician had developed a genius for pathos and violence.

CHASED EVERYWHERE

Among the shows, I have saved *Candide* for last, and for two reasons: it is perhaps Bernstein's greatest work and the recording he led in 1989, near the end of his life, with the London Symphony Orchestra and a cast of opera singers (Jerry Hadley, June Anderson, Christa Ludwig), plus Adolph Green, pulls together and synthesizes all the different versions of the piece. "The final revised version"—that's what it's called, and the phrase suggests how much the score was, for a long time, in a state of becoming. *Candide* opened on Broadway on December 1, 1956, and closed after seventy-three performances—a good number for an operetta, though not for a Broadway show. It was probably a mistake from the beginning not to shape the material as a repertory item in an opera house. The failure left bitterness in its wake, and between 1956 and 1989, the material was cut, reconceived, extended, restaged, pushed around. At one time or another, a battery of writers worked on the lyrics, including Lillian Hellman, librettist John Latouche, poet Richard Wilbur, and then, in later versions, Broadway book writer Hugh Wheeler, Stephen Sondheim, and Bernstein himself. The honor roll of contributors suggests how much people of diverse talents believed that the music was worth saving, that the show had to be rewritten and rewritten in order, so to speak, to become itself. In the end, *Candide* is an homage to European music—references to Richard Strauss, Gioachino Rossini, and Charles Gounod, as well as many waltz composers, fly though the score. Unity is less the point than variety, allusiveness, brio. Candide travels through all of Europe, and all of Europe plays through *him*.

Voltaire's book is a satire of human stupidity, an attack on people who see God's justice in every terrible thing that happens in life. Candide, its young hero, gets repeatedly battered in his many adventures yet remains convinced, in the words of his master Pangloss, that this is "the best of all possible worlds." He loves the beautiful Cunégonde, but she's not very bright either; she's violated almost as frequently as one of de Sade's victim-ninnies.

The bitterness of Voltaire's text becomes tiresome, but Bernstein, a more sensitive and companionable artist than Voltaire, entertains us. We understand that the advantage of musical, rather than purely literary, satire is that the composer has greater emotional latitude than the novelist; he can coddle and console as well as tease and jibe, and great singers can inflect the lines in a way that tells us what's really going on inside the characters. Bernstein writes with tender pity, not just contempt, for human idiocy.

Until the very end, Candide learns nothing from experience. As Harvard musicologist Carol Oja has said, the opera could be taken "as an allegory of the wandering Jew," that is, a Jew knocked from pillar to post, at home nowhere yet somehow surviving. Other characters die and come back to life, but Candide, despite every accident and betrayal, never dies. You could think of him as a Jewish fool, trusting, oblivious—a *shlemiel*, and therefore a familiar figure in Yiddish theater and literature (as in Isaac Bashevis Singer's story "Gimpel the Fool"). But such a figure is something of an oddity as the creation of modern American Jews, since a *shlemiel* is exactly what people like Lillian Hellman, Stephen Sondheim, and Leonard Bernstein don't want to be. The character of Candide can be considered a projection of every dumb move and blind trust they had ever been led into. The show is a mordant and ironic tribute to Jewish survival triumphing over bouts of stupidity. You're not too bright, you get knocked around, but you always keep going.

In the Bernstein and Co. version, philosophically modernized, Candide and Cunégonde, exhausted, reach a state of humbled acceptance: the world is neither good nor bad but a mix of good *and* bad, unvisited by God, ungoverned by morality. Life just *is*, which we may regard as a twentieth-century existentialist revision of an eighteenth-century anticlerical satire. The composer blesses them at the end. He places Candide and Cunégonde at the center of a very grand choral apotheosis called "Make Our Garden Grow." This choral finale is as close as Bernstein could get to the tremendous ending of Mahler's Symphony No. 2 (*Resurrection*), one of his signature pieces as a conductor. (In *Maestro*, Bradley Cooper restages Lenny's performance of it in the Ely Cathedral in England.) "Make Our Garden Grow" is extraordinarily moving, a paradoxically proud celebration of humility. The show is such a fabulous jumble-shop of styles that it seems odd to call it a masterpiece, but it's a great American musical work, a playful, one-of-a-kind American tribute to the music of the European past and the persistence of Europe's most battered minority.

A MAN AT FORTY

In the fall of 1958, at the age of forty, Leonard Bernstein took over as music director of the New York Philharmonic. Before Bernstein, European conductors held sway not only over orchestras but over the confidence of benefactors—the wealthy board members who raised money at high-society fundraisers. A conductor should have formal manners and a foreign accent. Rudeness and imperiousness were expected, even valued as a form of authenticity. But here was an American conductor whose Americanness came out as informality, a nourishing warmth. His Jewishness came out, too, in his rabbinical desire to teach anyone who would listen. He spoke, for heaven's sake, he *spoke*, giving little lectures before the Thursday night subscription concerts (critics not invited), describing the music about to be played. If music and sensuality could be drawn together, so could emotion and pedagogy. His constant melding of things normally kept apart upset traditionalists; they claimed he was humiliating music, but it was really their own humiliation they were describing.

He was a public man, erudite, endlessly articulate. He read a great deal and spoke out on the great issues of the day. In the sixties, he would become a high-minded crusader for world peace, a strenuous advocate of civil rights, a passionate adherent of the new state of Israel. These activities were mostly harmless, though the FBI took an active interest in them. The agency's interest was sheer Cold War paranoia. Lenny was no revolutionary, but rather a liberal humanist who hated prejudice and hoped for world peace. You might say Beethoven's Ninth with its message of universal brotherhood was constantly playing in his head, as if tolerance, love, and music could solve the world's problems. He took the New York

Philharmonic on tours of South America, Europe, the Soviet Union, and he made a trip with the orchestra to Berlin (in 1960), where he played and conducted Beethoven's Piano Concerto No. 1 and spoke for a while to the audience—German students—in Hebrew. They were puzzled at first and then burst into applause. They got it. These trips, backed by the American government, were political in a benign, world-peace way. Art, he believed, was at once the herald, the message, and the conclusion. "I believe in art for the warmth and love it carries within it, even if it be the lightest entertainment, or the bitterest satire, or the most shattering tragedy"—an American view that went both high and low. What mattered was intensity.

Unlike many public men, he was aware of his obsessions and excesses, aware of the impression he made on others. He could be soulfully self-critical, a good-humored American product of psychoanalysis and its attendant self-consciousness. When he traveled to, say, Rome, New Zealand, or Israel, he registered with warmth and spoofing excitement the details of landscape, architecture, and social life, the play of personalities in the background of his concert tours, enjoying and deploring, for instance, "two weeks of Princesses & Maharanees & phony Barons, parties without end, villas to make you gasp. I was the kid of the moment: it was all insane, ignoble, absurd & vastly entertaining."

NOT EVERYONE LOVED him. The New York music press was often rude, even contemptuous. Intellectuals were not much interested; he wasn't part of the musical avant-garde—John Cage in America and young Pierre Boulez in France—and his emotionalism mortified them. With some notable exceptions (Miles Davis, for one), artists who patrolled the borders of hip considered him a square. He was everywhere, an embarrassment almost, though many people, at first with a laugh, and then with rueful acknowledgment, allowed themselves to be impressed. He invited everyone into the glory of being Leonard Bernstein, which some have misinterpreted as narcissism. He was egotistical, of course, but he consistently drew out the best in other people, which is not a skill associated with narcissists.

By the time he was forty, he had written all four of his successful shows (in the case of *Candide*, the success was achieved gradually, through many revivals). He had composed, in 1949, a little piece for Woody Herman's band, "Prelude, Fugue, and Riffs," with its pell-mell excitement and rushed alarm. Herman never played it, so it became a nifty jazz-at-the-symphony piece. There was the *Serenade* for violin, strings, percussion, and harp, from 1954, a concerto in all but name. *Serenade* has pages of impassioned writing for violin (all the virtuosi now play it) and a great mocking stride that brings the work to a jaunty conclusion. It is perhaps his best classical piece. His Symphony No. 2, *The Age of Anxiety* (1949), inspired by the long Auden poem, is a work for piano and orchestra that opens with exploratory, thoughtful passages for two clarinets. It has eloquent moments of yearning and lamentation in the strenuous big-orchestra style of American symphonic writing in the forties and fifties. But the best music is the fifth movement, "Masque," in which the piano and the xylophone, lithe and happy together, produce the exhilarating effect of needles flashing through the air. The piece ends with a thunderous affirmation of "faith."

FAITH IN MARRIAGE

Faith of a different kind was central to his determination to marry. He met Felicia María Montealegre Cohn in 1946 at a party in New York given by the Chilean piano virtuoso Claudio Arrau. (Felicia was then studying with him but soon moved on to acting lessons with Herbert Berghof.) Lenny was twenty-seven, Felicia almost twenty-four. Her mother was Costa Rican and Catholic; her father, a wealthy industrialist, was an American Jew. Raised in Chile, she was an aristocrat in all but name, beautiful, with small perfect features. And she was bright and witty in a way that delighted Lenny. She could keep up with his propensity for tangled jokes and the word games that he and his friends loved. Full of fun, she was also vulnerable and anxious, a dramatic and emotional woman. They spent a great deal of time together in 1946 and 1947, wrote each other fervent and amusing letters, and became engaged—and then, in 1947, Felicia, tired of waiting for Lenny to commit to marriage, called the affair off. Soon after, she began a relationship with a married actor, Richard Hart, a strikingly handsome man but a hopeless alcoholic.

The difficulty in Lenny's getting married was hardly a mystery. He spoke about it to friends and to his sister, Shirley; he talked to his psychoanalyst, Marketa Morris, about his needs and his guilt. Deep into summer vacation (sacred among shrinks), Morris summoned her mighty powers and interpreted his dreams as follows: "You are seeing Felicia and the day she leaves you *have* to see a boy. The same old pattern. You can't give it up." Well, yes, how perceptive. That he was attracted to men, he had always known; the question was how to manage that attraction in marriage. One has to remember that in the Freudianized mid-forties, however free the sexual life in musical circles, homosexuality was still widely seen, including by many gay men, as a weakness, a character fault; or as a case of arrested development; or as a potential career disaster. Lenny's friends referred to his homosexuality in letters as "your perversity," a term he occasionally used as well.

He wanted to put cruising and short affairs with men behind him. A few years before meeting Felicia, he had written as much to Copland.

> And then this need for closeness always manifests itself in a sexual desire, the more promiscuous the better—giving rise to experiences like being taken by (PfB of course) to a Bain Turc (or is it Turque) and seeking out the 8th Street bars again. But I'm not attracted any more to anyone I find there, and it's just as horrible as if I hadn't gone at all.

PfB was Paul Bowles, the composer and writer. What Lenny describes is not a happy state, and not a state easily conquered. But in 1947, whatever his nights were like, he was in love with Felicia and unhappy over the breakup. In the next few years, he sought a reconciliation. He relied on Shirley, as a kind of sounding board and intermediary, writing her detailed letters about his hopes, including the following, from Tel Aviv, in May 1950.

> I have been engaged in an imaginary life with Felicia, having her by my side on the beach as a shockingly beautiful Yemenite boy passes—inquiring into that automatic little demon who always springs into action at such moment—then testing: If Felicia were there, sharing with me that fantastic instant when the Khamsin is suddenly gone, and a new wind, west from the sea, comes in to cancel the heat with its most holy approach—and the test works. . . . Not that the demon absents himself: he still pokes at me when his occasions arise—the French horn player, the artist in Jerusalem; but the old willingness to follow him, blind to any future, blind to the inner knowledge of the certain ensuing meaninglessness—that is gone. So the demon diminishes.

Despite the self-conscious literary flourishes, this has the sound of truth—the sound, that is, of a faithfully reported internal struggle. In the years 1947 to 1950, Lenny and Felicia would get together now and then in New York for concerts. After much intervention and assorted pressures from family and friends, they finally agreed, in 1951, to marry. Richard Hart, Felicia's alcoholic lover, had died in January of that year; Serge Koussevitzky, Bernstein's substitute father, died in June. They were free.

Felicia, who was half-Jewish, formally converted to Judaism, and they were wed at Lenny's old synagogue, Mishkan Tefila, now in Newton, Massachusetts, on September 8, 1951. Sam and Jennie and Felicia's Catholic mother, Clemencia, were in attendance. On their honeymoon, the couple drove to Wyoming and then to Cuernavaca, Mexico, one of Lenny's favorite vacation spots. Felicia's English was actually very good, but on the road, day after day, Lenny gave his bride formal lessons in English grammar, doing irregular verbs, perhaps, on route 95.

Lenny strayed with men soon after the wedding. As Nigel Simeone, the editor of Bernstein's letters, put it, Lenny regarded marriage "as a kind of experiment." There were wrenching scenes between husband and wife, in which it became clear that he was unhappy with the constraints of heterosexual monogamy. For her part, Felicia demanded discretion. She was hardheaded about such things, and she wrote him an extraordinary letter.

> You are a homosexual and may never change—you don't admit to the possibility of a double life, but if your peace of mind, your health, your whole nervous system depends on a certain sexual pattern, what can you do? . . .
> I am willing to accept you as you are, without being a martyr or sacrificing myself on the L.B. altar.

But he did live a double life, admitted or not. And Felicia, despite her protestations, wound up both martyring herself and tending the altar.

FAMILY MAN

Felicia Montealegre was an accomplished actress in an elevated elocutionary style that was losing out in the early fifties to naturalistic modes like the Method. She had serious work for a while on the stage and in the burgeoning field of live TV drama (she played Nora in *A Doll's House* on television). She was good at narrating oratorios. But her career stalled when she was still young, and, as she and Bernstein had children—Jamie (born in 1952), Alexander (1955), and Nina (1962)—she retreated from it. The family lived in fine apartments on Park Avenue and later in the Dakota, on West Seventy-Second Street and Central Park; they eventually bought a comfortable house in Fairfield, Connecticut (the setting for parts of *Maestro*). Felicia became a hostess, formal in her table and clothes, a mistress of splendid entertainments, a style setter and therefore a principal force in helping Lenny become a social as well as musical success in New York. Their letters to each other when they were apart were funny and conspiratorial; they enjoyed their preeminence and were amused by the fuss other people made over them. But they may have underestimated the kind of derision that builds up against Americans leading high-class lives. Carey Mulligan's great performance in *Maestro* captures Felicia's intelligence, her playfulness, her indignation when she's traduced by her husband, but the movie gives little evidence of how important a social figure she was in New York, nor of the liberal political activities that eventually got her in trouble.

At home (when he *was* at home), Leonard Bernstein was an ardent family man, attentive and affectionate, and, of course, an unrelenting didact, cramming his kids with poetry, music, and Hebrew lessons. In her excellent book *Famous Father Girl: A Memoir of Growing Up Bernstein* (2018), Jamie Bernstein remembers him in New York, half awake and fragrant in the mornings. "In my mind's eye, my father is always in a scruffy brown wool bathrobe; my cheek still prickles at the memory of his scratchy morning hugs." You couldn't say of this father, as you might of John Cheever (as revealed in his daughter Susan Cheever's somberly brilliant *Home Before Dark*), that he was unreachable at times or that his art absolutely came first. On the contrary, family was emotionally central to Bernstein, as it had been when he was a child in the Boston suburbs. And family meant not just Felicia and the kids but his loving and voluble immigrant parents; his talented brother, Burton, a *New Yorker* writer; and the ebullient Shirley, who ran a theatrical literary agency. Even in mid-career, Lenny would go off on holiday with Burtie and Shirley, the three of them joined in hilarity over childhood memories, complete with an invented nonsense language they spoke together—Ribernian, it's called, apparently an improvement on Elvish.

In Jamie Bernstein's account of her childhood, one detects something like the fervent nostalgia of Russian expatriates for life before the revolution. There was glory then, ample country as well as city luxury, faithful servants, tennis with Isaac Stern, the Macy's Thanksgiving Day Parade seen from the windows of their apartment in the Dakota; and also live music, much of it generated by Lenny sitting at the piano—Lenny the college-dorm *wunderkind*, still going in middle age, playing everything from Bach to new pop tunes. The family gatherings were a conspiracy to have fun. Parents and children together created rhyming nonsense songs; they made clowning home movies ("What Ever Happened to Felicia Montealegre?," an overwrought salute to Bette Davis and Joan Crawford). Lenny was devoted to anagrams, palindromes, acrostics; he pursued definitions and derivations and foreign tongues, very useful when conducting in Vienna, Milan, Paris—he was as much obsessed with words as he was with music.

If his effusiveness and omnivorousness were sometimes hard to bear, plenty of smart people, including Mike Nichols, Richard Avedon, Betty Comden, Adolph Green, and the young Stephen Sondheim, couldn't get enough of him. Playwright Lillian Hellman, terrifying to Jamie, was a growling presence. With that crew around, however, and L. B. driving the entertainments, the long evenings could become barbed. The word games were played as life-and-death matters, and more than one participant, Jamie says, left the room in tears.

In some ways—leaving sexuality aside for a minute—Lenny and Felicia were temperamentally at odds: she required rules and order, while he luxuriated in his own habits, some disciplined, some not. And, adoring her as he did, he still needed young men. He may have also needed, in a general way, to break from the upper-bourgeois confinements that his wife so skillfully established. He enjoyed their social success, but for all his reveling in family life, a part of his desire was always somewhere else.

MY FIRST NAZI AND MY FAVORITE NAZI

In 1938, when he was thirty, Herbert von Karajan had conducted Wagner's transcendent *Tristan und Isolde* in Berlin performances that elicited the newspaper headline, "*Das Wunder Karajan*." Ten years later, at forty, the miraculous Karajan was well into his extraordinary career as a conductor of the standard symphonic and operatic repertory. He was also a world-class careerist who had joined the Nazi party in 1933 and remained a member until 1945. After the war, he passed through a denazification examination at the hands of the Russians and Americans, and by 1947, he was conducting the Vienna Philharmonic. A few years later, he would be in demand as a conductor all over Europe, and still before him lay his years with the Philharmonia of London, La Scala, the Vienna State Opera, and the Berlin Philharmonic (where he spent more than thirty years as music director). He sold more records than any other classical conductor.

In 1954, Bernstein was working with Maria Callas at La Scala, and the two men met for the first time. They had a long talk, emptying a bottle of Ballantine's in the middle of the night. Soon after, Lenny wrote Felicia: "I became real good friends with von Karajan, whom you would (and will) adore. My first Nazi." Lenny's way of appropriating ex-Nazis has an element of both seduction and triumph. In the sixties, he had to deal with the repulsive truth that a man named Helmut Wobisch, a former trumpet player in the Vienna Philharmonic, was now the manager of the orchestra. This Wobisch had worked for the SS during the war, expelling Jewish members from the Philharmonic. Lenny referred to Wobisch *in public* as "my favorite Nazi," and there are multiple photos of a Wobisch happily greeting the maestro at the airport as he arrives in Vienna. Lenny made grim jokes, but he wanted to woo these men away from their pasts, their guilt; he would win them over, asserting not only Jewish talent but Jewish forgiveness. He and Karajan developed a friendly rivalry. On different occasions, when they were working in Vienna and Salzburg at the same time, they took turns upstaging each other in public.

Von Karajan was a dedicated music businessman, fully conscious of money, organization, and administration as he deliberately set about consolidating the classical tradition with his innumerable recordings of Beethoven, Brahms, Tchaikovsky, Bruckner, Sibelius, Verdi and Wagner operas, the tone poems of Richard Strauss. Each change in technology was an excuse to record again his entire repertory. But Lenny, searching always, left business details to others; he liked to move on and explore. One was a perfectionist who gave performances of great power that sometimes became smoothed out and even bland through repetition; the other was full of surprises—always discovering things, a sensibility always in the making. For years, they represented two versions of musical culture—

the authoritarian essence of the Old World and the democratic essence of the Jewish immigrant New World.

MUSIC DIRECTOR

At first glance—and Bernstein conducting was what everyone experienced at first glance—he was certainly a bit much. There was the massive, grandly sculpted head (Rodin couldn't have done better), the chin raised in exultation, the mane both abounding and clipped, all framing a virile Jewish beak and sizable ears. There was the kinesthetically mobile body, acting out the emotional significance of the score in a kind of parallel narrative to the music itself. He shaped the music with his arms and shoulders, his hips, mouth, and eyebrows—anticipating, summoning, triumphantly discharging. He did not move that way when conducting Mozart, Haydn, or Stravinsky's neoclassical compositions but, in general, he employed a vocabulary of gesture and movement that was often bigger, more emotionally explicit than any other conductor's. Now and then, he leaped upward, and on one occasion he landed among the cellos. "Keep on playing!" the Israel Philharmonic heard.

For years, his manner in front of an orchestra caused embarrassment and even anger. Critic and composer Virgil Thomson, writing in the *New York Herald Tribune* when Bernstein was young, complained of "corybantic choreography" and "the miming of facial expressions of uncontrollable states." In the arts, embarrassment may be the superego of emotion: this liberated Jewish body dismayed not only Thomson but the fastidious descendants of German Jews in New York, especially Harold C. Schonberg, the chief music critic of the *Times* after 1960, who gave Bernstein terrible reviews for years. In the eyes of Schonberg and others, Bernstein was hammy, overexpressive, undignified; he was Broadway, he was show business, he lacked seriousness.

One thing that bothered these men was obvious enough: Bernstein was introducing an unwanted eroticism into classical conducting, an art whose joys should be spiritual and, well, *clean*. He was young and more than handsome—"beautiful" many people said—with the moistly ripe sensuality of a second-level movie star of the forties and fifties. (Think of Victor Mature or the young Tony Curtis.) With bold, eager glances, he took in the orchestra, the audience, and, if a camera was present, the camera, frankly acknowledging his pleasure in being the center of everything and his assurance that he would not disappoint.

As he stood in front of the orchestra, showmanship and art came together. The beginning of a piece had to come not a second too early, not a second too late, but at just the moment when the bond between conductor and orchestra, conductor and audience, was at its strongest. Once he launched the piece, he would slip into a kind of exalted reverie in which he was triumphantly in his body but also outside it, communing with God, maybe, or at least with the composer. In such moments, he wasn't "miming" anything. The gestures were unselfconscious and entirely sincere. The extraordinary conductor Carlos Kleiber noted that "maybe the great thing about [Bernstein] was his kindness." He gave appreciative nods to soloists and whole sections as he cued in one passage after another. When everything worked, he was one of the most technically proficient and emotionally overwhelming conductors who had ever lived.

IN THE 1940S, classical music—it's hard to believe this now—was part of American popular culture. It was commonly taught in schools. There was a flood of books and radio commentary devoted to "music appreciation," much of it, alas, unctuous, pretentious, and boring. The CBS radio network had regular classical concerts, and NBC formed a virtuoso orchestra, the NBC Symphony, for Arturo Toscanini in 1937 and kept it on the air (and later on the NBC television network) for seventeen years. In Hollywood, distinguished European composers-in-exile wrote for the movies; classical music was treated with jaunty affection in the Disney extravaganza *Fantasia* (1940) and, more tellingly, in such Warner Bros. cartoons as the Looney Tunes series.

All of this was beginning to fade when Bernstein took over the Philharmonic in 1958. For decades, people with ears had known that jazz was an American art equal in spiritual and musical worth to the greatest of all music. The old hierarchies, in which loving classical was not only an ethical and aesthetic attainment but a sign of social status, mattered less and less, and, in the sixties, after the Beatles, the Stones, and Bob Dylan, the hierarchies collapsed altogether. No one with cultural ambition needed to feel guilty about ignoring classical music. After its long ascendency in high society, in the schools, on the radio, and elsewhere, classical music was on the defensive. Rock was the culturally charged music of the sixties.

Bernstein knew this as well as anyone, and perhaps his critics, knowing it too, were made nervous by Lenny's presence. *Tradition, which had to be preserved, was now in the hands of this glamorous young man.* The critics said in effect that they weren't going to be fooled by national pride into pushing a young American. No, not at all. Years later, Harold C. Schonberg recalled that "There was a time, for many years, when he could not get a good review in a New York paper, in either the *Times* or the [*Herald*] *Tribune.*"

I went to a lot of Philharmonic concerts in Bernstein's early days as music director, and I heard some things that were under-rehearsed and overdriven, a little coarse, without the discipline and mastery of orchestral technique that was so extraordinary in his later years. But the playing was always vital, the programs exciting. He conducted the standard repertory of the nineteenth century, but he also moved back to Haydn and revealed a robust, fearless genius whose roots lay in peasant dances and folk music. He revived Sibelius and championed Danish symphonist Carl Nielsen. And there was Mahler's heir Shostakovich, whom he conducted with full devotion to the martial uproar of a composer who had to please Stalin in order to survive and the lyricism and anguish of a composer who hated totalitarianism and created the most intimate and heartbreaking resistance to it. Bernstein was anything but careless in his relation to classical tradition.

And there was one concert, given on April 2, 1961, that changed my life. It was a performance of Mahler's Symphony No. 3, a monster with six movements, ninety-five minutes of outrageously stentorian swagger and odd, folkish nostalgia, capped by a lengthy *adagio* marked *Langsam—Ruhevoll—Empfunden* (slowly—tranquil—deeply felt). Bernstein took the *adagio* at a very slow tempo indeed, considerably slower than did many subsequent conductors, who, I dare say, would have had trouble holding it together at that speed. But the tempo wasn't remarkable in itself. What was remarkable was the sustained tension and momentum of the movement and the sense of improvisation *within* the sustained momentum—the slight hesitations, the phrases explored, caressed, and also the singing tone of the entire orchestra at those impossibly slow speeds, including the trumpets and trombones and even the timpani, all of it leading to the staggering climax at the end.

The audience erupted into applause, and I remember thinking (I was seventeen), "Anyone who doesn't know that this man is a great musician can't hear a thing"—or something like that. (The Mahler Third was recorded in the next few days, in the Manhattan Center, on West Forty-Second Street, and you can hear what I heard on a Sony CD.) After the concert, I went home shaken. That last movement opened gates of sensation and feeling that I had never experienced before, at least not outside of dreams. I was a very repressed and frightened teenager, and the music granted permission, a kind of encouragement to come out of myself and meet the world. The word *awakening* sounds banal, but I don't know how else to describe what happened. Bernstein had that effect on many people. But it took Bernstein's first journey to Vienna to awaken New York's critics, which became one of the great ironies of American musical taste.

VIENNA SPEAKS TO NEW YORK

I began by describing what occurred when Bernstein was rehearsing the Vienna Philharmonic in Mahler's Symphony No. 5 in 1972, and I noted that the Philharmonic's resistance was surprising after his great success with the orchestra in 1966. At that time, he was eight years into his directorship in New York, and often, despite his great performances of Mahler and many other composers, getting those sarcastic reviews at home. In 1966, in Vienna, he conducted Verdi's *Falstaff* (at the Staatsoper, the orchestra's parent organization), and, with the Philharmonic, he did some Mozart and Mahler, too—*Das Lied von der Erde*, the song cycle with orchestra that the orchestra actually knew very well. (It was the convoluted and violent later symphonies—masterpieces, all—that the orchestra didn't know or love.) The ovations in 1966 went on forever, in a strange kind of release that even Lenny, who certainly enjoyed acclaim, thought was a bit odd. "I'm sort of a Jewish hero who has replaced Karajan," he wrote Felicia. And a couple of weeks later, making a report to Sam and Jennie, he wrote, "You never know if the public that is screaming *bravo* for you might contain someone who 25 years ago might have shot me dead. But it's better to forgive, and if possible, forget. . . . What they call the 'Bernstein wave' that has swept Vienna has produced some strange results; all at once it's fashionable to be Jewish."

That an American conductor of any kind was enjoying acclaim in

Vienna was itself cause for wonder. From Bernstein's point of view, the odds had always been stacked against him. A few years after that 1966 triumph, he wrote the great German conductor Karl Böhm: "You were born in the lap of Mozart, Wagner, and Strauss, with full title to their domain, whereas I was born in the lap of Gershwin and Copland, and my title in the kingdom of European music was, so to speak, that of an adopted son." But by 1972, the positions of son and elders were reversed, and Bernstein's tone as he fought the Vienna Philharmonic in that rehearsal of the Mahler Fifth was anything but abashed. Bernstein did not, of course, walk out of the turbulent rehearsal. He stayed, and he drove the Vienna Philharmonic hard. An American Jew would make them *play* this music.

A decade or so later, in a video lecture, "The Little Drummer Boy," Bernstein insisted that Mahler's genius depended on combining the strengths of the Austro-German symphonic line with specifically Jewish elements recalled from his youth in Bohemia. All those wild, exultant horn calls—were these not the remembered tones of the shofar sounded from a distance on the High Holidays? The banal village tunes that Mahler altered into sinister mock vulgarities—did these not recall the raffish klezmer bands, the wandering musicians who played at shtetl weddings? The ambiguity, the exaltation and sarcastic self-parody, the gloom alternating with a yearning for simplicity and even for redemption—all of that reflected the split consciousness of Jews who could never belong and turned revenge upon themselves. In a remark that Lenny often quoted, Mahler said, "I am thrice homeless, as a native of Bohemia in Austria, as an Austrian among Germans, and as a Jew throughout the world. Everywhere an intruder, never welcomed."

Shame, Bernstein said—the shame of being a Jew—played an enormous role in Mahler's temperament. Leading the Vienna Philharmonic and other orchestras, Bernstein unleashed the late Mahler symphonies with a violence and tenderness that could be devastating, ending the shame forever. And by so doing, he helped restore to Europeans a part of the Jewish contribution to Austrian-German culture and life, and perhaps also a range of emotions, including access to the bitter ironies of self-knowledge that had been eliminated from consciousness during the Nazi period. Mahler died in 1911, but Bernstein believed Mahler *knew*; he understood in advance what the twentieth century would bring of violence and harrowing guilt. "Marches like heart attacks," he wrote in his score of the apocalyptic Sixth

Symphony. The tangled assertion and self-annihilation, the vaunted hopes and apocalyptic grief—that was our modern truth. It was all there in the music. Bernstein was not the only conductor playing Mahler after the war. Bruno Walter, Rafael Kubelik, and Dimitri Mitropoulos, Lenny's old mentor, campaigned for Mahler. But it was Leonard Bernstein who galvanized the revival that has never ceased.

In 2018, the Jewish Museum in Vienna mounted an exhibit called "A New Yorker in Vienna." The accompanying catalog included the words, "Vienna wanted *him* to put an end to the Nazi image and restore the city's glamorous and cosmopolitan image." Yes, exactly. The ovations for Lenny went on forever in 1966 and afterward in part because the audience was celebrating its release from infamy. Perhaps only an American Jew, open, friendly, but a representative of a conquering power, could have produced the effect that Bernstein did.

HE RETURNED TO New York in 1966 after his initial Vienna triumph, and a comedy ensued. The *Times*'s Harold C. Schonberg, who had been so critical of Lenny for years, immediately announced, "Maturity seems to be creeping in." It turned out that despite the heady initial celebration of an American conductor as music director, the old snobbery in favor of European musical taste had been operating in New York. But once Vienna applauded, New York changed its mind. In effect, Vienna taught Harold Schonberg and other critics how to listen. Some years later, the German avant-garde composer Karlheinz Stockhausen, whose compositions could frighten the hardiest music lover, wrote that Lenny possessed *Unbefangenheit* (unembarrassed openness), not to mention *Aufgeräumheit* (cheerfulness, clarity of mind). The Europeans were enchanted by the emotional fluency that the New York critics had thought vulgar.

After 1966, the condescension and embarrassment pretty much ended. Everyone but the prigs realized that Bernstein's gestural munificence was both utterly sincere and very successful at getting what he wanted. He wasn't out of control; on the contrary, he was asserting control. Karajan worked out the detail in rehearsal and then, in performance, stood there with his eyes closed, beating time, thrusting out his aggressive chin and mastering the orchestra with his stick and his left hand, sometimes in a clenched fist, sometimes in an angry claw. He was fascinating but almost frightening to watch. Karajan radiated power when he conducted; Bernstein radiated love. Smiling, imploring, flirting, and commanding, he cued every section, almost every solo, and often subdivided the beat for greater articulation. If you were watching him, either in the hall or on television, he pulled you into the structural and dramatic logic of a piece. He was not only narrative in flight, he was an emotional guide to the perplexed. For all his egotism, there was finally something selfless in his work. Alex Ross, in a 2008 *New Yorker* piece, put it this way:

> Musicians must be cajoled into creating a particular kind of unison: not a robotic sameness of execution but a deeper unanimity in which spontaneous activities on the part of each player viscerally realize the conductor's vision. . . . The players fall in line—that trembling, hurtling line in which Bernstein seemed the most inspired follower rather than the leader. Although he basked in fame, he never accumulated power: each night, he gave away everything he had.

BROKEN COMPACT

Buried within Bernstein's flamboyance was that naturally didactic temperament, the Jewish instructional mania he had inherited from Sam, now mixed with his own manias. He had to teach always. Many of the programs he devised in the early Philharmonic years were part of elaborate thematic festivals. An American was taking over, and music history had to be summarized and reconfigured, directions suggested, hopes held out. He designed programs that would both educate and electrify the audience—a survey of the concerto form, music for the theater, and the symphony, especially the symphony. By its very nature, the symphony, he thought, was a noble, even heroic invention, for the symphony was devoted to conflict and resolution, to difficulties met and overcome.

But apart from Shostakovich, what was the great symphonic music of the postwar period? He would have loved to have succeeded Koussevitzky as the benefactor of important new work. But the Big American Symphonies of the thirties and forties, written by Copland, Roy Harris, William Schuman, and Bernstein himself, high-powered, sometimes ardently lyrical music, celebrating American confidence and might—that kind of American symphony had petered out by the sixties. Indeed, after the

war and the Holocaust, the very form of the symphony, with its passage
through turmoil and triumph, had begun to seem pompous and beside
the point. What victory could we celebrate? For some, the form smacked
of hollow cultural reaction in the style of Soviet "socialist realism."

Among advanced European and American composers, the mood after
the war was often one of apocalyptic despair. Theodor Adorno, the Marxist philosopher and music theorist who wrote eloquently about Wagner
and Mahler, laid out a gloomy prescription: "[New music] has taken upon
itself the darkness and guilt of the world. All its happiness comes in the
perception of misery." Adorno had an almost vindictive contempt for
pleasure; he believed pleasure was amoral if not politically reactionary.
Yet he was not wrong in his characterization of the sullen mental state
of serious composers. Those who followed the atonal and serialist gospel
of Arnold Schoenberg had taken over much of the avant-garde and the
universities. Prim revolutionaries, they pushed aside the tonal composers
popular in the war period and immediately after. They spoke in experimental and mostly nonheroic work to a small, scarily exclusive group of
people. In 1958, in a notorious article, "Who Cares If You Listen?" written
for the magazine *High Fidelity*, the composer Milton Babbitt, in residence
at Princeton, declared, "I dare suggest that the composer would do himself and his music an immediate and eventual service by total and resolute
and voluntary withdrawal from this public world to one of private performance and electronic media, with its very real possibility of complete
elimination of the public and social aspects of musical composition."

Complete elimination of the public. Babbitt's bullying exclusiveness was
absurd (and intentionally outrageous), but his article highlighted what
was obvious to everyone, especially to Leonard Bernstein: the compact
between composer and audience had broken down. Up to the late eigh-
teenth century, there were congregations eager for a new cantata, mass, or
motet, and an aristocratic audience eager for opera, orchestral work, elegant party music, and then, in the nineteenth century, a bourgeois public
eager for a new symphony, concerto, or opera. Composers wanted to offer
emotional power and spiritual sustenance, or at least, putting it crassly,
to fill a market need and make a living. This compact between composer
and audience had existed, in different forms, for hundreds of years. But
after the Second World War, the public no longer looked forward to new
classical music. "The hideous fact remains," Bernstein wrote in 1966, "that

composer and public are an ocean apart." Not only was classical music losing its prestige, it was losing its audience. In 1963, Bernstein gave a speech before musicians honoring Koussevitzky, who had commissioned all that great work by Bartók, Stravinsky, Prokofiev, and Copland. But now the situation was gloomy. "Does anyone care anymore—really care—if anyone of us here ever writes another note?"

It's a strange, bitter question. In the following season, as if looking for an answer, he and the Philharmonic put on an avant-garde festival, with works by John Cage, Morton Feldman, Iannis Xenakis, and others—electronic music, music governed by chance, and so on. He gave the avant-garde a moment. In Cage's *Atlas Eclipticalis*, eighty instrumentalists played with small microphones leading to a preamplifier on the floor; the music was then mixed and fed to speakers positioned throughout the hall. It lasted eight minutes. Bernstein's rubric for the concert series was "The Search for Nothingness," which was apparently not meant ironically. In effect, composers were writing music that came close to annihilating music. All of which sounds (to me) both naive and megalomaniacal. In practice, the works played by the Philharmonic were too fragmentary and japeish to make much of an impression, and audiences were often derisive. The avant-garde festival didn't work, but it represents Bernstein's effort to at least sample, if not embrace, music that was temperamentally distant from his own work. He gave it a shot, and he sometimes played with serial or atonal composition—there are patches of it in his *MASS* (1971)—before returning, in consolation, to B-flat major or some other familiar key.

Throughout his years as music director of the Philharmonic (from 1958 to 1969, with one year off), Bernstein played very little new music that has lasted, and, at the end of his tenure, in 1969, he returned to the weightiest masterpieces, including Beethoven's *Missa Solemnis*, the Verdi *Requiem*, and, once again, Mahler's Third Symphony (with an even slower tempo for the last movement). Over the next twenty-one years, until his death in 1990, he virtually gave up on new music (except his own). Conducting in Tel Aviv, Munich, London, Paris, Berlin, Boston, and Chicago, as well as in Vienna and New York, he devoted more and more of his time to European masterworks. As much as Karajan, he had become a conservator. America had something to prove in Europe, and he was the vehicle of that proof.

He was one of the world's great conductors, revered everywhere, but in his work on the podium alone he could not solve what had gone wrong in the direction of music itself. Classical music was growing forlorn, abandoned; the love for it had to be created from the ground up.

TEACHING AS AN ART I

In 1948, Columbia Records introduced its version of the long-playing record, a wondrous affair of notched microgrooves pressed into a newly developed plastic called vinyl. One of the new records could play as much as forty-five minutes on its two sides and in good sound, too, a technological miracle that worked particularly well for classical music, whose proudest invention, the symphony, apart from the monster cases, lasted anywhere from twenty-five to forty-five minutes. You could get two Mozart symphonies on an LP, or all of Beethoven's *Eroica*, or, on two LPs, Beethoven's Ninth.

Toscanini and his NBC Symphony sold a million copies of their version of the Ninth, and Bernstein, with Columbia Records as his producer and distributor, plunged in, recording hundreds of works from the Philharmonic's repertory—sometimes after arduous rehearsal and three or four repetitions in concerts, sometimes without any rehearsal at all, just winging it, propelling themselves through light classics with Lenny's enthusiasm and the orchestra's discipline and memory carrying all before it. These performances, both serious and spontaneous, have been endlessly repackaged and reissued as CDs by Sony, which bought Columbia in 1988 and kept the Bernstein catalog active. The principal channel for distributing music now, of course, is streaming music services. Almost all of Bernstein's early work with the Philharmonic, with CD-quality sound, can be downloaded from such services as TIDAL and Qobuz.

Television had been available in various experimental forms since the late 1920s. After the war, in the United States and Britain, broadcast television made its way into homes as a mass medium, the bulky cathode-ray tubes producing 625 lines of black-and-white images, sometimes crisp, often not. Within a few years, television had changed the world—the way culture was conveyed, our consciousness of society and ourselves, our sense of time. Television was something radical we were doing to ourselves. For classical music, it was a brief shining moment. Beginning in 1948, NBC began broadcasting some of Toscanini's concerts. The great man would emerge from the wings, barely acknowledge the audience, glare at the musicians of the NBC Symphony for a few seconds, and then begin beating time in his inexorably energetic way. The extra lights needed for broadcast made him sweat; the entire presentation was both heroic and stiff, but the stiffness only fed Toscanini's mystique as an ultimate musical authority.

But Lenny wanted to talk, he wanted to smile and charm; most of all he wanted to dramatize and explain. On November 14, 1954, in prime time, on CBS's high-class program *Omnibus*, he devoted a show to Beethoven's Symphony No. 5. Dear God, Beethoven's Fifth! Revolutionaries and imperialists had exploited it, children had endured it being stuffed down their throats. So why begin his TV career with a cultural meme?

He stands on a studio floor that reproduces the opening pages of the score. Behind him, the musicians, holding their instruments, are positioned on the staves. Then he starts moving them around: Beethoven didn't want the sound of a flute in the opening phrases, so the flute player walks off, the timpanist leaves, and so on, until the remaining musicians generate the right sound, dark and gruff. The Fifth is always praised for its terse, unrelenting drive—what Lenny called, speaking of Beethoven in general, "the inexplicable ability to know what the next note has to be." But that sense of inevitability was produced, as he shows us, by endless revision. He points to Beethoven's score, with its ugly blots ("the bloody record of tremendous inner battle"), and then he turns to a full orchestra and conducts some of the early drafts—a discarded development section, a discarded ending. The discarded bits are truly terrible—Beethovenian drivel, furious but directionless pounding of a few notes.

By now we're ready for the real thing. He conducts the final version of the first movement, and the "inevitability" becomes an achieved miracle, not something taken for granted. By shuffling the musicians around, he makes the compositional choices physically palpable; he almost causes us to feel we've had a hand in writing the symphony ourselves. *His* physicality, of course, is also part of the excitement. He is thirty-six, slender, with a full head of dark hair, which he brushes back in the manner of a Brazilian gigolo. Well, a Jewish Brazilian gigolo, a teacher. He is more than a little nervous, but decisive and enormously friendly at the same time.

The 1954 broadcast was as much a triumph as his Philharmonic debut a decade earlier. He ends the show with an eloquent evocation of genius, eloquence earned by the demonstration we have witnessed.

> For reasons unknown to him or anyone else, [the composer] will give away his energies and his life just to make sure that one note follows another *inevitably*. It seems rather an odd way to spend one's life, but it isn't so odd when we think that the composer, by doing this, leaves us at the finish with the feeling that something is right in the world, that something checks throughout, something that follows its own laws consistently, something we can trust, that will never let us down.

Omnibus offered programs on science, theater, and architecture. Bernstein did seven shows on music, stretching from 1954 until 1958. He had become a national television star, a hypercultivated voice endlessly talking of music and emotion. It was the kids, however, he most wanted to reach. For them, he wanted to be at once pied piper and music master; he wanted to create them as emotional beings in a way that only music could do. Didacticism morphed into Jewish evangelism—instruction became a form of deliverance.

In 1958, as television's saturation of American households was nearing 90 percent, Bernstein and the Philharmonic gave the first of his *Young People's Concerts*. He faces the boys and girls—the boys, hair combed, in tightly fitted light-colored suits, the girls in jumpers and rounded white collars—and smiles broadly, teasing and flirting, an irrepressible uncle singing Mozart one moment, Elvis the next. In these broadcasts, he recognizes no bounds, mounting programs on melody, symphonic development, folk music, and jazz; on Latin American music; on humor in music and sonata form.

The televised children's concerts sold lots of records for Leonard Bernstein and the New York Philharmonic. But mere commercial calculation cannot explain the desire to do so many of these programs—fifty-three in all from 1958 to 1972, each one produced by exhausting hard work and carried off live under high-stress conditions. Watching the shows now, you feel present at an act of creation—the development, rarely attained before or since, of what can only be called pedagogical art. For here was the moldiest of genres—music appreciation—electrified by the spirit of play. Bernstein gets the Philharmonic to play Haydn in the wrong style, slowly and thickly, with soupy romantic emphasis. He has the voluptuous flute solo at the beginning of Debussy's "Afternoon of a Faun" played by a trumpet. He deconstructs passages, alters their instrumentation, clothes and unclothes them, and then, finally, plays them as complete pieces, with the correct orchestration, and with great brio.

Karajan might have said, "What could be the point of such foolish demonstrations?" And Bernstein would have retorted that for an American who had inherited so little, music was never a static series of masterpieces. Music was always in a state of becoming, and possession of it had to be earned. Of course, this American modesty was crested with defiance. Its implication was: America is where the action is. We aren't stuffy and reverential like the Old World; we can fool around with the classics, only to love them that much more by showing they were something *made*. We enjoy playing them badly so we can play them well.

But he had an intention even larger than repossession. If something had gone wrong in the relationship between composer and public, he wanted to close that awful gap. He couldn't alter music history, but he could create music lovers ready to listen to difficult things, ready to listen to *anything*, including dissonant work, even twelve-tone music. He tells the children (and everyone watching on TV) that music is the way you experience joy and pain and loneliness and even estrangement. Music is central to our being; it can create *selves* where before there was only the human equipment of receptivity, ready but unformed. The more music you know, the fuller human being you become. (My soul-forging experience with his performance of the Mahler Third Symphony in 1961 might be an example of what he meant.) And that receptivity, and how to cultivate it, is central to what he was to tell us some years later in the Norton Lectures, an even larger foray into the formerly cloying wastes of Music Appreciation.

MESSENGER TO THE JEWS

After the Second World War, until 1950, the United States occupied the southern part of Germany, an administrative arrangement that allowed traditional German culture to come back to life. In May 1948, the Bavarian

State Opera in Munich, up and running, offered Bernstein a chance to direct the company's orchestra. He was not quite thirty years old.

When he got to the city, he was shocked: many buildings lay in ruins, and people in the audience and even musicians in the orchestra didn't have enough to eat. The misery of the city where Nazism was born oppressed him but, still, he had something to prove—that an American Jew could conduct German music with passionate understanding. He chose Robert Schumann's Symphony No. 2, one of his favorite pieces, and the concerts were a great success. "Shrieking Germans—what a delight!" he wrote his sister Shirley. And to his secretary Helen Coates he wrote of the acclaim, "It means so much . . . since music is the Germans' last stand in their 'master-race' claim."

But then he was jolted again. An outfit called the American Jewish Joint Distribution Committee (JDC) was sending artists into Europe to help survivors recover from the traumas of war. The JDC, working with the United Nations Relief and Rehabilitation Administration, asked Bernstein, as part of his appearance in Munich, to conduct something called the Jewish Representative Orchestra, a twenty-piece group made up of survivors of the Dachau concentration camp. The musicians, who called themselves the Orchestra of the Last Survivors, were living in utmost despair in a Benedictine monastery.

Two days after the Munich concert, Bernstein somehow rehearsed and conducted this ensemble in two camps near the city, Feldafing and Landsberg. The audience was composed of stateless people, mostly Jewish, unable to leave the camps three years after the war. The program included Weber's overture to *Der Freischütz*, some Bizet, Verdi, and Puccini arias (with a local soprano), and then, with Lenny at the piano, Gershwin's *Rhapsody in Blue*. According to one witness (and a letter Lenny wrote home), he conducted parts of the program in tears. At one point, the audience started shouting "Bernstein! Bernstein!" and Lenny himself was so moved he needed to be helped from the makeshift stage. But if he had done his job lifting morale, he knew he wasn't helping people to achieve what they really wanted, which was "to get out of these rotten camps to Palestine. It's a mess. Everything's a mess except music."

It was not the first time he had experienced such emotions. In 1947, accompanied by his father and his sister, he had made his initial visit to Palestine. Arriving in Tel Aviv, he conducted the Palestine Symphony

Orchestra, a group of Eastern European refugees, some very talented, some ordinary, who had first formed an orchestra in 1936. The ensemble later evolved into the excellent Israel Philharmonic but, in 1947, Lenny generated the enthusiasm to carry the players past the rough spots. The enthusiasm of the audience was remarkable, too. In the Palestine concerts—and at the Displaced Persons Camps a year later—considerably more was at stake than the task of restoring musical pleasure to people who had suffered. The arrival of a great young American Jewish conductor solidified what was shaky, emotionally unstable, and often doubtful in Jewish survival itself, and in the two most significant places—Germany, where God's seeming abandonment of the Jews was most grievous; and Israel, where survival seemed more than possible. Bernstein himself, in his own way, had become essential to the Jews as a people.

In 1947, the Palestine orchestra asked him to become music director; he considered the offer, refused, then accepted it in 1948, after the Boston Symphony chose Charles Munch as its new leader. Then he pulled out again. Despite all these flirtations and much love on both sides, he never became music director of the Israel Philharmonic. But one can say that a good part of his soul always lived in Israel. He was there in September 1948, during the War of Independence, running around the country with the musicians, giving concert after concert (forty concerts in sixty days, he claimed), some of them in danger zones, with the sounds of artillery breaking through the music. "My last trip was up through Galilee almost on the heels of the victorious Israeli Army," he wrote his parents.

Two decades later, in the wake of the Six-Day War of 1967, he drove into Jerusalem in an open car, as if he had conquered the Arab armies himself, singing Jewish and Arabic songs, joking with wounded Israeli army vets. One of them, born in America, gleefully jumped out of his wheelchair—at least for a moment—to greet Bernstein. Lenny conducted Mahler's gigantic Symphony No. 2 (*Resurrection*) with the Israel Philharmonic on Mount Scopus, which was part of the "newly unified" city of Jerusalem. For Israelis, he had become a kind of messenger, bringing the news of endurance, reconnecting Jews with old emotions or introducing them to emotions they didn't know they had. He did it for himself, too—not just to assert, over and over, his Jewish identity, but to feel the music in ways that were new for him.

Conducting the *Resurrection* symphony was always an exalting experience for him, but in Israel he was able to conduct it outdoors. A year
later, in 1968, when he brought the New York Philharmonic to Israel, they
played at a Roman amphitheater in Caesarea. Was this longing for open
air just restlessness? Or was it Lenny's way of adapting to the informal
arrangements of a new country? Yes, both things, but he also wanted to take
music out of the ritualized bourgeois setting of the concert hall—to bring it
closer to earth and sky, to make it literally elemental, nearer to organic life
and death in the land where Judaism began.

TEACHING AS AN ART II

Tailored and coiffed, he wears an elegant jacket garnished with a maroon
Harvard tie and matching breast-pocket handkerchief. He sits at a table in
a darkened room, consulting papers before him. Music students in jeans
and sweaters are all around him; a piano is off to the side. He looks more
like an investment banker at a cocktail party than a professor, but it's very
much a professorial occasion: Lenny is holding forth in an academic chair,
the Charles Eliot Norton Professorship in Poetry, a position previously
taken by, among others, T. S. Eliot, E. E. Cummings, and Igor Stravinsky
(the notion of poetry extends to all the arts). He prepared for the Norton
Lectures throughout the academic year 1972–73, taking up residence in
his old Harvard dorm, Eliot House, where, much to the chagrin of his
daughter Jamie, who was then a junior at Radcliffe, he stayed up half the
night talking and playing music and fooling around with undergraduates.
Professor daddy, the campus stud! Jamie was appalled.

In the lectures, taped in the fall of 1973, he's in full "Fair Harvard"
mode: he even uses that dreary alma mater song as a musical example,
ringing it through harmonic changes in his Jewish-boy-on-the-Charles
accent, as rich as ever. Every word was scripted, and the musical examples
(played by the Boston Symphony) were perfectly fitted into the spoken
discourse, which was relaxed but voluminous, self-deprecating but bristling with allusions to music history, literary history, and everything else.
Byron, Delacroix, Victor Hugo . . . he almost croons the great names. He
comes off as a kind of humanist rabbi, the ultimate potent square.

The title of the lecture series, "The Unanswered Question," comes from
a disturbing little piece for orchestra that Charles Ives wrote in 1908.

Over a quietly breathing mass of strings, a solo trumpet repeatedly asks a "question," which is then answered by jangled chords from a group of woodwinds—each response more and more discordant and uncertain. The last question receives no answer at all, and the music fades away. "The Unanswered Question" is an incomparable avant-garde piece, but what question does it pose? Many have said it is, "What is the meaning of life?" But Lenny took the question to mean, "Where is music going?" Meaning: What comes after tonality?

At the beginning, Lenny engages a fundamental question: Is there a universal language of music and common emotions—tones and combinations of tones—that we all respond to? He reaches out to the linguistics of Noam Chomsky, who posited, in the late 1960s, an innate grammatical competence—a genetically endowed biological system, derived from the structure of the brain (not from experience) that allowed children of many cultures to understand the general meaning of sentences before they had *heard* all that many sentences. Was there not something comparable in music? The answer, of course, is yes.

The connections to linguistics become strained after a while, and some of us may be thinking, "Dear God, get to the piano." Which he does, for long, astonishing stretches, jumping from one piece to another, playing examples of virtually everything—schoolyard teases (*na-nya-na-nya*); Hindu ragas and African chants; passages both short and long of Mozart, Beethoven, Berlioz, Wagner, Debussy, and much else. No musical sound is alien to him; he would sing electronically if he could, and then analyze the structure of the electrons. Tom Wolfe famously lampooned him in 1970 as a "Village Explainer," without adding that he was the greatest explainer in the history of villages, really a saint of lucidity once he got going.

At the piano, he groans and roars during powerful passages. If you're discomforted, that's your problem—he wants to tell us why we feel the way we do. He connects music to our very beings, our hearts and souls. Even odd, indefinable feelings count, or frightened or negative feelings. Before he finishes the Norton Lectures, he voices—and acts out—his profound connection to emotions of doubt, even despair. This ultimate rabbi was a twentieth-century man in touch with the emotional forces of life; music was the way he found those moments of doubt and despair and learned to live with them.

He leads us to the breakdown, the moment when, by ordinary standards, music becomes tough to listen to. He takes us through Arnold Schoenberg's atonal works, right into the twelve-tone system (serialism) and the abandonment of a key center, and then through the works of Alban Berg, Schoenberg's disciple, the composer of the extraordinary operas *Wozzeck* and *Lulu* and the heartbreakingly beautiful Violin Concerto, which Lenny analyzes in considerable detail. But then, a big surprise: having taken us to the brink and then over the edge, he doesn't denounce the radical break with tonality. In the Berg concerto, he urges us to hear a mix of thorny experimentalism and such borrowed traditional forms as a Bach chorale and a rustic peasant waltz. He marvels over the most beautiful passages: "Isn't that *fantastic*?"

Schoenberg and Berg may have violated human nature by ignoring what was inherently pleasing in the combination of tones, but they loved music too much to escape the "magnetic pull" of tonality: they kept brushing up against a key center and traditional forms, and this habit of part rejection, part acceptance is what makes their music so haunting—so filled with longing, so moving, so close in spirit to the soulful Mahler, whom they both adored. For composers, and particularly for the followers of Schoenberg in the universities and elsewhere, the lecture is implicitly a warning: don't give up on beauty. If you are going to embrace serialism and atonality, you had better possess as strong a lyrical streak as Schoenberg and Berg. It's the absence of that lyricism, more than the harshness of atonality, that caused the break between composer and public. He had delivered his message. "The Unanswered Question," whatever its longueurs, is a superb creation of pedagogic art, a monumental triumph in the dismal wastes of music appreciation. And it may have had more of an effect on American composers than anyone in the early seventies could have imagined.

A MAN OF ACTION SEEKING HIMSELF

Throughout his entire life, Lenny loved meeting new orchestras and new audiences; he needed the adulation from them—needed it physically as well as financially. It kept him going through bouts of back pain and asthma and his increasing unhappiness over what he believed he was failing to accomplish as a composer. Every few years, he would resolve to take stock, examine himself, find time to rest and compose. He must relinquish conducting, if not for good, at least for a season! By 1966, after eight years on the job, he had resolved to quit the New York Philharmonic as music director (and did, in 1969). "I can't go on this way," he told two members of the orchestra's administration, "I can't be pinned down for so many weeks at a time. I'm really a composer, and I don't have my time to do my other work." On those breaks, he was determined, as he had said before, "to get acquainted with myself," as if he thought that truly knowing himself would make his compositional difficulties disappear.

But this was a mistake. He couldn't simply know himself—he was too diverse in his interests and abilities, he had many selves to draw on, and this, I insist, was his *strength*. He hoped that all his varied interests and experiences would somehow resolve themselves into music, and this did indeed happen with *Candide*, an unprecedented everything-but-the-kitchen-sink masterpiece. But are self-knowledge and self-consciousness some necessary road to composition? To speak of Bach knowing himself sounds absurd. He knew *God*; he thought of himself as His servant. Three hundred years ago, people did not understand self-consciousness the way we do now. Nor did they in the nineteenth century. Did Wagner know himself? He was a monster of ego. Verdi, by contrast, was a master of ego. Did Richard Rodgers, with his predatory behavior around young actresses, know himself? Self-knowledge, or the absence of it, probably has little relation to creative power. Bernstein found composing difficult, I suspect, for mostly musical reasons; indeed, his efforts to know himself may have led him astray when he attempted to write opera.

His vacations in Mexico, Key West, and Italy became sensual feasts of sun, swimming, and sex, but they were not times of *rest*. He loved the sea and the desert, Japanese gardens and Connecticut lawns. But he suffered at the same time. After a few weeks in Fairfield, in 1966, he wrote his secretary Helen Coates: "August here has been my usual dubious vacation: lots of tennis, lots of insomnia, some score-studying, no composing at all. As you can imagine, this leaves me suffused with guilt." A year later, after that conducting tour of Israel at the end of the 1967 war, he joined his family for a vacation in Ansedonia, on the Tuscan coast. He sounded the same desolate note in a letter to Copland.

Haven't found a work to write (after almost a month of *dolce-far-niente* in this beautiful house): not a note on paper, not a score studied, a very few books read: no thoughts to speak of, no nothin. . . . And no sleep. Somewhere in all this I must be restoring my soul, recharging my transistors, "resting." I never have rested well. I'm happy only when I work. But I can't work. And there you are.

At times, he was convinced that he had failed as a serious composer, failed even as a conductor. On one occasion, Craig Urquhart, his assistant in his later years, found him in his Vienna hotel, sitting at his desk in the morning with a glass of scotch and a tray full of cigarette butts, sleepless, agitated, lamenting that he didn't know Beethoven's Seventh well enough to rehearse it that day. "But of course he did know it—and conducted it beautifully," Urquhart said to me. In fact, Bernstein's recording for Deutsche Grammophon of the Seventh Symphony with the Vienna Philharmonic, made at a concert in 1978, was one of his best performances of Beethoven.

What are we to make of these self-accusations? Apart from his difficulties in composing, one wonders if his bouts of self-criticism and self-dismay were not some aspect of his Jewish heritage. He had found, in Gustav Mahler, an ambivalence pushed to extremes, supreme exultation giving way to despair, and then back again—found it, in part, because the same oscillations were present in himself. One has also to consider his relation to another great artist from early in the twentieth century. Writing of his doubts, he sounds at times like Franz Kafka, who constantly assailed himself with his inadequacies and failings. Kafka, again! He was a great writer, utterly himself and no one else, but he was also the twentieth-century Jewish soul in extremis, and one looks to him for guidance of a sort. Obviously, Kafka—the despairing and self-annihilating writer with his secret immense pride burrowed within immense doubt—is very different from the ebullient Lenny, who would perform for a kindergarten class, if he could. But they are alike in one powerful way: they both feared a nonexistent God. Lenny searched for faith but did not find it; in its place was judgment. But not God's judgment.

In an extraordinary remark, Kafka stated that "Only our concept of time makes it possible for us to speak of the Day of Judgment by that name. In reality it is a summary court in perpetual session." The summary court in perpetual session is the self-imposed verdict on one's merit, on one's *being*, the verdict that cannot be escaped or appeased, a judgment implacable, impersonal, and absolute. The summary court may evoke the wrathful God who instructed Moses in Exodus, but this condemnation comes from inside. "The state in which we find ourselves is sinful," Kafka wrote, "irrespective of guilt." Such a state can be called, I suppose, a specifically Jewish guilt, but there are many Jews who do not feel it. Lenny did feel it, and it was a humbling pressure on him despite all his heady and bodily flights into ecstasy.

COMING APART

In 1971, during a revival of *Candide* in San Francisco, Bernstein, then fifty-three, met and fell in love with a twenty-four-year-old man named Tommy Cothran, the music director of a local classical music station. Cothran's letters to Bernstein suggest that he was bright and funny, and something more than that: he understood Bernstein's strengths and weaknesses; he could be critical as well as fond. When Bernstein checked into Harvard, in 1972, to prepare for the Norton Lectures, Cothran was sometimes with him. Bernstein was becoming indiscreet, a violation of his agreement with Felicia to keep his gay life private. In the seventies, he went back and forth between defiant public pronouncements that he would live his life as he liked and sorrow over the humiliations that he caused his wife to suffer.

Throughout the decade, he rushed from Tel Aviv to Paris to Milan to Vienna, from special events to filmed concerts. He met the pope, he met everyone—ministers and mayors and assorted dignitaries and social lions. He was the toast of the town everywhere, even when he noisily intervened (with his opinions) in the national politics of his host countries. Many of the concerts were galas or parts of festivals rather than regular programs. Disorder, misery, gluttony—none of these sins or his frequent illnesses lessened his energy or the quality of his work as a musical performer and teacher.

His torment: he could not live openly as a gay man; nor could he stop loving his wife. In the seventies, after more than twenty years of marriage, Felicia was not doing well. Willing to serve as "Mrs. Maestro," as she put it, she had given up most of her career and had then developed eccentricities and odd illnesses; she engaged in passionate busywork (collecting, decorating, gardening); she made paintings and threw them away. Her judgment wasn't always sound. Back in January 1970, meaning well, she had stepped into the social disaster of the century—a fundraising party for the legal defense of the Black Panthers.

The party was held in the Park Avenue family apartment (the Dakota came later). The *New York Times* struck first, with a satirical account of the event, followed by a severe editorial ("This so-called party, with its confusion of Mao-Marxist ideology and Fascist paramilitarism . . ."). The event was attended by Tom Wolfe, who published in *New York* magazine, five weeks after the party, a poisonously funny lampoon called "Radical Chic: That Party at Lenny's." ("Do the Panthers like little Roquefort cheese morsels wrapped in crushed nuts this way, and asparagus tips in mayonnaise dabs, and *meatballs petites au Coq Hardi*?") Wolfe writes that Donald Cox, the Panther field marshal, made revolutionary proposals, and Lenny responded with "How? I dig it. But how?"

Lenny, who was accustomed to brickbats, picked himself up after the articles came out and kept his conducting dates, but Felicia, despite supporting notes from Jacqueline Onassis, Gloria Steinem, and Coretta Scott King, was badly hurt by the public ridicule. Jamie Bernstein is not alone in believing that she was never the same.

At dinner one night, Felicia pronounced a curse upon her husband: "*You're going to die a lonely, bitter old queen!*" Jamie says she uttered it as a joke, in the self-parodying tones of theatrical high camp. Maybe so, but it still sounds like the *maledizione* from *Rigoletto*.

BUMMER

An entire book could no doubt be written about the Leonard Bernstein musical projects that never happened—musicals based on Thornton Wilder's play *The Skin of Our Teeth*, two projects with music based on the Bertolt Brecht plays *The Exception and the Rule* and *The Caucasian Chalk Circle*. He spoke on and off about a Holocaust opera. He worked earnestly on these projects, usually with talented collaborators, and composed a lot of music for them, but, as Stephen Sondheim noted, the desire to make a grand statement was an impossible way to begin working on anything, and he came a cropper again and again. The abandoned projects have the dismaying half-life of untenanted mansions, haunted by ambition without sense, effort without discipline. In the end, as composers often do with abandoned projects, Bernstein cannibalized some of the music written for them, feeding the music into other pieces; conductor Kent Nagano, working with the family estates of Bernstein and librettist Alan Jay Lerner, was able to pull together *A White House Cantata* from the wreckage of *1600 Pennsylvania Avenue*. It's a lovely record, the only memorial we have of that ponderous and awkward work.

There is, alas, more failure to note, and it derives, I believe, not only from Bernstein's compositional difficulties but also from habits of self-consciousness and guilt that he carried around with him.

In that nine-year period between *On the Town* (1944) and *Wonderful Town* (1953)—the period of his pledge to Koussevitzky—Lenny wrote no new Broadway shows. But he did think constantly about creating an opera. What would a specifically *American* opera sound like? He came up with the strange idea: to set a short opera in one of the new bedroom communities—an opera set in suburbia. In 1951, in one of his good working vacations, he produced most of *Trouble in Tahiti*, a theater work for two singers, a chorus of three, and a chamber orchestra of brass, winds, and percussion. The ironic title refers to a made-up movie that one of the characters sees and complains about—the kind of forties Hollywood *kitsch* in which Dorothy Lamour lounges in a sarong among "natives" in the South Seas. The number Bernstein wrote ridiculing the film ("What a Movie!") is very funny and close, in spirit, to the satirical pieces he had concocted with Comden and Green for *On the Town*. This time he wrote the lyrics himself.

His overall satiric point is that the idealization of the suburbs, common in *Life* magazine and other media at the time, was little more than a lie, a case of consumerism and vanity writ large—pretty much what Betty Friedan would capture so devastatingly more than a decade later in *The Feminine Mystique*. There are two singing characters: the husband, Sam (arrogant, adulterous, and hapless), and the wife, Dinah (lost, bored, and complaining). Dinah has a lovely moment when she relates a dream of herself standing in a garden and longing for something transcendent—a moment of hope. But it's no more than a hint of what she could have been.

Sam's music is bullying and loud. He seems beyond redemption. In the quiet ending, the two of them long to get back to what they had. But what *is* it that they had?

Why in the world make an *opera* about these piss-out characters? In the past, comic operas were generated out of flirtation and lust, scheming servants and preposterous disguises; tragic operas were galvanized by myth, romantic passion, blood quarrels, political and religious strife. Opera needs characters heroic in foolishness or courage. But this opera, which mixes comic and trying-to-be-tragic moments, is devoted to *the failure to communicate* and *the loss of love*—the earnestly forlorn clichés of forties and fifties upper-middle-class life; especially, I'm sorry to say, upper-middle-class Jewish life, where psychoanalysis shrouded so many conversations. The piece has been performed from time to time, but a length of forty-five minutes is hard to place in an evening's entertainment. And school groups, who might like the length, are not likely to take up the subject of a failed marriage.

Tahiti was an experiment that didn't really work, but Bernstein, amazingly, wouldn't let it go. Thirty years later, collaborating with the librettist Stephen Wadsworth, he wrote *A Quiet Place*, a full-length sequel devoted to the descendants of this terrible marriage—the couple's semipsychotic son, his sister, and her husband (who may be the son's former lover). Sam is still alive, but Dinah has died in an automobile accident (perhaps as a suicide). All of them, with various family retainers, gather together and chew things over. But who cares about this poisonous crew? There is much wrangling and emotional cruelty, and again, the opera is about the failure to communicate, the failure to love. When the premiere (in Houston in 1983) fizzled, disappointing creators and critics alike, Bernstein and Wadsworth compounded the folly by dropping the short, satirical *Trouble in Tahiti* into the longer opera.

A stunning paradox: the twentieth century's greatest communicator and most publicly loving man devotes two operas to the absence of love, the absence of communication. Can a more self-defeating project be imagined? Bernstein wrote some spooky music for *A Quiet Place*, and a long powerful orchestral interlude that evokes Berg's *Wozzeck*. But most of the score is uninteresting.

The Jewish guilt and self-consciousness that Lenny oddly thought were opera subjects wound up destroying his operas. And this misjudgment in a man so worldly and charming—and so shrewd about what gave other people pleasure—makes one think that his own miseries must have been unappeasable and inescapable, defeating ordinary judgment.

If he never really resolved the question of "What is an American opera?" he had already answered two different questions—and good questions, too. The first was, "What is an American operetta?" and the answer was *Candide*, which he wrote in the mid-fifties and brought to its final form in 1989, near the end of his life. And the second question was, "What is an American sacred work?" His obsession with liturgy in the absence of faith found two dramatic answers. They were both Jewish works cast in Christian settings, blasphemous and reverential at once.

SACRED TEXTS

In 1964, the reverend Walter Hussey, the dean of Chichester Cathedral, in Sussex, wanted a new work for the cathedral's boys' choir. Hussey was a patron of the arts with some unconventional ideas. He wrote to Bernstein offering a commission, adding that "many of us would be very delighted if there was a hint of *West Side Story* about the music." In other words, the piece needn't sound like traditional English church music. Lenny then made an inquiry: How would Hussey feel about hearing Hebrew sung in an Anglican cathedral? It would be fine, Hussey said, and Bernstein set to work, using multiple verses from the book of Psalms as his texts. He was drawing on the Hebrew Bible again, as he had in the *Kaddish* symphony, finished the year before. "Obviously, something keeps making me go back to that book," he said a few years later. Yes, he kept going back to it, as the Jews had done for almost two millennia, trying to make sense of a text that is ferocious and sweet in bewildering alteration.

In the end, he took up Hussey's suggestion. In the work that came to be known as *Chichester Psalms*, Bernstein, in the second movement, set the Twenty-Third Psalm for boy soprano and chorus. The music begins very gently, but there's a shocking interruption—violent interjections for chorus and percussion to the words not of the Twenty-Third but of the Second Psalm ("Why do the nations rage"). That music was originally written for the first act of *West Side Story*. As Allen Shawn explains in his excellent analysis of *Chichester Psalms* in *Leonard Bernstein: An American Musician* (2014), much of this wonderful score is recycled from compositions that

Bernstein had abandoned. (Not an uncommon practice among composers. Handel did it.) Yet *Chichester Psalms* feels all of a piece.

The startling shift of tone in this second section of *Chichester Psalms* breaks up any possibility of merely conventional piety. After doubt and stress disrupt the serene setting of the Twenty-Third Psalm, Bernstein returns to the boy tenor and his sweet melody. The juxtaposition of gentleness and violence is characteristic of the entire work, which, in a general way, alternates rushing syncopated passages and percussion explosions with slowly unfolding melodies of caressing loveliness. Hussey's dream was fulfilled: *Chichester Psalms* is recognized (and enjoyed) as a classic modern sacred work—a Jewish work in a Christian form, both fierce and solacing, not a piece as great as Stravinsky's devastating *Symphony of Psalms* but still very satisfying as a representation of the Hebrew Bible's contraries. *Chichester Psalms* ends with a sustained quiet passage for unison chorus and just a few instruments. It's as if the composer were saying to himself, *Peace, Lenny.*

BUT OF COURSE there was no peace, not for this man, and, as he would say, not for our world either. Nor was there an end to his pursuit of the God he didn't quite believe in. Throughout his life, he wanted to dramatize his obsession, the *loss* of religion in the twentieth century. In 1966, a few years after his success in Chichester, Jacqueline Kennedy asked Bernstein to write a theatrical work for the new John F. Kennedy Center for the Performing Arts in Washington, DC. For his text, this very Jewish composer selected the words of the Latin Mass. "I've always had a deep interest in Catholicism in all its aspects, its similarities and dissimilarities to Judaism," he once said. Gearing up to compose, he was pleased by the liberalizing Second Vatican Council, which decreed in 1965 that the Jews were also the people of God, rejecting as slander the notion they were collectively responsible for the death of Jesus Christ.

For years, he struggled with *MASS*, finally enlisting, as the deadline approached, the young composer and lyricist Stephen Schwartz, who had created the Broadway hit *Godspell*. The work premiered in Washington, DC, in September 1971, and it was both loved and despised. *MASS* is part Broadway, part oratorio, part avant-garde experiment, part circus, part everything. Cultural historian Larry Wolff, in the *New York Review of Books* ("I Feel Pretty," September 27, 2018), made a case for the work as a post–Vatican II "questioning of religious faith that transcended denominational boundaries." But how do you pursue a God you don't believe in? In Lenny's case, with everything you've got.

The first time you hear it, you may think you are losing your mind. *MASS* opens with a prerecorded "Kyrie Eleison." We hear a soprano cartwheeling through drums and xylophone, accompanied by a baritone in cross-rhythm. We are in the realm of serious mischief. Soon after, a marching band of street kids jumps into the theater and picks up the Kyrie. "The Celebrant" (i.e., a priest), a male singer holding a guitar, then sings a lovely Bernstein melody, "A Simple Song." And so the battle is joined. The Celebrant struggles to complete the mass and is repeatedly interrupted by the music and street radicalism of the period.

Bernstein was excited by the sixties tumult—by rock, so much more communicative in his view than new classical music; by the protests against racism and the Vietnam War; by the renegade priests Dan and Philip Berrigan. He wanted to be "with it," which greatly embarrassed his daughter Jamie and many other people and caused President Nixon's political adviser Pat Buchanan to ask for a translation of the text (a translation of the Latin Mass?). Buchanan and other Nixon advisers thought that Bernstein's work was some sort of plot to embarrass the president with an anti-war message; in the event, Nixon didn't go. Others thought the piece was simply a *mishigas*—a mess ("a complete disaster" in the words of Stephen Sondheim). There are dancers writhing on all sides of the stage, episodes of syncopated jazz, some rhythm and blues, patches of fresh music appearing in antiphonal bursts. *MASS*, a fully ignited set of fireworks is possibly the wildest mix of classical and pop ever put together. The effect is jangled, unsettling.

Bernstein attacks the hypocrisy of the triumphant Church, the failure of ritual and piety to change our behavior. It is a Jewish view of religious futility—and the score, as Bernstein's musical assistant Jack Gottlieb has pointed out, has many motifs from Jewish liturgical music. The Celebrant, at the end of his tether, throws the chalice to the ground and falls into a long, tortured monologue—Bernstein's "mad scene," as many have called it.

I feel every psalm that I've ever sung
Turn to wormwood, wormwood on my tongue.
And I wonder, oh I wonder
Was I ever really young?

The Celebrant imagines his own death, and even the death of God. In the end, spent, he is renewed by a boy soprano, who makes a kind of return appearance from *Chichester Psalms*. The boy sings, "Sing God a secret song"—not "a simple song" this time, but a *secret* song. The child is joined by the chorus, which very beautifully, and prayerfully, brings the mass to a close. The truth lies in secrecy, buried, but available, perhaps, to the people willing to suffer for it.

In *MASS*, Bernstein again ridicules contemporary cynicism and shallowness, as he did in his operas, but he celebrates rebellion and blasphemy as well, which gives the project some strength, and he moves, in the end, toward healing. The emotional arc is similar to that in his earlier Symphony No. 3 (*Kaddish*): a revolt against God, combat with God, which leads to acceptance of faith, or at least the search for faith. By making the quarrel personal, in the tradition of Abraham and Job questioning God's will, Bernstein Judaizes Christianity; in making it an expression of a cultural crisis, he enlarges religious disbelief into disbelief in authority, society, justice.

At home, *MASS* is daunting to listen to; it overwhelms the speakers, overwhelms the listening space. It works better live, but it's hard to find a performing space big enough to accommodate the dancers and everyone else surrounding the Celebrant. *MASS* bursts the stage—bursts mere theater. It's tumultuous, clumsy, but, at times, a very moving piece.

FINALE

By the mid-seventies, Felicia was ill with cancer, and Lenny, having broken up with Thomas Cothran, nursed Felicia in the family apartment and then in a house in East Hampton. In that house, Felicia died, at the age of fifty-six, on June 16, 1978. In *Maestro*, Felicia fights with great concentration and courage, and Lenny and the children are always with her. But the complete story of this marriage may never be known. The movie shows us Felicia's physical suffering, but not the internal struggle—the cage fight of doubt, rebellion, fervent hope—that must have dominated her mind and spirit for years.

Lenny held himself responsible for Felicia's death, which doesn't make any kind of literal sense—fidelity would not have saved her. Yet he was grief-struck, and guilt-ridden, too, as if he needed to pay for damages wrought upon his wife with his own suffering. In his last decade, he continued his furious schedule in Europe and America, flying from one capital to another; and he composed some very good music. But a combination of indulgence and misery altered his body, his manners, his spirit. He was literally demoralized.

The body electric no longer charmed everyone in sight. Adonis had become Silenus, gut-heavy, sometimes drunk and mean, talking of sex too much, his hands too active, his tongue placed down unwilling throats. When he mixed alcohol and Dexedrine, he would say cruel things to people who had known him for years, embarrassing his children and his friends. He had always needed adulation; now he mainlined it. In some distant foreign city, the after-concert party would include his manager, his publicist, various musical assistants, his audio engineer, his video director, local notables and social lions, handsome young men, and assorted hangers-on. The reception had become a champagne-and-caviar version of a Rolling Stones tour stop.

He was often exhausted. The extraordinary craving for sensation, for love, for contact, which he converted, refined, and fed back to his audience in lavishly expended musical effort—a gift to everyone—was wearing him out. Despite every medical warning, he smoked incessantly, even in doctors' offices. In that last decade, when he was in his sixties—normally a golden time for a musician—he was often agitated, overwrought, as if something was eluding him. He wouldn't go to bed but then would have an even harder time than usual getting up in the morning. When he was at home in the Dakota, he sometimes slept for an entire day.

He turned seventy in 1988, and there were worldwide celebrations and a huge event at Tanglewood with the Boston Symphony, at the conclusion of which, Jamie Bernstein writes, "everyone was awash in emotion." But Lenny, incontinent, "was awash from the waist down. And of course he had to go on stage and hug everyone. On camera." The difficulties in his last decade figured as both the ordinary disasters of old age and the awe-inspiring decay of a national monument. Everyone noticed his difficulty breathing, the distension of his belly. In thinking of his later years, however, one has to invoke the mysteries of artistic will, its capacity to redeem and transcend many kinds of failure. Perhaps only Thomas Mann could have mastered the ironies of Bernstein's story. As he fell apart physically and morally, he not only wrote some demanding and beautiful music (including the song cycle *Arias and Barcarolles* and the orchestral piece *Jubilee Games*), but his work on the podium became ever more disciplined, often profound, even visionary.

Almost from the beginning, television was a kind of second home for him. The glories of early American network TV were behind him, but for Unitel, the German media company in Hamburg, he recorded dozens of concert films as well as detailed expositions of the works he was conducting. His intimacy with us, his viewers, had been charming and flirtatious when he was young; now it was gravely serious, a last attempt to conquer the sterilities of music appreciation. The late performances were sometimes slower, riper, and more detailed than the earlier ones, spontaneous in matters of phrasing but very grand in their overall architecture. Not everything from the 1980s is at the same level, but the best ones put him among the conducting immortals. There were late Mozart and Haydn symphonies with the Vienna Philharmonic, played with a glorious happy sweetness very much in opposition to the fashionably lean and hard sound of period-instrument performances; a fresh Mahler cycle recorded in Vienna, Amsterdam, and New York; and many of his favorites redone—symphonies by Schumann, Sibelius, Copland, and Shostakovich. And there was that last recording of his own much-revised operetta *Candide.*

Again and again, he pulled himself together for a performance. On Christmas Day in 1989, as the Wall between East and West was crumbling, he led a powerful Beethoven's Ninth in Berlin, which was broadcast all over the world. The orchestral players were drawn from London, New York, Munich, Dresden, Paris, and Leningrad, in a kind of universal shout of joy that Soviet Communism was finished at last. On the podium, the superb bone structure of his handsome brow was intact; a tuxedo pulled in the belly; his movements were not as fluent as earlier—he used his fists more—but he was completely in command. He was an American Jew standing exactly where he wanted to be, in the former Nazi and East German Communist capital at exactly the moment in which everything the totalitarian states stood for was being universally renounced. Music put a seal on the great turning point. An American Jew would bind up the world with music. It was his last great public event.

APART AND TOGETHER AT THE CLOSE

Herbert von Karajan also continued right to the end, conducting for audiences in Berlin and Vienna and on tour. But Karajan wanted a kind of immortality that went past good performance. Working with Sony in the mid-eighties, he retreated into a kind of music bunker where he recorded Beethoven and Brahms yet again, the music emerging from a featureless nowhere space, with Karajan in a potent shuttered trance, communicating only with Apollo, or perhaps only with himself. The Sony films were Karajan's way of turning death into an irrelevance; Beethoven and Brahms weren't so much performed as cryogenically preserved. But Bernstein's concert films and recordings, in his last decade, are as exploratory as they are grand.

The two men met on and off, and, in 1989, when both were close to death, they had a secret talk in a Vienna hotel. Karajan, the former Nazi who had disdained Mahler's tormented music for decades, had taken up the composer in his sixties and eventually produced two glorious recorded performances of the great Ninth Symphony. Karajan could no longer afford to ignore Mahler; he had become too central to concert life, to twentieth-century consciousness, and Bernstein had helped produce that shift. Ill and tired, they spoke of touring together with the Vienna Philharmonic, and I am moved by the thought of the two old men, all rivalries and differences forgotten, murmuring to each other in a hotel room and conspiring to make music.

But Karajan died on July 16, 1989. And Lenny died a year later, on October 14, 1990. He was seventy-two years old, which is young for a conductor. He was not alone, as Felicia had predicted, but attended by family and friends at home, and saluted, as the cortege passed through the city streets, by New York hardhats shouting "Goodbye, Lenny!" Charles Ives and Aaron Copland were great composers, but Bernstein was by far the greatest American musician.

"God, the number of things I have not done," he told a reporter in 1985, when he was in his late sixties. But the number of things he *did* is beyond comprehension. He conducted 1,247 concerts of the New York Philharmonic, 197 of the Vienna Philharmonic, and he had sustained relations with the Boston Symphony Orchestra, the London Symphony Orchestra, the Israel Philharmonic, and many other groups. He recorded more than 500 pieces of music (in some cases, recording the same piece more than once) and made more than 150 videos. He made music with Louis Armstrong and other jazz greats—he loved jazz. He wrote three exciting symphonies; the *Serenade* for violin, strings, percussion, and harp; the ballets *Fancy Free* and *Dybbuk*; the Broadway classics *Candide* and *West Side Story* as well as *On the Town* and *Wonderful Town*. He wrote the impassioned score for *On the Waterfront*, the lovely choral work *Chichester Psalms*, the tumultuous theater piece *MASS*, and the late song cycle *Arias and Barcarolles*. All of these works are now active repertory pieces, and he wrote quite a bit more, some of it still being exhumed, sorted, and reevaluated. His reputation as a composer has gone way up since his death in 1990. History's judgment of him as a composer may be kinder than his own.

In 2018, his hundredth birthday was marked all over the world. On a single day, June 23, 2018, there were concerts and theater performances in such places as Kansas City, Bilbao, and Klingenberg am Main. The event was celebrated in Asia as well as in America and Europe. In that centenary year, there were, all told, more than five thousand events.

MAHLER FOR THE LAST TIME AND FOREVER

A few days after struggling with the Vienna Philharmonic over Mahler's Fifth in 1972, Bernstein and the orchestra performed and filmed the work in Vienna. The orchestra was no longer holding back; it's a very exciting performance. Fifteen years later, in 1987, Bernstein and the Vienna Philharmonic returned to the Fifth, taking it on tour. The performance in Frankfurt on September 8, 1987, was recorded live by Deutsche Grammophon, issued as a CD in 1998, and is widely considered the greatest recording of the symphony.

But it is not the greatest recording of the symphony. Two days later, on September 10, at the mammoth Royal Albert Hall (5,200 seats) in London, Leonard Bernstein and the Vienna Philharmonic played the work yet again. The BBC recorded the performance for broadcast, and in recent years the recording (audio only) has been posted on YouTube, where anyone can listen to it for free.

The symphony, in any performance, is a compound of struggle, despair, tenderness, and triumph; the heroic cast of the Fifth is why it's so central to the career of the fictional Lydia Tár, who conducts it in Berlin and quotes Lenny about meaning in music. But in many performances, much of its detail can seem puzzling or pointless—vigorous or languorous note spinning between the overwhelming climaxes. Bernstein clarifies and highlights everything, sometimes by slowing the music down so that one can hear and emotionally register such things as the utter forlornness of the funeral march in the first movement, the countermelodies in the strings that are close to heartbreak, the long silences and near silences throughout the score in which the music struggles into being, tentatively at first, then with greater assurance—struggles against the temptation of nothingness, which for Mahler was very real. The symphony now makes complete sense as an argument about the unstable nature of life. Near the end of it, after a passage slowing the music almost to a halt, Mahler marks an abrupt tempo change *accelerando*. In Bernstein's personal score, lodged at the New York Philharmonic Archives, he writes at this point in the score, "GO." Just . . . *Go*. In London, the concluding pages, with the entire orchestra hurtling in a frenzy to the end, releases an ovation in the Royal Albert Hall that has the same intensity of joy as the music itself.

Mahler's music is the dramatized projection of Jewish sensibility into the world. Bernstein carried the thrice-homeless Mahler home, yes, home to the world, where he now lives forever. Lenny may have been frustrated in some of his ambitions, but he flourished in a time of American power, and he blended in his soul what he knew of Jewish sacred texts, Jewish family life, and emotion—blended all that with the ready forms of the Broadway musical, the classical symphonic tradition, Christian choral music, and the formerly tepid music-appreciation lecture. He took advantage of new media ways of reaching out—particularly television—without cheapening anything he had to say. He died too young, dissatisfied, full of ideas and projects, a man still being formed, yet through his half-century career he brought the richness of American Jewish sensibility into the minds and emotions of millions of people.

EPILOGUE:
AT HOME IN AMERICA II

A MIXED WELCOME

The Jews' early reception in America was a combination of angry repulsion and rueful acceptance.

Solomon Franco, a Sephardic Jew from Holland, a scholarly fellow and a trader, arrived in the Massachusetts Bay Colony in 1649, and made himself useful as a supplier to one Edward Gibbons, a major general in the Massachusetts Militia. But Franco was expelled in that year by a Massachusetts court and sent back to Holland with an allowance of six shillings per week. One cannot help but speculate: Did not the appearance of Jews present an awkward problem for the Puritans who dominated the colony? The Puritans believed that they were the true Israelites; they were children of God, and America was their promised land. Actual Jews, in this scheme, were an annoyance or worse.

In New Amsterdam (i.e., New York), the situation was quite different. The settlers from Holland were in America to make money, not to find God's kingdom on earth. They were not, however, without religious feeling. In 1654, a group of twenty-three Dutch Sephardic Jews showed up from Brazil (a colony that the Dutch had lost to the Portuguese). Peter

Stuyvesant, the governor of New Amsterdam, wrote an indignant letter to his masters at the Dutch West India Company in Amsterdam. "Owing to their present indigence," he wrote, "they [the Jews] might become a charge in the coming winter, we have for the benefit of this weak and newly developing place, and the land in general, deemed it useful to require them in a friendly way to depart." This feint at civility ("a friendly way") was almost certainly disingenuous: in the same letter, he described the Jews as "repugnant" and "enemies and blasphemers of Christ."

In Amsterdam, Stuyvesant's superiors had a different view. The Jews, they informed him, were prominent among the investors in the company; the Jews in Brazil had been helpful to the Dutch in their losing fight with Portugal over the colony. Let them stay in New Amsterdam. Let them live, let them trade, let them worship. As Arthur Hertzberg characterized the moment in *The Jews in America*, "American Jewish history thus began with no ringing debates about religious freedom or about the right of individuals." No, it began with disgust and then a frank acknowledgment by powerful people that the Jews had talent, they understood trade, they belonged in the New World.

In the next 130 years or so, the small communities of Sephardic Jews in America helped settle the western part of the country; they fought in the French and Indian Wars, and a significant number joined the rebellion against Britain. Their citizenly life in America was rarely easy. But the Jews were gratified by a momentous event: the passage in 1789 of the Constitution of the United States, which guaranteed freedom of conscience to all citizens. A year later, President George Washington put his personal stamp on the new assurances. Washington was eager to express his gratitude to the Jews for their support during the Revolutionary War, so he visited the Jewish community in Newport, Rhode Island. The leadership of the community wrote him an appreciative letter. Washington replied as follows:

> All possess alike liberty of conscience and immunities of citizenship. It is now no more that toleration is spoken of, as if it was by the indulgence of one class of people, that another enjoyed the exercise of their inherent natural rights. For happily the government of the United States, which gives to bigotry no sanction, to persecution no assistance, requires only that they who live under its protection shall demean themselves as good

citizens. . . . May the children of the Stock of Abraham, who dwell in this land, continue to merit and enjoy the good will of the other inhabitants, while everyone shall sit in safety under his own vine and fig tree, and there shall be none to make him afraid.

Every time I read Washington's letter I have to fight back tears. Washington proclaims an American ethos with both protective kindliness and the hard brilliance of steel: this country will celebrate not mere "toleration" of others but active embrace of all good citizens. In *Unsettled: An Anthropology of the Jews* (2003), Melvin Konnor writes that America "was to be the first and only diaspora in which Jews did not live by someone else's sufferance."

The Jews had lived with some freedom in Islamic North Africa; they had enjoyed a "golden" period in Moorish Spain and the benefits of emancipation under Napoleon in the nineteenth century. But all these periods of relative safety and well-being had ended disastrously. In the modern era, the Zionists wanted all the Jews to "come home" to Israel. But there is another home. The right to worship as one pleased was not the only reason that America was the right place for a wandering people—the necessary place, perhaps the inevitable place.

Consider it this way: Judaism offers a God who cannot be seen, a God ineffable, unknowable, mysterious. Reciting prayers and making vows of obedience are essential to Judaism, but they are only one part of it and perhaps not the most important part. The unseen God must be engaged; he must be interpreted; his will may be questioned and argued with. Abraham bargains with God over the smiting of Sodom; Jacob wrestles with the angel; Job protests against God's severity; and in the Talmud, wrangling over the Law never ends. A religious Jew can never be sure, of course, that he or she is getting through, but the attempt to reach God never stops; and the habits of *study*, which means questioning and skepticism, never end either. *Yearning and inquiry rather than grace is the essential Jewish state.* You are never entirely satisfied with yourself; you are always in a condition of becoming. You can ask forgiveness of God on Yom Kippur, but you have no guarantee of receiving it. These habits, lasting two millennia, have influenced secular as much as religious Jews. Those who lack faith nevertheless live within the temperament that faith has created. Many irreligious Jews have a fierce desire to know themselves and the world, a drive that is anything but disrespectful or wicked. Except for the Orthodox, Jews do not expect to arrive at ultimate truths, a habit of mind that often leads to liberal politics and the slow movement toward a better life.

In his magisterial book *The Jewish Century*, Yuri Slezkine demonstrates that the modern Jewish character is a product of both religion and two millennia of fraught Jewish history. Think of the Ashkenazi Jews entering America from the middle of the nineteenth century on: they were by necessity adaptable (they knew what it was to be chased); they were largely an urban group; and they were more than fluent with information, money, and trade, as the leaders of the Dutch West India Company understood about the Sephardic Jews in the 1650s. There weren't many farmers among them, but the immigrants were little hurt by what they didn't know of agriculture. The American economy in the early part of the twentieth century was just beginning its momentous shift from rural work to urban work, from manual labor and primary production to service, distribution, and management. In that economy, as Slezkine insists, the Jews were equipped to survive and even to succeed. The twentieth century the Jewish century? Is Slezkine joking? No he's serious. Despite the horrors in the middle of it, the twentieth century was the right time for the Jews. They were made for it.

In America, the Jews entered a country whose economic life was structured by market capitalism and whose Constitution guaranteed freedom of conscience. There was something else that suited the Jews to America, and America to the Jews: the Constitution also established a government of warring parts: the executive, the legislative, and the judicial. The very contestation that was so much part of the Jewish religion was built into the American system. Jews love to argue; the separate parts of government are often in dispute. In sum, the Jews were able to flourish in a civil society offering the unceasing activity of markets, the rule of law, divided government, and religious liberty.

THE NEW JEWISH AMERICAN

Except for Leonard Bernstein, these four did not imagine themselves as acting out some grand project of building Jewish culture in America. They wanted to think, write, play, direct, speak as themselves, *for* themselves. But they acted as Jews nonetheless. Their relation to Judaism was less formal than emotional and temperamental, and, as they made art, advanced their ideas, they jumped away from elements in Jewish cultural tradition even as they gained strength from it. They were free in ways that Jews had never been free in any society of the past.

Mel, unconquerably assertive, was perhaps the proudest and noisiest Jew in the country. Mel created an uproarious scandal out of the body's needs, hungers, and agonies; he bordered on saturnalia and made comedy out of death. He revived the crude humor of the the immigrant streets, thrusting it into the lives of college students and sophisticated people all over the country. Humor moved *down* and *in*, destroying hypocrisy and false gentility. Betty, whose ethical drive had Jewish roots, wanted to end women's confinement in the home, liberate women's brains and spirits as well as their physical freedom, a belief that put her in contention with traditional Jewish notions of a woman's role. Norman, at first a sweet, middle-class boy from Brooklyn, believed that Americans needed to live fully in their senses to overcome the postwar blight of conformity and consumerism. Brawling and breaking literary forms, he defined the kind of Jewish intellectual he wanted to be in opposition to middle-class restraint, all the while embracing what he took to be Jewish habits of inquiry and serious thinking. He was obsessed with violent young men who had grand ideas and lived outside of society, yet he was a Jewish family man always. Lenny had the easiest development. He may have been unable to decide at twenty which path to follow (before deciding to follow all of them), but his body was his guide, and as fellow conductor John Eliot Gardiner said of him years later, "There was a lot of music in that body." His polymorphous-perverse conducting style confounded and frightened certain listeners, even as he exercised greater and greater control over orchestras. His *West Side Story* took risks with race and violence and joined thrilling Latin dance rhythms to exquisite pathos.

In some ways, demanding not restraint but freedom, they violated the middle-class Jewish traditions they grew up with. Intentionally or not, they broke the Freudian hammerlock on American Jewish assumptions after the war. They lessened the high prestige of psychoanalysis, with its minimal estimation of women's capabilities, its dreary advocacy of "adjustment" to a repressive society. They also, unwittingly, overturned the Freudian assumption that civilization could be sustained only through suppression of violent and erotic instincts. In different ways, they liberated the Jewish body, releasing the unconscious of the Jewish middle class, ending the constrictions and avoidances that the immigrants and their children, so eager to succeed in America, imposed on themselves. They did so both in their lives and in their work. People didn't go to Betty's exhortations, Norman's books, Mel's movies, and Bernstein's concerts and *West Side Story* for displays of rectitude or even good taste. Their work might succeed, or it might fail (as expression, proportion, dramatic effectiveness), but it was work that disrupted the old ideas of what was proper. The elements in these four of wildness, anger, public exaltation, gross burlesque are a good part of what audiences wanted from them.

But here's the miracle, which I think of as a Jewish miracle: if their activities marked the end of tribal shame, it did not mark the end of conscience. A certain moral strenuousness emerged in all of them, an impulse toward exhortation and even prophecy. Some might find this laughable or hypocritical. In Yiddish: *Ven der putz shteht ligt, der sechel in drerd*, or "When the putz stands up, the brain goes to sleep." By "putz" in this case, I mean ego in general. But the brain doesn't sleep forever; it may even dream. I have taken their tendency to exhortation seriously as a natural impulse and a cultural demand. Jewish ethical ardency—the desire to make life better—got mixed into the bursting energies and claims of liberation; the combination of asserted freedom and ethical purpose unites these four as examples of a new kind of American Jew.

Leonard Bernstein's music making was part of a spiritual mission: if you could only *hear* Beethoven or Mahler, if you could only see how pain and pleasure were mixed together in ethnic gang violence, it would change you in some way. He would teach anywhere—on the podium, in front of TV cameras, in bed—and his "message" always was that music creates human souls. Betty led women out of fear and (in some cases) half-being. Norman tried in every way to awaken the country from its spiritual torpor in the fifties, its new imprisonment by technology, and he saw and deplored what was coming: the great divide between rural and urban America, between the aggrieved and the elite. He engaged in prophecy, even when he was rude and obscure. Mel was an entertainer, always going where the laughs were. But a lot of the laughs he went after were about death; and one of his ways of cheering up the Jews was to confront them with the disasters of their history. Not a prophet, exactly, an entertainer first and always but also a tough-minded man.

As they liberated themselves, they became sages, secular rabbis without shawl and tefillin, exemplars of full-bodied, fearless life, unrespectable but still demanding the utmost of themselves and other people. Though assimilated in many ways, they were not, as descendants of Russian and Eastern European Jews, entirely tame (unlike some of the German Jews). The Eastern Jews would continue to prize the qualities of temper, humor, and fantasy characteristic of their forebears. In the anti-Semitic thirties and early forties, much of this, out of fear, was suppressed. It reemerged after the war in many ways, most obviously in the work and character of such people as Mel Brooks, Betty Friedan, Norman Mailer, and Leonard Bernstein. And all four of them opened doors for Americans of many kinds who came after them.

INFLUENCERS

The careers of these four can't be separated from certain markers of postwar prosperity: the evident shrinking and near disappearance of the Jewish working class and the data assembled by Nobel laureate Simon Kuznets in 1956 in *Jewish Economies*, volume 2, showing that "the median money income per Jewish family was more than 20 percent higher than that of all other families. . . . Jewish per capita income was about thirty-five percent higher." Jews were understandably cautious about appearing to boast, but both the Catholic sociologist Andrew Greeley and the African American economist Thomas Sowell noted a couple of decades after Kuznets that Jewish American economic and social mobility after the war was unprecedented. By the 1980s, more than 80 percent of young Jews said they wanted to go to college. All of this created a large Jewish audience for the arts in the big cities and the suburbs. Working out the social and economic patterns, and their intersection with cultural figures, is a task for scholars. What I can do is gather a few plums that have fallen from the tree. There was a period in the fifties, sixties, and seventies when American culture seemed almost Jewish. Mel Brooks's influence can't be separated from this larger movement—an event, in truth, worthy of another book (by someone else). But I would like to mention in passing just a few things. First, there was the astonishing postwar spread of Yiddish. In a 1965 article in *Esquire* ("The Yiddishization of American Humor,"), novelist Wallace Markfield noted that "Yiddish, a language and a culture teetering on the rim of oblivion . . . has for the past several years quietly infiltrated the American scene and syntax," and Markfield, citing one among many examples, reported hearing Sid Caesar, in a parody of Italian neorealist movies, saying "Whosa' wearin' my gatkes?" [long underwear]. A second phenomenon, chosen almost at random: Jeremy Dauber, in his study of Jewish comedy, evoked the early years of *Mad* magazine, which was started by four Jewish boys in 1952—*Mad* magazine, a semi-scurrilous, all-out attack on propriety that became enormously influential on the counterculture that emerged a decade later. *Mad* did such things, Dauber recalls, as whittle pop culture icons down to size "by presenting them as neurotic, overemotional, hyperverbal manics: in short, Jews." The most famous neurotic Jew for over thirty years was of course Woody Allen, whose self-satire at times amounted to masochism, not an emotion ever indulged by Mel Brooks, whose ego was robust, extensive, and unending.

Mel was part of the larger Jewish influence that made public expression more candid, more physically explicit, and funnier. Every boy who realized that a fart was something to celebrate was in debt to Mel Brooks. Mel's loosening up of language and behavior in American film comedy shaped what Jim Abrahams and the Zucker Brothers (David and Jerry) perpetrated in the disaster-film spoof *Airplane!* (1980); and it influenced the Farrelly brothers in their tease of buddy movies *Dumb and Dumber* (1994). At a much higher level, Mel's soulfulness can be seen directly in Judd Apatow's messy, profane, sweet-tempered work as producer and director, including *The 40-Year-Old Virgin*, *Knocked Up*, *Superbad*, and *Funny People*. Larry David's epic TV crankfest *Curb Your Enthusiasm*, a catalog of unsuppressed infamies, is impossible to imagine without Mel Brooks. The brilliant and sometimes excruciatingly candid comedy of Joan Rivers and Sarah Silverman owes a lot to Mel. (Sarah: "My nanna was a survivor of the Holocaust—sorry, I mean the *alleged* Holocaust. One of the better camps," a joke that cuts two ways.) Sacha Baron Cohen, who presents himself as Kazakhstani journalist "Borat" (and other things), preys on the unsuspecting, who haplessly spill out their hostilities and prejudices. Cohen pushes Mel's aggressive attack into hostile undermining irony.

"What I gave them," Mel Brooks said to me, speaking generally of the comics after him, "was the take-a-chance-attitude. It may be very private and yours and never reach an audience. Take a chance." And he added, "I didn't want cheap laughs. I wanted twisted and crazy to work."

Betty Friedan's principal influence on America is the widespread belief that women must work if they are to be happy; they must work if the economy is to be fully productive and creative. Betty and many other writers and activists, as well as millions of women acting without theory, have permanently altered American society for the better.

There is a very potent cultural marker of where we have been—*Mad Men*, the great TV series (2007–15) devoted to the New York advertising world in the sixties. Creator Matthew Weiner and his cohort caught the sour misogyny of the account executives and the way some of the women struggled against contempt. But then there is Betty Draper, the wife of the ad genius Don Draper. Imprisoned in her suburban home, baffled, selfish, and ineffective, Betty Draper fits exactly the portrait of suburban futility that Friedan had created decades earlier. (Matthew Weiner has admitted the Friedan influence.) Social historian Stephanie Coontz reported in the *Washington Post* ("Why 'Mad Men' Is TV's Most Feminist Show," October 10, 2010) that some women were so upset by the accuracy of the series that they couldn't bear to watch it. Older men watched it with grim acknowledgment of their past selves and perhaps something like relief if they had moved to a better place in their relations with women. This extraordinary period re-creation was shaped by a forty-year-old book, a kind of posthumous reaffirmation of Betty Friedan's perceptions.

Norman Mailer, as we have seen, had trouble with plot; his novels become stalled midriver, paddle wheels pulling furiously in opposite directions. And Mailer had trouble finding a voice for his fiction—until he adopted the drastic solution of taking his voice entirely out of *The Executioner's Song*. In his nonfiction masterpieces, he created *himself*, a character in the action whose collaboration with the surrounding scene he could master for drama, irony, comedy, and disgust without loss of detail. He was the lens, the object, the atmosphere. No one had the full-ranging intellectual interests that Mailer had, but that experimental streak in his output was certainly an influence on Hunter S. Thompson's "gonzo" (stoned) journalism, such as *Fear and Loathing in Las Vegas* (1971); an influence, too, on half the male writers for the *Village Voice* in its glory days of the sixties, seventies, and eighties. Even a reporter as straitlaced as the *Times*'s Tom Wicker made himself a character in his book on the 1971 Attica prison revolt, *A Time to Die* (1976). After Mailer's many triumphs of political journalism—especially the pieces about the national conventions in the sixties and seventies—no one could read predictably astute, delegate-counting reports by other journalists without impatience. In so many areas of interest, Mailer substituted evocation and inspiration for what he despised as "acumen"—the inside dope that revealed nothing.

His soulfulness, however eccentric or profane, was never less than earnest in intent. His deep mining of the American underlife, his evocation of the American spirit that was present (or stunningly vacant) at any given moment, allied with such emotions as foreboding, contempt, euphoria—those insistent qualities in Mailer's writing found a powerful echo in the novels of Robert Stone (*Dog Soldiers*, 1974), in the journalism of Joan Didion (*We Tell Ourselves Stories in Order to Live*, 2006), and best of all in the fiction of Don DeLillo, whose acclaimed *Underworld* (1997), which links public events and political figures to individual destinies and the dream life of the nation, may have been the large-scale masterpiece of fiction that Mailer wasn't able to pull off.

At the end of my discussion of Leonard Bernstein's Norton Lectures, I said that he was putting young American composers on notice, saying, in effect, "Don't give up on beauty. If you are going to embrace serialism and atonality, you had better possess as strong a lyrical streak as Schoenberg and Berg."

The warning was heard. The indifference of the audience to much advanced composition was heard, too. By the eighties, in America, atonality and serialism had lost their grip, and composers were reaching for a more immediate and emotional connection with music lovers. In *The Rest Is Noise* (2007), Alex Ross traces the many branches of new music after 1980, including work by the popular minimalists Steve Reich and Philip Glass, whose motoric repetitions and chant-like melodies put listeners in a pleasurable trance. A challenging new work, like George Benjamin's opera *Written on Skin* (2012), may be harshly dissonant, but tonality has found a home in Benjamin's work. After the eighties, American classical music was influenced by many things, including African chanting and Hindu ragas, but Bernstein's work as a teacher and composer was also churning around in the unconscious of young artists. American classical music came alive and found an audience again, and Bernstein deserves part of the credit. In musicals, Lin-Manuel Miranda, creator of the electrifying *In the Heights* and *Hamilton*, has acknowledged his debt to *West Side Story.*

Two of Bernstein's assistants when he was music director of the New York Philharmonic became renowned conductors: Claudio Abbado, who later became music director of La Scala in Milan, music director of the Vienna State Opera, and chief conductor and artistic director of the Berlin Philharmonic; and Seiji Ozawa, who became the longtime music director of the Boston Symphony. Lenny's protégé and close friend Michael Tilson Thomas became the conductor of the San Francisco Symphony and a great Mahler interpreter in his own right. Tilson Thomas conducted and recorded many of Bernstein's works. So did Marin Alsop, whom Bernstein mentored and who was music director of the Baltimore Symphony from 2007 to 2021, the first American woman to have a major career as a conductor, followed by the fictional Lydia Tár, who, we're told, was a Bernstein protégé.

Among today's great conductors, Simon Rattle (the Bavarian Radio Symphony), Gustavo Dudamel (newly appointed music director of the New York Philharmonic), and Yannick Nézet-Séguin (music director of the Philadelphia Orchestra and the Metropolitan Opera) have acknowledged Bernstein's greatness and have recorded his works. The influence is temperamental as much as musical. The old image of the conductor as the ill-tempered European, bristling with the authority of three hundred years of tradition, has given way to a more welcoming and relaxed man or woman, enthusiastic, approachable, easy with the audience but just as demanding of orchestras as the older tyrants.

IN THE 1940S, the Jewish population in the United States peaked at about 3.7 percent. In a country of about 140 million people, there were about 4.5 million Jewish men and women. In the 2020s, after decades of intermarriage and a relatively low birth rate, Jews are now only about 2.3 percent of the population, or 7 million out of 330 million Americans. Many scholarly and journalistic observers are obsessed with that proportional decline. I am not. Seven million Jews in one place is a lot of Jews! In terms of ethnic economic behavior, the Jews may no longer be top dog. As a group, Asian

Americans may now be the highest earners. Still! In the 2020s, as before, Jewish accomplishments in certain areas of the economy—retail business, real estate, finance, the professions, entertainment, the arts, scientific and medical research, university and secondary-school teaching—continue to be way out of proportion to their numbers. In the postwar period, synagogue attendance surged and Jewish associations of all kinds sprang up or grew larger—charities, community groups, Hadassah groups, research institutes, university Jewish studies departments. Centers, alliances, institutes! In the past, Jewish survival has seemed shaky—a wish built out of despair or fervent hope—but in this country it is not under serious threat.

It is no exaggeration to say that Jewish culture was reborn in America. It was reborn in religious observance and in artistic, intellectual, and entrepreneurial activity of every kind. By the 1960s, the descendants of the Eastern Jews, religious and unreligious alike, were strong and unapologetic. They exercised religious and intellectual freedom; they possessed their bodies. The notion of what was American, present in the Constitution, and in our manners and popular culture, expanded still further to include the Jews, who with manic intensity built ever so much more of America. The Jews sensed how to accept the American embrace without giving up on their past. They were not behaving like everyone else. They were behaving like Jewish Americans. They were 100 percent American, and 100 percent Jewish.

SOURCES

GENERAL SOURCES

American Jewish Year Book 60 (1959), edited by Morris Fine and Milton Himmelfarb.

Baer, Jean. *The Self-Chosen: "Our Crowd" Is Dead. Long Live Our Crowd.* New York: Arbor House, 1982.

Baum, Devorah. *Feeling Jewish (a Book for Just about Anyone).* New Haven, CT: Yale University Press, 2017.

Bellow, Saul. "A Jewish Writer in America—II." *New York Review of Books*, November 10, 2011.

Dauber, Jeremy. *Jewish Comedy: A Serious History.* New York: W. W. Norton, 2017.

Diner, Hasia R. *The Jews of the United States, 1654 to 2000.* Berkeley: University of California Press, 2004.

Feingold, Henry L. *A Time for Searching: Entering the Mainstream 1920–1945.* Baltimore: Johns Hopkins University Press, 1992.

Foer, Franklin. "The Golden Age of American Jews is Ending," *Atlantic*, April 2024.

Freud, Sigmund. *Moses and Monotheism.* New York: Vintage, 1990. First published London: Hogarth Press, 1939.

———. "On Narcissism." *The Standard Edition of the Complete Psychological Works of Sigmund Freud.* Vol. 14. London: Hogarth Press, 1916.

Galbraith, John Kenneth. *The Affluent Society.* New York: Houghton Mifflin, 1958.

Glazer, Nathan. *American Judaism.* 2nd ed. London: University of Chicago Press, 1972.

Goldscheider, Calvin, and Alan S. Zuckerman. *The Transformation of the Jews.* Chicago: University of Chicago Press, 1984.

Gornick, Vivian. *The Odd Woman and the City.* New York: Farrar, Straus and Giroux, 2015.

Grubin, David, writer, producer, and director. *The Jewish Americans.* PBS, 2008.

Hertzberg, Arthur. *The Jews in America: Four Centuries of an Uneasy Encounter; A History.* New York: Simon and Schuster, 1989.

Hodgson, Godfrey. *America in Our Time: From World War II to Nixon—What Happened and Why.* Princeton, NJ: Princeton University Press, 2006.

Hollinger, David A. *Science, Jews, and Secular Culture: Studies in Mid-Twentieth-Century American Intellectual History.* Princeton, NJ: Princeton University Press, 1996.

Holtz, Barry W., ed. *The Schocken Guide to Jewish Books: Where to Start Reading about Jewish History, Literature, Culture, and Religion.* New York: Schocken, 1992.

Horn, Dara. *People Love Dead Jews: Reports from a Haunted Present.* New York: W. W. Norton, 2021.

Howe, Irving. *World of Our Fathers: The Journey of the East European Jews to America and the Life They Found and Made.* New York: Harcourt Brace Jovanovich, 1976.

Kazin, Alfred. "The Jew as Modern American Writer." Introduction to *The Commentary Reader: Two Decades of Articles and Stories*, edited by Norman Podhoretz. New York: Atheneum, 1966.

———. *New York Jew.* New York: Alfred A. Knopf, 1978.

Kirsch, Adam. *The Blessing and the Curse: The Jewish People and Their Books in the Twentieth Century.* New York: W. W. Norton, 2020.

———. *The People and the Books: 18 Classics of Jewish Literature.* New York: W. W. Norton, 2016.

Kobrin, Rebecca, ed. *Chosen Capital: The Jewish Encounter with American Capitalism.* New Brunswick, NJ: Rutgers University Press, 2012.

Konner, Melvin. *Unsettled: An Anthropology of the Jews.* New York: Viking Penguin, 2003.

Lederhendler, Eli. *Jewish Responses to Modernity: New Voices in America and Eastern Europe.* New York: NYU Press, 1994.

Lévy, Bernard-Henri. *The Genius of Judaism.* Translated by Steven B. Kennedy. New York: Random House, 2017.

Lipset, Seymour Martin, and Earl Raab. *Jews and the New American Scene.* Cambridge, MA: Harvard University Press, 1995.

Muller, Jerry Z. *Capitalism and the Jews.* Princeton, NJ: Princeton University Press, 2010.

Ozick, Cynthia. *Art and Ardor.* New York: Knopf, 1983.

Rosenberg, Harold. "Is There a Jewish Art?" *Commentary*, July 1966.

Rosenthal, Erich. "Jewish Fertility in the United States." *American Jewish Yearbook* 62 (1961): 3–27.

Rosten, Leo. *The New Joys of Yiddish.* New York: Three Rivers Press, 2001.

Sarna, Jonathan D. *American Judaism: A History.* 2nd ed. New Haven, CT: Yale University Press, 2019.

Sartre, Jean-Paul. *Anti-Semite and Jew.* Translated by George J. Becker. New York: Schocken, 1948.

Schoener, Allon. *The American Jewish Album: 1654 to the Present.* New York: Rizzoli, 1984.

Shapiro, Edward S. *A Time for Healing: American Jewry since World War II.* Baltimore: Johns Hopkins University Press, 1992.

Silberman, Charles E. *A Certain People: American Jews and Their Lives Today.* New York: Summit Books, 1985.

Sklare, Marshall. *America's Jews*. New York: Random House, 1971.

———, ed. *The Jews: Social Patterns of an American Group*. New York: Free Press, 1958.

———. *Observing American Jews*. Waltham: Brandeis University Press, 1993.

Slezkine, Yuri. *The Jewish Century*. Princeton, NJ: Princeton University Press, 2004.

Wakefield, Dan. *New York in the Fifties*. New York: Greenpoint Press, 1992.

Wex, Michael. *Born to Kvetch: Yiddish Language and Culture in All of Its Moods*. New York: St. Martin's Press, 2005.

Whitfield, Stephen J. *In Search of American Jewish Culture*. Hanover, NH: Brandeis University Press, 1999.

Wisse, Ruth R. *No Joke: Making Jewish Humor*. Princeton, NJ: Princeton University Press, 2013.

SOURCES FOR MEL BROOKS

BROOKS MOVIES DISCUSSED IN THIS TEXT

The Producers (1967).

The Twelve Chairs (1970).

Blazing Saddles (1974).

Young Frankenstein (1974).

Silent Movie (1976).

History of the World, Part 1 (1981).

To Be or Not to Be (1983).

Spaceballs (1987).

Robin Hood: Men in Tights (1993).

CDS AND VIDEO

The Incredible Mel Brooks: An Irresistible Collection of Unhinged Comedy. Shout! Factory, 2012. (Includes interviews, TV appearances, reflections on his movies, essay by Robert Brustein, etc.)

The 2000 Year Old Man: The Complete History. Shout! Factory, 2009.

Pearlstein, Ferne, director. *The Last Laugh* (documentary), 2016.

BOOKS AND ARTICLES ABOUT BROOKS

Adler, Renata. "'The Producers' at Fine Arts." *New York Times*, March 19, 1968.

Apatow, Judd. *Sick in the Head: Conversations about Life and Comedy*. New York: Random House, 2016.

Bernstein, Richard. *Only in America: Al Jolson and* The Jazz Singer. New York: Knopf, 2024.

Brooks, Mel. *All About Me! My Remarkable Life in Show Business*. New York: Ballantine Books, 2021.

———. Interview by Brad Darrach. *Playboy*, February 1975.

Brooks, Mel, and Rebecca Keegan. *"Young Frankenstein": The Story of the Making of the Film*. New York: Black Dog and Leventhal, 2016.

Brooks, Mel, and Tom Meehan. *"The Producers": The Book, Lyrics, and Story behind the Biggest Hit in Broadway History! How We Did It*. New York: Miramax Books, 2001.

Bruce, Lenny. *How to Talk Dirty and Influence People*. Chicago: Playboy Press, 1965.

Daniel, Douglass K. *Anne Bancroft: A Life*. Lexington: University Press of Kentucky, 2017.

Dauber, Jeremy. *Mel Brooks: Disobedient Jew*. New Haven, CT: Yale University Press, 2023.

Denby, David. "Portrait of an Artist as an Old Man: Mel Brooks in His 90s." *Atlantic*, July 22, 2018.

Hoberman, J., and Jeffrey Shandler. *Entertaining America: Jews, Movies, and Broadcasting*. Princeton, NJ: Princeton University Press, 2003.

Kael, Pauline. "A Generation's Clown." *New Yorker*, March 3, 1973.

———. "O Pioneer!" Review of *The Producers*. *New Yorker*, March 23, 1968.

Kafka, Franz. *Selected Stories*. New York: W. W. Norton, 2007.

Kanfer, Stefan. *A Summer World: The Attempt to Build a Jewish Eden in the Catskills, from the Days of the Ghetto to the Rise and Decline of the Borscht Belt*. New York: Farrar, Straus and Giroux, 1989.

Kazin, Alfred. *A Walker in the City*. New York: Harcourt, Brace, 1951.

Kimmelman, Michael. "The Führer Returns to Berlin, This Time Saluted Only by Laughs." *New York Times*, May 18, 2009.

Lahr, John. "Gold Rush." Review of *The Producers* [play]. *New Yorker*, April 29, 2001.

———. "Joy Ride." Profile of Susan Stroman. *New Yorker*, March 24, 2014.

McGilligan, Patrick. *Funny Man: Mel Brooks*. New York: HarperCollins, 2019.

Mikics, David. "On Jewish Vulgarity." *Tablet*, December 13, 2022.

Nachman, Gerald. *Seriously Funny: The Rebel Comedians of the 1950s and 1960s*. New York: Pantheon Books, 2003.

Parrish, James Robert. *It's Good to Be the King: The Seriously Funny Life of Mel Brooks*. Hoboken, NJ: John Wiley and Sons, 2007.

Scheinfeld, Marisa, Stefan Kanfer, and Jenna Weissman Joselit. *The Borscht Belt: Revisiting the Remains of America's Jewish Vacationland*. Ithaca, NY: Cornell University Press, 2016.

Silverman, Stephen M., and Raphael D. Silver. *The Catskills: Its History and How It Changed America*. New York: Knopf, 2015.

Simon, Neil. *Laughter on the 23rd Floor*. New York: Samuel French, 1995.

Tynan, Kenneth. "Frolics and Detours of a Short Hebrew Man: Mel Brooks's Indestructible Comedy." *New Yorker*, October 22, 1978. Reprinted in Kenneth Tynan. *Profiles*. New York: Random House, 1995.

SOURCES FOR BETTY FRIEDAN

BOOKS AND ARTICLES BY FRIEDAN

The Feminine Mystique. Norton Critical Edition. Edited by Kirsten Fermaglick and Lisa M. Fine. New York: W. W. Norton, 2013. First published 1963.

"Up from the Kitchen Floor." *New York Times*, March 4, 1973.

It Changed My Life: Writings on the Women's Movement. New York: Random House, 1976.

"Friedan at 55: From Feminism to Judaism," *Lilith I*, Fall 1976.

"Women as Jew/Jew as Woman." *Central Conference of American Rabbis Yearbook*, 1979.

The Second Stage. New York: Summit Books, 1981.

"Women and Jews: The Quest for Selfhood," *Congress Monthly*, February–March 1985.

Beyond Gender: The New Politics of Work and Family. Washington, DC: Woodrow Wilson Center Press, 1997.

The Fountain of Age. New York: Simon and Schuster, 1998. First published 1993.

Life So Far: A Memoir. New York: Simon and Schuster, 2000.

Interviews with Betty Friedan. Edited by Janann Sherman. Jackson: University of Mississippi Press, 2002.

BOOKS AND ARTICLES ABOUT FRIEDAN

Antler, Joyce. *Jewish Radical Feminism: Voices from the Women's Liberation Movement.* New York: NYU Press, 2018.

———. *The Journey Home: How Jewish Women Shaped Modern America.* New York: Free Press, 1997.

Beauvoir, Simon de. *The Second Sex.* Translated by Constance Borde and Sheila Malovany-Chevallier. New York: Vintage, 2010. First published as *Le Deuxième Sexe*, 1949.

Blair, Elaine. "A Woman's Work." *New York Review of Books*, November 7, 2019.

Brownmiller, Susan. "Sisterhood Is Powerful." *New York Times*, March 15, 1970.

Collins, Gail. *When Everything Changed: The Amazing Journey of American Women from 1960 to the Present.* New York: Little, Brown, 2014.

Coontz, Stephanie. *A Strange Stirring: "The Feminine Mystique" and American Women at the Dawn of the 1960s.* New York: Basic Books, 2011.

———. "Why 'Mad Men' Is TV's Most Feminist Show." *Washington Post*, June 30, 2010.

Deutsch, Helene. *The Psychology of Women: A Psychoanalytical Interpretation.* Two volumes. Boston: Allyn & Bacon, 1944–45.

Diner, Hasia R., Shira Kohn, and Rachel Kranson, eds. *A Jewish Feminine Mystique? Jewish Women in Postwar America.* New Brunswick, NJ: Rutgers University Press, 2010.

Donegan, Moira. "The Catalyst." *New Yorker*, September 11, 2023.

Ephron, Nora. *Crazy Salad: Some Things about Women; and Scribble Scribble: Notes on the Media.* New York: Vintage, 2012.

Erikson, Erik H. *Young Man Luther: A Study in Psychoanalysis and History.* New York: W. W. Norton, 1958.

Faludi, Susan. *Backlash: The Undeclared War against American Women.* New York: Crown, 2006. First published 1991.

———. "Death of a Revolutionary." *New Yorker*, April 8, 2013.

———. "Feminism Made a Faustian Bargain with Celebrity Culture. Now It's Paying the Price." *New York Times*, June 20, 2022.

Firestone, Shulamith. *The Dialectic of Sex: The Case for Feminist Revolution.* New York: William Morrow, 1970.

Goldin, Claudia. "The Quiet Revolution That Transformed Women's Employment, Education, and Family." *American Economic Review* 96, no. 2 (2006): 1–21.

Greer, Germaine. *The Female Eunuch.* New York: HarperCollins, 1970.

Heilbrun, Carolyn G. *The Education of a Woman: The Life of Gloria Steinem.* New York: Ballantine Books, 1995.

Hennessee, Judith. *Betty Friedan: Her Life*. Random House, 1999.

Heschel, Susannah, ed. *On Being a Jewish Feminist: A Reader*. New York: Schocken, 1983.

Horowitz, Daniel. *Betty Friedan and the Making of "The Feminine Mystique": The American Left, the Cold War, and Modern Feminism*. Amherst: University of Massachusetts Press, 1998.

———. "Jewish Women Remaking American Feminism / Women Remaking American Judaism: Reflections on the Life of Betty Friedan." In *A Jewish Feminine Mystique?: Jewish Women in Postwar America*, edited by Hasia Diner, Shira Kohn, and Rachel Kranson, 235–56. New Brunswick, NJ: Rutgers University Press, 2010.

Jewish Women's Archive. Newton, MA. https://jwa.org/.

Kevles, Bettyann. "A Feminist in the Late 80s." *Los Angeles Times*, May 17, 1987.

Levy, Ariel. "Lift and Separate." *New Yorker*, November 8, 2009.

Menand, Louis. *The Free World: Art and Thought in the Cold War*. New York: Farrar, Straus and Giroux, 2021.

Merkin, Daphne. "Sister Act." *New Yorker*, June 14, 1999.

Millett, Kate. *Sexual Politics*. New York: Doubleday, 1970.

Morgan, Robin, ed. *Sisterhood Is Forever: The Women's Anthology for a New Millennium*. New York: Washington Square Press, 2003.

———, ed. *Sisterhood Is Powerful: An Anthology of Writings from the Women's Liberation Movement*. New York: Random House, 1970.

Oliver, Susan. *Betty Friedan: The Personal Is Political*. New York: Pearson, 2007.

Ozick, Cynthia. "Notes Toward Finding the Right Question." *Lilith* 6 (1979).

———. "Toward a New Yiddish." In *Art and Ardor*, 151–77. New York: Knopf, 1983.

Plaskow, Judith. *The Coming of Lilith: Essays on Feminism, Judaism, and Sexual Ethics, 1972–2003*. Boston: Beacon Press, 2005.

———. *Standing Again at Sinai: Judaism from a Feminist Perspective*. San Francisco: Harper-SanFrancisco, 1990.

Rich, Adrienne. *Of Woman Born: Motherhood as Experience and Institution*. New York: W. W. Norton, 1976.

Rosen, Ruth. *The World Split Open: How the Modern Women's Movement Changed America*. New York: Viking, 2000.

Shteir, Rachel. *Betty Friedan: Magnificent Disrupter*. New Haven, CT: Yale University Press, 2023.

Shulevitz, Judith. "Kate Millett: 'Sexual Politics' & Family Values." *New York Review of Books*, September 29, 2017.

Shulman, Alix Kates, and Honor Moore, eds. *Women's Liberation! Feminist Writings That Inspired a Revolution & Still Can*. New York: Library of America, 2021.

Steinem, Gloria. *My Life on the Road*. New York: Random House, 2015.

Willis, Ellen. *No More Nice Girls: Countercultural Essays*. Hanover, NH: Wesleyan University Press, 1992.

Witchel, Alex. "At Home with Betty Friedan: Beyond Mystique, a Frank Memoir." *New York Times*, May 11, 2000.

SOURCES FOR NORMAN MAILER

MAILER WORKS DISCUSSED IN THIS TEXT
The Naked and the Dead. New York: Rinehart, 1948.
Barbary Shore. New York: Rinehart, 1951.
The Deer Park. New York: Putnam's, 1955.
Advertisements for Myself. New York: Putnam's, 1959.
The Presidential Papers. New York: Putnam's, 1963.
An American Dream. New York: Dial, 1965.
Cannibals and Christians. New York: Dial, 1966.
Miami and the Siege of Chicago. New York: World Publishing, 1968.
The Armies of the Night. New York: New American Library, 1968.
Of a Fire on the Moon. Boston: Little, Brown, 1970.
The Prisoner of Sex. Boston: Little, Brown, 1971.
Marilyn: A Biography. New York: Grosset and Dunlap, 1973.
The Fight. Boston: Little, Brown, 1975.
The Executioner's Song. Boston: Little, Brown, 1979.
Ancient Evenings. Boston: Little, Brown, 1983.
Tough Guys Don't Dance. New York: Random House, 1984.
Harlot's Ghost. New York: Random House, 1991.
Oswald's Tale: An American Mystery. New York: Random House, 1995.
The Gospel According to the Son. New York: Random House, 1997.
The Castle in the Forest. New York: Random House, 2007.
"Interview with Norman Mailer." *Der Spiegel*, October 23, 2000.
"The White Man Unburdened," *New York Review of Books*, July 17, 2003.
Selected Letters of Norman Mailer. Edited by J. Michael Lennon. New York: Random House, 2014.
The Mind of an Outlaw: Selected Essays of Norman Mailer. Edited by Phillip Sipiora. New York: Random House, 2014.

BOOKS, ARTICLES, AND FILMS ABOUT MAILER
Abbott, Jack Henry. *In the Belly of the Beast*. New York: Random House, 1981.
Abbott, Jack Henry, and Naomi Zack. *My Return*. New York: Prometheus, 1987.
Baldwin, James. "The Black Boy Looks at the White Boy." *Collected Essays*. New York: Library of America, 1998.
Bernstein, Mashey. "Judaism." In *Norman Mailer in Context*, edited by Maggie McKinley, 246–56. Cambridge, UK: Cambridge University Press, 2021.
Bloom, Harold, ed. *Norman Mailer*. New York: Chelsea House, 1986.
Braudy, Leo, ed. *Norman Mailer: A Collection of Critical Essays*. Englewood Cliffs, NJ: Prentice-Hall, 1972.
Corrigan, Maureen. Keynote speech at the 20th Annual Conference of the Norman Mailer Society. Austin, TX, April 22, 2023.
Denby, David. "The Contender." *New Yorker*. April 12, 1998.

——. "A Great Writer at the 1968 Democratic Disaster." *New Yorker*, August 26, 2018.

——. "Mr. Mailer Goes to Washington." *Harper's Magazine*, January 2018.

Dickstein, Morris. *Leopards in the Temple: The Transformation of American Fiction, 1945–1970*. Cambridge, MA: Harvard University Press, 2002.

——. "A Trip to Inner and Outer Space." *New York Times*, January 10, 1971.

Didion, Joan. "I Want to Go Ahead and Do It." *New York Times*, October 7, 1979.

Gerson, Jessica. "Sex, Creativity, and God." In *Norman Mailer*, edited by Harold Bloom, 167–82. New York: Chelsea House, 1986.

Kael, Pauline. "Marilyn: A Rip-Off with Genius." Review of *Marilyn: A Biography*. *New York Times*, July 22, 1973.

Kazin, Alfred. "The Trouble He's Seen." Review of *The Armies of the Night*. *New York Times*, May 5, 1968.

Lennon, J. Michael, ed. *Conversations with Norman Mailer*. Jackson: University Press of Mississippi, 1988.

——, ed. *Critical Essays on Norman Mailer*. Boston: G. K. Hall, 1986.

——. *Mailer's Last Days: New and Selected Remembrances of a Life in Literature*. Wilkes-Barre, PA: Etruscan Press, 2022.

——. *Norman Mailer: A Double Life*. New York: Simon and Schuster, 2013.

Lennon, J. Michael, and Donna Pedro Lennon. *Norman Mailer: Works and Days*. Edited by Gerald R. Lucas. Norman Mailer Society, 2018.

Loving, Jerome. *Jack and Norman*. New York: St. Martin's Press, 2017.

Lucid, Robert F., ed. *Norman Mailer: The Man and His Work*. Boston: Little, Brown, 1971.

Mailer, Adele. *The Last Party: Scenes from My Life with Norman Mailer*. Fort Lee, NJ: Barricade Books, 1997.

Mailer, Norris Church. *A Ticket to the Circus*. New York: Random House, 2010.

Mailer, Susan. *In Another Place: With and Without My Father, Norman Mailer*. Northampton, MA: Northampton House Press, 2019.

Manso, Peter. *Mailer: His Life and Times*. New York: Simon and Schuster, 1985.

McKinley, Maggie, ed. *Norman Mailer in Context*. Cambridge, UK: Cambridge University Press, 2021.

Menand, Louis. "Beat the Devil." Review of *The Time of Our Time*. *New York Review of Books*, October 22, 1998.

——. "The Norman Invasion." *New Yorker*, October 14, 2013.

Mikics, David. "Let's All Celebrate Norman Mailer." *Tablet*, January 30, 2023.

Oates, Joyce Carol. "Out of the Machine." *Atlantic*, July 1971.

O'Hagan, Andrew. "Oswaldworld." Review of *Oswald's Tale: An American Mystery*. *London Review of Books*, December 14, 1995.

——. "The Reviewer's Song." Review of *Norman Mailer: A Double Life*, by J. Michael Lennon. *London Review of Books*, November 7, 2013.

Podhoretz, Norman. "Norman Mailer: The Embattled Vision." *Partisan Review*, Summer 1959.

Poirier, Richard. *Norman Mailer*. New York: Viking Press, 1972.

——. *Trying It Out in America: Literary and Other Performances*. New York: Farrar, Straus and Giroux, 1999.

Ricks, Christopher. "Mailer's Psychopath." Review of *The Executioner's Song*. *London Review of Books*, March 6, 1980.

Siegel, Lee. "Maestro of the Human Ego." *New York Times*, January 21, 2007.

Stone, Robert. "The Loser's Loser." Review of *Oswald's Tale: An American Mystery*. *New York Review of Books*, June 22, 1995.

Trilling, Diana. "The Radical Moralism of Norman Mailer." *Encounter*, November 1962.

———. *We Must March My Darlings*. New York: Harcourt Brace Jovanovich, 1977.

Wood, James. "He Is Finished." Review of *The Gospel According to the Son*. *New Republic*, May 12, 1997.

Wood, Michael. "Kissing Hitler." *New York Review of Books*, September 20, 1973.

Zimbalist, Jeff, director. *How to Come Alive with Norman Mailer* (documentary portrait). Zeitgeist/Kino Lorber, 2023.

SOURCES FOR LEONARD BERNSTEIN

BOOKS BY BERNSTEIN

The Joy of Music. Pompton Plains, NJ: Amadeus, 2004. First published New York: Simon and Schuster, 1959.

The Infinite Variety of Music. New York: Simon and Schuster, 1966.

The Unanswered Question: Six Talks at Harvard. The Charles Eliot Norton Lectures, 1973. Cambridge, MA: Harvard University Press, 1976.

Findings: Fifty Years of Meditations on Music. New York: Simon and Schuster, 1982.

Young People's Concerts. New York: Amadeus, 2006.

The Leonard Bernstein Letters. Edited by Nigel Simeone. New Haven, CT: Yale University Press, 2013.

BOOKS AND ARTICLES ABOUT BERNSTEIN

Aucoin, Matthew. "Performance as Immolation." *New York Review of Books*, February 23, 2023.

Bernstein, Burton. *Family Matters: Sam, Jennie, and the Kids*. New York: Summit Books, 1982.

Bernstein, Burton, and Barbara B. Haws. *Leonard Bernstein, American Original: How a Modern Renaissance Man Transformed Music and the World During His New York Philharmonic Years, 1943–1976*. New York: HarperCollins, 2008.

Bernstein, Jamie. *Famous Father Girl: A Memoir of Growing Up Bernstein*. New York: Harper, 2018.

Botstein, Leon. "The Tragedy of Leonard Bernstein." *Harper's Magazine*, May 1983.

Burton, Humphrey. *Leonard Bernstein*. New York: Doubleday, 1994.

Burton, William Westbrook, ed. *Conversations about Bernstein*. New York: Oxford University Press, 1995.

Clark, Philip. "The Bernstein Enigma." *New York Review of Books*, February 8, 2024.

Cott, Jonathan. *Dinner with Lenny: The Last Long Interview with Leonard Bernstein*. New York: Oxford University Press, 2013.

Denby, David. "Leonard Bernstein through His Daughter's Eyes." *New Yorker*, June 18, 2018.

————. "The Trouble with Lenny." *New Yorker*, August 17, 1998.

Flugel, Jane, ed. *Bernstein Remembered.* New York: Carroll and Graf, 1991.

Gabler, Neal. *An Empire of Their Own: How the Jews Invented Hollywood.* New York: Crown, 1988.

Glazer, Nathan, and Daniel Patrick Moynihan. *Beyond the Melting Pot: The Negroes, Puerto Ricans, Jews, Italians, and Irish of New York City.* 2nd ed. Cambridge, MA: MIT Press, 1970.

Gottlieb, Jack. Interview for *Leonard Bernstein: Reaching for the Note*, PBS American Masters, March 18, 1998. https://www.pbs.org/wnet/americanmasters/archive/interview/jack-gottlieb/.

————. *Working with Bernstein: A Memoir.* New York: Amadeus Press, 2010.

Hanak, Werner, and Adina Seeger, eds. *Leonard Bernstein: Ein New Yorker in Wien; A New Yorker in Vienna.* Wolke Verlag. Published in conjunction with the exhibition of the same name at the Jewish Museum Vienna, October 17, 2018–April 28, 2019.

Harmon, Charlie. *On the Road and Off the Record with Leonard Bernstein: My Years with the Exasperating Genius.* Watertown, MA: Imagine, 2018.

Horowitz, Joseph. *Artists in Exile: How Refugees from Twentieth-Century War and Revolution Transformed the American Performing Arts.* New York: Harper, 2008.

————. "Professor Lenny." *New York Review of Books*, June 10, 1993.

Jowitt, Deborah. *Jerome Robbins: His Life, His Theater, His Dance.* New York: Simon and Schuster, 2004.

Lebrecht, Norman. *The Maestro Myth: Great Conductors in Pursuit of Power.* New York: Birch Lane Press, 1991.

Mauceri, John. *Leonard Bernstein: A Centenary Celebration.* Kindle Books, 2019.

Mordden, Ethan. *Broadway Babies: The People Who Made the American Musical.* New York: Oxford University Press, 1983.

————. *Coming Up Roses: The Broadway Musical in the 1950s.* New York: Oxford University Press, 1998.

Myers, Paul. *Leonard Bernstein.* London: Phaidon Press, 1998.

Oja, Carol J. *Bernstein Meets Broadway: Collaborative Art in a Time of War.* New York: Oxford University Press, 2014.

Osborne, Richard. *Herbert von Karajan: A Life in Music.* Boston: Northeastern University Press, 2000.

Porter, Andrew. Liner notes. *Candide.* London Symphony Orchestra, conducted by Leonard Bernstein. Recorded December 1989, Deutsche Grammophon.

Ross, Alex. "The Legend of Lenny." *New Yorker*, December 7, 2008.

————. "Leonard Bernstein and the Perils of Hero Worship." *New Yorker*, September 10, 2018.

————. "'Maestro' Honors the Chaotic Charisma of Leonard Bernstein." *New Yorker*, December 17, 2023.

————. *The Rest Is Noise: Listening to the Twentieth Century.* New York: Farrar, Straus and Giroux, 2007.

Sarna, Jonathan D. "Leonard Bernstein and the Boston Jewish Community of His Youth: The Influence of Solomon Braslavsky, Herman Rubenovitz, and Congregation Mishkan Tefila," in "Leonard Bernstein in Boston," special issue, *Journal of the Society for American Music* 3 (February 2009): 35–46.

Shawn, Allen. *Leonard Bernstein: An American Musician*. New Haven, CT: Yale University Press, 2014.

Simeone, Nigel. *Leonard Bernstein: "West Side Story."* Farnham, UK: Ashgate, 2009.

Sondheim, Stephen. Interview for *Leonard Bernstein: Reaching for the Note*, PBS American Masters, February 26, 1998. https://www.pbs.org/wnet/americanmasters/archive/interview/stephen-sondheim-2/.

Thomson, Virgil. *Music Chronicles: 1940–1954*. New York: Library of America, 2014.

Wolff, Larry. "I Feel Pretty." *New York Review of Books*, September 27, 2018.

EXHIBITIONS

Leonard Bernstein at 100. New York Public Library for the Performing Arts, December 9, 2017–March 24, 2018.

Leonard Bernstein: The Power of Music. National Museum of American Jewish History, Philadelphia, 2018.

Leonard Bernstein: Ein New Yorker in Wien; A New Yorker in Vienna. Jewish Museum Vienna, October 17, 2018–April 28, 2019.

SELECTED RECORDINGS AND VIDEOS

CDs available from Amazon or as digital downloads from TIDAL or Qobuz; videos available from Amazon or YouTube.

BERNSTEIN WORKS

Leonard Bernstein Wunderkind. Pearl. (Includes the Revuers, *On the Town*, *Fancy Free*, "Facsimile," and Symphony No. 1, *Jeremiah*.)

On the Town. Original Broadway cast. Columbia.

Wonderful Town. Original Broadway cast. Decca.

The Three Symphonies; Chichester Psalms. Israel Philharmonic Orchestra. Deutsche Grammophon.

Bernstein Conducts Bernstein. New York Philharmonic, New York City Ballet Orchestra. Sony.

Jubilee Games. Israel Philharmonic. Deutsche Grammophon.

West Side Story. Original Broadway cast recording. Sony.

Candide (final revised version). London Symphony Orchestra. Deutsche Grammophon.

MASS. Alan Titus, Orchestra, the Norman Scribner Choir, the Berkshire Boy Choir. Sony.

A White House Cantata. London Voices, London Symphony Orchestra, Kent Nagano, conductor. Deutsche Grammophon.

OTHER COMPOSERS

Leonard Bernstein's New York Philharmonic Debut, November 14, 1943. New York Philharmonic. (Includes Schumann's "Manfred" overture; Rozsa's Theme, Variations, and Finale; and Strauss's "Don Quixote.")

Bartók: Concerto for Orchestra, Music for Strings, Percussion, and Celesta. New York Philharmonic. Sony.

Beethoven: Symphony No. 3, "Eroica." New York Philharmonic. Sony.

Beethoven: Symphony No. 7. Vienna Philharmonic. Deutsche Grammophon.

Copland: Appalachian Spring, Rodeo, Billy the Kid. New York Philharmonic. Sony.

Copland: Symphony No. 3. New York Philharmonic. Deutsche Grammophon.

Harris: Symphony No. 3. New York Philharmonic. Deutsche Grammophon.

Haydn: Paris Symphonies (nos. 82–87). New York Philharmonic. Columbia.

Ives: Symphony No. 2. The Unanswered Question. New York Philharmonic. Deutsche Grammophon.

Liszt: Faust Symphony. Boston Symphony. Deutsche Grammophon.

Mahler: Symphony No. 3. New York Philharmonic. Deutsche Grammophon.

Mahler: Symphony No. 5. Vienna Philharmonic. Deutsche Grammophon.

Mahler: Symphony No. 6. Vienna Philharmonic. Deutsche Grammophon.

Mahler: Symphony No. 7. New York Philharmonic. Deutsche Grammophon.

Mozart: Symphonies 25, 29, 35–41. Vienna Philharmonic. Deutsche Grammophon.

Nielsen: Symphonies Nos. 3 & 5. Royal Danish Orchestra, New York Philharmonic. Sony.

Schumann: Symphonies Nos. 1–4. Vienna Philharmonic. Deutsche Grammophon.

Shostakovich: Symphonies No. 5 & 9. New York Philharmonic. Sony.

Sibelius: Symphony No. 5. Vienna Philharmonic. Deutsche Grammophon.

Stravinsky: The Rite of Spring. New York Philharmonic. Sony.

SELECTED VIDEOS

Mindlin, Michael Jr., director. *A Journey to Jerusalem.* Maysles Films, Inc., and MGM, 1968.

Burton, Humphrey, and Tony Palmer, directors. *Four Ways to Say Farewell.* Mahler's Symphony No. 9. Unitel, 1971.

Burton, Humphrey, and Tony Palmer, directors. *The Little Drummer Boy: An Essay on Gustav Mahler.* Retitled *Bernstein on Mahler.* Unitel, 1985.

Leonard Bernstein: Omnibus (complete). Archive of American Television. E1 Entertainment, 1990.

The Unanswered Question: Six Talks at Harvard by Leonard Bernstein (the Charles Eliot Norton Lectures). Kultur, 1992.

Burton, Humphrey, director. *The Love of Three Orchestras.* Unitel, 1993.

Leonard Bernstein's Young People's Concerts (complete). Kultur, 1993.

Hohlfeld, Horant H., director. *The Gift of Music: An Intimate Portrait of Leonard Bernstein.* ITTC and Unitel, 1993.

Lacy, Susan, director and producer. *Leonard Bernstein: Reaching for the Note.* PBS American Masters. Educational Broadcasting Company, 1998.

Burton, Humphrey, and Horant H. Hohlfeld, directors. *Leonard Bernstein Rehearses Gustav Mahler.* Unitel, 2005.

ACKNOWLEDGMENTS

I would like to thank my wife, novelist Susan Rieger, who heard every idea, read many drafts, endured my doubts and hesitations for years. She is the companion—and a creative force herself—that any writer would be lucky to have. I would also like to thank my agent and friend Kathy Robbins and her husband, Richard Cohen, writer and publisher (and also friend), for unending support of what has been a difficult project. Without their constructive nudging and extreme patience, the book might never have been written.

I'm indebted to Gillian Blake, who believed in this book, and to Sarah Crichton, of Holt, who edited it, sticking to it through thick and thin, improving it in large ways and small. Tim Duggan graciously took over the project when Sarah Crichton left and masterfully steered it home. Jane Haxby did a superlative job as copy editor; Alex Foster and Zoë Affron were invaluable in many ways.

I would like to express my gratitude to J. Michael Lennon, whose extraordinary biography *Norman Mailer: A Double Life* is the essential resource for anyone with serious interest in Norman Mailer. Mike Lennon, a man blessed with outsize talent, energy, and goodwill, answered all my queries, made unpublished Mailer manuscripts available to me, and was helpful in countless ways. At the annual conferences of the Norman

Mailer Society, Lennon and Maggie McKinley, director of the society, as well as the risk-taking members of that group, provided stimulation and scholarly expertise.

Just as Mike Lennon's biography is essential to understanding Norman Mailer, Humphrey Burton's *Leonard Bernstein* is the unending source of information about Bernstein. The word "fair" sounds like faint praise. But this book turns fairness into heroic strength; it omits nothing of glory and weakness in its subject. Patrick McGilligan's *Funny Man* is by far the most informed and useful of the biographies devoted to Mel Brooks. Rachel Shteir's *Betty Friedan: Magnificent Disrupter* pulls together the many facets of Betty's life.

Friends and scholars (often both at once) read parts or all of the manuscript and gave me various forms of encouragement and criticism: Bernard Avishai, Peter Blauner, Jane Booth, Robert Caserio, Jonathan Cole, Andrew Delbanco, Nicholas Delbanco, Susan Faludi, Henry Finder, Owen Gleiberman, Molly Haskell, Gerald Howard, Jean Howard, Ira Katznelson, Rebecca Kobrin, John Lahr, Nicholas Lemann, J. Michael Lennon, David Mikics, Jerry Muller, Daniel Okrent, Kit Rachlis, David Ratzan, Frank Rich, Alex Ross, Stephen Schiff, Cathleen Schine, Stephen J. Whitfield.

I would like to express my appreciation for the welcoming attentions and skills of the archivists and librarians at two extraordinary institutions—the Schlesinger Library at Harvard University (Betty Friedan's papers) and the Harry Ransom Center at the University of Texas (Norman Mailer's papers). At the New York Philharmonic Archives, Barbara Haws and Gabryel Smith allowed me to examine Leonard Bernstein's personal scores of the Mahler symphonies. The Leonard Bernstein holdings of the Library of Congress yielded a number of treasures. The Theatre on Film and Tape Archive of the New York Public Library for the Performing Arts made certain Mel Brooks materials available to me. The Mailer family allowed me to print some unpublished writings of Mailer.

I had fruitful and enjoyable conversations with many people about these subjects, but I especially treasured speaking with the following: Bernard Avishai, Andrew Bergman, Jamie Bernstein, Mashey Bernstein, Jane Booth, Mel Brooks, Robert Caserio, Muriel Fox, Emily Friedan, Jonathan Friedan, Werner Hanak, Charlie Harmon, Molly Haskell, Barbara Haws,

Daniel Horowitz, Helen Lefkowitz Horowitz, Martha Lear, John Buffalo Mailer, Michael Mailer, Norman Mailer, Susan Mailer, David Mikics, Kit Rachlis, Frank Rich, Kevin Salter, Jonathan Sarna, Stephen Schiff, Gabryel Smith, Stephen Sondheim, Susan Stroman, Michael Tilson Thomas, Craig Urquhart, Steven J. Whitfield, Gail Winston, Naomi Zack.

ILLUSTRATION CREDITS

Bettye Goldstein, college photo (1942): Smith College Special Collections.

Norman Mailer in his army uniform (1944): Norman Mailer Estate Archives.

Leonard Bernstein rehearsing (1949): I. W. Schmidt / Bettmann / Getty Images.

Mel Brooks with Sid Caesar (early 1940s): reprinted with permission from Patrick McGilligan, *Mel Brooks: Funny Man* (HarperCollins, 2019).

Bernstein with Aaron Copland (1945): Library of Congress, Music Division.

Bernstein with wife, Felicia (1960): Henry Clarke / Condé Nast / Getty Images.

Bernstein conducting the Vienna Philharmonic for the last time, Carnegie Hall, New York (1990): © Steve J. Sherman.

Brooks and Anne Bancroft (1963): Dan Farrell / NY Daily News Archive / Getty Images.

Brooks at the TCL Chinese Theatre, Hollywood (2014): Frank Trapper / Corbis / Getty Images.

Brooks with a bust of Peter Boyle as *Young Frankenstein*'s monster (1974): Steve Schapiro / Corbis / Getty Images.

Gary Gilmore (1977): Lawrence Schiller / Polaris Communications / Getty Images.

Jack Henry Abbott (1981): David Handschuh / AP Photo.

Lee Harvey Oswald (1963): AP Photo.

Mailer announcing his libel suit against the *New York Post* (1982): Bettmann / Getty Images.

Friedan commemorating the fiftieth anniversary of women's suffrage, New York (1970): Fred W. McDarrah / MUUS Collection / Getty Images.

Friedan with husband, Carl (1947): Schlesinger Library, Harvard Radcliffe Institute.

Friedan, Abzug, and Steinem, Democratic National Convention, Miami (1972): Schlesinger Library, Harvard Radcliffe Institute / © Estate of Bettye Lane.

Mailer with wife Adele Morales (1960): Anthony Camerano / AP Photo.

Mailer with wife Norris Church (1977): Robert Belott / Alamy.

Bernstein in Israel (1977): Patrick Jarnoux / Paris Match / Getty Images.

Brooks, Allen, Tolkin, and Caesar (undated): Everett Collection.

Friedan (1995): Tao-Chuan Yeh / AFP / Getty Images.

Mailer (2000): Chris Felver / Getty Images.

Bernstein (1990): © Eiichiro Sakata, image courtesy of Akio Nagasawa Publishing.

Brooks (2015): © Andy Gotts / Camera Press London.

INDEX

ABOUT THE AUTHOR

David Denby is the *New York Times* bestselling author of *Great Books*. His other books include *American Sucker* and *Lit Up*. He was a film critic for *New York* magazine and the *New Yorker*, where he is now a staff writer. His essays have appeared in the *New Republic* and the *Atlantic*. He lives in New York City with his wife, novelist Susan Rieger.